THE POSTCOLONIAL MIDDLE AGES

THE NEW MIDDLE AGES

BONNIE WHEELER

Series Editor

The New Middle Ages presents transdisciplinary studies of medieval cultures. It includes both scholarly monographs and essay collections.

PUBLISHED BY PALGRAVE:

THE POSTCOLONIAL
MIDDLE AGES

Edited by Jeffrey Jerome Cohen

palgrave

First published in hardcover in 2000 by St. Martin's Press
First PALGRAVE™ edition: April 2001
175 Fifth Avenue, New York, N.Y. 10010 and
Houndmills, Basingstoke, Hampshire, England RG21 6XS
Companies and representatives throughout the world.

PALGRAVE is the new global publishing imprint of St. Martin's Press
LLC
Scholarly and Reference Division and Palgrave Publishers Ltd (formerly
Macmillan Press Ltd).

ISBN 0–312–21929–6 hardcover
ISBN 0–312–23981–5 paperback

Library of Congress Cataloging-in-Publication Data
The postcolonial Middle Ages / edited by Jeffrey Jerome Cohen.
      p.   cm. (New Middle Ages)
   Includes bibliographical references and index.
   ISBN 0–312–23981–5
   1. Middle Ages—History.   2. Colonies.   I. Cohen, Jeffrey Jerome.
D113.5.P65   2000
909.07 21—dc21   99–044203
                                                                      CIP

A catalogue record for this book is available from the British Library.

Design by Letra Libre, Inc.

First paperback edition: May 2001
10   9   8   7   6   5   4   3   2   1

Printed in the United States of America

CONTENTS

SERIES EDITOR'S FOREWORD

The New Middle Ages contributes to lively transdisciplinary conversations in medieval cultural studies through its scholarly monographs and essay collections. This series provides new work in a contemporary idiom about precise (if often diverse) practices, expressions, and ideologies in the Middle Ages. In *The Postcolonial Middle Ages,* the eighteenth book in the series, Jeffrey Jerome Cohen invites readers to rethink basic presumptions about time as well as other such terms of positioning as race, class, and nation in order to destabilize hegemonic identities. The fourteen new studies included here collectively urge readers to reconsider the central place accorded progress narratives about Europe and Christianity. In fact, these essays go further, encouraging readers to decenter even the usual intellectual positioning of Europe and Christianity so that we can avoid typecasting all non-European, non-Christians as Others who live in cultural interstices and whose geography is the periphery or frontier. From the perspectives of these essays, if the center can hold, then, it will be because our gaze will become as capacious as it is dynamic.

Bonnie Wheeler
Southern Methodist University

INTRODUCTION

MIDCOLONIAL

Jeffrey Jerome Cohen

"Where time unfolds irregularly and resists being captured by the cycles of clock and calendar . . ."[1]

Dante, Joan of Arc, Malcolm X: Postcolonial Time

Due north of the White House along 16th Street rises the steep incline of Meridian Hill. Famous for a public park designed by Frederick Law Olmstead, the slope's expanse of cascading fountains and green lawns bears an alternate name, Malcolm X Park. In the 1960s the District of Columbia was torn apart by riots following the assassination of Martin Luther King, Jr. Since Meridian Hill Park marked a boundary between poor, "colored" Washington and the wealthy, "white" sections of Upper Northwest, renaming the area to honor another slain hero of the civil rights movement was a small way for some citizens to countercolonize the space. Twenty years later the hill bears traces of other struggles as displaced and diasporic communities (especially African and Caribbean) settled in the District. The surrounding area is also now the home of many Latin American families who fled the U.S.-aided strife in their homelands. At night the park becomes a gay cruising ground, a place where drugs are sold, and the location of community concerts and festivals. Multiple histories are being lived along the hill as multiple cultures make use of its geography.[2]

Meridian Hill and its park are hybrid places where heterogeneous cultures mingle, compete, coexist. Less obvious, perhaps, is that Malcolm X/Meridian Hill Park is composed of multiple, hybridized temporalities.

Although its latinate name reveals an origin in the European colonization of the Americas, the hill bears witness through that title to another genealogy: The Native Americans who once inhabited the area considered its summit a meridian, prompting Thomas Jefferson to propose the hill as the prime meridian for the entire planet. Although his recalibration of universal time along an American axis failed, Jefferson's colonization of Native American time-space demonstrates that there is more than one way to live "American" time. The citizens who displaced the "Meridian" from the Hill to create Malcolm X Park likewise recognized that not every group narrates history according to the same *telos*. Meridian Hill embodies the conflicting ways in which contiguous cultures in their difference and overlap struggle not simply over space as *patria* and colony, but over time in its fetishization as objects and its linearization as chronology.

These disparate, thick, "colonial intimacies" in which time unfolds differently at different vantage points, according to disparate "logics of origin," is materialized by the local architecture.[3] The park's design is a mixture of French and Italian Renaissance styles. Neoclassical monuments, 1970s-style apartment houses, nineteenth-century mansions, and twentieth-century public housing overlook its walls. More significantly for the purposes of this volume, displayed prominently within the park are statues of two medieval figures: an enormous bronze of a robed Dante, clutching his *Divine Comedy*, and an equestrian Joan of Arc, sword raised to the sky. What do a medieval poet obsessed with language and desire and a cross-dressing heretic/heroine/saint have to do with the mixed cultural moment in which they find themselves?

As a little fragment of the medieval lodged in the heart of the postcolonial, these two statues in their surprising affiliation (with each other, with the minority and dominating histories that surround them) suggest that while contemporary critical theory has developed a sophisticated vocabulary for dealing with that which is *unheimlich* ("uncanny," "un-homely," "out of place"), a problem that has yet to be explored sufficiently is that posed by the *untimely*. The progress narratives of that traditional history that has left its traces in the names assigned to the major epochs of the West declare that the Middle Ages began in darkness and ended at a rebirth that made them obsolete. Yet, as the strange alliance among Dante, Joan of Arc, Native Americans, El Salvador, and Malcolm X suggests, a progressive or teleological history in which time is conceived as mere seriality and flat chronology is inadequate to the task of thinking the meanings and trauma of the past, its embeddedness in the present and future. Once homogeneity and progressive or hierarchizing "developmental" models are denied history—once simple, linear sequences of cause and effect are abandoned for more complicated narratives of heterogeneity, overlap, sedimentation, and multiplicity—time itself becomes a problem for postcolonial studies, and the medieval "meridian" or "middle" becomes an instrument useful for rethinking what postcolonial might signify.

The adjective "postcolonial" has been accommodated comfortably enough into the contemporary critical lexicon for the hyphen that used to divide its constituent parts to vanish. This disappearing punctuation, like all ghosts, tells an interesting story about time. "Post-colonial" suggests straightforwardly enough that a historical period exists that is after colonialism. "Postcolonial," the hyphen digested but its constituent elements bumping against each other without synthesis, has come to signify a temporal contiguity to, rather than an evolutionary difference from, the noun that forms its linguistic base. Just as postmodernism no longer signifies that which historically follows modernism in some binary of opposition, but is instead something that always-already existed alongside (and perhaps before) the modern, the postcolonial could be said to originate "from the very first moment of colonial contact," as a "discourse of oppositionality which colonialism brings into being."[4] Vijay Mishra and Bob Hodge describe the postcolonial as "a splinter in the side of the colonial itself," leading Michelle R. Warren to conclude that postcolonial theory opens a window "into any time or place where one social group dominates another."[5] Just as there was never a time before colony, there has never yet been a time when the colonial has been outgrown. For this reason Gayatri Spivak has suggested replacing "postcolonial" with "neocolonial," but for accuracy's sake it would make more sense to speak of the "midcolonial": the time of "always-already," an intermediacy that no narrative can pin to a single moment of history in its origin or end.[6]

Anne McClintock has cautioned that the term "postcolonial" is nonetheless haunted by a "commitment to linear time and the idea of 'development.'"[7] One could go further and argue that postcolonial theory in practice has neglected the study of the "distant" past, which tends to function as a field of undifferentiated alterity against which modern regimes of power have arisen. This exclusionary model of temporality denies the possibility that traumas, exclusions, violences enacted centuries ago might still linger in contemporary identity formations; it also closes off the possibility that this past could be multiple and valuable enough to contain (and be contained within) alternative presents and futures. No definition of postcolonial theory has gained the same citational weight as that by Homi Bhabha: "Postcolonial criticism bears witness to the unequal and uneven forces of cultural representation involved in the contest for political and social authority within the modern world order."[8] Postcolonial interventions into the "discourses of modernity" fragment the clean and easy identity narratives that cultures tell themselves, offering "critical revisions" that

stress difference, conflict, and (to cite Bhabha citing Habermas) "widely
scattered historical contingencies." "Bearing witness" would seem to be an
activity one does in the present in order to address a recent past—thus the
haunting of Bhabha's definition by the modern. Yet there is nothing especially recent about the "differential, often disadvantaged, histories of nations, races," social antagonism, and irreducible difference he describes.
Indeed, the temporal boundaries Bhabha draws seem especially arbitrary in
that an important challenge offered by his essay is a rethinking of temporality itself from a postcolonial perspective.

Perhaps it is unsurprising to find that some medievalists follow Benedict Anderson to declare that "medieval colonialism [is] oxymoronic, indeed anachronistic."[9] If the Middle Ages have been characterized too often
as a field of undifferentiated otherness against which modernity (and
therefore the possibility of a premodern postcoloniality) emerged, medievalists have to accept some blame for the blanket terms in which their
disciplines have been defined. The supposed "hard-edged alterity" of the
medieval for which some scholars have argued not only provides an astig-
matic lens through which to examine such an enormous and heterogeneous time span, but—as Kathleen Biddick has shown—also manages to
avoid confronting the colonialist traumas that mark the emergence of medieval studies as a discipline.[10] Such a characterization of the period as
wholly other repeats an exclusionary model of temporalization at least as
old as the construction of the "Renaissance" as an epoch of classical rebirth. By establishing a continuity between the pre- and postmedieval, this
periodization precipitated the Middle Ages as middle while at the same
time banishing them from any kind of center.[11] As "the West's shadowy
'other'" against which modernity-as-difference is defined, the Middle Ages
becomes, in the words of Freedman and Spiegel, "a space of empty waiting and virtual death until the reawakening of the West to its proper nature and purpose."[12]

It does not take a medievalist armed with philology, codicology, textual
and cultural theory, and history to point out that any delimitation of a field
of knowledge that stresses its internal homogeneity (even as a field of difference) is likely to be, at best, reductive. Such delimitations can be useful
to the extent that they arrange a set of previously dispersed truths in order
to construct a history that may not yet have been thought within that particular configuration. Such delimitations are dangerous, however, when
they begin to seem the singular Truth of that history, abandoning for a
monocular view of the past a perspectivism that offers a nontotalizable
"multiplicity of vantage points or positions" rather than fixed, "exclusive,
and privileged access to true representations and valid methods of knowing reality."[13] Postcolonial theory has long been urging just such a local-

ized, contextual critical perspectivism on geography, culture, recent history. A criticism that has detailed the imperialistic colonization of space surely must now turn to an examination of the epistemological colonizations of time. As the revolutionary psychoanalyst of racial oppression Frantz Fanon famously argued, "colonialism is not simply content to impose its rule upon the present and future of a dominated country."[14] Time and history are always-already colonized and never an inert, innocent Otherness waiting to be excavated.

It makes little sense to choose between continuist and alterist approaches to the study of the Middle Ages when both these metanarratives contain truths about the relation of the medieval to the modern and postmodern. Hybrid, uncanny bodies like those of the medieval giant (too exorbitant to be human, too recognizable to be anything else), the Donestre (a ferocious cannibal as well as a sympathetic auditor for homesick travelers), and the cynocephalus (a man-dog composite, as domestic as outlandish) suggest that even if the period is alluringly strange, it is at the same time discomfortingly familiar.[15] Lacanian psychoanalysis speaks of *extmité,* the "extimacy" or "intimate alterity" that characterizes whatever inassimilable remainder results when the raw Real of the world is transformed into the Symbolic structure of culture.[16] Paradoxically this abjected, traumatic otherness is lodged deep within social and individual identity, a foundational difference at the heart of the selfsame. The time-space of this intimate alterity could accurately be described as a middle in an absolute sense: an unbounded center generative of identity through that constant movement of irresolvable relations that constitute its traumatic effect, an ever-expanding line that arcs back through what has been even as it races toward what shall be.[17] Just as the monster in its spectacular corporeality has long served as the embodiment of the medieval itself, the Middle Ages as a formal effect of their very middleness could likewise be located as extimate to the modern: intimate and alien simultaneously, an "inexcluded" middle at the pulsing heart of modernity.[18] This ontological ambivalence does not mean that the Middle Ages are all things to everyone, an empty vessel rather than a point of friction and queer contiguity.[19] Rather, both "in and of themselves" and through their constitution as a distinct object of study, the Middle Ages in their mediacy confront the modern with powerful trauma conjoined to the possibility of transhistorical alliance and mutual transformation.

Medieval studies as interminable, difficult middle must stress not difference (the past as past) or sameness (the past as present) but temporal interlacement, the impossibility of choosing alterity or continuity (the past that opens up the present to possible futures). Something more than simple common sense, which always advises against choosing between extremes, this formulation of the Middle Ages as intimate alterity could spur both medievalists and those outside medieval studies to hesitate (as postcolonial studies urges) before embracing any methodological framework that is comfortable only with singular truth and precise boundaries. *Extimité* is the guarantee that only a localizing, perspectivist epistemology can hope to do justice to the heterogeneity of the past, refusing to bend it to some master narrative of progress and complete differentiation. If this Borromean knot that entwines disparate temporalities, supplanting the teleological chronology of more traditional history, seems uncannily similar to the theoretical displacement of linear history within postcolonial studies, that is no coincidence, since the "middle" of the Middle Ages is already forging a productive alliance with the nontemporal "post" of postcolonial theory, both in this volume and elsewhere.[20] It makes sense, then, to explore the complex ways in which the medieval touches the "midcolonial," making both more familiar and more strange.

The Medieval Future

How might postcolonial theory encourage an opening up of what the medieval signifies, and how might that unbounded "middle space" then suggest possible futures for postcolonial theory? How can medieval studies with its turn to the "distant" past bring about the new? Medievalists have at least five overlapping suggestions:

1. Continuously rethink the keywords of postcolonial theory's collective discourse by insisting on cultural, historical, even textual specificity. As I have suggested, of special urgency to medievalists is an engagement with terms involving time. Much work has been done on the atemporality of postcolonial theory's nonperiodizing "post," and this inquiry could be extended when paired with a rethinking of the Middle Ages' temporally perturbed "middleness." Other keywords that medievalists and postcolonial theorists are reconsidering in tandem include: race, nation, translation, spirituality, rhetoric, location, ghettoization, and internal heterogeneity.
2. Rethink history as effective history, as history that intervenes within the disciplinization of knowledge to loosen its sedimentation. Edward Said demonstrated well how knowledge itself often has an invidious history: The seeming naturalness of "truth" can be an effect of accumulating acts of power, especially colonialist power.[21] Postcolonial theorists and medievalists alike are critically reexamining the genealogy of contemporary disciplinary configurations, demonstrating the complex webs of nationalism and othering in which

they are caught. Kathleen Biddick calls this encounter with interior trauma "the work of mourning in medieval studies" and argues that without it, medievalists risk being trapped in identity politics and "elegiac loops" that render an open future impossible.[22]

3. Destabilize hegemonic identities (racial, sexual, ethnic, religious, class, age) by detailing their historical contingency. Anne McClintock has argued that nationalism constitutes identities in ways that are "frequently violent and always gendered."[23] Medievalists are demonstrating that this violent gendering of the nation is not a recent invention. Historians of sexuality have argued the relative modernity of the "homosexual vs. heterosexual" divide. Medievalists are exploring how sexuality and gender could be constructed otherwise (e.g., along a "sexual vs. celibate" axis) not in order to reestablish such categories but to take sexuality back from the biological determinists and give it the uncertain, open future it deserves. Other identity categories receiving an urgent rethinking include slaves, sex workers, laborers, people of compound ethnicity—even human identity.

4. Displace the domination of Christianity. For the Middle Ages and for contemporary scholarship, that means more work not only on Islamic, Jewish, and other non-Christian cultures, both in their relationship to Christianity and in their particularities, but also the jettisoning of progress narratives that speak of "pre-Christian" eras and "the triumph of Christianity," as if such colonization were inevitable or inherently desirable.[24] Benedict Anderson notoriously downplayed nationalism in the Middle Ages by describing Christianity as a monolithic and transnational identity, but a "post-Christian" Middle Ages means more focus on Christian heterogeneity, the ways in which *Christianitas* differed within itself. Christianity then becomes a conflicted nexus of discourses, lacking uniformity and full cohesion, mutable over time. The Gregorian reform, for example, was a massive colonization of sexualities still being felt today.

5. Decenter Europe. A postcolonial Middle Ages has no frontiers, only heterogeneous borderlands with multiple centers. This reconfigured geography includes Asia, Africa, and the Middle East not as secondary regions to be judged from a European standard, nor as "sources" from which to trace influence, but as full participants in a world simultaneously larger and more fragmented—a world of intersecting, mutating, incommensurable times and places. The supposed margins of Europe must also be rethought, so that "peripheral" geographies like Wales, Ireland, Brittany, the Midi, Catalonia become their own centers.

Underwriting all five of these imperatives is a conviction that the past need not function as a field of simple origin, as a time of mythic wholeness that underwrites contemporary fantasies of ethnic, national, or even epistemological homogeneity.[25] Janus-faced, *biformis,* the postcolonial Middle Ages performs a double work, so that the alliance of postcolonial theory and medieval studies might open up the present to multiplicity, newness, difficult similarity conjoined to complex difference.

Although most of the chapters collected here engage several of these imperatives at once, it must be admitted from the start that they accomplish some better than others. Because they take as their starting point the decolonization of "Europe" from within and employ discursive modes of analysis over other possible methodologies, the fourteen contributions to *The Postcolonial Middle Ages* tend to stress the internal heterogeneity of the West and its fantastic textual construction of the East over the necessary project of opening medieval studies to medieval India, Africa, China, and the Islamic world. Although many of the chapters displace Europe by refusing the center/margin game of subordination and unequal comparison, arguing that Jewish communities (Tomasch), Wales (Cohen, Ingham), Cilician Armenia (Burger) are centers in their own right, the non-Christian Middle Ages are approached mainly through European contact and colonization (Akbari, Biddick, Heng, Kruger, Uebel). Taken together, these chapters suggest that "Europe" as a unifying concept is a fairly recent fiction that travels back in time problematically. Indeed, the very notion of "time travel" (or the spatialization of time) is never innocent or ungendered, as Kathleen Davis demonstrates. Although England looms disproportionately large in the shared critical imaginary of this volume, this imbalance was a deliberate choice, accomplished because England has such a tight grip on the critical imaginary of North American medievalists (and postcolonial theorists). One of the volume's objectives is to loosen that stranglehold a little by demonstrating the violences and internal colonizations upon which Englishness was founded (Bowers, Robertson, Sponsler, Tomasch) as well as the postcolonial histories behind contemporary disciplinary configurations (Ganim, Ingham, Kruger). Together the contributors to this collection realize that their total effort amounts to no more than some few steps along a long road being built by many hands.

Chapter 1, by Suzanne Conklin Akbari, begins with Edward Said's thesis that East and West have always been arranged along a binary axis, where the Orient exists only to the extent that it mirrors fantastically its colonizer. Arguing against medievalists who uncritically transport this duality back into their period, Akbari excavates a medieval division of the world that is uneven, tripartite: Asia, Europe, Africa. While some medieval cartographies fixed the earth within a stable geography and history, others stressed the "flux and process essential to the development of nations." The *orbis terrarum* was for the most part oriented through a mapping of climatic extremes, with Asia as the happy middle. Only in the fourteenth century was the world shifted to render the cold North the desirable West; the once-temperate East becomes the overheated mirror of this newly invented Occident.

In chapter 2, Kathleen Biddick argues that Edward Said's critique of racialized geographies in *Orientalism* depends on an unthought series of racialized *temporalities*. Said locates the originary moment of Orientalism in Dante, producing the Middle Ages as "a fantastic origin that sets in motion a progressive history," as an adolescence linked to exile and homelessness. The medieval is conflated with exile throughout Said's work, where "exile" is glossed as an atemporal, purified, immobile space. Biddick argues that medievalists need to be attentive to postcolonial critiques of exile, such as that by Orhan Pamuk in *The New Life,* which suggest different, living temporal orders. These complex, engaged temporalities undercut Orientalist binaries and invite medievalists out of their own disciplinary exile to engage postcolonial time.

John M. Bowers, in chapter 3, excavates the formation of "English" identity in Chaucer's late writing. English at the close of the fourteenth century was a colonized language in a state of transition, absorbing a new French vocabulary and fractured into a variety of regional dialects. Chaucer's exclusive use of London English is somewhat surprising, considering that French was for him both a domestic and a courtly language; even the five Canterbury pilgrims who would have been bilingual never speak a word of French. Bowers argues that Chaucer resists easy binaries of identification. He never imagines a country united in an essential Englishness because to do so would have validated the otherness of the English as a subaltern people against the French. Chaucer's English nationalism is the product of a "crowded pageant of uniquely crafted personalities," a present-looking and eclectic multiculturalism. At the same time, Chaucer resolutely refuses to voice the Norman origins of the contemporary nation, deconstructing all discourses of origin instead. The temporality in which he sets his *Canterbury Tales* is not the official chronology of the liturgical calendar, by which secular events become saturated with religious meaning, but instead an "in-between" period constructed by coincidence and cut off from ritual. The imagined community of his pilgrims is contingent, fragmented, multiple—and unified in its unstoppable drive to possess.

In chapter 4 Glenn Burger calls attention to Hetoum's *La Fleur des histoires de la terre d'Orient,* a widely popular medieval text, the "disorienting discontinuities" of which precipitated a long struggle to assimilate

its difference into familiar Christian sameness. Hetoum's work embodies
the cultural multiplicities of its origin in a Cilician Armenian diasporic
community, where Christian heterogeneity intersected with conflicting
Islamic empires (Egyptian and Mongol). The text intervenes into crusade
discourses with a cross-cultural negotiation exceeding anything Europe
was capable of imagining. Cilician Armenia frustrates any attempt to articulate a singular ethnic, religious, political identity, even as this middle
space becomes (in Hetoum's text) a "productive sign of renewal and
strength for Armenia, Outremer, and Europe." Between the two worlds
of Europe and Asia while belonging to neither, Hetoum resisted essentialized identities and easy formulations of otherness, emphasizing diversity and alliance over singular visions of domination in order to challenge
European dreams of a monolithic Orient.

In chapter 5 Jeffrey Jerome Cohen uses the writings of Giraldus Cambrensis to argue that the concept of "hybridity" derived from postcolonial
treatments of English India does not fully capture the force of the phenomenon in the twelfth century Welsh March. The son of an Anglo-Norman father and a half-Welsh mother, Gerald was trained as a cleric in Paris
and served Henry II as court chaplain. Multiple allegiances and possible
identifications course through his mixed blood, spurring a lifelong fascination with *mixta,* hybrid bodies that cannot assimilate their constitutive
histories. With their spectacular, corporeal insistence on historical context
and the simultaneous existence of multiple colonialisms, these medieval
monsters are similar to those examined by Gloria Anzaldua in her analysis
of the function of contemporary cultural borderlands. Medievalists, Cohen
argues, can usefully put themselves in dialogue with those working in Chi-
cana/o studies and other postcolonialist fields that at first might seem unlikely allies in opening up the past to the future.

Kathleen Davis's chapter conducts a postcolonial inquiry into the signification of conflicting medieval temporalities within contemporary
colonialism. This three-part chapter brings together a recent political documentary, Edward Said's *Orientalism,* and Chaucer's *Man of Law's Tale* as it
examines the interrelations of the gendered temporalities in contemporary
and medieval Orientalisms. A critical apprehension of colonial violence
upon women's bodies requires a disruption of the temporal logic that underwrote colonialism and is being reproduced in both critical theory and
globalizing rhetoric today. Davis argues that medievalists are uniquely positioned to disrupt temporal oppositions, to demonstrate how every monolithic origin is cut through with other cultural presences, other gendered
times.

In chapter 7, John M. Ganim explicates the tension between myths of
foundational purity inherent in critical constructions of the Middle Ages

and the "actual," historical overlap of what would now be called Western and non-Western cultures during the medieval period. The struggle over what constitutes occidental culture and what is to be excluded from its composition has long been waged through the Middle Ages, especially in arguments over "foreign" influence on Gothic architecture and romance narrative. To the eighteenth century, fascinated by Oriental exoticism, the medieval world was a site of both native continuity and exorbitant alterity. Colonialism, especially in India, pervasively hierarchized racial difference, and the Middle Ages was called in to serve as a happy model for the control of "inferior" civilizations by their conquerors. Anthropology turned from the frontiers of empire to the otherness within European history, leading to a Middle Ages full of folk ritual and custom. Ganim finds in the unresolved controversies over the Celtic origins of Arthurian literature and the Arabic origin of courtly love a protracted battle over the Europeanness of the medieval past, over its dual status as both origin and rupture.

Geraldine Heng in chapter 8 details the cultural work of cannibalistic jokes in the Middle English romance *Richard Coer de Lyon.* When King Richard learns that some pork he ate was actually the flesh of a Saracen, he laughs and declares his army will never be hungry again with such delicious meat abounding. The thirteenth century conjoined a new zeal for bodily discipline with an obsession for making deviance visible: Discourses to mark racial, religious, and bodily difference circulated as instruments for an emergent nationalism embodied by the king. Heng argues that Richard's joke and the exorbitant visualization of black flesh that surrounds its telling are directed toward the English nation, offering a spectacular racial otherness to precipitate a collective cohesion. This alterity is not only Muslim but Jewish. Heng links Richard's cannibalism of Islamic bodies to contemporary aggression against English Jews, highly visible communities upon which the economic vitality of the nation depended. She also sees in the romance a rewriting of historical class inequality within a utopian imaginary of English justice, abundance, and solidarity. *Richard Coer de Lyon* is an experiment in literary fiction that aids in bringing about a fiction of another sort: the nation itself, "an experiment that has not yet seen its conclusion."

Patricia Ingham begins chapter 9 with an account of Matthew Arnold's "sponsorship" of Celtic studies. Arnold constructed medieval Welsh literature as a fragment of a majestic tradition now lost to (impersonal, relentless) "Time," thus effacing a colonialist history. Although his pro-Celtic scholarship undermined contemporary racism, Arnold argued in the same breath that Celtic culture was to be preserved only as an academic object of study, thus denying it a vitality in the present. Ingham argues that colonialist desires are still embedded in "dispassionate" methodologies, especially in a view of time as an irresistible progress that demands submission and loss. The archaic in this formulation of temporality is inhabited by marginal cultures that must inevitably surrender their identity to the assimilationist demands of modernity; cultural difference is rich so long as it is contained by the past, and—because it has been irrevocably lost—impossible for the present and future. "Branwen, Daughter of Llyr" entwines Welsh culture and loss but (unlike Arnold) insists that this loss is the contingent product of "geopolitical and historical actions." Doubleness, fragmentation, and a vexed chronology characterize the story, eluding colonist progress narratives while implicating them in inconsolable loss. Ingham finds in the tale's insistence on particularity a possibility for a reconfigured understanding of time as well as the promise of a more compassionate future.

Chapter 10, by Steven F. Kruger, unfolds the multiple temporalities embedded in a key term of postcolonial theory. By examining the traces of racialized discourse haunting Freud's explication of the fetish, Kruger maps the traces of the race-obsessed "age of discovery" within psychoanalysis, then demonstrates how both these moments depend on the medieval even as they deny it. The word "fetish" is etymologically linked to the European colonization and enslavement of Africa, and this earlier, still dominant "anthropological/religious" discourse is one that Freud represses, only to have it return in his racialized treatment of sexual perversions. Kruger argues for a parallel to this disavowal in the "fetish accusations" of medieval religious polemic, with its anxious disavowal of Jewish disbelief. The dissemination of the word "fetish," further, assists in a program of making the experience of Africa seem new, disavowing a historical continuity between the commercial and religious situation of the early modern period and that of the medieval. That which is premodern is not necessarily left behind at the advent of the modern but in fact survives within and substantiates that modernity.

Kellie Robertson argues in chapter 11 that in late-fourteenth-century England, the rise in vernacular translation and expansion of the mercantile economy were not (as has been previously assumed) causally related but were rather cognate developments. Drawing on postcolonial language and translation theory, Robertson details how both vernacularization and trade were "suspect activities" that overcame official opprobrium to occupy and redefine the public space. Justifications for the use of English in writing were intimately tied to social dissent. Lollard writers, for example, exposed how the Church's resistance to translation of the Bible fortified contemporary class structures. Translation as the "merchandizing" of knowledge was analogous to trade. Both terms were redefined by their relation to "common profit," which through this commingling became a hybrid concept in Homi Bhabha's sense of the word: a resistant site where authority is deformed and subverted. "In translation, as in trade," Robertson writes, "there were no essences," leading to the wide circulation of a worldview (condensed materially into books and manuscripts) very unlike the clerical belief in fixed meanings and values which it challenged.

In chapter 12 Claire Sponsler analyzes public spectacle in Lancastrian England to map transformations in the representation of foreignness. John Lydgate's mummings intervene into London's potentially xenophobic mercantile communities to perform a new set of relations that phantasmatically unites native and alien merchants, even if only temporarily. London was a large city whose ethnically and linguistically diverse population was susceptible, in times of economic stress, to fragmentation, scapegoating, and violence against the smallest and least powerful groups. At a time when hostility toward aliens was high, Lydgate's performances of cosmopolitan inclusion constructs a generous, open world where cultural difference is accommodated into the fellowship of the guilds, although subordinated and distanced at the same time. London is figured as a Mecca that draws grateful outsiders into its folds, where they are absorbed into a newly inclusive Englishness in "fantasy of easy solutions to the complex problems facing urban manufacturing and trading communities."

Sylvia Tomasch insists in chapter 13 that Chaucer's work is haunted by the Jew, corporally absent but paradoxically central to late fourteenth-century English identity. The colonialist moment of 1290, when the country's entire Jewish population was expelled, endured well into the next century by turning inward to colonize the English as subjects. In Chaucer's *Canterbury Tales,* Jews lose their religion, their community, their bodies as anti- and philo-Semiticism combine into a dangerous "allosemitism" that divorces the historical Jew from reality. Tomasch's formulation of "virtuality" draws from the representational theories of Homi Bhabha and Marie-Laure Ryan to push postcolonial theory to consider how absences and eradications performed in the past inhabit the present: The expulsion of the Jews in 1290 is part of a "postcolonial continuum" that entangles medieval trauma in contemporary identities.

In chapter 14 Michael Uebel traces the linking of fetishism and imperialism in two twelfth-century narratives of magical gifts, Christopher Columbus's journal, and an early twentieth-century book for boys. The *Letter of Prester John* announced to a medieval West dispirited by the failure of the second crusade that a Christian sovereign already ruled in the East. The fabulous and extended lists of gifts in the letter compensated for the lost Holy Land while conserving the Orient by fragmenting it into discrete *facta.* These lists perform a fantasy for the "meeting of self and other across the space opened up by their putative differences," so that in some narratives misunderstandings about the value of Prester John's gems open up the possibility of restructuring relations to that other. Uebel allies this ecstatic leap into new phantasmatic spaces with Russian filmmaker Sergei Eisenstein's idea of montage; both share a utopic impulse capable of altering reality. Columbus was beckoned to the New World by Prester John, who functioned as a fetish, "an impassioned object" concentrating multiple social and psychological values, while enabling an imaginary, ideal union of religion and conquest. John Buchan found in the same figure a symbolic ideal of resistance to imperialism, an anticolonialist Prester John who restores difference and enables a revolutionary leap. The oscillation between these possibilities, Uebel concludes, reveals the dynamic nature of the fetish from the twelfth to the twentieth century.

Notes

1. Antonio Benítez-Rojo, *The Repeating Island: The Caribbean and the Post-modern Perspective,* 2nd ed., trans. James E. Maraniss (Durham, NC: Duke University Press, 1996), p.11. Benítez-Rojo is writing specifically of the Caribbean as a "meta-archipelago," a figuration I have found especially useful in struggling toward a language in which to collect an entity as big as "the Middle Ages" even while insisting on the violence generalization performs.

2. The hill and its multiple histories are located within the larger political space of the District of Columbia, which has been described as an interior colony of the United States. Unlike the residents of the fifty states, citizens of the District of Columbia do not elect a voting member of Congress to represent their interests in either the Senate or the House of Representatives. Democracy in the District is allowed only at the whim of Congress: At any time an elected mayor and city council can be replaced by a federally appointed control board; local governance (including the city's budget) is overseen by a congressional committee.

3. The quotations are from Sara Suleri's excellent analysis of postcolonial time in *The Rhetoric of English India* (Chicago: University of Chicago Press, 1992), p. 9. My discussion of time is also informed by the work of Anne McClintock in *Imperial Leather: Race, Gender, and Sexuality in the Colonial Conquest* (New York: Routledge, 1995), esp. p. 10, and "'No Longer in a Future Heaven': Gender, Race and Nationalism," in *Dangerous Liaisons: Gender, Nation, and Postcolonial Perspectives,* ed. McClintock, Aamir Mufti, and Ella Shohat (Minneapolis: University of Minnesota Press, 1997), pp. 89–112.

4. See the thoughtful anthology compiled by Bill Ashcroft, Gareth Griffiths, and Helen Tiffin, *The Post-Colonial Studies Reader* (New York: Routledge,

1995), p. 117. The section on "Postmodernism and Post-Colonialism" (pp. 117–47) contains selections from essays by Kwame Anthony Appiah, Simon During, Linda Hutcheon, Diana Brydon, and Kumkum Sangari that explore the imbricated but different temporalities of these two supposed "post-"s. Anne McClintock ("The Angel of Progress: Pitfalls of the Term 'Post-Colonialism,'" *Social Text* 31–32 [1992]: 84–98) has cautioned that the term "postcolonial" is still haunted by a "commitment to linear time and the idea of 'development'" (85), which postcolonial theory argues against, and therefore should be deployed with caution (if at all).

5. Vijay Mishra and Bob Hodge, "What is Post(-)Colonialism?" in *Textual Practice* 5 (1991): 399–414, quotation at p. 411; Michelle R. Warren, "Making Contact: Postcolonial Perspectives through Geoffrey of Monmouth's *Historia regum Britannie*," *Arthuriana* 8.4 (1998): 115–34, quotation at p. 115.

6. For Gayatri Spivak on neocolonialism, see "Neocolonialism and the Secret Agent of Knowledge: Interview with Robert Young," in *Oxford Literary Review* 13.1–2 (1987): 220–51.

7. McClintock, "The Angel of Progress," p. 85.

8. Bhabha's delimitation has so powerfully affected the critical imaginary of the field because it appears in two texts fundamental to the institutionalization of postcolonial studies, especially within literary studies: first in the collection *Redrawing the Boundaries: The Transformation of English and American Literary Studies,* ed. Stephen Greenblatt and Giles Gunn (New York: Modern Language Association of America, 1992), where Bhabha's essay is made to speak for all postcolonial criticism; the essay was then republished as "The Postcolonial and the Postmodern" in Bhabha's widely influential book *The Location of Culture* (New York: Routledge, 1994), pp. 171–97. I quote here from the latter version.

9. See Benedict Anderson, *Imagined Communities: Reflections on the Origin and Spread of Nationalism* (London: Verso, 1983). Kathleen Biddick argues against this perspective in a typically rich footnote to her essay "The ABC of Ptolomy: Mapping the World with the Alphabet," in *Text and Territory: Geographical Imagination in the European Middle Ages,* ed. Sylvia Tomasch and Sealy Gilles (Philadelphia: University of Pennsylvania Press, 1998), pp. 268–93, quotation at p. 291. For a historical refutation of the view, one need look no further than Joshua Prawer, *The Latin Kingdom of Jerusalem: European Colonization in the Middle Ages* (London: Weidenfeld and Nicolson, 1972); as Bruce Holsinger pointed out to me when I began putting this collection together, medievalists have unselfconsciously been engaged with a kind of postcolonial criticism for a very long time. On Anderson's thesis, recent postcolonial theory, and medieval studies, see also Kathleen Davis's valuable discussion in "National Writing in the Ninth Century: A Reminder for Postcolonial Thinking about the Nation," in *Journal of Medieval and Early Modern Studies* 28:3 (1998): 611–37.

10. These traumas are specifically related to the imperialist moments during which British and North American medieval studies articulated their

self-identity. See Kathleen Biddick, *The Shock of Medievalism* (Durham, NC: Duke University Press, 1998), pp. 3–12, and Paul Freedman and Gabrielle M. Spiegel, "Medievalisms Old and New: The Rediscovery of Alterity in North American Medieval Studies," *American Historical Review* (June 1998): 677–704. "Hard-edged alterity" is Stephen G. Nichols' term in "Modernism and the Politics of Medieval Studies," in *Medievalism and the Modernist Temper,* ed. R. Howard Bloch and Nichols (Baltimore: Johns Hopkins University Press, 1996), p. 49, and is also used by Marina S. Brownlee, Kevin Brownlee, and Nichols in *The New Medievalism* (Baltimore: Johns Hopkins University Press, 1991), p. 12. The phrase is cited as definitive of a certain approach to the Middle Ages by both Biddick (*Shock of Medievalism,* p. 4) and by Freedman and Spiegel in their influential survey of the state of the North American field ("Medievalisms Old and New," p. 677).

11. On the critical significance of the break performed by the construction of the Renaissance as the other of the medieval, see Lee Patterson, "Critical Historicism and Medieval Studies," in *Literary Practice and Social Change in Britain, 1380–1530,* ed. Patterson (Berkeley: University of California Press, 1990), p. 2.

12. Freedman and Spiegel, "Medievalisms Old and New," p. 678.

13. On feminist epistemologies and perspectivism (which is not at all the same thing as relativism), see Elizabeth Grosz, "Bodies and Knowledges: Feminism and the Crisis of Reason," in *Space, Time, and Perversion* (New York: Routledge, 1995), pp. 25–43; quotation at p. 30.

14. Frantz Fanon, *The Wretched of the Earth,* trans. Constance Farrington (New York: Grove Press, 1963), p. 210.

15. For my work on medieval monstrousness (which this sentence summarizes), see "Monster Culture (Seven Theses)" in *Monster Theory: Reading Culture,* ed. Jeffrey Jerome Cohen (Minneapolis: University of Minnesota Press, 1996), pp. 3–25, and *Of Giants: Sex, Monsters, and the Middle Ages* (Minneapolis: University of Minnesota Press, 1999).

16. On "intimate alterity," see Charles Shepherdson, "The Intimate Alterity of the Real: A Response to Reader Commentary on 'History and the Real,'" in *Postmodern Culture* 6:3 (1996). I discuss the term at greater length in *Of Giants,* p. xii.

17. For the Middle Ages as middle in an absolute sense, see Jeffrey Cohen and Bonnie Wheeler, "Introduction: Becoming and Unbecoming," in *Becoming Male in the Middle Ages,* ed. Cohen and Wheeler (New York: Garland, 1997), pp. xii-xiii.

18. On the intertwining of the Middle Ages and monstrousness, see John Ganim, "Medieval Literature as Monster: The Grotesque Before and After Bakhtin," *Exemplaria* 7.1 (1995): 27–40.

19. On the alluring, disturbing, denaturalizing touch of the queer (a concept inherently allied with the postcolonial), see Carolyn Dinshaw, "Chaucer's

Queer Touches / A Queer Touches Chaucer," *Exemplaria* 7.1 (1995): 75–92.

20. In addition to the work already cited, see Maria Rosa Menocal, *The Arabic Role in Medieval Literary History* (Philadelphia: University of Pennsylvania Press, 1987), and Menocal, *Shards of Love: Exile and the Origins of Lyric* (Durham, NC: Duke University Press, 1994).

21. Edward Said, *Orientalism* (New York: Random House, 1978, reprinted 1994).

22. Kathleen Biddick, *The Shock of Medievalism,* pp. 10–11.

23. Anne McClintock, "'No Longer in a Future Heaven,'" p. 89.

24. It also means no longer leaving Christianity as the "unmarked" religion, so that books about "medieval popular religion" no longer assume that "religion" transparently means "Christianity." On this point see Steven F. Kruger, "Conversion and Medieval Sexual, Religious, and Racial Categories," in *Constructing Medieval Sexuality,* ed. Karma Lochrie, Peggy McCracken, and James A. Schultz (Minneapolis: University of Minnesota Press, 1997), pp. 158–79, esp. pp. 158–59.

25. For this specific formulation of what the postcolonial Middle Ages might accomplish, I am grateful to Stephen Slemon's paper presented at the Postcolonial Middle Ages workshop at the University of Alberta, Edmonton (April 1999). Reflecting on the five imperatives I have outlined, Slemon argued that medieval studies is well situated to address the political imperatives of postcolonial theory by undermining contemporary discourses of origin, arguing against the transhistoricity of normative liberal discourses of unified subjectivity, and cautioning against myths of purity and wholeness.

CHAPTER 1

FROM DUE EAST TO TRUE NORTH:
ORIENTALISM AND ORIENTATION

Suzanne Conklin Akbari

This chapter examines how the East/West duality came into being, finding in Asia a third term that calls into question medieval "Orientalism."

Since its publication in the late 1970s, Edward Said's masterful study *Orientalism* has been the foundation of virtually every effort to characterize literary descriptions of the Near and Middle East. Said argues that the Orient and the Occident mirror one another, locked in a mutually self-sustaining fiction.[1] Yet, as Aijaz Ahmad has pointed out, Said's account of the origins of the idea of the Orient is, at best, plural; at worst, contradictory. The Orient is simultaneously both a product of Western European colonization of Egypt and the Levant during the eighteenth and nineteenth centuries and a concept that has existed almost since the beginning of time.[2] Said devotes little space to accounts of the Orient found in medieval texts,[3] a peculiar omission in view of the fact that Western efforts to conquer Jerusalem during the Crusades can be seen as an early manifestation of modern efforts to colonize the Orient.[4]

Even studies of the East in modern literature that are critical of Said's arguments accept both the ambiguous origin of Orientalism and the mirroring binary of Orient and Occident that he posits.[5] Medievalists have pointed out the presence of something like more modern manifestations of Orientalism in the richly nuanced portrayals of a luxurious Orient, characterized by sexual and economic surplus, found in medieval texts.[6]

Yet even these studies have done little to disrupt the dichotomy of Asian Orient and European Occident generally taken for granted. A medieval source for the dichotomy is rarely offered; and when it is, the dichotomy proves to be hardly straightforward. For example, one otherwise useful study of the Orient in the fourteenth-century Middle English *Wars of Alexander* bases the dichotomy of Orient and Occident on the opposition of Muslim East and Christian West attributed to the twelfth-century theologian Peter the Venerable.[7] Yet Peter's account of the geographical parameters of the clash of Christianity and Islam is more nuanced. He opens one work with a comment on how "strange" it is that he "write[s] from the far parts of the West to men who inhabit the lands of the East and South."[8] Elsewhere Peter describes a Christendom penned into one corner of the known world by an Islamic empire encroaching on its borders, occupying "the greatest part of Asia, with all of Africa and a part of Spain."[9]

It is true that medieval Christian texts such as polemics against Islam, Crusade chronicles, and *chansons de geste* emphatically articulate a dichotomy of good Christian and bad pagan, "us" and "them."[10] It would be a mistake, however, to conflate a binary overtly based on religious difference with the binary of Orient and Occident. The East is where "they" are; it is, as Mary Campbell puts it, "essentially Elsewhere."[11] It does not follow, however, that the West is where "we" are. In the following pages, I show how the designation of the Orient as a fixed point permits the generation of its own Other, opposite to it in every respect. That Other, however, is not our modern West. Instead, medieval geography divides the world not into two but three. As Augustine puts it, "the whole world is divided into three parts: Asia, Europe, and Africa; but they are not divided equally . . . [I]f you divide the world into two parts, Orient and Occident, Asia is in one and, in the other, Europe and Africa."[12] This schema is echoed throughout the encyclopedic and patristic traditions, in both maps and descriptive geographies. A whole, homogeneous East is posited, which only gradually gives rise to its mirror image: a cold (because northerly) European West.

Medieval world maps, or *mappaemundi,* depict the world as simultaneously whole and divided. It is whole because the known world is linked genealogically, due to mankind's common descent from Shem, Ham, and Japheth, whose names appear on *mappaemundi* next to or even in place of the names of the three continents.[13] Further, it is whole because the world is linked spiritually, due to mankind's collective redemption by Christ. Such unity is manifest in the Ebstorf *mappamundi,* where the head, hands, and feet of Jesus appear at the margins of the known world, affirming the coterminousness of the body of Christ and the earth itself. In the schema of the *mappamundi*, the world is divided not only into three parts, the three known continents, but also into four: the cardinal directions. *Oriens,* usually located at the top of the map, designates the place where the sun rises; *occidens,* where it sets; *septentrio,* the location of the North Star; and *meridies,* the area closest to the equator.

The primacy of the Orient on these maps is illustrated not only by their eastern "orientation" but by the illustration of the Garden of Eden frequently found at the top, signaling the location of the now-forbidden earthly Paradise.[14] Moreover, the primacy of the Oriental continent of Asia is reflected in the positioning of Jerusalem, which often is depicted prominently at or near the center of *mappaemundi,* especially after the beginning of the Crusades.[15] On such maps Jerusalem appears less as a place of origin than as a place of return, the objective of every assault on the Holy Land and the conjectured site of the Last Judgment.[16] In this context, it is interesting to note that the map of the Holy Land included in Matthew Paris's *Chronica majora* (ca. 1270) emphasizes the centrality not of Jerusalem but of the last crusader stronghold of Acre (lost in 1291), signaling the imperative of conquest essential to the world maps created during the Crusades.[17]

The centrality of Jerusalem is affirmed in the descriptive geographies of medieval encyclopedias. Isidore of Seville states that Jerusalem is located at the center of the province of Judea, "quasi umbilicus regionis totius."[18] His assertion is based on biblical references to the city's position "in the middle of the earth" (Psalm 73:12; cf. Ezekiel 5:5), emphasized in the early-fifth-century commentary on Ezekiel written by Jerome.[19] Isidore's statement is echoed by other encyclopedists, including (in the ninth century) Hrabanus Maurus and (in the thirteenth century) Vincent of Beauvais and Bartholomaeus Anglicus. Hrabanus Maurus amplifies Isidore's descriptions, stating that Jerusalem is the navel "of the region and of the whole earth" [quasi umbilicus regionis et totius terrae].[20] Vincent of Beauvais follows Isidore closely,[21] as does Bartholomaeus Anglicus: "In the myddel of this Judea is the cite of Jerusalem, as it were the navel of all the cuntrey and londe."[22]

Diagrams of the world impose order by establishing both a fixed center and a periphery. In her study of medieval wind diagrams, which, like the *mappaemundi,* have an eastern orientation, Barbara Obrist shows that "the main role of the cardinal winds in the medieval view was to contribute to the coherence and stability of the universe."[23] The world depicted on the *mappaemundi* is similarly ordered by its boundaries, marked by the four cardinal directions. The fourfold division of the earth has biblical as well as cosmological foundations: In Revelation 7:1 John relates that he "saw four angels standing on the four corners of the earth, holding

the four winds of the earth." This fourfold geographical schema found its
way into the medieval encyclopedic tradition as well. The natural universe
was seen as fundamentally quadripartite: Matter was divided into the four
elements, time into the four seasons, while human health was regulated by
the balance of the four bodily humors. Hrabanus Maurus bases the account
of the world in his *De universo* on this fourfold schema, stating that there
are four cardinal points within which the whole circle of the earth is contained (12.2, col. 333B). Hrabanus immediately adds that the earth can,
moreover, be divided into three parts (Asia, Europe, and Africa) and also
into two (Orient and Occident [col. 333D]). Yet Hrabanus Maurus, like the
other encyclopedists, fits the three continents into the four cardinal directions only awkwardly: Asia is said to extend from the South along the East
as far as the North; Europe from the North along the West; Africa from the
West as far as the South (col. 333C).[24] The uneven distribution of the three
continents into the four corners of the earth is heightened in medieval accounts of the population of the continents by the sons of Noah, whose dispersal is similarly unequal.

As Benjamin Braude has demonstrated, the association of each of the
three sons of Noah with each of the three known continents has been far
from consistent. The assumption that Shem is to be invariably associated
with Asia, Ham with Africa, and Japheth with Europe has so influenced
modern readings of medieval texts that in at least one case, the readings of
an otherwise authoritative manuscript of *Mandeville's Travels* have been
wrongly amended to associate the sons with their "proper" continents.[25]
Braude rightly asserts that "the medieval understanding did not simply and
consistently allot Africa to Ham, Asia to Shem, and Europe to Japhet."[26] Yet
as Braude himself acknowledges, a number of medieval texts do baldly assert the standard distribution of the three continents among the sons of
Noah (e.g., Vincent of Beauvais, 1.62; Bartholomaeus Anglicus, 15.1), while
medieval maps use the names of the sons interchangeably with the names
of the continents. Even as a stable one-to-one correspondence between the
sons of Noah and the continents is asserted (as in the *mappaemundi* and general prefatory statements by the encyclopedists), more nuanced accounts of
the sons' migration (as in the ninth book of Isidore's *Etymologies*) emphasize
the flux and process essential to the development of nations.

The essentializing tendency evident in the correspondence of Noah's
sons to the continents also appears in the association of one son, Ham, with
one cardinal direction, and the consequent association of his brothers with
different climates. The association of Ham with heat goes back at least to
Jerome: "Ham, id est calidus."[27] His etymological essentializing of Ham is
repeated throughout the patristic and encyclopedic traditions. Hrabanus
Maurus follows Augustine in explaining the allegorical significance of the

etymology: The heat associated with Ham represents "the primordial passions of the Jews and heretics, which disturbs the peace of the holy."[28] Ham's progeny can be understood allegorically, as Hrabanus does, or literally, as in Isidore's account of the predominant distribution of Ham's offspring in the southern continent of Africa.[29] The association of Noah's other sons with other climatic conditions follows from the association of Ham with the heat of the south. Isidore identifies the regions related to Japheth as not simply the northern continent, Europe, but the northern regions of Asia (14.3.31).[30] The offspring of Shem are not identified in terms of climate due to the much grander scale of his land allotment: His patrimony, Asia, includes both northern and southern lands.

In view of his dominant role among the sons of Noah—firstborn, receiving the first fruits of the blessing of Noah (Gen. 9:26)—it is appropriate that Shem is heir to the greatest portion of the world. In Bartholomaeus Anglicus's thirteenth-century account of the division of the continents among the sons of Noah, Shem's primacy is emphasized by immediately following an explanation of how each of the three sons of Noah was heir to each of the three continents with a brief account of Asia, Shem's inheritance; all the nations of the world (and the other two continents) follow, "sequendo ordinem alphabeti" (15.1, 15.2). Bartholomaeus's ordering principle gives prominence only to Asia rather than to each of the three continents. Both Isidore, in book 14 of the *Etymologies,* and Vincent of Beauvais, in his *Speculum historiale,* treat the nations of Asia, Europe, and Africa in three separate groups, placing Asia first. For Bartholomaeus, however, Asia alone serves as a point of orientation according to which all other locations are ordered: Shem's portion is the greatest in terms of both size and centrality. In his twelfth-century commentary on the Pentateuch, Hugh of Saint Victor follows Isidore in assigning the sons of Japheth "the northern part of Asia and all of Europe" and the sons of Ham "the southern part of Asia and all of Africa." Shem's sons, by contrast, inherit the middle ground: "Medium autem Asiae, quae major est quam Europa et Africa, filii Sem possederunt."[31] For Hugh, Asia is "middle" in the sense that it is centrally located: It is most desirable and is predominant in terms of size.

For Bartholomaeus Anglicus, however, the middle ground comes to seem less desirable. At the end of his chapter "Europa," Bartholomaeus compares the three types of peoples who inhabit the known world. Following Isidore (*Etym.* 9.2.105), he states that the men of Africa are adversely affected by the heat of the sun, which discolors their bodies and weakens their spirit:

[T]he sonne abideth longe over the Affers, men of Affrica, and brennen and wasten humours and maken ham short of body, blacke of face, with crispe

here. And for here spirites passe oute atte pores that ben open, so they be
more cowardes of herte.

An the cuntrarye is of men of the northe londe: for coldenes that is with-
oute stoppeth the pores and breedeth humours of the bodye maketh men
more ful and huge; and coolde that is modir of whitnesse maketh hem the
more white in face and in skynne, and vapoures and spirites ben ysmyten
inwarde and maken hatter withinne and so the more bolde and hardy. An
the men of Asia ben meneliche disposed in that, and here firste londe is by
eeste.(15.50; pp. 752–53)

This passage is remarkable in a number of respects, not least because it re-
defines the middle ground of Asia in a pejorative sense. The men of Asia
are "meneliche disposed," or in Bartholomaeus' original Latin, "mediocriter." The heat of southern men is expressed outwardly, leaving them
"cowardes of herte"; the heat of northern men is expressed inwardly, making them "bolde and hardy." The visible signs of cowardice and boldness
are dark skin and white skin, for the heat of the sun makes men "blacke of
face," while coldness is the "modir of whitness."

In his account of the extremes of heat and cold and their visible manifestations in men, Bartholomaeus follows Isidore closely. His account dif-
fers, however, from that of the seventh-century bishop in the context
within which those extremes are placed: specifically, the way in which the
white men of the North and the dark men of the South are located relative to the encyclopedist's own homeland. This difference can be appreci-
ated only in the context of each encyclopedist's method of ordering his
work. In keeping with his method of etymological exegesis, Isidore emphasizes the interrelation of the development of languages and the growth
of nations, taking these as his dual theme in the ninth book of the *Etymologies.* He treats geography separately in the fourteenth book, although
he alludes there as well to the names of the sons of Noah and their descendants in explaining the etymological origin of place-names. The thirteenth-century encyclopedist Vincent of Beauvais similarly conflates the
origin of languages and the origin of peoples; his innovations relative to
Isidore take place on the level of content rather than form. Vincent abbre-
viates, integrating into a single book the account of peoples, languages, and
the world geography treated by Isidore separately in books nine and fourteen of the *Etymologies.* Bartholomaeus' treatment of the material, by contrast, is more innovative: He omits the focus on the development of
languages central to Isidore's account. Instead, Bartholomaeus emphasizes
the role of geography in generating national identity.

Isidore had stated that "nations grow out of languages, not languages out
of nations." For Bartholomaeus, language is not involved at all: Instead, na-

tions grow out of the soil they are planted in. That is, for Isidore, the diversity of languages comes first; the migration of peoples follows; finally, the physical qualities of a nation are altered by the climate its members inhabit. For Bartholomaeus, however, climate is the only factor that determines the characteristics of a nation. Yet the most important difference between Isidore's and Bartholomaeus' accounts of the effect of climate on nations can be found in the context in which each encyclopedist embeds the comparison of northerners and southerners. In his account of the white-complected Gauls and the dark-skinned Mauritanians, Bartholomaeus follows Isidore closely. Gaul has its name due to the "whittenes of men. For *Gallia* is grew [Greek] and is to menynge 'melke.'" Galicia is similarly named after the "wy3tnes of men, for they ben more wy3te than men of the othere cuntreis of Spayne" (15.66; p. 763). Just as the Gauls are named on account of their milky white skin, so the Mauritanians are named after their black skin: "Mauritania hath that name of the colour of men, as it were to menynge 'blacke.' For as Fransshe men ben yclepede Galli and han that name of whitnes of men, so men of this londe ben yclepede Maury and han that name of blacke colour" (15.93; p. 780). These etymologies are based on Isidore (9.2.104, 14.4.25; 9.2.122, 14.5.10), and Bartholomaeus explicitly cites the ninth book of the *Etymologies* in explaining how the qualities of the people of a nation are determined by its climate: "For by the dyversite of hevene, face and colour of men and hertes and witte and quantite of bodyes ben dyvers. Therefore Rome gendreth hevy men, Frece li3t men, Affrica gyleful men, and Fraunce kyndeliche fers men and sharpe of witte" (15.67, p. 763; cf. Isidore 9.2.105). Bartholomaeus expands upon Isidore's account of the effect of a land's climate on the physical traits of its inhabitants, as when he describes how the Ethiopians are darkened by the sun; his fourteenth-century translator, Trevisa, in one of his relatively few departures from literal translation, amplifies this aspect even further, stating that the sun "rosteth and tosteth ham [them]" (15.52; p. 754).[32]

Bartholomaeus' and Isidore's treatments of the Gauls and Mauritanians differ in the way in which each encyclopedist relates these peoples to his own homeland. Unlike Bartholomaeus, Isidore describes the geography of the world as if he were following the contours of a map: He enumerates the lands of Asia, beginning in the farthest east with Paradise (14.3.2), India (14.3.5), and Parthia (14.3.8), in that order. His account of Asia finishes up in the northeast and resumes with Europe, beginning with Scythia (14.4.3) in the easternmost part of Europe and ending with Spain (14.4.28). An account of Africa follows, moving from Egypt to the farthest regions, "unknown to us due to the heat of the sun" (14.5.17).

Throughout Isidore's descriptive geography, lands are located relative to their proximity to the sun. This is seen both in the descriptions of the peoples, variously disposed both physically and mentally depending on their climate, and in the description of where the lands are to be found. The people in the farthest north are least marked by the heat of the sun, while those farthest south are most marked: "Ethiopia has its name from the color of the people, who are scorched by being so near to the sun" (14.5.14). The sun serves as an ordering principle that allows the encyclopedist to differentiate between peoples and between disparate territories. Isidore's geography is schematized according to the principle of the sun. He begins with Paradise, located in "Oriens" itself, where the sun rises; India is placed near it, enclosed on the west by the river Indus (14.3.5); Parthia extends from India as far as Mesopotamia (14.3.8), and so on. The area farthest east is defined as the land most proximate to the sun (Asia is "ab Oriente ortu solis" [14.3.1]), but so is the area farthest south: Africa is said to have its name from "*apricam,* that is, open to the sky and the sun, and without any bone-chilling cold" [sine horrore frigoris (14.5.2)]. Ethiopia, located "circa solis ardorem" (14.5.3), is said to have two parts, one nearer Mauritania, one located "circa solis Ortum" (14.5.16), that is, "toward the East" or "toward the rising of the sun." That farther Ethiopia is "exusta solis ardoribus" (14.5.17), scorched by the heat of the sun; in Trevisa's translation of Bartholomaeus Anglicus, this regions is said to be located "a3ens the cours of the sunne, in the southe" (15.52; p. 754). This land is doubly marked by the effects of the sun, by its southern exposure as well as its eastern orientation.

Isidore both begins and ends his geographical survey in "ortu solis": first, in the easternmost region of Asia and finally in the extreme southeastern reaches of Ethiopia located "circa solis Ortum" (14.5.16), beyond which lie only lands "unknown to us due to the heat of the sun" (14.5.17). Such ordering gives Isidore's world geography a circular structure patterned about the location of the sun; simultaneously, however, it defines the sun's location in a double way. The Orient, location of the rising sun (*sol oriens*), is the farthest east; yet the region most visibly scorched, both in its desert land and in the blackened faces of its people, is the southern extreme of Africa. The former region of the sun is the place of origin not only for the sun but for humanity, because Eden, mankind's ancient cradle, is located there. The latter region of the sun is a place currently unknown, knowledge of which lies at some unspecified point in the future, if at all: The "fabled Antipodes," as Isidore calls them (14.5.17), await exploration. Yet the distant lands of Africa, for Isidore, are not so distant as they may at first seem. Isidore concludes his survey of the three known continents with a summary: "Mauritania is the nearest to Spain, then Numidia, then the area of Carthage, after that we find Getulia, and thereafter Ethiopia, that place scorched by the heat of the sun" (14.5.17). The dark-skinned Mauritanians, for the Spanish bishop, lie just to the south; the fair-skinned Gauls and Galicians, just to the north.

Bartholomaeus Anglicus' adaptation of Isidore's schema departs from his model in several respects. The former's alphabetical ordering, while facilitating the use of his encyclopedia as a reference tool,[33] omits the maplike survey of the world employed by Isidore and followed by Vincent of Beauvais.[34] Bartholomaeus does not move smoothly from East to North and down into the South; instead, his alphabetical geography skips about, ranging from Aragon to Babylon to Crete. Significantly, where Isidore had discussed the islands of the world in a separate section, Bartholomaeus integrates them into his alphabetical schema, allowing him to gives the same prominence to "Anglia" that he does to, for example, "Italia" or even "Europa" itself. He notes Isidore's etymology of "Anglia" as "*angulo* 'a corner' as it were a londe ysette in the eends or a cornere of the worlde" (15.14; p. 733). But, says Bartholomaeus, the fabulous etymology of Angles/angels in the story of Pope Gregory more accurately reveals the extraordinary quality of the nation. If it is a corner, says Bartholomaeus, "Inglonde is a stronge londe and sterne and the plenteuouseste corner of the world" (15.14; p. 734). For Isidore, the extremes of heat and cold function as an ordering principle that does not, however, geographically alienate those lands from his own homeland: The white-skinned Galicians inhabit one portion of Spain, while the black-skinned Mauritanians inhabit the southern land nearest Spain. Isidore's own space is a mean, but one surrounded closely by climactic extremes.

Bartholomaeus' schema of the world, conversely, emphasizes the climatic extremes that make distinct the various parts of the world. In his chapter "Europa," Bartholomaeus suggests that Europe, not Asia, is the dominant continent, for its people are better formed by their native climate "thanne men of the cuntres and londes of Asia other of Affrica" (15.50; p. 752). The cold northern climate of Europe breeds men who are physically "more ful and huge" and, in spirit, "more bold and hardy" (15.50; p. 753). This development of a cold, northerly European identity marks a crucial point in the development of an Occident that will mirror the Orient. The northern chill produces white-complected men whose bodily heat, says Bartholomaeus, is turned inward to produce men who are "bold and hardy." Asian men, by contrast, are "meneliche disposed in that": with some interior heat and some exterior, only moderate boldness, and only moderate marks of the heat of the sun. Bartholomaeus' Asia is still central in that its people are "meneliche disposed"; yet at the same time its position is supplanted by the men of the North Bartholomaeus praises. Asia is primary ("regio prima est"), but the Asians are "mediocriter."

In John Gower's *Confessio Amantis,* written during the last decades of
the fourteenth century, a brief descriptive geography appears that is worth
comparing to Bartholomaeus' depiction of the bold, white European men
of the North. Gower declares that his geographical description is "After
the forme of Mappemounde" (7.530),[35] and, accordingly, Gower follows
the conventional tripartite division of Asia, Europe, and Africa, distributed
among the three sons of Noah. As in the encyclopedias, Asia is the largest
portion ("double as moche as othre two" [7.559]) and thus belongs by
rights to the eldest son (7.557). The continent of Asia is, as usual, defined
in terms of the sun, and—unusually—is defined as coterminous with the
Orient itself: "Asie . . . lay to the Sonne / Upon the Marche of orient,
/ . . . / And schortly for to speke it so, / Of Orient in general / Withinne
his bounde Asie hath al" (7.554–55; 572–74). The other continents are subsequently defined in terms of direction:

> And thanne upon that other side
> Westward, as it fell thilke tyde,
> The brother which was hote Cham
> Upon his part Aufrique nam.
> Japhet Europe tho tok he,
> Thus parten thei the world on thre. (7.575–80)

So far, Gower's account is in keeping with the basic division of the world
among the sons of Noah found in the encyclopedias. The world is in three
parts, the continents; but it is also divided into two parts, as Augustine,
Isidore, Hrabanus Maurus, Vincent of Beauvais, and Bartholomaeus Anglicus all declare. The two parts are, of course, Orient and Occident, occupied by Asia, on one side, and Europe and Africa, on the other.

Beginning with Isidore, the encyclopedic tradition develops a geographical schema that juxtaposes a northern Europe, inhabited by fair-
skinned men, with a southern Africa, inhabited by dark-skinned men. For
Isidore, these diverse peoples are proximate to his own location in Spain;
for Bartholomaeus, these peoples are more distant, and the northerly climate of Europe is explicitly stated to breed men who are more "bolde and
hardy" due to their inwardly directed heat. Bartholomaeus thus claims that
not the East but the Northwest is the place of greatest potency, which sets
the stage for Gower's extraordinary recasting of the "forme of Mappe-
monde." Gower concludes his brief geography by evoking the conventional two-part division of the world into East and West:

> Bot yit ther ben of londes fele
> In occident as for the chele,

In orient as for the hete,
Which of the poeple be forlete
As lond desert that is unable,
For it mai noght ben habitable. (7.581–86)

To a modern reader, it may not seem peculiar to associate the Orient with heat. But as we have seen, medieval encyclopedias universally describe the South in terms of the sun's heat, its people blackened and its earth scorched. While they naturally define the Orient in terms of the sun, the quality of heat is associated with the South rather than the East.

A similar pattern appears in medieval allegory, both sacred and profane. One twelfth-century account of the north and south winds identifies the latter with "the throne of the Almighty," where "the flame of love" [ardor] is found: "the south wind denotes the grace of the Holy Spirit . . . the warmth [Its] love" [calor amor].[36] Similarly, the description of the Castle of Love in Andreas Capellanus's twelfth-century *Art of Courtly Love* includes an account of the moral character of the ladies at each of the four gates. Unsurprisingly, it is the ladies at the south gate who "always linger around the open door" and are receptive to love: "Those at the south, then, are those women who wish to love and do not reject worthy lovers; this is proper since, being all in the south, they are worthy to be illuminated by a ray from Love himself who lives in the east."[37] It is only in the fourteenth century, as seen here in Gower's account, that the Orient comes to be known as a place of overwhelming heat, understood in both a literal and a moral sense. By characterizing the Orient in terms of (formerly southern) heat, it becomes possible to characterize its opposite, the Occident, in terms of (formerly northern) cold. It is thus only during the late fourteenth century that something like our modern notion of a European "West" appears in literature: an Occident characterized by cold, and the external whiteness and internal fortitude born of it.

Thus it is ultimately unsurprising that Kathryn Lynch has recently analyzed Chaucer's *Squire's* and *Franklin's Tales* in terms of the dichotomy of Orient and Occident, in spite of the fact that she herself draws attention to the significance of the cold environment and Arveragus' journey northward in the latter tale.[38] Lynch's application of this dichotomy to Chaucer's text is the result not only of its centrality in more modern manifestations of Orientalism but also of the participation of Chaucer's own text in the construction of a cold, dispassionate, northerly Occident. The formation of this Occident can be witnessed in Bartholomaeus Anglicus's comparison of the "bolde and hardy" white men of the North with the southern men, "blacke of face," who are "cowardes of herte"; in Gower's opposition of deserts found "in occident as for the chele, / In orient as for the hete"; and in Chaucer's contrast of the setting of the *Squire's Tale* with that of the *Franklin's Tale*. In the former tale, the sun, "ful joly and cleer," causes "lusty . . . weder" (V.48, 52), while in the latter, the sun is "hewed lyk laton" and "shoon ful pale" (V.1245, 1249), coldly illuminating a world where fraternal exchange takes precedence over carnal desire. Throughout the *Canterbury Tales,* the reader is "oriented" by the sun, which, as it were, rises in the *Squire's Tale,* where the steamy "vapour" rising from the earth causes "the sonne to seme rody and brood" (V.394). The Oriental sun is reflected in those who inhabit its regions, so that the movement of "Phebus" is simultaneous with the movement of the "Tartre kyng" (V.263–67), while his daughter Cánacee rises "As rody and bright as dooth the yonge sonne" (V.385). According to Bartholomaeus Anglicus, the people of the Orient are "disposed meneliche," characterized by neither of the extremes of hot and cold; in the Squire's Tale, however, the East rather than the South is the location of "lusty . . . weder" (V.52), where "dauncen lusty Venus children deere" (V.272). They are shaped by the heat of the sun.

The development during the fourteenth century of an idea of the Occident that is the mirror image of the Orient is accompanied by a concomitant change in the figurative meaning of the cardinal directions. The North had long been associated with evil, based on the biblical tradition identifying it with the realm of Lucifer (Jeremiah 1:14, 6:1; Isaiah 14:13). In his twelfth-century *De naturis rerum,* Alexander Neckam explains the allegorical significance of the magnetic compass, which points to the North Pole: "Sailors crossing the sea . . . put a needle above the lodestone; and the needle revolves until, after its motion has stopped, its point faces due north. So should a prelate guide his subjects in the sea of life, so that his reason may set them facing that north of which it is written, 'From the North is all evil spread' [Jeremiah 1:14]."[39] With the increasing practical use of the magnetic compass during the thirteenth and fourteenth centuries, however, the cardinal direction North came to be representative not of the presence of evil but of locatability. This shift is most clearly visible in the transition from *mappaemundi* to more modern-looking, north-oriented maps influenced by portolan charts. It would be an oversimplification to suggest that a linear progression from one kind of map to the other took place; as John Friedman, among others, has pointed out, conventional *mappaemundi* are "works of art of a didactic and cultural sort, rather than rigid and unsuccessful attempts to portray geographical features,"[40] while later, portolan-influenced maps function as practical guides to navigation. Yet the portolan-influenced map is, like the *mappamundi* (and, indeed, every map), also a symbolic image of the world. This symbolic value is evident in the ornate presentation copies of some portolan-influenced maps, where compass roses appear in which the arrow pointing north is richly embellished.[41] The shift from maps oriented toward the East to those oriented toward the North is meaningful: It illustrates a transition from a view of the world based on sacred geography, which tells you mankind's collective destination (Jerusalem), to a view of the world that tells you individually where you are, and hence enables you to choose where to go and how to get there. The transition from East to North is a transition from the primacy of the sacred object to the primacy of the seeing subject.

As increasing numbers of medievalists have discovered, Orientalist and postcolonial theory (in all its many varieties), although developed on the basis of modern manifestations of colonialism, can nonetheless be used to analyze premodern texts. Inevitably, a disjunction between modern theory and medieval practice is bound to appear; yet this disjunction can be seen not as a moment of theory's inadequacy in the face of medieval culture but rather as a gap that reveals a site where medieval culture has participated in the generation of a norm taken for granted in the construction of the modern theoretical paradigm. One such gap has been discussed here: The dichotomy of Orient and Occident essential to modern theory has been shown to be the product of the late-medieval reorientation of the extremes of hot south and cold north, aligning them respectively with the Orient and the Occident. The "West," as we know it, appears to be an invention of the fourteenth century.

Issues of place and space have received increasing attention in the field of postcolonial theory.[42] The geographer David Harvey has welcomed the proliferation of interest in such issues, yet cautions against using maps as cultural artifacts without situating them in their proper context. Specifically, Harvey insists that maps and other schemata must be understood as participating in a dialectical process in which apparently permanent entities (e.g., the Orient, the Occident) are constructed, taking their place in the generation of "a landscape of knowledge seemingly impermeable to change."[43] Medieval efforts to map the world—both in the images of the *mappaemundi* and the words of descriptive geographies—reveal moments of "crystallization," as Harvey puts it, when the process of mapping brings an entity into apparent being. The Orient is continually in the process of being re-formed while the Occident, it seems, was born just yesterday.

Notes

1. Edward W. Said, *Orientalism* (New York: Random House, 1978, reprinted 1994) p. 5.
2. Aijaz Ahmad, *In Theory: Classes, Nations, Literature* (New York: Verso, 1992), p. 181.
3. See Ahmad's account of Said's treatment of Dante, pp. 187–90.

4. Joshua Prawer, *The Latin Kingdom of Jerusalem: European Colonization in the Middle Ages* (London: Weidenfeld and Nicolson, 1972), pp. 469–533.

5. See, for example, Ali Behdad, *Belated Travelers: Orientalism in the Age of Colonial Dissolution* (Durham, NC: Duke University Press, 1994), and the special issue of *L'Esprit Créateur* on Orientalism edited by Behdad (vol. 34, 1994).

6. See, among others, Mary B. Campbell, *The Witness and the Other World: Exotic European Travel Writing, 400–1600* (Ithaca, NY: Cornell University Press, 1988); Sheila Delany, "Geographies of Desire: Orientalism in Chaucer's *Legend of Good Women*," *Chaucer Yearbook* 1 (1992): 1–32, and *The Naked Text: Chaucer's* Legend of Good Women (Berkeley: University of California Press, 1994); Iain Macleod Higgins, *Writing East: The "Travels" of Sir John Mandeville* (Philadelphia: University of Pennsylvania Press, 1997); Kathryn L. Lynch, "East Meets West in Chaucer's Squire's and Franklin's Tales," *Speculum* 70 (1995): 530–51; Susan Schibanoff, "Worlds Apart: Orientalism, Antifeminism, and Heresy in Chaucer's Man of Law's Tale," *Exemplaria* 8 (1996): 59–96.

7. Christine Chism, "Too Close for Comfort: Dis-Orienting Chivalry in the *Wars of Alexander*," in *Text and Territory: Geographical Imagination in the European Middle Ages,* ed. Sylvia Tomasch and Sealy Gilles (Philadelphia: University of Pennsylvania Press, 1998), pp. 116–39, esp. p. 121.

8. Peter the Venerable, "Liber conta sectam sive haeresim Saracenorum," ed. and trans. James Kritzeck, *Peter the Venerable and Islam* (Princeton, NJ: Princeton University Press, 1964), p. 231; trans. p. 161.

9. "Summa totius Haeresis Saracenorum," in ibid., p. 208; trans. p. 140.

10. See Norman Daniel, *Heroes and Saracens: An Interpretation of the* Chansons de Geste (Edinburgh: Edinburgh University Press, 1984), and his *Islam and the West: The Making of an Image* (London: Oneworld, 1960, rev. ed. 1993).

11. Campbell, *The Witness and the Other World,* p. 48.

12. Augustine, *City of God,* 16.17, p. 521, in *Sancti Aurelii Augustini De civitate Dei Libri xi-xxii,* ed. Bernardus Dombart and Alphonsus Kalb, Corpus Christianorum Series Latina 48 (Turnhout: Brepols, 1955).

13. Williams notes that this convention first appears in Isidoran world maps of the ninth century (13). John Williams, "Isidore, Orosius and the Beatus Map," *Imago Mundi* 49 (1997): 7–32.

14. David Woodward, "Medieval *Mappaemundi*," in *The History of Cartography,* vol. 1, ed. J. B. Harley and David Woodward (Chicago: University of Chicago Press, 1987), pp. 286–370; quotation at p. 337.

15. Ibid., pp. 341–42.

16. More specifically, the Valley of Josaphat, based on Joel 3:12, identified after the fourth century with Cedron, located just outside the walls of Jerusalem. See "Josaphat" in *The Catholic Encyclopedia,* ed. Charles G. Habermann *et al.* (15 vols., New York: Encyclopedia Press, 1913), 8: 503; also J. Rivière, "Jugement," *Dictionnaire de Théologie Catholique,* ed. A. Vacant *et al.* (15 vols., Paris: Letouzey et Ané, 1923–46), vol. 8, part 2, col. 1721–1828, esp. col. 1819.

17. Woodward, "Medieval *Mappaemundi*," pp. 341–42; noted in Iain Macleod Higgins, "Defining the Earth's Center in a Medieval 'Multi-Text': Jerusalem in *The Book of John Mandeville*," in *Text and Territory*, ed. Tomasch and Gilles, pp. 29–53; quotation at p. 49.

18. Isidore, *Etymologies* 14.3.21, cited from *Isidori Hispalensis Episcopi Etymologiarum sive Originum Libri XX*, ed. William Lindsay (Oxford: Oxford University Press, 1911, reprinted 1989); subsequently cited parenthetically in the text.

19. Jerome, *Commentari in Hezechielem*, ed. Francisci Glorie, Corpus Christianorum Series Latina 75 (Turnhout: Brepols, 1964), pp. 55–56.

20. Hrabanus Maurus, *De universo* 12.4, cols. 9–614, in *B. Rabani Mauri Opera Omnia*, ed. J.-P. Migne, Patrologia Latina Cursus Completus III (Paris, 1864) col. 339C; subsequently cited in the text. On the place of the *De universo* in the encyclopedic tradition, see Elisabeth Heyse, *'De rerum naturis.' Untersuchungen zu den Quellen und zur Methode der Kompilation*, Münchener Beiträge zur Mediävistik- und Renaissance Forschung 4 (München: Arbeo-Gesellschaft, 1969).

21. Vincent of Beauvais, *Speculum historiale* 1.67; cited from vol. 4 of *Speculum quadruplex sive Speculum maius* (Graz: Akademische Druck- und Verlagsanstalt, 1624, reprinted 1964), p. 25.

22. Bartholomaeus Anglicus, *De proprietatibus rerum* 15.78; quoted from the late fourteenth-century translation by John Trevisa, *On the Properties of Things: John Trevisa's translation of "Bartholomaeus Anglicus, De proprietatibus rerum." A Critical Text*, 3 vols., ed. M. C. Seymour *et al.* (Oxford: Clarendon, 1975–78), II: 772; subsequently cited parenthetically in the text.

23. Barbara Obrist, "Wind Diagrams and Medieval Cosmology," *Speculum* 72 (1997): 33–84.

24. Cf. Isidore 14.2.2 and Bartholomaeus Anglicus 15.1.

25. Benjamin Braude, "The Sons of Noah and the Construction of Ethnic and Geographical Identities in the Medieval and Early Modern Periods," *William and Mary Quarterly* 54 (1997):103–42; quotation at pp. 116–20.

26. Ibid. p. 114.

27. Jerome, *Liber interpretationis hebraicorum nominum*, ed. Pauli de Lagarde, pp. 57–161 in *S. Hieronymi Presbyteri Opera*, Corpus Christianorum Series Latina 72 (Turnhout: Brepols, 1959), p. 63; echoed in Hrabanus Maurus, *Commentariorum in Genesim* 2.6 (PL 107, cols. 439–670), col. 513C.

28. Hrabanus Maurus, *Genesis* 2.9, col. 526A; cf. Augustine, *City of God* 16.2, pp. 498–99.

29. Isidore states that three of the four sons of Ham gave rise to the nations of Ethiopia, Egypt, and Libya. The fourth, Canaan, gave rise not only to the "Afri," but also to the (Asian) Phoenicians and Canaanites (9.2.10–12).

30. Cf. Hrabanus Maurus, who states that Japheth's offspring are "Aquilonis partem habitant" (*Genesis* 2.10, col. 526D).

31. Hugh of Saint Victor, "Adnotationes elucidatoriae in Pentateuchon" cols. 29–86 in *Hugonis de S. Victore Opera Omnia*, ed. J.-P. Migne, Patrologia Latina Cursus Completus 175 (Paris: 1879), col. 49A.

32. On the consistently literal fidelity of Trevisa's translation, see David Greetham, "The Fabulous Geography of John Trevisa's Translation of Bartholomaeus Anglicus' *De proprietatibus rerum*" (Ph.D. diss., City University of New York, 1974), p. 261.

33. On the independent use of book 15 of the *De proprietatibus rerum,* see ibid., p. 188.

34. See also Hugh of Saint Victor's *Descriptio mappe mundi,* which, Dalché has argued, follows very closely a particular *mappamundi.* See Patrick Gautier Dalché, ed., *La "Descriptio mappe mundi" de Hugues de Saint-Victor* (Paris: Etudes Augustiniennes, 1988).

35. In volume 3 of *The Complete Works of John Gower,* 4 vols., ed. G. C. Macaulay (Oxford: Clarendon Press, 1901); cited parenthetically in the text.

36. *The Medieval Book of Birds: Hugh of Fouilloy's* Aviarium, ed., trans. and comm. Willene B. Clark (Binghamton: Medieval and Renaissance Texts and Studies, 1992), pp. 138–39 (ch. 14).

37. Andreas Capellanus, *The Art of Courtly Love,* trans. John Jay Parry (New York: Columbia University Press, 1990), pp. 73–74 (fifth dialogue).

38. Lynch, "East Meets West," p. 547.

39. *De naturis rerum* 2.98, ed. Thomas Wright, *Alexandri Neckam De naturis rerum libri duo,* Rerum britannicarum medii aevi scriptores 34 (London, 1863), p. 183. Translated in Julian Smith, "Precursors to Peregrinus: The Early History of Magnetism and the Mariner's Compass," *Journal of Medieval History* 18 (1992): 21–74; quotation at p. 37.

40. John B. Friedman, "Cultural Conflicts in Medieval World Maps," in *Implicit Understandings: Observing, Reporting, and Reflecting on the Encounters Between Europeans and Other Peoples in the Early Modern Era,* ed. Stuart B. Schwartz (Cambridge: Cambridge University Press, 1997), pp. 64–95; quotation at p. 64.

41. See Woodward, "Medieval *Mappaemundi,*" p. 315 and plate 17. Increasingly striking examples appear during the course of the fifteenth century; see Tony Campbell, "Portolan Charts from the Late Thirteenth Century to 1500" in *The History of Cartography,* ed. J. B. Harley and David Woodward (Chicago: University of Chicago Press, 1987), vol. 1, pp. 371–463; quotation at p. 396.

42. See Homi K. Bhabha, *The Location of Culture* (New York: Routledge, 1994), and his "Minority Maneuvers and Unsettled Negotiations," *Critical Inquiry* 23 (1997): 431–59.

43. David Harvey, *Justice, Nature and the Geography of Difference* (Oxford: Blackwell, 1996), pp. 80–83; quotation at p. 81. For a more blithely enthusiastic view, see J. B. Harley, "Deconstructing the Map," *Cartographica* 26 (1989): 1–20, and the useful reply, outlining "process cartography," by Robert A. Rundstrom, "Mapping, Postmodernism, Indigenous People and the Changing Direction of North American Cartography," *Cartographica* 28 (1991): 1–12.

CHAPTER 2

COMING OUT OF EXILE:
DANTE ON THE ORIENT EXPRESS*

Kathleen Biddick

> *This chapter rereads Edward Said's* Orientalism *(twenty years after) as a crisis in imperial temporality and reimagines exile by bringing Said's work in contact with a recent rewriting of Dante's* Vita Nuova *by the Turkish writer Orhan Pamuk.*

Orientalism **and Exile**

Does *Orientalism* ever let go? The twentieth anniversary of its publication brought me back to Edward Said's text.[1] I could recall the exhilaration of first encounter in the early 1980s, when a colleague chose it for our reading group. *Orientalism* exposed different cultural and institutional ways in which Europeans fabricated objects of study by assigning and hierarchizing boundaries between East and West and unmasked "Europe" as a "theatrical stage whose audience, manager, and actors are for Europe" (p. 71). Its critique of imaginary racialized geographies hooked me.

Upon first reading, it was less clear to me how Said thought about imaginary *temporalities.* It seemed to me that just as racialized geographies guaranteed the West as a powerful spatial fabrication, so too racialized temporalities fashioned the fantastic present tense of the West—the West *is* the best. The "East," Said seemed to argue, was the imaginary past tense of the West ("unimaginable antiquity, inhuman beauty, boundless distance," p. 167). Yet this past tense had its origins for Said in the poetry of Dante

(1265–1321), which epitomized for him the stronger "articulation," the more careful "schematization," and the more dramatically "effective" moment of placing the Orient in Western imaginative geographies (pp. 68–70). Dante enacted in his notorious image of the riven "Maömetto" (Mohammed) the violence of an Orientalist spatial binary: "no barrel staved-in, and missing its end-piece ever gaped as wide as the man I saw split open from chin down to the farting-place" [giá veggia, per mezzul perdere o lulla, com'io vidi un, così non si pertugia, rotto dal mento infin dove si trulla].[2] As for Dante's redemption of "good" Muslims in Limbo (Avicenna, Averröes, Saladin), Said identified this "tolerance" as evidence of the "discriminations and refinements" of Orientalist vision, in which Islam is the "creature of the West's moral apprehension" (p. 69). Dante, in effect, provided Said with an originary moment for Orientalism perfectable in the "secularizing elements in eighteenth-century European culture" (p. 120). Said tells the history of Orientalism according to the highly conventionalized chronologies of an Enlightenment history of progress. *Orientalism* thus paradoxically produces the Middle Ages as a medievalism, that is, a fantastic origin that sets in motion a progressive history.[3]

How could Said, his brilliant grasp of spatial forms of Orientalist power notwithstanding, emplot the Middle Ages as the "adolescent" stage preparatory to a fully mature, "modern," imperialist Orientalism? Nor is he alone in the grip of this fiction. Consider, for example, Benedict Anderson's acclaimed book *Imagined Communities,* which directly addresses the question of temporality as a form of knowledge. Anderson imagines a sharp break between medieval (read religious) "apprehensions of time" and Enlightenment (read technological) temporalities capable of thinking the progress of the nation.[4] Medieval time, as described by Anderson, is synchronous, meaning that all events are organized around the same eschatological vanishing point; it is always, therefore, the same time in the Middle Ages until the eschaton. Anderson thus reduces the Middle Ages to a space from which the progressive Enlightenment history of the nation may unfold. Enlightenment temporality imagines time as metrological coincidence defined by the calendar and the clock. These different forms of temporal knowledge formulated by Anderson actually work as a spatial binary without contiguity. The ambivalence and complexity of temporal contact, and of history, is thus held at bay.

Why did Said foreclose critique of temporal practices in *Orientalism?* I closely reread his text in an effort to understand.[5] First, it intrigued me that in this capacious work that crosses the borders of so many genres (poetry, travel-writing, novels, anthropology, lexicography, to name a few), Said leaves the question of history-writing virtually untouched. The opening words of the first chapter, "on June 13, 1910" (p. 31), assert that Orientalist temporality can be reduced to chronology, the empty, homogeneous time of Western historiography. On one hand, Said claims that "instability suggests that history, with its disruptive detail, its currents of change, its tendency towards growth, decline, or dramatic movement, is possible in the Orient and for the Orient" (p. 240). On the other hand, he not only avoids the study of history-writing but relies on the binaries of what he calls "latent" and "manifest" Orientalism to describe its temporality. In fact, these distinctions, like the comparable ones made by Anderson, are spatial rather than temporal. Latent Orientalism means that representations of the Orient are organized by the same vanishing point; thus this ideology is synchronous (it is always the same time in Orientalism). Its content, like a stage set, might change (Said's manifest Orientalism), but we are always watching the same play, on the same proscenium. Indeed, to this day, Said continues to separate what he calls a spatial tradition of thinking (represented for him by Vico and Gramsci) from a temporal one (de Man, Derrida, Lukács).[6]

To avoid temporal critique in *Orientalism,* Said linked the "adolescence" of the Middle Ages inherent in his emplotment to one of the most central and powerful metaphors of his life and oeuvre, that of *exile.* Sara Suleri has drawn our attention to the importance of such a connection: "the connection between the idioms of exile and adolescence has long haunted the literature of empire—the classic text in this mode is *Lord Jim*—but perhaps it is time for critical discourse to examine more rigorously the idiom of exile."[7] It seemed to me that efforts to rethink the Middle Ages in Said's *Orientalism* would require a critical understanding of his rhetorical use of exile.

My close reading concentrated on this problem and established that Said used two exemplary figures of exile in *Orientalism* and returns to them again and again in his subsequent writings. They are especially relevant to medievalists, because they come from the Middle Ages and the discipline of medieval studies respectively. These exiles of such importance to Said are Hugh of St. Victor (a German cleric from Saxony who emigrated to Paris, d. 1140) and Erich Auerbach (renowned German Jewish philologist and medievalist, d. 1957). From Said's earliest academic publications, his two exemplary figures of exile occur together.[8] In 1969 he and his wife, Maire, translated Auerbach's essay "Philology and Weltliteratur." Auerbach closed this essay, in which he argued that his "philological home is the earth: it can no longer be the nation," with the following famous words of Hugh of St. Victor:

It is, therefore, a great source of virtue for the practiced mind to learn, bit by bit, first to change about in visible and transitory things, so that afterwards it may be able to leave them behind altogether. The man who finds his homeland sweet is still a tender beginner; he to whom every soil is as his native one is already strong; but he is perfect to whom the entire world is a foreign land (*exsilium*).[9]

A decade later in *Orientalism,* Said cites Auerbach (p. 259), in a crucial but very condensed discussion that attempts to distinguish the estrangement of European Orientalists during their fieldwork from the humanistic estrangement of the exile, so valued by him (pp. 259–60). He argued that the former sense of alienation came from the fieldworker's inherent sense of superiority, and he contrasted such haughtiness to the humanistic detachment exemplified by Auerbach. Why is Said so anxious to make these distinctions? I argue that as an ardent believer in humanism, and also a critic of its orientalist practices, Said faces the following conundrum in *Orientalism:* "Yes, I know from my study of Orientalism that humanism helped to construct Orientalism, but even so humanism is innocent." Said tries to resolve such incommensurabilty by turning to exemplary exiles as a way of *purifying* humanism and *exempting* it from historic taint of collaboration.

Throughout subsequent publications Said continues anxious invocations of these exemplary exiles. At the close of *Culture and Imperialism* (1993: 335–36), his elaboration of *Orientalism,* Said again emphasizes exile as the motivation for his work. He returns to Hugh of St. Victor and repeats his tribute to Erich Auerbach's exile at the University of Istanbul from 1936 to 1947. Hugh's words, Said wrote, are a model "for anyone— man and woman—wishing to transcend the restraints of imperial, national or provincial limits" (p. 335). In his recent interview with *boundary 2,* Said also invoked Hugh: "I find myself, in a funny way, sort of living the way that passage describes—you know the passage I've quoted it many times— from Hugh of Saint-Victor, where the person who is a stranger everywhere is somehow at home but not loving the world too much—you know—you're moving on" (p. 23). The repetition of these citations suggests that Said strongly identifies the atemporal and purified place of exile with the medieval and with mimesis. As the last citation suggests, Said "performs" Hugh of St. Victor.

In his important "Reflections on Exile," Said yet again couples these two exemplary figures, articulating exile as a deeply painful spatial problem: "much of the exile's life it taken up with compensating for disorienting loss by creating a new world to rule" (p. 167).[10] He staunchly opposes the metaphor of exile to the concept of diaspora, which for Said intimates the temporal dimension of a return, associated with a history of both Gentile and Jewish Zionism. Cutting exile off from temporality demands, however, a price. To freeze the past as lost (and therefore melancholically

timeless) denies the possibilities (albeit mournful) of making the past now,
in the present. By immobilizing the past, Said's exile forecloses those complex actions of cultural reinscription that move back to the future.

The temporal resistances intrinsic to *Orientalism* have affected the efforts of medievalists to rethink Orientalist practices. By and large medieval
critiques have tended to reproduce the temporal problems of *Orientalism*.
Two strands of recent disciplinary response can be briefly summarized
here. First, many medievalists have avoided the problems posed by the intimate, but nevertheless violent, entanglements of orientalism with medievalism by celebrating aspects of the Middle Ages as a non-Orientalist
Golden Age free of the appropriations inventoried by Said. In a reparative
wish to distance medieval studies from Orientalism, they inadvertently re-
install medieval/modern binaries, which can be diagnosed as a version of
"postcolonial Orientalism."[11] A second strategy has been to engage in critical disciplinary histories, which often end up with the distancing claim
"We are not they" (our scholarship is not that of nineteenth-century im-
perialists) and thus stop short of disciplinary transformation.

In the studies in which medievalists identify with a medieval Golden
Age, the authors often manifest a great difficulty in dealing with the ambivalence of their exemplary texts. By ambivalence I mean anxieties about
the intimacy of difference and the porosity of the border purportedly defining "almost the same, but not quite."[12] Recent approaches to Petrus Alfonsi
and Gerald of Wales, both border figures, can be cited as illustrative of this
problem of "postcolonial Orientalism." When taken as a figure of a twelfth-
century Golden Age, Petrus Alfonsi (an Arabic-trained Jew who converted
to Christianity in the early twelfth century) is praised for his fabulous *Dis-
ciplina clericalis,* a book of wisdom, which disseminated to a Christian audience moral fables from Arabic and Hebrew sources. Such a celebratory
reading overlooks Alfonsi's ambivalence about the intimacy of difference he
embodies and overlooks his murderous attack on Judaism and Islam in his
Dialogi contra Judaeos, a text that had greater circulation than his book of
wisdom.[13] Likewise, Gerald of Wales, a cleric who accompanied Henry II
on his expedition to Ireland and wrote the *Topographia Hibernica* (1180s),
confronts medievalists with the ambivalence of intra-Christian identity politics (Welsh, English, Norman, Irish). Medievalists seeking a non-Orientalist history of cognition in the Middle Ages appreciate his expressions of
wonder at the Irish. Other medievalists have analyzed his text as an ethnographic turning point in the historical fabrication of hierarchical differences
within medieval Christendom.[14] These hierarchies, dismissive of the intimacies of intra-Christian identity politics, were used to legitimate conquest
and oppression of fellow Christians. Such contrasts in interpretation cannot
be dismissed simply as the conundrum of the glass half full, half empty.

Rather, the intersections of wonder with the clerical work of constructing the barbarian within Christendom cleave wonder with the intimate disturbance of writing medieval colonialism.[15]

Medieval economic histories also have carefully traced and celebrated a Golden Age of exchange among Christians, Muslims, and Jews in the Mediterranean up to the end of the twelfth century. These histories concentrate on "peoples of the book" and tend to reduce history to their interactions. They generally fail to link how peoples not of the book came to be fabricated as Others (pagans) in order to ensure the integrity of people of the book. Implicit in this short-circuit is the urgent need to rethink the medieval slave trade as a shared undertaking among peoples of the book both materially and fantastically directed against "pagans."[16]

Over the last decade, energetic examinations of nationalist and imperialist genealogies of medieval studies have offered much potential for transformation, which has been adumbrated by rituals of disciplinary purification.[17] These edited collections and conference proceedings seem to have made it safe for medievalists to say "we are not they." Such exorcism has obviated the ongoing challenge of examining the persistence of such historic disciplinary structures in the academy today. Recent and important disciplinary syntheses such as *The Making of Europe* or *Writing East* avoid debate over *Orientalism* altogether.[18]

Coming Out of Exile

How can medievalists intervene in the politics of temporality so far delineated? What follows is an effort to retemporalize Said's exemplary but immobilizing image of Auerbach's exile in Istanbul during World War II by putting it into contact with a lively critique of exile written 50 years later in that same city by Orhan Pamuk. His novel, *The New Life,* not only returns to the Istanbul of the 1930s encountered by Auerbach, who fled there from the Nazi-controlled University of Marburg, where he as a Jew could no longer teach; it also rereads Dante, another famous exile on whom Auerbach showered his critical attention. This crisscrossing of Auerbach's and Pamuk's Dante in Istanbul, then and now, is intended to set in motion Said's atemporal notion of exile and also render intimately contiguous Islam-within-Europe and Europe-within-Islam, bridged by this city that straddles two continents.[19]

When Auerbach arrived in Istanbul in 1936, the modernization program of Mustafa Kemal Atatürk had already proclaimed the secular Turkish republic in 1923; changed writing from Ottoman Arabic to Roman alphabet in 1928; founded a system of public education; given voting rights to women; banned the fez; moved the capital; and suppressed mystic orders, among other things. (October 29, 1998, marked the seventy-fifth anniversary of the Republic of Turkey.)[20] Indeed, Auerbach's invitation to teach at the University of Istanbul is of a piece with this program. Auerbach lamented Atatürk's modernization, which he viewed as destructive of traditional Arabic culture and as undertaken only to "beat an admired and hated Europe with its own weapons" [um das verhaßte und bewunderte Europa mit den eigenen Waffen zu schlagen].[21] In this crossfire of German fascism and Turkish modernization, between 1942 and 1945, Auerbach wrote his renowned book *Mimesis*. Auerbach's hero is Dante, whose artistry he regarded as "a well-nigh incomprehensible miracle" [Dantes Sprache nahezu ein unbegreifliches Wunder].

Fifty-odd years later, in the same city, Orhan Pamuk wrote *The New Life* (1997), a meditation, among other things, on Dante's *Vita Nuova* (1292–94).[22] Pamuk takes up the legacy of Turkish modernization commented on by Auerbach, by tracing the afterlife of a book written by the protagonist's Uncle Rifki. The latter was a railroad engineer of the cohort growing up under Atatürk's rule, a generation that faces old age and death in the 1990s.[23] Pamuk's novel suggests a way of thinking about Turkish modernization with outcomes other than the apocalyptic plot imagined by Auerbach. At the same time, the novel invites a reading of the "yet to be read" in Dante studies. Joined together, Pamuk's *New Life* and Dante's *Vita Nuova* form a double lens that renders visible an invisible history of technology and temporality relevant to medieval studies and the critique of Orientalism.

Atatürk's policy to "modernize" literature haunts the writing of Uncle Rifki's book. The library collection upon which he drew included "translated works of Dante, Ib'n Arabi, and Rilke from the world classic series published by the Turkish Ministry of Education and sometimes distributed free of charge to directorates, and ministries" (p. 256).[24] When readers read this book they are transformed. They leave their families, old friends, and familiar neighborhoods and go into exile. Exile is both far away and within an eternal present; the past is left behind: "the glow of the new life I felt inside me existed in a faraway place, even in a land that was unattainable, but I sensed that as long as I was in motion, I was getting closer. I could at least leave my old life behind me" (p. 11).

What interests me in particular is how Pamuk frames the exile undertaken by his protagonists who are seeking the "new life" as a technological catastrophe. In spite of the importance of technology to Orientalism as the material means and media of rendering visible the representations of its imaginary geographies and temporalities, both Said and medievalists grappling with critiques of Orientalism overlook it. Pamuk brings the crucialness of technologies to the reader's attention.

Technologies of "communication-translation" (railroads, cars, buses, etc.) that move the body in space become his metaphors for the exile of the New Life sought by his protagonists. They have "slipped off the tracks" (p. 285) upon reading the book; they travel on long bus trips to find the New Life. For several months the protagonist with his sometime companion Janan pass the time on interminable bus trips by watching films played on video monitors. Pamuk thus enfolds a second modern technology, that of "communication-expression" (radio, films, television, video) within the first. Lest the reader miss the point about the importance of these technologies, the protagonist kills Janan's old boyfriend in a movie theater, and he himself dies in a final bus accident that ends the novel.[25] After shooting his friend and rival Mehmet, the protagonist asks himself "why, in our language, the same French loanword, *makinist,* designates both the person who runs films and the person who runs railway engines" (pp. 230).

The reader wonders why Pamuk insists on understanding the New Life as a form of technological exile. He certainly lets the reader know that, as technologies of communication-translation give themselves up to pure speed (instantaneous time), they grow more militaristic and policing. Technologies of communication-expression also have their own unsettling temporal anxieties, which the protagonist unfolds in the story of his search for the source of the image of the angel printed on the wrapper of New Life Caramels. The latter were a favorite sweet of his childhood, redolent with memories of his Uncle Rifki. In his efforts to track down the sources for this image, he collects pictures of angels from "East" and "West" and searches for clues about angels in literature. When he finally locates their octogenarian confectioner, he learns that a special face, that of Marlene Dietrich fondly remembered from the film *The Blue Angel,* inspired the man to print a blue angel on the wrapper. *The Blue Angel,* shot in both English and German versions by the Jewish-German émigré Joseph von Sternberg, premiered in 1930. Auerbach might have seen the film in Germany; the fictional caramel maker saw the film in Turkey and translated the face of Marlene Dietrich into the angel adorning the wrapper. This paper angel thus becomes a kind of still of the film *The Blue Angel,* a kind of "second encounter" between modern European film technologies and modernizing under Atatürk.

The still on the candy wrapper returns us in a compelling way to the problems of orientalist temporality we are concerned with here. Because the still throws off the material constraints of filmic time (i.e., the constraint that reels cannot go faster or slower than the motor of the projecting mechanism without losing perceptibility), it materializes a different temporal order: "the still by instituting a reading that is at once instantaneous and vertical, scorns logical time (which is only an operational time); it teaches us how to disassociate the technical constraint from what is the specific filmic and which is the 'indescribable' meaning."[26] This still fabricated by Pamuk serves as his brilliant map for rereading Dante's *Vita Nuova*.[27]

Pamuk is posing a question of Dante that has been a concern of recent Dante criticism: "medievalists need to develop a stance that will allow us to attend to Dante's narrative strategies as well as to ponder the repercussions of our blinkered praise."[28] Pamuk is asking how we can read Dante without undergoing conversion, becoming his disciples, his narrative believers, and his companions-in-exile.[29] Inspired by Pamuk's question, I want to consider changing technological media of representation in Tuscany from Dante's childhood to the time of his writing the *Vita Nuova* between the ages of 27 to 30 years (1292–1295). I do so in order to explore further Pamuk's untangling of technology and exile or, perhaps better, *technologies of exile*.

Dante lived in a visual world that had undergone a radical transformation in the cultic media.[30] A palpable and corporeally referential world of relics (bone, tooth, hair, etc.) and their complementary reliquaries transformed into the painted surface of devotional panels. These panels had become increasingly popular in Tuscany after the Crusader sack of Constantinople in 1204, which disseminated Byzantine icons and Greek artists more widely in Italy. The significant impact of this deterritorialization of the cultic body to the iconic painted surface can be gauged in the new Franciscan cult of St. Francis of Assisi, which developed rapidly after his canonization in 1228. Dissemination of that cult did not rely on relics poached from his corpse but rather on the fabrication of official icons that represented both his sainthood and its material proof in the paint itself (representing the blood of the stigmata). Dante would have known of the icon of St. Francis in S. Croce in Florence. Its shimmering painted surface produces a palimpsest in which the saint is Francis and Francis is Christ.

From around the mid-thirteenth century, Tuscan confraternities vied with each other to commission ever-larger icon panels for their religious festivals. Before Dante sat down to write his *Vita Nuova* he would have seen Duccio's *Madonna Rucellai*, commissioned by the Laudesi, a confraternity located in S. Maria Novella. That panel (450 x 290 cm—larger than any young Beatrice) depicts the Madonna and Child flanked by six angels. They are garbed in richly textured fabrics that float against the fabric fields of curtains and gold leaf. Such luminous representations acquired the tactile powers once possessed by relics. For instance, the images of the Virgin painted on the walls of the civic loggia of Or San Michele, in Florence, became famous in 1292 for healing the sick.

I propose that, when Dante beheld Beatrice (whom he always describes as both a face and fabric), he perceived a "still" of the icons that increasingly surrounded him as authoritative images in his visual world. He tells the reader that when he was nine years old (1274), he witnessed an apparition. He saw a nine-year-old girl, Beatrice, who appeared "humbly and properly dressed in a most noble color, crimson, girded and adorned in the matter that befitted her so youthful age" [apparve vestita di nobilissimo colore, umile e onesto, sanguigno, cinta e ornata a la guisa che a la sua giovanissima etade si convenia] (2.3). This vision initiates Dante into obeying the rubric (incipit vita nuova) of his imagined book of memory.

Dante marks the violence of the translation at stake in these new representational technologies in his famous vision in the opening pages (3.5–3.7) of the *Vita Nuova*. Love (Amor), who appears to Dante holding in his arms a naked Beatrice loosely wrapped in red cloth, takes Dante's glowing heart and feeds it to Beatrice. At this moment of cannibalism Beatrice performs the deterritorialization of corporeality (Dante's heart in this example). Here Dante produces for the reader his first lyric of the *Vita Nuova*. Dante thus writes the lyric just as a body part is in the process of becoming a representational surface.[31]

References to this new media of cultic representation punctuate the *Vita Nuova*. Dante recounts how he accompanied a friend to a wedding meal, where he was overtaken by a "wondrous tremor" [uno mirabile tremore] (14.4) in his left side, where his heart used to be. Dante then leaned against "a painting that went round the walls of the house" [io poggiai la mia persona simulatamente ad una pintura la quale circundava questa magione] (14.4). Trembling there, a body against a painted surface, a part of the wall painting, he beholds Beatrice and is transfigured [de la mia trasfigurazione] (14.7). At this moment Dante writes his famous lines that Pamuk cites in his *New Life* (p. 258): "I have set my feet in that part of life beyond which one cannot go with the intention of returning" [Io tenni li piedi in quella parte de la vita di là da la quale non si puote ire più per intendimento di ritornare] (14.8). On the first anniversary of Beatrice's death, Dante finds himself again involved with the new technology of signifying surfaces. He reports that he was sketching an angel on a panel [disegnava uno angelo sopra certe tavolette] (34.1). Following an interruption by friends, he returns again to designing figures of angels [disegnare figure d'angeli] (34.3), at which point he is inspired to write another lyric. Once again the surface of painting and the writing of lyrics join together.

Dante condenses the power of these new representational surfaces upon which the relic has been reterritorialized and upon which he also attaches his authority as vernacular lyricist at the close of the *Vita Nuova*. There he invokes the Veronica Veil, or Holy Face, the veil upon which Christ wiped his bloody visage, only to leave a perfect impression, a photograph of his face. This image is thus the original of the original—not made by human hands: "that blessed image that Jesus Christ left to us as an exemplum of his most beautiful countenance" [quella imagine benedetta la quale Iesu Cristo lasciò a noi per essemplo de la sua bellissima figura] (40.1).[32] Dante identifies with this image, and uses it, in an important moment in the *Vita Nuova,* to mark himself as an *exile,* a "peregrini" in the broadest sense, that is, as "anyone outside one's country" [peregrino chiunque è fuori de la sua patria] (40.6). And so Dante fashions himself as an exile *before* his political banishment from Florence would become a reality. In this complex moment of the *Vita Nuova,* Dante chains to his vernacular lyric the notion of pilgrimage, understood as a form of exile, with the concept of the "original," the Veronica Veil, an image that authorizes painted surfaces, translations of corporeality into paint. The surface of the new visual technologies of thirteenth-century Tuscany thus give birth to the artist-in-exile, Dante, in whom Western criticism has believed so long and fervently. Dante is always already in exile in the *Vita Nuova.* Dante uses exile to suspend his "contract with the future." (Consider his obsessions with time in this text in which there is no future).[33] Just as the painted panels of the icon reterritorialized the relic onto the painted surface, Dante would use exile to reterritorialize the lyric of the *Vita Nuova* into the epic enterprise of empire and the demise of memory in the *Divine Comedy.*

A suspicion of murder haunts Dante's fashioning of exile in the *Vita Nuova.* Critics have been curious about the whereabouts of Guido Calvacanti, Dante's best friend ("primo amico") and fellow poet in the work. The reader hears no more of him from chapter 30, just after Beatrice's death.[34] Guido is thus disappeared textually by Dante well before 1300, when, as a member of the City Council of Florence, Dante signed the proclamation that banished Guido (a banishment from which he never recovered) and before 1302, when Dante himself was sent into exile.

Why must Guido be disappeared by Dante? The *New Life* provides a compelling clue. Just before Osman is about to kill his rival Mehmet, he hesitates. He remembers that in the adventure comics he loved in his youth (and drawn by his many-talented Uncle Rifki) the protagonists, Pertev and Peter, after going through many battles, realize they have fallen in love with the same girl, yet they do not harm each other: "they sit down and solve the problem amicably" (229). As Osman fondly recalls these negotiated endings, he wonders why he needs to kill Mehmet. For one moment of intense identification he actually imagines Mehmet as Pertev: "Pertev had them weigh for me a kilo of the famous large white grapes grown in Viran Bag" (229). But *pace* Uncle Rifki's comics, that moment of identification cannot be sustained "amicably" and Osman shoots Mehmet. Likewise

Dante cannot sustain his "amicable" relation with Guido. Their linked versions of the same lyric voice (Dante and Guido), just as Pertev and Peter's linked versions of adventure, retain an ineradicable ambiguity, an intimacy, that has to die. Better exile and elision than ambivalent intimacies.

An exile that shoots Mehmet in a cinema, an exile that disappears Guido in a new world of iconic representation: Pamuk's play with the still of *The Blue Angel* printed on the candy wrapper of the New Life caramels reminds us that Orientalist temporalities have to do with representational technologies and their combinations whose mechanical regularities result in the "swallowing-up of contact . . . by the copy, is what ensures the animation of the latter, its power to straddle us."[35] Exile, as a guiding concept for Said and for Dante, becomes a way of ensuring the original and of eschewing the original's contact with the copy, which is always ineradicably ambiguous. Pamuk reminds us that in its frozen purity, exile can run the risk of becoming a dangerous way of keeping out of touch, out of time.

Fourteen years after the publication of *Orientalism,* Edward Said chose to come out of exile. Faced by a terminal diagnosis, Said decided in 1992 to return to the city of Jerusalem that he had fled with such anguish as a young boy.[36] Much of his visit in 1992 reminded him of the "eerie finality of history" (50). As his memoir of the visit opens, it offers little evidence of a sense of other histories open to the future, but his apocalyptic tone changes as he enthusiastically relates his last anecdote, a story about an invited lecture given at the Palestinian University of Bir Zeit on the West Bank. For the first time Said accomplishes what he tells his reader he has imagined for years: "translating my type of cultural criticism into the language and concerns of Palestinian students. And that, more even than the fact of residence, could become my contribution to a Palestine that would be neither insular nor ruled by orthodoxy" (55). After his talk, two campus Islamic leaders ask to speak to Said. He agrees, "expecting the worst" (55). He was "thunderstruck" when the leaders acknowledge their differences and nevertheless thank him and invite him back to campus. It is at this moment that the possibility for a second encounter for *Orientalism* takes place, one that disrupts Said's own tendencies toward atemporal Orientalist forms of power. Not only has he come out of exile in this encounter with Palestinian students, he has agreed to speak to Islamic "fundamentalists" for whom he, as a "secular critic," has born militant scorn.[37] Said's coming out of exile creates other temporal potentials and new complex spaces that belie Orientalist binaries. His own complicated and changing relations to Orientalist critique and exile offer an invitation to medievalists to come out of disciplinary exile and to engage complex temporalities of postcolonial histories.

Notes

*A fellowship at the Stanford Humanities Center and its lively collegiality generously supported the work for this chapter. I am indebted to the following fellows for their readings and critical advice: Donald Carter, Sean Keilen, Alexander Nemerov, Ruth Nissé, Aron Rodgrique, Cynthia Steele, Jennifer Summit, and Deanne Williams. The comments of Bob Franklin, Lisa Rofel, Joan Scott, and Kerry Walk proved invaluable. Jeffrey Cohen offered unstinting editorial generosity during a time of grief.

1. I have used the 1994 edition of Edward Said's *Orientalism* (New York: Random House, 1994) which prints his afterword. References to Said's book are italicized in this essay to distinguish that volume from general discussion of phenomena of Orientalism (capitalized in this essay) which he analyzes. Appreciation of the book abounds at this anniversary. The following references offer a guide to debate: Robert Young, *White Mythologies: Writing History and the West* (New York: Routledge, 1990); Gyan Prakash, "Orientalism Now," *History and Theory*, 34 (1995): 119–212; Bart Moore-Gilbert, *Postcolonial Theory: Contexts, Practices, Politics* (New York: Verso, 1997), pp. 34–73; also the special issue of *boundary* 2 (Summer 1998) on Edward Said, edited by Paul A. Bové. I am grateful to the editors for making the galleys of this issue available to me.

2. *The Inferno of Dante: A New Verse Translation* by Robert Pinsky (New York: Farrar, Straus and Giroux, 1994), Canto XXVIII, p. 294. On the "tolerance" of Dante's depiction of Mohammed in viewing him only as a schismatic, see James Kritzeck, *Peter the Venerable and Islam* (Princeton, NJ: Princeton University Press, 1964), p. 144. Such a diagnosis neglects to see how Christianity is normalized in such a view as hegemony from which everything "not Christian" is viewed as schism.

3. The term "medievalism" has grown more complex in recent critical work. For an overview see my *Shock of Medievalism* (Raleigh, NC: Duke University Press, 1998); Paul Freedman and Gabrielle M. Spiegel, "Medievalisms Old and New: The Rediscovery of Alterity in North American Medieval Studies," *American Historical Review* 103 (June 1998): 677–704; Louise O. Fradenburg, "'Voice Memorial': Loss and Reparation in Chaucer's Poetry," *Exemplaria* 7 (1995): 41–54.

4. Benedict Anderson, *Imagined Communities: Reflections on the Origins and Spread of Nationalism* (London: Verso, 1991), pp. 22–25.

5. Early criticism of Orientalism remarked on the absence of a critique of temporal forms of power. I now appreciate more acutely the relevance of this critique to medieval studies. Homi Bhabha has concentrated on problems of temporality in postcolonial studies; in an essay published in 1983, he commented on Said's hesitations to interrogate temporality as a form of power in *Orientalism:* "The Other Question," *Screen* 24 (1983): 18–36, reprinted in *The Location of Culture* (London: Routledge, 1994), pp. 66–84. Bhabha has joined his concept of ambivalence with the notion of the

borderline proximity, the one in the other in a recent essay, "Front Lines/Border Posts," *Critical Inquiry* 23 (1997): 431–59.

6. Said discusses this "pedagogic typology" in an interview with W. J. T. Mitchell published in the special issue of *boundary* 2 (1998): 21.

7. Sara Suleri, *The Rhetoric of English India* (Chicago: University of Chicago Press, 1992), p. 184.

8. Erich Auerbach, "Philology and Weltliteratur," trans. Maire and Edward Said, *Centennial Review,* 13 (1969): 1–17. The essays in *Literary History and the Challenge of Philology: The Legacy of Erich Auerbach,* ed. Seth Lerer (Stanford, CA: Stanford University Press, 1996), provide an excellent starting point for the extensive bibliography on Auerbach.

9. The epigraph comes from Hugh of St. Victor's treatise, *Didascalion,* book 3, chapter 19: "magnum virtutis principium est, ut discat paulatim exercitatus animus visibilia haec et transitoria primum commutare, ut postmodum possit etiam derelinquere. delicatus ille est adhuc cui patria dulcis est; fortis autem iam, cui omne solum patria est; perfectus vero, cui mundus totus exsilium est" (p. 69), cited here from the edition by Charles Henry Buttimer in *Studies in Medieval and Renaissance Latin,* X (Washington, DC: Catholic University of America Press, 1939). For translation, see Jerome Taylor, *The Didascalicon of Hugh of St. Victor* (New York: Columbia University Press, 1991). Hugh of St. Victor composed his treatise in the late 1120s, at the Abbey of Saint Victor in Paris. For an important historical introduction to this Christian tradition of exile, see Gerhart B. Ladner, "Homo Viator: Medieval Ideas on Alienation and Order," *Speculum* 42 (1967): 233–59; for the links with Hugh's scholarly interests in cosmology as representation and his moral views on attachments to the world, see Richard Bultot, "Cosmologie et 'contemptus mundi,'" in Dom Hildebrand Bascour, *Sapientiae Doctrina: Mélanges de théologie et de littérature médievales offerts à Dom Hildebrand Bascour* (Leuven: Abbaye du Mont César, 1980), pp. 1–2. Herman Hailperin argues that Hugh was familiar with the Jewish exegesis of Rashi, where he might have drawn on his emphasis on exile: see Hailperin, *Rashi and the Christian Scholars* (Pittsburgh: University of Pittsburgh Press, 1963), p. 107.

10. Said's most sustained commentary on exile can be found in his essay "Reflections on Exile," *Granta* 13 (1984): 159–72. Said is careful to prefer exile to diaspora. He links the latter to the idea of a redemptive homeland; see his "On Palestinian Identity: A Conversation with Salman Rushdie," reprinted in his *Politics of Dispossession* (New York: Pantheon Books, 1994), p. 114. For an important discussion of temporality and diaspora and an emergent critique of exile, see James Clifford, *Routes: Travel and Translation in the Late Twentieth Century* (Cambridge, MA: Harvard University Press, 1997), pp. 244–78; for a recent critical survey of the postcolonial use of diaspora, see Jaqueline Brown, "Black Liverpool, Black America, and the Gendering of Diasporic Space," *Cultural Anthropology* 13 (1998): 292–325. (I am grateful to my colleague Lisa Rofel for this reference.) Daniel and

Jonathan Boyarin offer important insights into the problems of temporality within diaspora and exile in their essay "Diaspora: Generation and the Grounds of Jewish Identity," *Critical Inquiry* 19 (1993): 693–725.

11. The problem of postcolonial orientalism is the subject of compelling commentary in Lisa Lowe, *Critical Terrains: French and British Orientalisms* (Ithaca, NY: Cornell University Press, 1991), pp. 136–89.

12. I am relying on the work of Homi Bhabha (see his *Location and Culture*) and Suleri (*Rhetoric of English India*) in this usage of ambivalent.

13. For different approaches to cross-cultural exchanges in the world of Petrus Alfonsi, compare and contrast: Maria Rosa Menocal, *Shards of Love: Exile and the Origins of the Lyric* (Raleigh, NC: Duke University Press, 1994); John Tolan, *Petrus Alfonsi and His Medieval Readers* (Gainesville: University of Florida Press,1993); and my essay, "The ABC of Ptolemy: Mapping the World with the Alphabet," in *Text and Territory: Geographical Imagination in the European Middle Ages,* ed. Sylvia Tomasch and Sealy Gilles (Philadelphia: University of Pennsylvania Press, 1998), pp. 268–94.

14. The following studies can be read together for ways in which the ambivalence of Gerald is either ignored or elaborated: Caroline Walker Bynum, "Wonder," *American Historical Review* 102 (February 1997): 16; John Gillingham, "The Beginnings of English Imperialism," *Journal of Historical Sociology* 5 (1992): 392–409; Robert Bartlett, *Gerald of Wales* (Oxford: Oxford University Press, 1982).

15. It is in the space between this escalating violence within Christendom and between Christians and Jews, Muslims, and pagans that the provocative images analyzed by Jacqueline de Weever can be read even more complexly; see *Sheba's Daughters: Whitening and Demonizing the Saracen Woman in Medieval French Epic* (New York: Garland Publishing, 1998).

16. For a brilliant introduction to new ways of thinking about medieval slavery, see Benjamin Braude, "The Sons of Noah and the Construction of Ethnic and Geographical Identities in the Medieval and Early Modern Period," *William and Mary Quarterly* 54 (1997): 103–42. Because I am focusing on problems of Orientalism's temporal forms of power, I do not address the important minoritarian and majoritarian questions at issue in recent work on religious and ethnic groups and economic history in medieval Iberia, which have rich implications for recent work on postcolonial translingual practices: Thomas E. Burman, *Religious Polemic and the Intellectual History of the Mozarabs, c. 1050–1200* (New York: E. J. Brill, 1994); Olivia Remi Constable, *Trade and Traders in Muslim Spain: The commercial realignments of the Iberian peninsula 900–1500* (Cambridge: Cambridge University Press, 1994); Mark D. Meyerson, *The Muslims of Valencia in the Age of Ferdinand and Isabella: Between Coexistence and Crusad*e (Berkeley: University of California Press, 1991); David Nirenberg, *Communities of Violence: Persecution of Minorities in the Middle Ages* (Princeton, NJ: Princeton University Press, 1996). For a thoughtful meditation on colonial linguistic interactions, see Lydia H. Liu, *Translingual Practice: Literature, National*

Culture and Translated Modernity, China, 1900–1937 (Stanford, CA: Stanford University Press, 1995).

17. For a discussion of these recent anthologies, see the introduction to my *Shock of Medievalism;* also, see Peter Monaghan, "Medievalists, Romantics No Longer, Take Stock of their Changing Field," *Chronicle of Higher Education* 45.10 (1998): A15–A17.

18. Robert Bartlett, *The Making of Europe: Conquest, Colonization and Cultural Change 950–1350* (Princeton, NJ: Princeton University Press, 1993); Iain Macleod Higgins, *Writing East: The "Travels" of Sir John Mandeville* (Philadelphia: University of Pennsylvania Press, 1997).

19. For an important discussion of how the Turkish bid to enter the European Community has resulted in anxious reassertions of "Europeanness," see Talal Asad, "Representing Islam in Europe," in *Cultural Encounters,* ed. B. Street and E. Mallami (forthcoming). I am grateful to my colleague Donald Carter for sharing this reference with me.

20. See Stephen Kinzer, "Safranbolu Journal," *The New York Times,* October 29, 1998, p. A4.

21. From a letter of Erich Auerbach to Walter Benjamin, written December 12, 1936, ed. Karlheinz Barck, "Neue Materialien," *Zeitschrift für Germanistik* 6 (1988): 692. In the same letter Auerbach also noted the "disturbing" intimacies of Istanbul: He describes the Pera, a new suburb, as "a caricature, a mimicry of a European settlement of the nineteenth century, now in decay. There are the ghastly remains of luxury stores, Jews, Greeks, Armenians, all tongues, a grotesque society." Said's views on modernization in Cairo are interesting to compare with Auerbach's. They appear in his essay, "Cairo Recalled: Growing Up in the Cultural Crosscurrents of 1940s Egypt," *House and Garden* 159 (1987): 20–32. In the course of describing the Cairo of his adolescence, Said only had a rare chance to have "contact with the Cairo that was neither pharaonic, nor European" (32). Said believes that such contact with the "latent promiscuity of this underground Cairo" is being lost by "Nasser's Arabization, Sadat's Americanization, and Mubarek's reluctant Islamization" (32). Such sentiments are close to those of the travelers to Egypt described by Ali Behdad, *Belated Travelers: Orientalism in an Age of Colonial Dissolution* (Raleigh, NC: Duke University Press, 1994).

22. Erich Auerbach, *Mimesis* (Bern: A. Francke, 1946), p. 175; translated Willard Trask, *Mimesis* (New York: Doubleday, 1953) p. 159. Orhan Pamuk, *The New Life* (Yeni Hayat), trans. Güneli Gün (New York: Farrar, Straus, and Giroux, 1998); reviewed in the *Times Literary Supplement,* October 10, 1997, p. 23, by Ronald Wright. I am using "second encounter" following Michael Taussig, who emphasizes the technologized colonial chain of mimesis and its crucialness to material construction of the shifting borders between "original" and "copy": *Mimesis and Alterity: A Particular History of the Senses* (New York: Routledge, 1993, p. 246).

23. Pamuk's own grandfather was a wealthy engineer who ran a factory and made a fortune on building the railway; see an interview with Pamuk in *Publisher's Weekly* 252 (December 19, 1994): 36–37.

24. Auerbach's pedagogical manual, *Introduction aux études de la philologie romane,* written in 1943 in Istanbul and published in French (1949) serves as a partial guide to this translation project mapped out by Uncle Rifki's library. Auerbach published his famous essay "Figura" in Istanbul in 1944 in the *Neue Dantestudien* (Istanbuler Schriften 5): 11–71; trans. Ralph Manheim and published in Erich Auerbach, *Scenes from the Drama of European Literature* (Minneapolis: University of Minnesota Press, 1984) pp. 11–78.

25. Gilles Deleuze shows the importance of the hybrid linking of these two modern technologies and the problem of the close-up and faciality in cinema in *Cinema 1: Movement-Image* (Minneapolis: University of Minnesota Press, 1986), p. 101; see also Gilles Deleuze and Felix Guattari, *A Thousand Plateaus: Capitalism and Schizophrenia* (Minneapolis: University of Minnesota Press, 1987), pp. 167–91.

26. Roland Barthes, "The Third Meaning," in his *Image, Music, Text* (New York: Hill and Wang, 1977), p. 68. I am grateful to my colleague Alexander Nemerov for remarking on the relevance of another essay by Barthe, "The Face of Garbo," printed in his *Mythologies* (New York: Hill and Wang, 1973). Barthes makes interesting links between the actress's face, exile, and temporality: "the Essence [of her face] became gradually obscured, progressively veiled with dark glasses, broad hats and exiles: but it never deteriorated" (57).

27. I have used the edition of the *Vita Nuova* edited by Dino S. Cervigni and Edward Vasta (Notre Dame, IN: University of Notre Dame Press, 1995); see also Robert Pogue Harrison, *The Body of Beatrice* (Baltimore: Johns Hopkins University Press, 1988).

28. Sylvia Tomasch, "Judecca, Dante's Satan, and the Dis-placed Jew," in Tomasch and Gilles, eds., *Text and Territory,* p. 264.

29. Teodolinda Barolini, *The Undivine Comedy: Detheologizing Dante* (Princeton, NJ: Princeton University Press, 1992), p. 16.

30. My summary is based on the work of Hans Belting, *Likeness and Presence: A History of the Image before the Era of Art* (Chicago: University of Chicago Press, 1994), especially chaps. 17 and 18.

31. Just as relics are translated onto painted panels, Dante "translates" his relics into prose in the *Vita Nuova:* "the lyrics thus chosen undergo not only a passive revision in the process of being selected for inclusion, but also an active revision at the hands of the prose narrative, which bends them into a new significance consonant with the poet's 'new life.' . . . The prose is the chief witness to the author's revised intentions, since through its agency poems composed as isolated love lyrics are forced into temporal sequence that places them in a predetermined and significant relation to each other." Quotation from Teodolinda Barolini, *Dante's Poets: Textuality and Truth in the Comedy* (Princeton, NJ: Princeton University Press, 1984), p.15.

32. For the Holy Face and Veronica's Veil, see Belting, *Likeness and Image,* pp. 208–25, and Joseph Leo Koerner, *The Moment of Self-Portraiture in German Renaissance Art* (Chicago: University of Chicago Press, 1993), pp. 80–126.

33. The topical index of the Cervigni and Vasta edition of the *Vita Nuova* conveniently indexes Dante's references to temporality under "time." The image of Dante's suspension of his contract with the future comes from Harrison, *Body of Beatrice,* p. 166.

34. The brilliant essay on the ghost of Guido Cavalcanti in Harrison's *Body of Beatrice* has guided my thoughts about these intersections between *Vita Nuova* and the *New Life.*

35. Taussig, *Mimesis and Alterity,* p. 22.

36. Edward W. Said, "Palestine, Then and Now," *Harper's* 285 (December 1992): 47–55.

37. For the damage that can be done by such militant secular criticism see the two perceptive essays by Talal Asad on the Salman Rushdie affair in his *Genealogies of Religion: Discipline and Reasons of Power in Christianity and Islam* (Baltimore: Johns Hopkins University Press, 1993), pp. 239–306.

CHAPTER 3

CHAUCER AFTER SMITHFIELD: FROM POSTCOLONIAL WRITER TO IMPERIALIST AUTHOR

John M. Bowers

> *This chapter examines the development of an English literary tradition in re-sponse to the long-standing dominance of French cultural models during the last decade of the fourteenth century. The study suggests ways in which this body of vernacular writing, particularly the Canterbury Tales, was quickly appropriated to the expansionist agenda of the new Lancastrian regime dur-ing the first decades of the fifteenth century.*

> The native is an oppressed person whose permanent dream is to be-come the persecutor.
>
> —Frantz Fanon, *The Wretched of the Earth*

When Geoffrey Chaucer as Clerk of the King's Works constructed lists for the 1390 Smithfield tournament, he took part directly in the aristocratic spectacle that Richard II staged as part of England's grand reentry into the European political arena.[1] King Richard's eager embrace of French culture, especially after his marriage to Isabelle of France in 1396, encouraged the appearance at his court of French chivalric poets such as Oton de Graunson and literary opportunists such as Jean Froissart. After Chaucer's "Italian period" of the 1380s, the poet was again induced to engage directly with this hegemonic French tradition. In addition to his burlesque of the courtly love vision in *The Legend of Good Women,* the *Canterbury Tales* represented his literary response as a postcolonial writer to these cultural challenges and, moreover, provided the materials of a nationalist English tradition ready-made for appropriation by a subsequent imperialist movement.

The feudal conquest begun in 1066 by William the Conqueror may have lacked the systematic acquisitiveness of nineteenth-century industrial powers, but it effected a permanent dislocation from any sense of Saxon identity. Sir Richard Southern's account of these cultural transactions through the twelfth century exposes the complexity as well as the long-term mutations of England's colonial identity.[2] Postconquest aristocrats came to identify with Frenchmen, or contrast themselves with the increasingly alien French nationals, but the other half of the geographical formula was always the same. *England* and *France* became fixed in a dynamic of binary opposition that reached an extreme of self-consciousness during the late fourteenth and early fifteenth centuries, midway in the protracted international struggle that came to be known as the Hundred Years War.[3]

By the time Chaucer began his decolonizing project, English itself showed two major characteristics of an indigenous language in transition under pressure of a ruler language imposed from outside its existing linguistic borders. The native language was spoken "badly," without a sure sense of correct usage, and it had begun borrowing extensively from French for its vocabulary and, to a lesser extent, its syntax. It is one of the ironies of literary history that Geoffrey Chaucer, "father of English poetry," was ideally situated to consider unproblematic—even advantageous—these neocolonial erosions in his native language, because they allowed such vast opportunities for linguistic inventiveness. He participated as a member of the ruling elite schooled in the French language. His Hainault wife probably spoke French exclusively in the home as she did in the household of Queen Philippa of England, who served as patroness to other French-speaking Hainault natives such as Jean Froissart. He operated within a state bureaucracy that used French as its official language, and he produced poems that had as their intended audience these same French-speaking courtiers and bureaucrats.[4] Because Chaucer had the greatest natural inducement to perpetuate French usage, his turn to English struck at the heart of francophone culture. Although there may have been some effort under Richard II to privilege the Cheshire dialect of the *Pearl* Poet—an effort that came too little and too late[5]—a variety of factors gave a natural advantage to Chaucer's London dialect, particularly the city's large population and its centrality in terms of governance and commerce.[6]

As a decolonizer of Anglo-Norman culture, however, Chaucer faced the quandary of so many postcolonial intellectuals. How was he to represent the distinctiveness of his native society without being fatally compromised as a bilingual reader whose primary literary authorities belonged to the nonindigenous tradition?[7] Active in the last decades of the fourteenth century when the conflict with France took several important turns, Chaucer became an agent of pivotal importance because he was placed in the dialogic position of reaction, competition, calculation, and innovation. Although his decision to compose his works exclusively in English forms a commonplace of literary history, political readings of his career will mean interpretation of an entirely different sort.[8] Postcolonial criticism means reading against the grain of Christian pedagogy, detecting significant interruptions in narrative probability, and exploring the interstices through which the text utters its sarcastic critiques, a sarcasm born of *ressentiment* and often merging with Chaucerian irony at its most characteristic. A sophisticated buffoonery attends the postcolonial performance as it seeks to evolve its own discourses of place, tradition, and bodily desire by miming the artistic forms of the foreign culture. Because Chaucer produced his works across several disjunctive moments in history and culture that anticipate in rough outline many events in the world today—in Eastern Europe and the former Soviet Union no less than in Africa, Asia, and the Caribbean—the strategic contents of his poetry, its antagonistic negotiations with prevailing authorities, and its later appropriations by those with more blatant political designs certainly have much to suggest.[9]

During the rapprochement with France inaugurated by the 1390 Smithfield tournament, Richard II himself was increasingly drawn to French literary styles of the sort embodied in the volume of poetry presented to him by Froissart in 1395.[10] Consequently, Chaucer's notion of himself as an English poet was subject to urgent redefinition. The Prologue to the *Legend of Good Women* bears witness that *Troilus,* which was meant to be acclaimed as a great English-language achievement, had fallen short of its author's high expectations. The court audience was not uniformly pleased. Chaucer retreated. His works of the 1390s show such dazzling audacity precisely because they were not written to be published for "courtly consumption" during the poet's lifetime. The *Legend* marked his permanent estrangement from royal literary culture for the remainder of his career.

John Dryden's admiration of the *Canterbury Tales* for encompassing "the whole English Nation of his Age"[11] hardly goes far enough in estimating Chaucer's newly aggressive Englishness. Although the Knight, the Squire, the Prioress, the Merchant, and the Man of Law would have been as bilingual as Chaucer himself in real life, significantly none of these Canterbury pilgrims ever lapses into French. When narratives are projected across the Channel and stories are set in Brittany, Flanders, and Lombardy, the speech and customs are thoroughly anglicized. The *Shipman's Tale* is situated in the town of Saint-Denis, but Chaucer resists political realities by rendering this French territory as a demilitarized zone, domesticating it as wholly English in terms of peacetime mercantile and matrimonial commerce. Whereas Chaucer the historian shows no inclination toward an ethnography based on cultural differences, Chaucer the nationalist does not invent an essential Englishness that would have homogenized his characters and trivialized them as mere types. Such an assertion of English identity was a trap. It would have validated the stereotype of "otherness" that a dominant culture maintains to render manageable a subaltern people. Whereas warfare became in Froissart's *Chronicles* the theater for displaying personal excellence according to a single chivalric model—which was basically a French model—Chaucer's English nationalism would be realized in an crowded pageant of uniquely crafted personalities.

Some of the literary alternatives Chaucer did not choose are revealing. He did not translate Old English poems such as *Beowulf* into Middle English, and he did not contribute his talents to the Alliterative Revival as a more authentic expression of English identity. Chaucer's well-known disinterest in the alliterative romances became a tactic for avoiding the asphyxiation of a constrictive literary provincialism. Similarly, Chaucer did not become a nativist or folklorist. The last item of his agenda was any ethnic revival appealing to some sense of hearty Saxon yeomanry.[12] His closest approximation was the *General Prologue's* most taciturn figure, the Knight's Yeoman, who is subsequently allowed to disappear from the tale-telling competition and the roadside drama of the frame narrative. Arguably Chaucer's most brilliant creation owes nothing to the native substratum. The Pardoner—who represents the Spanish religious house of Roncesvalles, has recently come from Rome, and preaches "in sondry landes" while belonging to none—becomes his true personification of an English multiculturalism that is as eclectic as it is eccentric.

Chaucer's most explicit attempt at a Celtic re-creation is the *Franklin's Tale*. The choice of this story's location—Brittany rather than Wales or Cornwall—and its obsessive concern with avoiding shipwreck on the coast's "blak rokkes" are more fully understood in terms of Brittany's strategic importance during the longstanding hostilities with France. Because sea travel from England to the south involved piloting the Breton coast and stopping at Breton ports, the rocky coast of Finistère had become the Gibraltar of military operations throughout the fourteenth century.[13] Stubbornly independent, the duchy demonstrated the reluctance of a *pays* to allow itself to be forced into a submissive status. It possessed a provincial nationalism based on claims of ancient historical origins, a distinct language, and a deep antagonism toward its more powerful neighbors.[14] The *Franklin's Tale* takes for granted the cultural and political separateness of Brittany as a fief that acknowledged no feudal ties with France. When Arveragus goes to seek honor in the exercise of arms, he turns his back on France and invests his service in a kindred land—"in Engelond that cleped was eek Briteyne" (*CT,* V, 810). And when Aurelius and his brother embark on their own quest, the romance's topography contrasting centric with liminal spaces renders the French town of Orléans as the wilderness place and the zone of dark instability, uncertain identities, dangerous dealings, and subtle illusions. In this adroit reversal of geographical meanings, Chaucer demonstrated cunning textual support for the independence of a Celtic homeland, so long as this breakaway territory caused disruption on the border of France, not England.

Unlike some modern nationalisms whose revolutionary leaders claim to represent the majority populace against an externally imposed state, the nationalist movement in late medieval England was an "inside job" undertaken by members of the ruling elite itself, Chaucer included.[15] The goal was the extension of a sense of collective belonging from the *polis* to the *patria,* from the face-to-face society of the city to the abstract community of the nation.[16] The key to such ambition was commonality: a common territory, a common language, a common culture, a common religion, and a common history. Since "replacement within the same time frame of representation is never adequate," as Homi Bhabha observes, the project of liberating national consciousness "requires a radical revision of the social temporality in which emergent histories may be written."[17] Despite an obsessive interest in the past, Chaucer's historiography renders completely invisible the Norman origins of the English state. Some massive denial has taken place. The great nineteenth-century French historian and Christian intellectual Ernest Renan long ago identified the twin processes for creating a national self-consciousness: "the essence of a nation is that all individuals have many things in common, and also that they have forgotten many things!"[18] Chaucer's "key of remembrance" opened the door to selective recall, which also meant tactical amnesia. The absence of the Norman Conquest from Chaucer's historical record spelled a retreat from any *grand récit* of national origins and an assault on the validity of originary discourse as the site of social authority. He aestheticizes the histories that he does invoke. He revels in playfulness and pastiche. The Garden of Eden, as the preeminent locale of human beginnings, is reduced to the sexual playground of the aged lecher Januarie in the *Merchant's Tale.*

Although the Man of Law has access to all legal decisions from the time of William I (*CT* I, 323–24), his tale reaches back much further, to King

Alla and the Northumbrian past. While erasing the Norman foundation, Chaucer prudently resists the temptation of an insurgent nationalism to create any version of the past as monolithic as the one it attempts to supplant. The *Man of Law's Tale* recalls the Northumbrian kingdom as a culture itself arising from an even earlier period of conquest when the native Britons were driven into Wales (*CT* II, 541–45). Although Celtic prehistory provides the time settings for the *Franklin's Tale* and the *Wife of Bath's Tale,* the myth of Trojan origins explicitly invoked in Chaucer's address to Henry IV—"O conquerour of Brutes Albyon"—reaches back even more remotely to a common European foundation, one that renders *Troilus and Criseyde* an episode from the earliest record of the British people. If insistence on the homogeneity of origins figures prominently in the ideology of colonial subjugation no less than in the narrative of the nation,[19] Chaucer explodes this foundational mythology by offering a baffling regression of originary societies: Anglo-Saxon, Celtic, Roman, Trojan. Yet even Troy is not the beginning *ante quem non*. Before Troy, as Lee Patterson has so powerfully demonstrated, there was Thebes.[20] None of these sites represented a lost Edenic purity, however, a place of moral and ethical wholeness, an uncontaminated mythological space that could be used for arguing redemption by way of return or revival. Further regression meant only further disenchantment, as John Lydgate's *Siege of Thebes* (ca. 1420–22) would make tragically clear.

These originary episodes do not affirm a single social model but contribute instead to separate categorical paradigms: governmental, military, religious, familial, matrimonial. "The cultural shreds and patches used by nationalism are often arbitrary historical inventions," Ernest Gellner points out.[21] Chaucer gathers many historical shreds because he pursues a multiple agenda in constructing a patriarchal community in which *pater* and *patria* become inseparable, although open to constant qualification and supplement. These anchoring moments create a fragmented anteriority whose causality, multiple and unconnected, disrupts any sense of serial continuity and frees the discourse of nationhood from a historical contingency in which England was always the loser. The effect was to produce an unstable but productive space in which an unfixed code of cultural meaning could emerge.[22] It follows that irrational story-structure and the frustration of Aristotelian cause-and-effect would characterize Chaucer's most diligent historical narratives in the *Knight's Tale* and *Man of Law's Tale*. Only fabliaux such as the *Miller's Tale* and the *Shipman's Tale* with contemporary settings could afford the discursive solidarity of truly coherent plots.

Any single historical underpinning probably was already doomed in a totalizing nationalist movement—and Chaucer may have understood this point all too well—because England then, like the United Kingdom today, was not really a nation but a state.[23] The fourteenth-century historian Ranulf Higden repeated commonplace observations on the linguistic differences within the British Isles as well as the temperamental dispositions of its peoples—southerners quiet and gentle, northerners restless and fierce.[24] Since there was no homogeneity, the process of state-making required centralization to enforce uniform practices. Tax collecting, accountancy, and financial transactions of the sort Chaucer himself conducted as Controller of the Custom contributed to this standardization for the entire realm.[25] In England, the domination of the center over the periphery meant the ascendancy of London/Westminster over the provinces, especially those in the north.[26] "Internal colonialism" becomes the process by which domination is spread from the state's center.[27] Since commonality is achieved only when the center is able to assert its superiority over the rest of the country, the universality of the Latin language actually worked against this process. Only the ascendancy of a single regional dialect would spell success.

The body politic was being radically redefined by the burgeoning middle strata represented by the assembly of pilgrims in the *General Prologue,* with the consequent recognition of what T. F. Tout characterized as a truly assertive "public opinion" during this period.[28] Toward these ends, an official corpus of vernacular writings such as Chaucer's would become essential for the cultural construction of nationhood as a form of social and textual affiliation. A native-language literature, created in such political circumstances, fictionalizes the national identity by ignoring, effacing, ridiculing, or domesticating ethnic and provincial differences, especially linguistic ones. The *Canterbury Tales* averts a continual splintering by anticipating an achievement usually credited to the later genre of the novel. It objectifies the nation's *composite* nature as a hodgepodge of different classes, a jumble of regional representatives, and a mixture of the jargons of gender, religion, and professional class—but *not* a mixture of regional dialects.

It is usually argued that the discourse of nationhood was made possible by the Enlightenment's destruction of the older medieval discourse of a divinely ordained hierarchy, which had precluded some strong sense of horizontal comradeship. Christian historiography, with its figural anachronism fostering a sense of simultaneity based on vertical relations with God, made a discourse of nationalism inconceivable in the Middle Ages—so the argument runs. What was required instead was a horizontal social discourse open to temporal coincidence and markable on the calendar. The emplotment of national destiny was dependent on an outlook in which sacral ontology was replaced by a greater arbitrariness of signs and the narrative "now" became a *meantime* rather than the penultimate moment in an

apocalyptic frame. Benedict Anderson has offered the most influential formulation of this view: "The idea of a sociological organism moving calen-
drically through homogeneous, empty time is a precise analog of the idea
of the nation."[29]

To situate these conditions in the modern world, however, means ignoring Chaucer's initiatives. The *Canterbury Tales* is set not in the liturgical
time of Easter but in the calendrical month of April. Its chronology is not
teleological but a true in-between time, a temporalizing zone cut off from
ritual moments and civic spaces, the open road deployed as a discontinu-
ous *somewhere* between London and Canterbury. The pilgrims have been
brought together by coincidence ("by aventure"), and their actions are
never rigorously marshaled under the discursive trope of pilgrimage narrative. As true members of an "imagined community," they do not have determined identities but are possessed of a radical contingency that emerges
from anonymity and is constantly deconstructed by deviances traditionally
discussed in terms of estate satire. The sum of the Canterbury fragments
represents "the collective voice of the people as a performative discourse
of public identification," just as Homi Bhabha discovers in the realistic
novel, which has been privileged as the literary analog to the larger social
discourse of nationhood.[30]

In his *De Vulgari Eloquentia,* Dante offered the prospect of a nationwide
language "which belongs to every city but seems to belong to none."[31]
There is no evidence that Chaucer would have dissented from a grand
scheme of this sort for England. More deliberate ideological work attends
the construction of national identity at the linguistic level precisely because there is so much riding on the populace's identification with the nation. The absence of London from Chaucer's poetry, except for brief
unflattering glimpses in the *Cook's Tale* and the *Canon's Yeoman's Tale,* becomes an authorial strategy to avoid splintering the nation into competing
cities.[32] Heavy-handed promotion of London would have worked against
any sense of English unity.

Of course this is a ruse. Although London is hardly mentioned in
Chaucer's works, every town is treated as if it were London, every household a London household, nearly every character a London speaker. London is nowhere but everywhere. This paradox frequently attends nationalist
campaigns that begin as urban movements but that seek authenticity in
rural or plebeian settings, while the instigators explicitly distrust the cosmopolitan upper classes and intellectuals (like themselves!) as those most
likely to embrace foreign fashions and ideas.[33] Chaucer's pilgrims derive
from many regions of England—the Wife of Bath, the Clerk of Oxford,
the Shipman of Dartmouth, the Reeve of Norfolk—but they gather in a
London suburb and are represented as speaking the London dialect of the

poet himself. One of the narrator's unstated duties is to translate provincial dialects into "Londonese." Even the Canterbury destination is close enough to the metropolis to promote a sense of regional preeminence. D. W. Robertson reminds us that St. Thomas à Becket's status as "London's most celebrated citizen" also carried political weight: "When Chaucer decided, therefore, to create a fictional pilgrimage to the shrine of St. Thomas at Canterbury beginning on the outskirts of London, he was making a deliberate appeal to the *pietas* of the City of London."[34] How would the poem's geographical consciousness have been altered if, instead, the pilgrims had journeyed to Glastonbury or Bury St. Edmunds?

Benedict Anderson has argued that "pilgrimage" provides a powerful organizing trope for the unification of a community *e pluribus unum*.[35] Pilgrimage draws together a great diversity of peoples and tongues, joins them in a sense of higher purpose, and maps their journey as an ad hoc society to some distant, unseen goal. The fact that Chaucer's pilgrims never reach their goal accords better with the narrative of a nation, which is always unfolding and never fulfilled, than with the stereotype of the pilgrimage narrative so richly documented by Donald Howard.[36] The one-way pilgrimage provided an even more specific metaphor for the careerism of those state functionaries like Chaucer himself whose efforts, although steadily self-serving, drove the machinery of nation-building. Interchangeability—the ability to switch from one post to another with minimum difficulty—placed these "new men" on the high road to success. "The last thing the functionary wants is to return home; for he *has* no home with any intrinsic value."[37] Speaking a single language of state, these careerists encountered eager fellow travelers who had also severed their ties to local roots and social origins. The Wife of Bath is a constantly displaced person, forever "wandrynge by the weye," and the roster of the entire Canterbury company is bracketed by the most relentless traveling professionals, the Knight and the Pardoner.

The prudishness of Richard II, who quite possibly practiced celibacy in his marriage with Queen Anne,[38] displaced sexual dalliance as the privileged theme of high culture and therefore encouraged Chaucer's move to redefine obsessive love and sexual play as the versatile themes of a "middle-strata" literature. In what would become his most effective rebuttal to the voice of official courtliness, his *Canterbury Tales* signals a detachment from royal maneuvering in a shift toward the "politics" of domestic relationships. The *Knight's Tale* begins in the broader social dimension of international conquest, but its central antagonisms are quickly reinscribed in the domestic sphere: Theseus's marriage to Hippolyta dispels the Amazonian threat, and Palamon's marriage to Emelye eliminates the Theban problem. Because politics existed as a category of morality for Chaucer no less than for Thomas Aquinas, all the paramount issues of desire, allegiance, compromise, and betrayal could be examined in the microcosmic environment of the married couple's household.

But is this the whole story? Whether the Greek siege of Troy, the Athenian conquest of Thebes, or the Christian colonization of the Western world from Syria to Northumbria, Chaucer's histories are retellings of imperial aggression. They are also accounts of failed imperialist ambitions: the stalemate of the Trojan conflict, the recursiveness of Theban violence, and the slippage of Christian cultures back into prior states of paganism. Chaucer discovered that the chambers of bourgeois acquisitiveness and enclosed gardens of sensual self-interest merely provided analogs for the feudal landscape of castles and battlegrounds that had become the mise-en-scènes of a militarist endgame. He represents the middle-class economic revolution as a cultural initiative of the first importance, and as an English innovation, it helped to fill the space of colonial dispossession and compensate for the lack of a noble native lineage. But having "invented" English society in the *General Prologue,* how was Chaucer to plot the narrative of this community of pilgrims when faced with a Christian teleology that rendered all political economies merely preliminary?

Instead of an aestheticizing project that might repeat the closed system of the dominant culture it sought to supersede, the *Canterbury Tales* entered its public life as an artifact so fragmentary, so jostled with competing voices, and so internally disrupted in its central discourse—in short, so fully embodying Edward Said's sense of a text's "worldliness"—that it was ripe for appropriation, domestication, and continuation. The underlying narrative of late-medieval chivalry had been the desire to acquire. The *Roman de la Rose* had relentlessly enacted this theme, and it haunted Chaucer's work from his earliest efforts. If there is a single obsessive theme of the *Canterbury Tales,* it is the drive to possess another man's property, his money, or most frequently his woman—followed always by the anxiety of losing what had been won. Chivalric discourse offered a model for acquisition only, not permanent possession. To the extent that Chaucer problematizes the urge to keep what had been seized, his final work bridges the worlds of the Knight as a campaigner in heathen lands and a later knight, Sir Walter Raleigh, as a colonizer of the New World.[39]

Envisioning a journey to the New Jerusalem at the end of the *Canterbury Tales,* the *Parson's Tale* partly stages the collection's closure and partly invites further initiatives of a political nature. From the foundational narrative of national origins in the Old Testament in which Moses leads the Israelites to the Jordan River, with the subsequent dispossession of the natives of Jericho, discourses of the Promised Land have been freighted with imperialist potentials—potentials obsessively pursued in a succession of crusades, including the one proposed by Chaucer's contemporary Philippe de Mézières in his *Epistre au Roi Richart* (1395). Any narrative that translates society into another realm of lived experience is ready-made for the ideology of colonization. The road to Canterbury, it should be remembered, was also the road to France.

The agency of Chaucerian writings and the construction of his status as an English author during the generation after his death in 1400 figure importantly in Henry V's larger campaign of aggressive nationalism, which asserted itself in imperialist claims across the Channel. When the next stage of hostilities was crowned with victory at Agincourt in 1415, the strategy of the *chevauchée* or military expedition was replaced by a campaign of territorial settlement and colonization.[40] The welfare of these colonists would become a major consideration during all Anglo-French negotiations following the Treaty of Troyes in 1420—a date associated, not coincidentally, with the production of the two most important Chaucerian continuations, the anonymous *Tale of Beryn* and John Lydgate's *Siege of Thebes,* the latter of which actually alludes to the language of the treaty in its final prayer for "pees and quyet / concord and unité."[41]

Amid the compendious contents of the *Canterbury Tales,* Chaucer's narration of nationhood was begun *in medias res* with English social history half-made, because it was still in the process of being made.[42] Especially after the large number of French captives arrived in England following Agincourt, an arena of cultural competition was created again for the first time since the decade following Poitiers in 1356. But the English were no longer at the same disadvantage. Unlike the large number of French noblemen who had arrived in England in 1360, the royal hostages who took up residence in the early fifteenth century actually learned the English language and became Chaucer's "captive audience." Jean of Angoulême supervised the production of his own copy of the *Canterbury Tales,* and his older brother Charles of Orléans wrote English poetry in the Chaucerian idiom. James I of Scotland, who was captured en route to the court of his French allies in 1406, became the author of the finest of all Chaucerian imitations, *The Kingis Quair.* These rulers were in effect "colonized" as surrogates for the lands they ruled over. Clearly the English poet who had positioned himself ideally to serve as the agent for this form of Lancastrian *cultural* imperialism was Geoffrey Chaucer.[43]

Notes

1. Nigel Saul, *Richard II* (New Haven, CT: Yale University Press, 1997), pp. 340–42 and 351–52, and *Chaucer Life-Records,* ed. Martin M. Crow and Clair C. Olson (Oxford: Clarendon, 1966), pp. 472–76.

2. R. W. Southern, "England's First Entry into Europe" (1966), in *Medieval Humanism* (New York: Harper & Row, 1970), pp. 136–57.

3. Kenneth Fowler, "Introduction," in *The Hundred Years War*, ed. Kenneth Fowler (London: Macmillan, 1971), p. 21, and V. J. Scattergood, "Nationalism and Foreign Affairs," in *Politics and Poetry in the Fifteenth Century* (New York: Barnes & Noble, 1971), pp. 35–106.

4. Rolf Berndt, "Period of Final Decline," in *Cambridge History of the English Language, vol. 1: 1066–1476,* ed. Norman Blake (Cambridge: Cambridge University Press, 1992), pp. 352–59, emphasizes that use of the prestige language virtually defined the courtly and professional elite.

5. Michael J. Bennett, "The Court of Richard II and the Promotion of Literature," in *Chaucer's England,* ed. Barbara A. Hanawalt (Minneapolis: University of Minnesota Press, 1992), pp. 3–20, and John M. Bowers, "*Pearl* in Its Royal Setting: Ricardian Poetry Revisited," *Studies in the Age of Chaucer* 17 (1995): 111–55.

6. Bernard Guenée, *States and Rulers in Later Medieval Europe,* trans. Juliet Vale (Oxford: Blackwell, 1985), "The Rise of the Capital," pp. 126–34, points out that increased record-keeping necessitated by Edward III's French wars encouraged the permanent settlement of the bureaucratic offices at Westminster.

7. Tejaswini Niranjana, *Siting Translation: History, Post-Structuralism, and the Colonial Context* (Berkeley: University of California Press, 1992), pp. 163–86.

8. See Jacques Derrida, "Otobiographies," in *The Ear of the Other,* trans. Peggy Kamuf (New York: Schocken, 1985), p. 32.

9. Anne Middleton, "Medieval Studies," in *Redrawing the Boundaries: Transformation of English and American Literary Studies,* ed. Stephen Greenblatt and Giles Gunn (New York: Modern Language Association of America, 1992), pp. 12–40, at 30 has identified what medieval studies share with postcolonial criticism.

10. Richard Firth Green, *Poets and Princepleasers: Literature and the English Court in the Late Middle Ages* (Toronto: University of Toronto Press, 1980), pp. 64–65 and 77.

11. *Chaucer: The Critical Heritage, Vol. I, 1385–1837,* ed. Derek Brewer (London: Routledge & Kegan Paul, 1978), p. 166.

12. Edward Said, "Yeats and Decolonization," in *Nationalism, Colonialism, and Literature,* ed. Seamus Deane (Minneapolis: University of Minnesota Press, 1990), p. 82: "Nativism, alas, reinforces the distinction by revaluating the weaker or subservient partner." See John M. Bowers, "Chaucer's Canterbury Tales—Politically Corrected," in *Rewriting Chaucer: Culture, Authority, and the Idea of the Authentic Text, 1400–1602,* ed. Thomas A. Prendergast and Barbara Kline (Columbus: Ohio State University Press, 1999), pp. 13–44, esp. 16–19.

13. Fowler, "Introduction," in *Hundred Years War,* p. 5.

14. *War, Literature, and Politics in the Late Middle Ages,* ed. C. T. Allmand (New York: Barnes & Noble, 1976), contains two pertinent studies: P. S. Lewis,

"Of Breton *Alliances* and Other Matters," pp. 122–43, and especially Michael Jones, "'Mon Pais et ma Nation': Breton Identity in the Fourteenth Century," pp. 144–68.

15. Ronald Wardhaugh, *Languages in Competition: Dominance, Diversity, and Decline* (Oxford: Blackwell, 1987), pp. 64–74, makes the point that because French always had been an official language, the king and the ruling elite could officially promote its disuse in favor of English. See also R. D. Grillo, *Dominant Languages: Language and Hierarchy in Britain and France* (Cambridge: Cambridge University Press, 1989), pp. 43–62.

16. John A. Armstrong, *Nations before Nationalism* (Chapel Hill: University of North Carolina Press, 1982), pp. 93–128.

17. Homi K. Bhabha, "Postcolonial Criticism," in *Redrawing the Boundaries,* ed. Greenblatt and Gunn, pp. 437–65, at 437.

18. Ernest Renan, "What Is a Nation?" (1882), trans. Martin Thom, in *Nation and Narration,* ed. Homi K. Bhabha (New York: Routledge, 1991), p. 11. See also Homi K. Bhabha, "DissemiNation: Time, Narrative, and the Margins of the Modern Nation," ibid., p. 310: "It is this forgetting—a minus in the origin—that constitutes the *beginning* of the nation's narrative."

19. Niranjana, *Siting Translation,* p. 39.

20. Lee Patterson, *Chaucer and the Subject of History* (Madison: University of Wisconsin Press, 1991), pp. 47–83 and 165–230; on the Trojan historiography behind *Troilus,* see pp. 84–164.

21. Ernest Gellner, *Nations and Nationalism* (Oxford: Blackwell, 1983), p. 56.

22. Bhabha, "Postcolonial Criticism," p. 438.

23. The classic formulation by Ernest Renan in "What Is a Nation?" is critiqued by Edward Said, "Islam, Philology and French Culture: Renan and Massignon," in *The World, the Text, and the Critic* (London: Faber, 1984), pp. 268–90.

24. *Polychronicon Ranulphi Higden Monachi Cestrensis,* ed. Churchill Babington and J. R. Lumby, 9 vols. (London: Rolls Series, 1865–86), 2:156–66.

25. Michael Clanchy, "Literacy, Law, and the Power of the State," in *Culture et Idéologie dans la Genèse de l'Etat Moderne,* ed. J.-P. Genet (Rome: Collection de l'Ecole Française de Rome, no. 82, 1985), pp. 25–34, and Richard Bean, "War and the Birth of the Nation State," *Journal of Economic History* 33 (1973): 203–21.

26. Crawford Young, *The Politics of Cultural Pluralism* (Madison: University of Wisconsin Press, 1976), pp. 23–24, and Armstrong, *Nations before Nationalism,* pp. 168–76.

27. Wardhaugh, *Languages in Competition,* pp. 56–63, and Michael Hechter, *Internal Colonialism: The Celtic Fringe in British National Development, 1536–1966* (Berkeley: University of California Press, 1975).

28. Thomas Frederick Tout, "The English Parliament and Public Opinion, 1376–1388," in *Collected Papers,* 2 vols. (Manchester: Manchester University Press, 1934), 2:173–90.

29. Benedict Anderson, *Imagined Communities: Reflections on the Origin and Spread of Nationalism,* rev. ed. (New York: Verso, 1991), p. 26.

30. Bhabha, "DissemiNation," p. 308. Timothy Brennan, "The National Longing for Form," in *Nation and Narration,* ed. Bhabha, pp. 49–56, discusses the relations between the novel and the formation of nationhood.

31. *De Vulgari Eloquentia: Dante's Book of Exile,* trans. Marianne Shapiro (Lincoln: University of Nebraska Press, 1990), pp. 65–66, prefers "an illustrious, cardinal, courtly, and curial Italian vernacular" that could be used in the textual drive toward centralized power: "for what power is greater than that which is capable of changing human hearts?"

32. David Wallace, "Chaucer and the Absent City," in *Chaucer's England,* ed. Hanawalt, pp. 59–90.

33. Bruce King, *The New English Literatures* (London: Macmillan, 1980), p. 42.

34. D. W. Robertson, Jr., *Chaucer's London* (New York: John Wiley & Sons, 1968), p. 217.

35. Anderson, *Imagined Communities,* pp. 53–56.

36. Donald R. Howard, *Writers and Pilgrims: Medieval Pilgrimage Narratives and Their Posterity* (Berkeley: University of California Press, 1980), esp. pp. 49–52 and 106–09.

37. Anderson, *Imagined Communities,* p. 55.

38. Caroline M. Barron, "Richard II: Image and Reality," in Dillian Gordon, *Making and Meaning: The Wilton Diptych* (London: National Gallery, 1993), p. 15, and John M. Bowers, "Chaste Marriage: Fashion and Texts at the Court of Richard II," *Pacific Coast Philology* 30 (1995): 15–26.

39. Stephen Greenblatt, *Marvelous Possessions: The Wonder of the New World* (Chicago: University of Chicago Press, 1991), reasserts the Medieval-Renaissance disjunction by contrasting *Mandeville's Travels* with later texts such as Raleigh's *The Discoverie of the Large, Rich, and Beautifull Empire of Guiana.*

40. Richard Ager Newhall, *The English Conquest of Normandy, 1416–1424* (New Haven, CT: Yale University Press, 1924), esp. pp. 143–89, and C. T. Allmand, *Lancastrian Normandy, 1415–1450: The History of a Medieval Occupation* (Oxford: Clarendon, 1983).

41. *The Canterbury Tales: Fifteenth-Century Continuations and Additions,* ed. John M. Bowers (Kalamazoo, MI: Medieval Institute Publication, 1992), esp. pp. 1–12 and 55–57.

42. Homi K. Bhabha, "Introduction: Narrating the Nation," in *Nation and Narration,* ed. Bhabha, p. 3.

43. See John M. Bowers, "The House of Chaucer & Son: The Business of Lancastrian Canon-Formation," *Medieval Perspectives* 6 (1991): 135–43.

CHAPTER 4

CILICIAN ARMENIAN MÉTISSAGE AND HETOUM'S *LA FLEUR DES HISTOIRES DE LA TERRE D'ORIENT*

Glenn Burger

> *The generic discontinuities and unexpected conjunctions of* La Fleur des histoires *bear witness to the complexities of its author's cultural location as part of a Cilician Armenian diasporic community. The text demonstrates an innovative cross-cultural negotiation in advance of modern European colonialism and in excess of medieval European attempts at cultural hegemony.*

Although little known today, *La Fleur des histoires de la terre d'Orient,* written by the Cilician Armenian prince Hetoum of Korikos, was a popular text throughout the late medieval and early modern period. Fifteen manuscript copies of the original French text and thirty-one copies of the scribal Latin translation survive.[1] The Latin text was later translated back into French: anonymously in British Library MS Cotton Otho.D.V, and then in 1351 by the monk Jean le Long, as part of a collection of Eastern travel literature and works relating to the Mongols.[2] Hetoum's work enjoyed a similar popularity with the early European printers. There were three undated, early sixteenth-century printings of the original French text, under the title *Sensuyrent les fleurs des histoires de la terre Dorient:* first in Paris by Philippe Le Noir, second in Paris by Denys Janot after Le Noir, and third in Lyon, also after Le Noir, for Benoist Rigaud. These editions show that Hetoum's text was considered more than a historical curiosity, for Le Noir attempts to bring the book up to date by replacing the original Book IV and its plan to reconquer the Holy Land with a new book entitled "des Sarrazins e des Turcz depuis le premier iusqus aux presens q'ont conqueste Rhodes Hongrye et dernierement assailli Austriche" [A history from the beginning to the present of the Turks who had conquered Rhodes, Hungary, and lately besieged Austria]. Also, in 1529, Le Long's French translation of the Latin text was published under the title *L'Hystoire merueilleuse plaisante et recreative du grand Empereur de Tartarie.* Editions of the Latin text were published six times throughout the sixteenth century.[3]

Even this brief outline of the publication history of *La Fleur des histoires* should make evident the extent to which its early readers viewed the text within the normalizing frames of European crusade propaganda or exotic travel narrative. Similarly Eurocentric tendencies mark the work's reception by modern audiences, but now work to maintain the text's obscurity on the margins of Western histories of the Crusades or European travel literature. Indeed, the scribal colophon ending *La Fleur des histoires* already provides such a hermeneutics of incorporation and colonization. Its inscription of the desires of its first European "readers"—Nicholas Falcon, Hetoum's scribe, and Pope Clement V, the supposed commissioner of the Latin translation—assimilates the potentially disorienting discontinuities and differences of Hetoum's text within an already known Western *Christianitas:*

> Here endeth the boke of Thistoris of Thorient Partes (compyled by a relygious man, Frere Hayton, frere of Premonstre order, somtyme lorde of Corc, and cosyn german to the Kyng of Armeny) vpon the passage of the Holy Land, by the commaundement of the Holy Fader the Apostle of Rome, Clement the V, in the cite of Potiers. Which boke, I, Nicholas Falcon, writ first in French as the Frere Hayton sayd with his mouth without any note or example; and out of Frenche I haue translated it in Latyn for our Holy Father the Pope, in the yere of Our Lorde God M CCC vii in the moneth of August. (G3v, p. 85)[4]

Falcon's account emphasizes both the text's translatability and Hetoum's serviceable position as native informant—this "relygious man" speaking French, intent "vpon the passage of the Holy Land," and working upon "the commaundment of the Holy Fader." In the process, this incorporation of Hetoum and his text within the European imaginary and its colonizing fantasies of the Middle and Far East flattens the text's diasporic and polycultural Cilician Armenian perspective. Hetoum's Western readers thus can ignore the potentially awkward differences generated by the complex relationships of Western ecclesiastical and secular desire vis-à-vis the crusade—differences within and between European and Middle Eastern Christian allies,[5] Western and Eastern cultures, Christian and non-Christian.[6]

Certainly the fiction that *La Fleur des histoires* was simply compiled by a "Frere Hayton" writing under papal commandment provides a useful disguise to cover the potentially awkward relationship of the book and its author to contemporary Cypriot and Armenian politics. For if Hetoum did indeed choose to retire to the monastic life in Cyprus, he did so for only a very brief period. Before 1305, as *La Fleur des histoires* makes clear, Hetoum actively participated in the succession of military campaigns necessary to the security of the increasingly beleaguered Cilician Armenian kingdom.[7] Given his close family connection to the royal house of Cilician Armenia and the successful careers of his children, one can presume that Hetoum played an important and dynamic role in the political life of the kingdom.[8] If so, he could not have cut himself off from the dynastic struggles dividing Cilician Armenia between 1295 and 1305, nor could he have failed to align himself with one or more of the feuding parties.

But the exact nature of his role is unclear and has been much disputed. The dates coincide with a period of civil war in Cilician Armenia between King Hetoum II and some of his brothers. In 1295–96 Hetoum II and his brother Toros were in Constantinople arranging the marriage of their sister Rita to Michael, son of the Byzantine emperor. During their absence their brother Sempad seized power, possibly with the support of the catholicos Gregory VII and Pope Boniface VIII. Hetoum II and Toros were arrested and imprisoned by Sempad after an unsuccessful visit to the court of Ghazan, Mongol ilkhan of Persia (and overlord and ally of Cilician Armenia), having been thwarted by a previous mission of Sempad. While in prison, Sempad had Toros strangled and Hetoum blinded. However, two years later, in 1298, another brother, Constantine, deposed Sempad, only to be ousted in turn by King Hetoum II, who had by then partially recovered his sight. Both Sempad and Constantine were exiled to Constantinople under the care of their sister Rita, now wife of Emperor Michael IX. These conflicts were finally resolved in 1305 by the recognition of the son of Toros as King Leon III and his uncle, Hetoum II, as regent. Unfortunately, the young king's reign was short-lived, for on December 7, 1307, both Hetoum II and Leon III were assassinated by the Mongol general Bilarghu. After a brief attempt by Constantine to seize power, Oshin, another brother of Hetoum II, ascended the throne.

According to the testimony of *La Fleur des histoires,* Hetoum of Korikos played a central role in restoring some measure of internal and external calm to Armenia during these years. At the end of Book Three, speaking of a victory of the Armenians and Mongol over the Egyptian forces invading Cilicia, Hetoum adds:

> And I, Frere Hayton, maker of this warke, was present to this thinges. And longe tyme afore that I was purposed to take the order of relygion, but I coude nat, for the great besinesse that the Kyng of Armeny had at that tyme; I coude nat, for myne honour, forsake my lordes and my frendes in all nedis. But sith God of his grace hath gyuen vs the victory agaynst our ennemys, and also gyuen grace to leue the realme of Armeny in suffycient good state, shortly after, I thought for to make an ende of my vowe. And than I toke leue of the Kyng and of my kynred and frendes, and in that tyme that Our Lorde gaue vs the victory agaynst the ennemys of our fayth I toke my way and cam into Cipres. And there, into Our Lady Delepiscopie chirch of the order of Premonstrey, I toke the abyte of religion—and longe I had ben knyght in this worlde—to thyntent for to serue God the remenaunt of my lyfe. And this was in the yere of Our Lorde God M CCC v. Grace and mercy to God, for the realme of Armeny is reformed in better state than it was, by the yonge kinge, my Lorde Lynon [i.e., King Leon III]. (E2r-v, p. 60)

However, the Cypriot chroniclers always have insisted that Hetoum's sudden departure for Cyprus in 1305 was the result not of a long-held religious vow but of his seditious activities against King Hetoum II.[9] Almost immediately on his return to Cyprus in May 1308, Hetoum proceeded to Armenia—within six days, according to Amadi.[10] His return was probably a consequence of the assassination of Hetoum II the previous December.

Moreover, Hetoum's supposed retirement to a religious contemplative life in Cyprus seems not to have prevented him from being drawn into its increasingly complicated political life. The Cypriot chroniclers also accuse Hetoum of being one of the principal agents in the insurrection of Amalric of Tyre against his brother, King Henry I of Cyprus. And Hetoum's arrival in Cyprus coincides with the first secret plans made against Henry, which culminated in April 1306 with Amalric's self-appointment as governor of Cyprus (supposedly at the request of the Cypriot barons). While Kohler points out that Hetoum was not a signatory of the baronial brief accusing Henry of incapacity to govern, Hetoum's abbot was probably the "frater Bartholomeus, abbas monasterii s. Mariae de Epyra" who did sign the brief.[11] And Hetoum's visit to the papal court in Poitiers a year later was at least in part as an unofficial ambassador of Amalric of Tyre. Hetoum's job (as with other more official emissaries of Amalric to the papal court) was to persuade Pope Clement V (a supporter of plans for a new crusade) that Amalric was the best choice as ruler of Cyprus.

Hetoum arrived in Poitiers sometime late in 1306 and remained there at least until February 8, 1308, when he is mentioned in four papal letters, none of which concern political matters. Nor is Hetoum referred to in them as an ambassador of Amalric; instead he is called by his Armenian title, "dominus de Curcho," or by his monastic position, "conversus monasterio sanctae Mariae de Episcopia." But a letter written between April 7 and June 4 by Raymond de Piis, papal legate to Cyprus, to Cardinal Rufati, referendary of Clement V, proves that Hetoum did play an important behind-the-scenes role on Amalric's behalf. The cardinal had authorized Raymond to collect the 10,000 florins Hetoum had offered the cardinal if he would help ensure papal recognition of Amalric's governorship. Amalric told Raymond "that he was prepared . . . to comply as far as the sum of the ten thousand florins was concerned for which I asked him in your name, and which the said lord of Curcus had promised you."[12] But Amalric refused to pay the much larger sum of 50,000 or 60,000 florins that Hetoum supposedly had offered to the cardinal on the pope's behalf. Later, when Raymond met with Hetoum in Armenia, the

> same lord of Curcus talked to me several times about these matters, and I to him; and . . . he said that he had made you no promise concerning the person of our lord aforementioned [i.e., Pope Clement], but had only made a promise for ten thousand florins payable to you (and to be paid within three years by the lord of Tyre), if our lord, through your good services, would confirm the same through a letter of his in his office of government.[13]

Whatever the personal reasons for Hetoum's support for Amalric, it would also make good strategic sense from an Armenian point of view. By all accounts Amalric had played an active role in attempts to stabilize Cilician Armenia and to oppose Egyptian incursians into Syria. Furthermore, he had shown himself willing to cooperate with the Mongol ilkhans of Persia. From an Armenian point of view his belligerent tactics in Cyprus would promise an aggressive Cypriot foreign policy and future support for the beleaguered Armenian state. Hetoum's diplomatic role also suggests a political motivation, at least in part, for writing *La Fleur des histoires.* One of Pope Clement's main reasons in opposing Amalric's insurrection was that civil unrest in Cyprus would hinder the chances for a new crusade. If Hetoum could show that the lord of Tyre's party was pro-crusade and, furthermore, more likely to have the strength to actively promote one, then Clement might be more inclined to favor Amalric's cause over Henry's.

The growing urgency of the Cypriot situation and the desire for Armenian involvement in it also may have contributed to Hetoum's speedy return to Cilician Armenia in 1308. In June of that year Amalric exiled several of Henry's leading supporters to Armenia and in 1309 took the extreme measure of placing King Henry in prison there under the guard of his brother-in-law King Oshin. It is perhaps this outright seizure of power that accounts for Amalric's vagueness about, and Hetoum's denial of, any promises of money to the pope, since the pope could hardly now recognize Amalric's blatant usurpation of his brother's throne.[14] All signs point to Hetoum's resumption of an active and influential role in the political life of his country. About this time his daughter Zabel married King Oshin, successor to Leon III, and Hetoum may have resumed his position as constable of the kingdom (if he is the "Haytonus dux generalis" present at the Council of Adana in 1314).[15]

Not only does Falcon's insistence on papal patronage disguise the complexities of the book's relationship to Armeno-Cypriot politics, but his claim that the book is centered "vpon the passage of the Holy Land" plain and simple ignores the fact that only a small portion of *La Fleur des histoires* actually falls into the genre of *passagium*. Of its four books, the first provides a brief geographical survey of the countries of Asia; the second, a brief history of the rulers of Asia until the ascendancy of the Mongols in the thirteenth century; the third (fully half of the total work), an account of the rise of Genghis (Ghinggis) Khan and of Mongol expansion across Asia, and especially of the subsequent conflicts between the Mongol ilkhans of Persia and the Muslim sultans of Egypt; and only the fourth (a mere 20 percent of the total), a proposal for a new crusade involving the Mongols and Latin and Armenian Christians, directions for the conduct of such an expedition, and an account of recent Egyptian history.

The variety of content and narrative forms that constitutes Hetoum's actual text thus forms a loose aggregration of material often only tangentially relevant to its scribe's stated aim of a passage to the Holy Land: Geography, chronicle history, crusade propaganda, military strategy seem, at times, an uneasy fit. But the very discontinuities and unexpected conjunctions of *La Fleur des histoires* bear witness to the complexities of Hetoum's cultural location as part of a Cilician Armenian diasporic community precariously situated on the borders of European Christian, Islamic Egyptian, and Islamic Mongol empires. Nor can Hetoum's text simply be dismissed as mere crusade nostalgia and colonial mimicry from a privileged member of a Frankish-influenced, Cilician Armenian ruling class. Instead I would argue that the record of *La Fleur des histoires* suggests something more complicated: For the text's interventions into European discourses of the crusade do not simply manifest the colonial stereotype, but rather mark an innovative cross-cultural negotiation in advance of modern European colonialism and in excess of medieval European attempts at cultural hegemony.[16]

When members of the First Crusade entered Cappadocia and Cilicia at the end of the eleventh century, they received unexpected assistance from Christians living there. These were Armenians who, for the most part, had drifted south and southwest from Greater Armenia after its conquest by the Seljuk Turks following the battle of Manzikert in 1071. These Armenians found refuge in the Taurus and Anti-Taurus Mountains or in the cities of the Cilician plain and northern Syria. For nearly a century after their arrival Armenians' political situation was confused and frequently precarious. Those scattered throughout the cities of Cilicia and Syria were under direct Turkish rule or under the control of semiautonomous governors of the Byzantine emperor. However, a few Armenian barons in the relative security of the Taurus and Anti-Taurus Mountains managed to preserve varying degrees of independence. By the early twelfth century two baronial families were beginning to gain ascendancy: The Hetoumids controlled the narrow western pass into Cilicia; the Roupenids, the wider eastern pass into the rich Cilician plain. While the Hetoumids remained loyal to their Byzantine overlords, the Roupenids aimed continually at the establishment of an independent Armenian kingdom in Cilicia.

Finally in 1198 Leon I, a Roupenid and a strong supporter of the Third Crusade, was crowned king, with Archbishop Conrad of Mainz, as the Holy Roman Emperor's representative, bringing the crown and bestowing the other royal insignia on Leon. At the same time the Armenian church submitted to the authority of the Western pope, although it retained its own liturgy and creed. Leon's Latin crown intensified the growing Western influence on the new Armenian kingdom and was a visible sign of Armenia's importance as one of the stronger and more vital of the Christian states in Outremer. For strategic reasons Leon also granted considerable territory in the west of Cilicia to the Hospitallers and Teutonic Knights, in order to free his forces for the struggle against Antioch and the Templars in the East. Leon also began the tradition of intermarriage between Armenians and the Frankish nobility of Outremer, most notably in 1214 with the marriage of his daughter Rita to John of Brienne, regent of the kingdom of Jerusalem.

After Leon's death in 1219, his daughter Isabel succeeded to the throne. She was quickly married to Philip, fourth son of Bohemond IV of Antioch, in the hope of maintaining internal stability and of easing tensions on the kingdom's insecure eastern border. But Philip's high-handed preference for Latin barons and the Latin ritual soon alienated his new subjects and resulted, in 1225, in his deposition and murder. Constantine of Lampron, regent and head of the rival Hetoumid clan, then married Isabel to his son Hetoum, who became king and ended a century of dynastic and territorial wrangling between the two Armenian factions. The accession of Hetoum I marks the beginning of Cilician Armenia's golden age. Throughout his reign the kingdom remained strong, free of dynastic quarrels and, for much of the time, free of foreign invasion. Armenia's ties with the Franks widened, especially with the kingdom of Cyprus. Hetoum's sister Stephanie married Henry I of Cyprus in 1237, and his daughter, Bohemond VI of Antioch in 1254. Hetoum's brother, Sempad the Constable, translated the Assizes of Jerusalem into Armenian, thereby providing the new kingdom with a basis in Frankish feudal law.

Cilician Armenian identity, then, evidences in a variety of ways a productive and complex métissage.[17] As a diasporic community, Cilician Armenia's point of cultural origin is Greater Armenia; however, as the only independent Armenian state, Cilicia is also the embodiment of a proud Armenian culture and history.[18] But its status as an independent kingdom depends in crucial ways on a Western European and Catholic recognition of the state—the crown comes from Western emperor and pope. Moreover, this recognition is achieved and maintained (as in crucial ways is the physical security and integrity of the Cilician state) by incorporation of Armenian bodies within the regimes of European feudal law, Frankish culture (most obviously by intermarriage between the ruling classes of Cilicia and Outremer), and Western Catholicism. That this struck some parts of the Cilician Armenian ruling class as miscegenation rather than métissage is evident from the periodic recurrence of factional violence and civil war among them. However, for Hetoum of Korikos (and for those he admires in its history) métissage is a productive sign of renewal and strength—for Armenia, for Outremer, and for Europe.

But this concerted Armenian engagement with European presence in the Middle East is matched with an equally open and astute engagement with the Mongols. By 1243 the Mongol invasion of Asia had reached Asia Minor. The Mongols had conquered the Seljuk kingdom of Iconium, devastating Greater Armenia and Georgia on their way. In 1247, facing the imminent demise of his kingdom at the hands of the apparently invincible Mongols, Hetoum I sent his brother, Sempad, on an official peace mission to the Great Khan's capital of Karakorum.[19] Sempad returned in 1250 with a promise of autonomy for the Armenian kingdom, but only under Mongol suzerainty. Three years later Hetoum I himself undertook the long journey across Asia to submit in person to the Great Khan Mongke. Such conditions were unacceptable to the crusader states (except for the Principality of Antioch, ruled by Hetoum's son-in-law); indeed the other crusader states roundly criticized Antioch for acknowledging Mongol authority and for joining the Armenians in fighting with these enemies of Chistendom during the successful Mongol invasion of Syria and Palestine in 1260.[20]

Any articulation of ethnic, religious, political, even geographical identity in Hetoum's text is thus complicated by the instabilities of the middle position occupied by Cilician Armenia and its ruling class. For, despite the newness of the Cilician Armenian kingdom, Hetoum's text makes no attempt to construct a narrative of origins for a ruling house or nation, or to construct Cilician Armenia as a colonial extension of a homeland, or to use *La Fleur des histoires* as the narrative of a *translatio imperii*. This absence of a proto-Armenian nationalism or Roupenid-Lusignan dynasticism may simply reflect the status of Hetoum's book as a "Frankish" text, written by a French-speaking inhabitant of a border zone of European hegemony and directed at a "Frankish" audience interested in securing the threatened borders of Christian Europe. Certainly Hetoum's identifications as a Cilician Armenian in *La Fleur des histoire* do at times focus on that kingdom's distinctiveness vis-à-vis its immediate Islamic neighbors in Syria and Palestine and provide points of association with the Frankish crusader states, especially Antioch and Cyprus. But these identifications also show a keen awareness of Cilician Armenia's location on the margins of several great empires and its potential assimilation by different cultures and religions.

Indeed, Cilician Armenia is a curiously absent presence in Hetoum's text. The description of the realms of Asia that occupies Book One lists the historical Greater Armenia as a separate realm, and Hetoum describes his own country simply as "Silyce," the fourth "prouince" of the realm of Syria, "now called Armeny; for, syth that the enemis of the Cristen fayth had taken this lande from the Grekes handes, the Armins traueyled so moche that thei recoverd the realme of Silyce, and now the Kyng of Armeny holdeth it by the grace of God." Moreover, Syria is marked by a great diversity of peoples—"Grekes, Armins, Iacobyns, Nestorins, Sarasins, and two other nations that is Syrisins and Maroins"—as well as a variety of Christian practices—Greek Orthodox, Maronite, Jacobite, Catholic (B1v, p. 18). Cilician Armenia is even more peripheral to Book Two's account of the history of Asia (as indeed is Europe, except vicariously through the Byzantine Empire, itself a signifier of decline and increasing marginality). And even in Book Three's account of the Mongols and of recent Middle Eastern history, where Hetoum was physically present at many of the events or had access to family members who would have been, the point of view is seldom a Cilician Armenian one. Instead, the narrative emphasizes again and again the vagaries of the circulation of power. No one man, no one country, no one race, no one religion is guaranteed military victory or cultural supremacy. In this sense the instability of the Cilician Armenia kingdom (whose borders are constantly threatened and open to enemy attack and occupation) might be seen as emblematic for its apparently more powerful neighbors.

Thus, King Hetoum I, as the embodiment of the paradoxes of the Cilician Armenian perspective, provides the closest thing to a heroic subject position that might orient the narrative. *La Fleur des histoires* describes his

historic visit to Mongke Khan in highly idealized terms, and the real reason for the visit—Hetoum's potentially humiliating acceptance of Mongol
overlordship in return for the Mongols' sparing his country the ravaging
that had taken place elsewhere—disappears behind the ritualized account
of him presenting Mongke with seven requests (conversion to Christianity, peace between Mongol and Christian, delivery of the Holy Land, destruction of the Caliph of Baghdad, Mongol military aid for Cilician
Armenia, and return of any Armenian lands conquered by the Mongols)
that Mongke accedes to with alacrity and goodwill.[21] Neither Mongke
nor any other Great Khan actually converted to Christianity. But the account does manage to convey the reality of Mongol religious tolerance as
well as the very real strategic value of such an "alliance" for the Armenian
state. Moreover, the values of diplomacy, moderation, and peaceful cooperation that this account celebrates in King Hetoum's heroism are quite
different from the pursuit of personal prowess and glory that Western
chivalric accounts so often emphasize and that so often proved disastrous
for the crusader cause.[22] Hetoum I's desire to work in concert with the
Mongol Great Khan is very different from the interactions of a William of
Rubrick or a European prince like Edward I, who display a will to domination and insistence on Western cultural preeminence in their interactions with the Mongols.

In *La Fleur des histoires,* Cilician Armenian métissage means that Hetoum and the imagined community he represents envisage a set of borders
permeable enough that the Cilician Armenian ruling class may intermarry
with the local Frankish ruling class, can be clearly conversant with French
language and culture, and can accept the overlordship of the Western pope
and the establishment of a Catholic Armenian church. But the same Cilician Armenians continue to be close collaborators with the non-Christian
Mongols (even when they become Muslim as the ilkhans of Persia did)
and remain far less dominated than Europeans by the *idea* of crusade (and
with it the idea of complete cultural and religious domination) as the motivating impulse for foreign policy and alliances.

Neither does Hetoum attempt to present Armenia's Mongol allies as Europeans before the fact. His account of the rise of Genghis Khan at the beginning of Book Three of *La Fleur des histoires* tells of a knight in armor
seated on a white horse coming to Genghis in a dream. The knight then
tells him: "the wyll of thy immortall God is suche that he oweth to be
shortli gouernor made vpon the vii natyons of the Tartas that ben called
Malgothz, and that by hym they shal be delyuerd oute of the saruage that
thei had longe ben in, and shall haue worship vpon theyr neighbours." Afterward, "Cangius rose vp merily, herynge the worde of Christ and rehersed
the vision that he se to all the gentilmen" (B5r, p. 26). While this story struc-

tures Mongol origins as monotheistic, pseudo-Christian, and beleaguered but for divine intervention—in other words, sufficiently like that of the crusaders to be readable by them, the tale also probably draws on a Mongol legend closely connected to fact. According to Mongol religious beliefs, a ruler could learn the will of Tengri (the ruler of heaven) only through the medium of a shaman. At the great gathering of the Mongols in 1206 that approved the election of Genghis as Great Khan, one such shaman, Kokocu Tab-tengri, claimed to have ridden up to heaven on a white horse, where he learned that Tengri had appointed Genghis as Great Khan. Hetoum may represent Genghis Khan and Mongol origins as inherently monotheistic and open to Christian arguments, but his account attempts to represent a rapprochement with, not colonization of, difference.[23] And unlike most Western observers who comment on the ugliness of Mongol's Asiatic facial appearance as a way of underscoring an often essentializing racial difference, Hetoum treats Mongol rulers in much the same way as the Europeans he describes. The moment that comes closest to such a negative Western representation of Mongol physical otherness actually works to underscore Ghazan Khan's military prowess and generosity in rewarding his men with the spoils of war: "And marueyll it was that so lytell a body myght haue so great vertu; for among a M [1000] men coud nat be so sklender a man, nor so euyl made, nor a fouler man. He surmounted all other in prowesse and vertue." Thus chivalric prowess is not imagined here as a specifically European attribute, nor is Mongol difference essentialized by such a representation of Ghazan's historical specificity.

Hetoum, then, acts as a go-between, presenting an Asia, complete with its own history, customs, religions, and peoples, to a European audience that should be interested. But he does so as one inhabiting both worlds yet not completely identified with either. And while Asia has its own integrity and continuities—where one can "know" the number and disposition of its countries and peoples—as Hetoum's own history makes apparent, ceaseless variability and change accompanies such continuity. Book Two's account of the history of Asia depicts one conqueror succeeding another, recognizing the circulation of power *tout court* rather than presenting a focused account that would establish some essential Asian character or historical otherness to Europe. Instead *La Fleur des histoires* emphasizes for its European audience the plenitudinous variety of Asia's geographic, linguistic, ethnic, religious, and cultural diversity. By implication, no one nation or ruler, no one religion will ever completely dominate it; hence the value of such knowledge in order to allow strategic intervention and alliance of Western and Asian forces. Similarly, Hetoum's descriptions of Islamic forces in Syria and Egypt at times draw on the language of Christian vituperation and otherness. But for the most part these Muslims are singled out for hatred because they are the *tactical* enemies of Armenia, and for this reason different from Muslim allies such as the Mongol ilkhans of Persia. It is thus necessary to pay attention to multiple differences in order to find security in such a complex landscape; simple binaries will not work. Hetoum's book, then, with its mixture of forms of knowledge, attunement to all points of the compass, and attention to the telling differences between peoples, chronicles the need to know the actualities of the lay of the land around one, to appreciate as many points of view as possible. Perhaps because there could be no one, transcendent point of view that marked a coherent, unified Cilician Armenian identity, Hetoum's narrative seems less concerned with chronicling in its history or charting in its geography a fixed, transcendent signifier, such as *Christianitas* or Europe.

Thus the explicit aim of Hetoum's fourth book may be to persuade the pope to lead a new crusade to the Holy Land and to provide useful practical information for the best way to conduct such a venture. But Hetoum's interest implicitly harnesses a European crusade ideology to "Eastern" tactical needs, focusing on the means by which significant external resources can be harnessed for the defence and security of the Cypriot and Armenian kingdoms. Moreover, this final section is a relatively small portion of a text largely given over to *Asian* concerns; most of the work focuses on a geography of Asia and a history of its rulers (in which recent Mongol and Egyptian history—and by extension, that of the crusader states—are but the latest instalment). In other words, Hetoum's propagandizing might be seen as much an attempt to change the European worldview, to realign it geopolitically, as an attempt to whip up European crusading spirit against a monolithic Oriental other.

Implicitly, Hetoum's text maps Jerusalem as one destination among many, sees it in a geographical context quite different from the usual European one: on the periphery of Asia, *strategically,* not *conceptually,* in the center of Egyptian, Mongol, Frankish, Armenian geopolitical interests. This Jerusalem therefore does not define a whole and originary *Christianitas* (and with it a supreme Latin Europe) by acting as mirror and *translatio.* In a more "standard" crusade or travel account from a European perspective, in "naturally" ending in Jerusalem one thereby proves who one truly is, that is, a Christian subject, and proclaims the centrality of that "I" and the inherent superiority of its point of view.[24] Hetoum's methodology is metonymic rather than metaphoric, a bringing close together into productive contiguity a variety of differences rather than a process of othering in order to define some crucial foundational difference. His Asia thus becomes a productive place of contiguity rather than orientalizing spectacle, part of the multiplicity of crosscultural identifications that *La Fleur des histoires* inscribes and encourages.

Notes

1. See *Receuil des historiens des croisades: Documents Arméniens,* vol. 2, ed. C.
    Kohler (Paris: Académie des Inscriptions et Belles-Lettres, 1906; reprinted
    Farnborough, England: Gregg, 1967), lxxxv–cxxxi, for detailed descriptions
    of the manuscript copies and printed editions of Hetoum's texts and their
    translations. Kohler's is the only modern edition of the French and Latin
    texts and is based on a collation of thirteen French and eight Latin manu-
    scripts. Kohler argues that Book IV of *La Fleur des histoires* was not part of
    the first French version of the text but was added as part of the Latin text
    prepared at the request of Pope Clement V and only later translated into
    French and added to the original three books (lxi–lxvii).
2. Five manuscript copies of the Le Long collection survive: listed by M. C.
    Seymour, *Mandeville's Travels* (Oxford: Oxford University Press, 1967), pp.
    277–78.
3. See Kohler, *Recueil des historiens,* cxxii–cxxvii, for a summary of these early
    printed editions. Numerous manuscript and print translations also testify to
    the text's continuing popularity throughout the late medieval and early
    modern period. A Spanish manuscript translation—*La Flor de la Ystorias de
    Orient*—was commissioned in the late fourteenth century by a grand mas-
    ter of the Order of St. John of Jerusalem (ed. Wesley Robertson Long
    [Chicago: University of Chicago Press, 1934]). Two Tudor English transla-
    tions—one manuscript (Royal 18.B.xxvi); the other, printed by Pynson—
    were produced before 1520. Books I and II of *La Fleur des histoires* were
    translated into English again in 1625 and included in Samuel Purchas's col-
    lection of travel texts titled *Haklvytus Posthumus, or Purchas his Pilgrimes.*
    There were also numerous translations into the other major European lan-
    guages published in the sixteenth century: German (1534), Italian (1556,
    1562 [twice]), Spanish (1595), Dutch (1563, and three more times in the
    late seventeenth century). Ironically, *La Fleur des histoires* was not translated
    into Armenian until 1842, as *History of the Tartars,* trans. Br. P. Mkrtitch
    [Jean-Baptiste Aucher] (Venice: Imprimerie de Saint-Lazare, 1842). See
    Kohler, cxxviii–cxxx.
4. G3v, p. 85. References to *La Fleur des histoires* (hereafter included in the
    text) are given first by folio number (as above) in Richard Pynson's six-
    teenth-century English translation (which can be found on STC micro-
    film, *Short-title Catalogue of Books Printed in England, Scotland, and Ireland,
    and of English Books Printed Abroad, 1475–1640,* No. 13256), and then by
    page number in *A Lytell Cronycle: Richard Pynson's Translation (c1520) of "La
    Fleur des histoires de la terre d'Orient" (c1307),* ed. Glenn Burger (Toronto:
    University of Toronto Press, 1988).
5. Thus any crusading endeavor included "foreign" European crusaders
    present for the limited duration of a given military action, members of
    the crusading orders (Hospitallers, Teutonic Knights, Templars) perma-
    nently based in the Middle East, and knights drawn from the Christian
    states of Outremer—the latter divided between a state like Cyprus (or

earlier, Antioch or Jerusalem) containing "native" populations (of Greeks, Jews, Armenians, Muslims, etc.) ruled by Frankish elites and a state like Cilician Armenia (with a diverse population ruled by a "native" Christ- ian elite heavily but not completely Frankicized).

6. As Hetoum's text makes clear, at least six different Christianities coexist in the East: (Roman) Catholic, Greek Orthodox, Armenian (with an Armen- ian Catholic Church in Cilician Armenia), Maronite, Nestorian, and Jaco- bite. Non-Christian forces included the Islamic Arabic states in Egypt and Syria as well as the different Mongol states (variously shamanistic, Bud- dhist, Islamic, and Christian leaning).

7. This makes him a firsthand observer of many of the events he describes and allows him, for earlier material, to draw on the experience of his un- cles, the great King Hetoum I and Sempad the Constable, both of whom visited the courts of Mongol great khans.

8. Hetoum probably did not assume the title "Lord of Korikos" until after the death of his brother Gregorios (around 1280). About this time, Hetoum married his Cypriot cousin, Isabel of Ibelin. At least six children resulted from the marriage, a daughter, Zabel, becoming the wife of King Oshin I of Cilician Armenia and a son, Oshin, regent during the minority of King Leon IV. See Count William Henry Rüdt-Collenberg, *The Rupenides, Het- humites and Lusignans: The Structure of the Armeno-Cilician Dynasties* (Paris: Calouste Gulbenkian Foundation Armenian Library, 1963), table III, after p. 48.

9. See *Chronique d'Amadi*, ed. René de Mas Latrie, in *Collection de Documents Inédits sur l'Histoire de France*, Première Série (Paris: Imprimerie Nationale, 1891). An earlier instance of piety on Hetoum's part is also open to varied interpretation. In a version of the third book of *La Fleur des histoires* found in only one French and eight Latin manuscripts, Hetoum tells of a pil- grimage he made "apud Vallem Viridem" (probably to France between 1297 and 129—see Kohler, *Receuil des historiens,* p. 330). This pilgrimage also took place during a time of civil strife and dynastic struggle in Cili- cian Armenia. And here too Hetoum's pilgrimage might have been a dis- guise for a diplomatic mission (to add his voice to those urging a new crusade, to shape papal intervention in Armenian politics, or as a polite term for an enforced exile). Kohler finds support for this accusation in the suppression by Hetoum in *La Fleur des histoires* of any direct reference to King Hetoum II and in Hetoum's passionate support of the young king Leon III (xxxvii–xxxviii). For discussions of Cilician Armenian politics during this period, see Serarpie Der Nersessian, "The Kingdom of Cilician Armenia," in *A History of the Crusades,* gen. ed. Kenneth M. Setton, vol. 2, *The Later Crusades,* ed. Robert Lee Wolff and Harry H. Hazard (Madison: University of Wisconsin Press, 1962), pp. 630–60; *The Cilician Kingdom of Armenia,* ed. T. S. R. Boase (New York: St. Martin's Press, 1978), pp. 28–33; Fr. H. François Tournebize, *Histoire politique et religieuse de l'Arménie* (Paris: A. Picard et fils, 1910); The *Cambridge Medieval History,* vol. 4, part 1, *Byzan-*

tium and Its Neighbours, ed. J. M. Hussey (Cambridge: Cambridge University Press, 1966), pp. 628–37.

10. *Chronique d'Amadi,* ed. Latrie, p. 280.

11. Kohler, *Receuil des historiens,* xxxix and note 3; "Epyra" is likely a misreading for "Episcopia."

12. "Paratus erat . . . usque ad summam decem milium florinorum per me ab ipso, vestro nomine, petitam et per dictum dominum de Curco vobis promissam complacere"; Vatican Archives *Instrumenta Miscellanea,* No. 484; printed in Charles Perrat, "Un Diplomate gascon au XIVe siècle: Raymond de Piis, nonce de Clément V en orient," *Mélange d'Archéologie et d'Histoire,* 44th year (1927): 73.

13. "Idem dominus de Curco pluries super hiis fuit mihi locutus et ego secum; et . . . diceret quod nullam promissionem personam dicti domini nostri contingentem vobis fecerat, nisi solum de decem milibus florinis vobis dandis et in tribus annis solvendis per dominum Tirensem, so idem dominus noster eidem officium gubernationis, vobis procurante, per suas litteras confirmaret" (Vatican Archives *Instrumenta Miscellanea,* No. 484).

14. For discussions of Cypriot history in this period, see Peter W. Edbury, *The Kingdom of Cyprus and the Crusades, 1191–1374* (Cambridge: Cambridge University Press, 1991), pp. 101–40; Setton, *History of the Crusades,* vol. 3, *The Fourteenth and Fifteenth Centuries,* ed. Harry W. Hazard (Madison: University of Wisconsin Press, 1975).

15. If this is so, then he was certainly dead by 1320 when his son Oshin, now lord of Korikos, became regent, for no mention is made of Hetoum's presence.

16. I have avoided using the term "multicultural" to describe any of the mixed cultural situations that Hetoum found himself in or attempts to describe in his book. Instead, I would argue, we need to distinguish between three different situations: (1) crosscultural contact, such as that obtaining between Cilician Armenia and the Mongols (especially the ilkhans of Persia); (2) métissage, such as the blending of Frankish and Armenian culture that characterized the Cilician Armenian ruling class during Hetoum's time; and (3) what I would call the polyculturalism that one finds in Syria, with its diverse "communities" of different racial, ethnic, and religious backgrounds living in often harmonious but bounded relationship to each other.

17. I emphasize métissage over diaspora in defining the ruling class of Cilician Armenia because, from Leon I onward, actual intermarriage with the Frankish nobility of Outremer is the foundation for a wider mixing of legal, social, linguistic, military, and religious forms with the Frankish West. What is produced, I am arguing through the case of Hetoum and *La Fleur des histoires,* is a set of identifications not strictly Western or Eastern, Armenian or Frankish—in short, the situation of the métis.

18. Kirakos of Ganjak, for example, describes in glowing terms the reception by King Hetoum I of Armenian dignitaries while on a visit to Greater

Armenia: "He received them all with love, for he was a gentle man, wise and learned in the Scriptures. And he gave them presents in accordance with his means and sent them all away happy: he also gave sacerdotal robes for the adornment of the churches, for he greatly loved mass and the church. He received the Christians of all nations and besought them to live in love with one another, as brothers and members of Christ, even as the Lord had commanded." See J. A. Boyle, "The Journey of Het'um I, King of Little Armenia, to the Court of the Great Khan Möngke," *Central Asiatic Journal* 9 (1964): 186; reprinted as No. X in Boyle, *The Mongol World Empire 1206–1370* (London: Variorum Reprints, 1977).

19. Sempad described some of his experiences during this visit in a letter to King Henry I of Cyprus: see *Recueil des historiens des Gaules et de la France*, ed. Martin Bouquet et al., vol. 10 (Paris, 1840; reprinted, Farnborough, England: Gregg, 1967), pp. 361–63; and Sir Henry Yule, *Cathay and the Way Thither*, rev. H. Cordier, vol. 1, The Hakluyt Society Second Series, No. 38 (London, 1913), pp. 162, 262–63.

20. See Steven Runciman, *A History of the Crusades*, vol. 3 (Cambridge: Cambridge University Press, 1954), pp. 307, 311–12. It was not until twenty years later, when the situation in the Holy Land had grown more desperate and when Abaga, Mongol ilkhan of Persia, had dropped the demand for suzerainty, that the possibility of a general alliance between Mongols and the West could be considered seriously (notably by Edward I of England during his crusade of 1271). The mediation of Cilician Armenians between the Mongols and Europeans and the Armenians' firsthand experience of alliance with the Mongols must have been an important factor in developing this European openness to some limited rapprochement with the Mongols.

21. Kirakos of Ganjak, in his account of the meeting, mentions only the guarantee of Hetoum's lands and the promise of religious freedom for all Christians living under the Mongols. See Boyle, "Journey of Het'um I," 181.

22. Lee Patterson notes that chivalry's "deepest ambition was to produce not a better world but a perfect knight. It was committed to codes of behavior not as programs of action but techniques of self-fashioning: the chivalric life was its own goal. . . . Hence the insistence throughout chivalric writing on the simplicity of chivalric selfhood. Chivalric heroes are represented as driven by a single, all-compelling desire. Peter of Cyprus is inspired by a youthful vision to found the Order of the Sword, 'and this was the goal of all his efforts.' Geoffroi de Charny, a preeminent chevalier who died defending his king's *oriflamme* at Poitiers, tells us in his authoritative *Livre de Chevalerie* that the youths who will become successful soldiers are those who have haunted the *mestier d'armes* from their earliest days and are driven solely by the desire 'to have the high honor of prowess.' . . . Machaut, for example, explains Peter of Cyprus's adoption of the sword as an emblem of his crusading order in these terms: 'For when an eminent prince

conquers by the sword, he acquires glory—honor and profit together—and a good name.'" Patterson, *Chaucer and the Subject of History* (Madison: University of Wisconsin Press, 1991), pp. 175–76.

23. See Mouradja d'Ohsson, *Histoire des Mongols depuis Tchinguiz-Khan jusqu'à Timor Bey ou Tamerlan,* vol. 1 (The Hague: Van Cleef, 1834), pp. 98–100; and R. P. Lister, *The Secret History of Genghis Khan* (P. Davies: London, 1969), pp. 191–95.

24. See Iain Higgins, "Defining the Earth's Center in a Medieval 'Multi-Text': Jerusalem in *The Book of John Mandeville,*" in *Text and Territory Geographic Imagination in the European Middle Ages,* ed. Sylvia Tomasch and Sealy Gilles (Philadelphia: University of Pennsylvania Press, 1998), pp. 29–53, for a discussion both of the tradition of Jerusalem as the centre of the world in some Western medieval *mappaemundi* and of the complexity with which such a concept actually plays out in a travel narrative such as *Mandeville's Travels.* Because Jerusalem is so often conceived as this originary point, pilgrimages "ended" with the arrival in Jerusalem. As a result, as Donald Howard has pointed out, the pilgrimage account of Friar Felix Fabri from the end of the fifteenth century is a rarity in dwelling on the return journey and the homecoming: "most writers barely mention it, and some do not at all. The same is true of 'voyages.'" *Writers and Pilgrims: Medieval Pilgrimage Narratives and Their Posterity* (Berkeley: University of California Press, 1980), pp. 46–47. In addition, a text like *Godefrey of Bouillon* "romances" crusade history so that Godfrey's identity as knight (and by extension, the identities of the other crusaders) is fulfilled by the conquest of Jerusalem and his coronation as its first Christian king. But such an ending also fantasizes the successful crusade as ending history, signalling a fulfilling stasis that colonizes not only Islamic/Christian difference but also those between Eastern and Western Christianity and between a Christian present and Jewish past. See William Caxton, *Godeffroy of Boloyne,* ed. M. N. Colvin, Early English Text Society Extra Series 64 (London: Kegan Paul, Trench, Trübner, 1893; reprinted 1987); see also another English translation even more focused on Godfrey as romance hero in BL MS Royal 18.B.xxvi, folios 6v–86v.

CHAPTER 5

HYBRIDS, MONSTERS, BORDERLANDS:
THE BODIES OF GERALD OF WALES*

Jeffrey Jerome Cohen

> *Through the writings of Giraldus Cambrensis, this chapter maps some monstrous embodiments of cultural hybridity. It argues that postcolonial medieval studies might find an unexpected ally in contemporary Chicana/o studies.*

If the European Middle Ages are that intimately alien, medial time that are not quite the lost past and not quite the modern West, something of both and wholly neither, then medieval temporality finds its contemporary analog in what postcolonial theory calls the hybrid. A composite figure derived from biology, botany, and the discourses of race, the hybrid conjoins differences without fully assimilating them. The hybrid is (in Robert Young's Derridean gloss) "difference and sameness in apparently impossible simultaneity."[1] If the medieval touches the postcolonial exactly at the point of hybridity, this conjunction reveals both a startling consonance and a productive dissonance. Some medieval hybrids could feel quite at home in the high theory of scholars like Homi Bhabha, who identifies in English India phenomena that have immediate analogs in the European Middle Ages. Yet medieval hybridity is, to paraphrase Bhabha, "the same but not quite." In the medieval occidental imaginary, the category admixture that hybridity represents is almost always conjoined with monstrousness, where *monstrum* has the doubled sense of "that which warns" (*monere*) and "that which reveals" (*demonstrare*).[2] Medieval monstrousness intimates an unthought epistemological limit to the widely influential postcolonial criticism derived from the study of English India, and suggests that an alliance might be usefully forged between medieval studies and what has been called borderlands theory. Derived mainly from Chicana/o studies, this growing body of work takes as its central figure not the all too literary hybrid, with his [*sic*] ambivalence, mimesis, and sly civility, but the provocative and proudly resistant *mestiza,* with her insistently embodied experience of that middle formed by the overlap among a multitude of genders, sexualities, spiritualities, ethnicities, races, cultures, languages.

The Grass-Eating Welshman

Like all imperialist powers, the Anglo-Norman rulers of England employed multifarious strategies to annex those territories that dared to stand so invitingly at their borders.[3] In Wales these tactics included strategic intermarriage to infiltrate the local political arena; resettlement of key areas with Flemish and English colonists to fracture indigenous culture; treaty and selective alliance; the frenzied building of castles (300 by 1215) in order to secure and Europeanize the landscape; slaying of livestock, destruction of buildings, seizure of property; torture, dismemberment, murder, imprisonment, and the selling of men and women into slavery. The Welsh fought this relentless invasion with whatever tools came to hand: swords, sabotage, and—in at least one case—the strategic deployment of colonialist stereotypes against those who circulated them. According to Giraldus Cambrensis ("Gerald of Wales"), when Henry II was preparing to seize Pencader, he sent a trustworthy knight from Brittany to reconnoiter the terrain and report on local defenses. This nameless noble was accompanied on his mission by Guaidan, dean of Cantref Mawr, who was instructed by the king "to lead the knight . . . by the easiest route and to make his journey as pleasant as possible [*per viam meliorem . . . et faciliorem militi praeberet iter*]."[4] Gerald describes the Breton's nightmarish sojourn as follows: "[The priest] made a point of taking him along the most difficult and inaccessible trackways. Whenever they passed through lush woodlands, to the great astonishment of all present, he plucked a handful of grass and ate it, thus giving the impression that in time of need the local inhabitants lived on roots and grasses" (I.10 140). When the knight from Brittany finally returned to Henry, he immediately declared that this inaccessible district is impossible to settle, yielding only enough nourishment for "a bestial race of people [*genti bestiali*], who were content to live there like animals [*bestiarum more viventi*]" (140). The king decided that region was not worth colonizing and released the captured Welsh prince Rhys ap Gruffydd to hold the land in tenure for him.

That the Breton knight should find the inhabitants of Pencader to be indistinguishable from animals is likely to have surprised no one in the royal entourage, since it only confirms a representation of the Welsh that their oppressors were themselves circulating. In promulgating an association between the people of Wales and beasts, England was employing a tactic already ancient by the twelfth century: An indigenous people are represented as primitive, subhuman, incomprehensible in order to render the taking of their lands unproblematic.[5] John of Salisbury called the Welsh "a people rude and untamed," declaring that "they live like beasts and despise the Word of Life" [*gens enim rudis et indomita bestiali more uiuens*].[6] The *Gesta Stephani* described Wales as a place that "breeds men of an animal type" [*hominum nutrix bestialium*] whom the Normans subdue and civilize.[7] While giving what he believes is a factual report to Henry, the unlucky Breton knight cites this same stereotype of the feral Welsh, even employing familiar Latin terms.[8]

Guaidan returns to the colonizers the very message they disseminate, reconfirming their knowledge in order to subvert their authority. He thereby brings about the release of the captive prince and prevents a more forceful subjugation of the land. For Gerald's readers, the stereotype is suddenly reversed. The would-be invaders demonstrate that they are the naïfs, and the Welsh become the clever manipulators of dominant representation and *idées fixes*. Homi Bhabha has called such subtle moments of mimicry and doubleness "sly civility."[9] Guaidan's strategic deployment of the Welsh stereotype effects a moment of ambivalence in the text during which the settlement of Wales becomes a problem rather than a program, capturing an uncertainty that Bhabha argues characterizes all colonialist demands and that always haunts Gerald's conflicted relation to his place of origin. The hybrid offspring of a Norman knight married to the granddaughter of a Welsh prince, Gerald is the product of the Welsh March, a border society fully allied with neither of its parents, a linguistic and ethnic *métissage*.

Competing allegiances conjoined with tortured abjections characterize Gerald's writing throughout his career but are especially prevalent in his Welsh texts.[10] In offering a description of the land he does and does not belong to, for example, Gerald suggests in a chapter entitled *Qualiter gens ista sit expugnanda* [How the Welsh can be conquered] that the country be cleansed of its barbarous inhabitants and transformed into a game preserve.[11] Shortly thereafter, he writes at length *Qualiter eadem resistere valeat, et rebellare* [How the Welsh can best fight back and keep up their resistance, II.10 273]. Tellingly, he completes the *Descriptio Kambriae* by returning to Pencader, the site of Guaidan's quietly seditious mimicry in the *Itinerarium*. King Henry asks an elderly Welshman serving in the royal army if he thinks that the native rebels, the soldier's kinsmen, will ever be subdued. The man's reply to the monarch is stunning. Wales may well be decimated by England, he says, just as it has been ravaged by other powers since the Trojan forebears of the Welsh settled the island long ago. Nevertheless, "I do not think that on the Day of Direst Judgment any race other than the Welsh, or any other language, will give answer to the Supreme Judge of all for this small corner of the earth" (II.10 274).[12] Gerald here resolves, at least for a moment, all of his identity ambivalence by crossbreeding Christian futurity (the Last Judgment) to secular history (the Welsh as bearers of the Trojan *imperium*) and articulating its resultant progeny in a language he himself conspicuously never uses: Although translated into clerical Latin, the final answer to God, which is in fact a "final" answer to Henry's colonialist demand, comes in a pure Welsh that binds past to future in order to forge a resistant temporality outside of Norman, Angevin, English fantasies of progress, colonization, and time. Sly civility indeed.

Guaidan inhabits the interstices between Wales and England, a place of overlap where "cultural differences 'contingently' and conflictually touch."[13] As his deployment of Welshness suggests, strategic mimicry and the moments of hybridity that result is not limited to English India, the historical moment from which Bhabha derives the concepts. If hybridity is a "revaluation of the assumption of colonial identity through the repetition of discriminatory identity effects," deforming and displacing the colonialist gaze while constructing an ambivalent site of discipline, dissemination, and disruption, then the Middle Ages were replete with such impurity.[14] Gerald is far from unique in connecting medieval colonialist projects of representation to their mimicry and subversion. The ethnicized Welsh in John of Salisbury and the *Gesta Stephani* are manifestations of an othering impulse also visible behind the racialized representations of Islam disseminated throughout the Latin West. "Saracens" are fantasy products of the Christian imaginary that, like all monsters, could take on an uncanny life and agency of their own. In at least one case they attained a certain amount of self-consciousness about their status as distorting representational project. In an episode from the fourteenth-century history of France known as the *Grandes Chroniques,* the Saracen army of Cordova employs a tactical mimesis to defeat the indefatigable cavalry of Charlemagne:

> At the point that our first contingent was about to join battle with the first contingent of the Saracens, a great crowd of their foot-soldiers placed themselves in front of the horses of our fighters; each one had a horned mask, black and frightening, on his head, that made him look like a devil [*et avoit chascuns en sa teste une barboire cornue, noire et horrible, resemblant à deable*]. In his hands, each held two drums [*tympanes*] together, making a terrible noise, so

loud and frightening that the horses of our soldiers were terrified, and fled madly to the rear, in spite of the efforts of their riders.[15]

The scene is magnificently illustrated in a manuscript now at the Bibliothèque Nationale (BNF FR 2813) in which uncertain French knights swathed in fleurs-de-lis retreat from black-skinned enemies with excessively racialized visages. Without reference to the surrounding text, a medieval observer of the minutely rendered scene might not guess that the Saracens are wearing masks, for their caricatured corporeality is wholly consonant with other textual and pictorial representations of Muslims as a monstrous cultural other. That stereotypes can be performed, that dominant representations and the bodies grouped beneath them do not necessarily coincide, is dangerous knowledge that can topple whole epistemological systems. And so in the *Grandes Chroniques,* Charlemagne destroys his Cordovan foe utterly: "the announcement was made throughout the army that everyone should cover his horse's head with cloth or sheets, so that they might not see the masks, and to stop up their ears, so that they could not hear the shouts of the Saracens, or the sounds of their drums."[16] Veiled eyes, earplugs, and a violence that is consequently both blind and deaf seem to be the only reply that the Christians can give to this message offered by the very Other it constructs but whose "truth" it does not wholly control.

The grass-eating Welshman is easy enough to accommodate within Bhabha's eminently civil gloss on hybridity: Guaidan is a medieval forerunner of the "natives" who so vexed the English missionaries with their subversive assent to Christian truth.[17] Yet the masked Saracens of Cordova suggest that there is more to hybridity than the clever admixture of two disparate cultures. Medieval hybridity is an impudent, relentlessly embodied phenomenon that brings together in a conflictual, "unnatural" union races (*genera*) in the medieval sense: not just different kinds of human bodies, with their competing determinations, but geographic, animal, "inanimate" bodies that incarnate heterogeneous histories of colonization, inscription, transformation. Gerald of Wales suggests that medieval hybridity is the admixture of categories, traumas, and temporalities that reconfigure what it means to be human. Medieval hybridity is inherently monstrous.

For an illustrative instance we need look no further than the text by Giraldus Cambrensis with which we began.

The Knight Who Gave Birth to a Calf

The *Itinerarium Kambriae* is a fascinating composite of travel narrative, imperialist cartography, and localized history. A record of the mission undertaken in 1188 by Gerald and Baldwin, Archbishop of Canterbury, to recruit soldiers and raise funds for the Third Crusade, the *Itinerarium* should no doubt be read as assisting in a transnational project of fostering a united Christian imaginary capable of transcending national, regional, and even sectarian differences—and capable as well of the most unspeakable violence to non-Christian cultures, especially Muslims and Jews.[18] At the same time, the journey through Wales achieved a variety of local political objectives. Baldwin's progress ensured that the church in Wales was publicly acceding to the power of Canterbury—a fact that Gerald must have found particularly galling, since he was a vocal proponent of an independent Welsh see at St. David's.[19] Once Welsh rulers and nobles (many of whom were Gerald's relatives) were transformed into *crucesignati,* they were forced to champion Henry II's crusade and therefore were more deeply under royal control.[20] The distant struggle over the Levant proved a useful distraction from nationalistic struggles closer to home, and even helped to empty Wales of men who were clearly a cause of domestic troubles—including, by Gerald's own admission, "robbers, highwaymen and murderers." The religious devotion that the Crusades inspired should not, however, be downplayed. The clerics recruited about 3,000 men. Gerald's companion, the elderly Baldwin, died surrounded by "desolation and despair" at the siege of Acre (*Itinerarium* II.14 208).

Formally structured around the route along which the two churchmen journeyed for six weeks, the text at times seems a loose collection of anecdotes held thinly together by shifting logics of association. An obsession with corporeal mutability characterizes Gerald's writing throughout. A boy steals pigeons from a church in Llanfaes and his hand adheres to the ecclesiastical stone in punishment, triggering an extended account of sinners who suffered similar fates: A woman of Bury St Edmunds attempted to take coins in her mouth as she kissed a saint's shrine, and her lips adhered to the altar for a day; in Howden church, a parson's *concubina* irreverently sat upon the tomb of St. Osana, and her buttocks became fastened to the wood; in Winchcombe, a monk was divinely rebuked for having had intercourse the previous night when the psalter he carried attached itself to his unclean hands; at the same abbey, a woman who blasphemed a saint was punished while reading the same psalter so that "her two eyes were torn from her head and fell plop on the open book, where you can still see the marks of her blood to this day" (I.2 84–86). What thematically connects these episodes widely scattered through geography and time is their fascinated gaze upon the body as the site for a public spectacle of truth. The flesh is suddenly possessed by an agency that does not originate from the soul inhabiting it and through a forced conjoining to sacred objects (church walls, altars, prayer books) is revealed as a medial space where the private and the spiritual cohabitate. Gerald's narrative disciplines these bodies by hybridizing them with a material fragment of the ecclesiastical institution whose regulatory power over themselves they must now recognize. The exorbitant punishment for the priest's concubine, for example, is wholly consonant with Gerald's goal of colonizing ecclesiastical sexualities, doing away with clerical marriage and enforcing celibacy to bring Wales in line with Rome.[21]

The narrative arc of punished flesh melded to sacred objects culminates in a second saintly blinding and a pair of impious lips fastened to the magic horn of St. Patrick. A few words about the numinous power of bells over those who take oaths are followed by the observation that when held to the ear, Patrick's horn makes a sweet noise like an aeolian harp. Next comes what appears to be another "pure" (i.e., extraneous) wonder: a wild sow "suckled by a bitch remarkable for its acute sense of smell" matures into a hunting pig that can track game better than most hounds (*Itinerarium* I.2 87–88). Gerald generalizes the episode into a truth about the power of the maternal body. Both man and beast, he says, are "greatly influenced by the dam whose milk they suck."[22] A seemingly unrelated story follows, told because it happened in the same region at about the same time. According to Gerald, a Welshman once quite literally had a cow. A certain knight (*miles*) named Gilbert Hagurnell, "after a long and unremitting anguish, which lasted three years . . . gave birth to a calf" (*Itinerarium* 1.2 88). Perhaps, Gerald observes, the event was an omen of some calamitous event yet to arrive, but more likely the monstrous birth was "a punishment for some unnatural act of vice."[23]

In isolation, the knight's difficult labor and strange progeny is yet another wonder offered for the reader's consumption, only slightly more remarkable than St. Patrick's horn and the pig that acts like a dog. Yet the anecdote in context tells an intriguing story about the relationship of hybridity to medieval postcoloniality. The story is introduced, after all, by the linking of somatic morphogenesis to a generative historicity (a wild sow suckled by a domesticated hound becomes a composite body, physically porcine while functionally canine; the flow of breast milk overcodes the biologically innate with the culturally contingent). The man–calf narrative in turn precedes a second story of interspecies procreation: In the ancient past, a mare belonging to St. Illtyd mates with a stag and gives birth to creature with a horse's head and deer's haunches. These narratives are immediately followed by a sexualized account of the mixed ethnicity of Brecknock, the Welsh county in which they occur. Bernard of Neufmarché, *primus Normannorum* in the area, seized the land from its inhabitants, then married the Welsh woman Nest. Norman on its father's colonizing side and Welsh through its mother's indigenous blood, Brecknock is an ethnic hybrid—exactly like Gerald himself.

Nest is named after her mother, Nest daughter of Gruffydd ap Llywelyn, emphasizing her royal Welsh ancestry. This younger Nest is also called Agnes, at least by the English (*materno Nestam vocavere, quam et Angli vertendo Anneis vocavere*). As her bilingual nomination suggests, the body of Nest/Agnes is a point of cultural ambivalence for Gerald's historical narrative. After her son Mahel mutilates the knight with whom she is having an adulterous affair, Nest/Agnes wrongly denounces her offspring to Henry I as the son of this disgraced lover. The king disinherits Mahel and happily bestows Bernard's land on Milo FitzWalter, a royal relation. Milo has five sons, including one named Mahel, but each dies upon succeeding to Brecknock.[24] Milo's inability to found a family that can hold the land through history is underscored by Gerald, who punctuates the episode by finally having King Henry admit to Milo that, even though England occupies Wales for the time being to "commit acts of violence and injustice" against its people, he knows full well that it is the Welsh "who are the rightful heirs" (I.2 95).[25] Brecknock's destiny, Henry and Gerald declare, is a Welsh future.

But not a *pure* Welsh future. The sow-hound, the man who gave birth to a calf, the deer-horse of St. Illtyd, Nest/Agnes, failures of inheritance in the Neufmarché and FitzWalter families, and the mixed heritage of Brecknock are bound by a logic of monstrous hybridity condensed in the history of the land as a history of unresolved Anglo-Norman/Welsh violence. Mixed ethnic identity is figured as ontologically difficult because it arises at that border where cultures meet in a violent, "unnatural" coupling. Gerald is not telling a reductive story about the eradication of native purity by some colonialist regime that overwrites the aboriginal with new forms, structures, narratives. The culture of south Wales is already impure, and Gerald is a living embodiment of its intermediacy. He is instead exploring how both Wales and England were changed when two bodies formed a third that carries with it something of both parents without fully being either. The knight pregnant with a calf through his alliance with a bull transforms a male into a maternal form, a human into an interspecies hybrid; the offspring of the mare and stag is simultaneously both and neither of its parents, a body that spectacularly displays its constitutive difference without resolving them; when translated into Agnes, Nest forgets her Welshness and so forgets that her son is half Welsh, then is rebuked into meaninglessness by history (her story ends when as Agnes she dispossesses her son); the English Mahel who replaces the Welsh-Norman Mahel dies when a rock strikes him on the head, poetic justice accomplished by the land itself. Gerald's sympathy clearly lay with the Mahel of mixed blood, son of the Norman knight Bernard and Welsh mother Nest. This hybrid body, at once native and alien, is the future of postcolonial Wales, a fact Milo FitzWalter and (presumably) Henry I learn too late.

Of course, this mongrel body is also Gerald's own. His father was the Norman knight William de Barri. His mother, Angharad, was the daughter of another Nest, who in turn was at once the daughter of Rhys ap Tewdwr, prince of South Wales; mistress to Henry I; and wife to Gerald de Windsor, grandfather and namesake of Gerald of Wales and a clever colonizer of the country. A cleric almost *ex nativate* (as a child his father called him "my bishop"), Gerald was schooled in Paris, where he became well versed in the dominant, transnational discourses of the Latin West.[26] Multiple, conflicting possibilities course through Gerald's mixed blood: "Cambro-Norman" citizen of the Welsh March; Welshman; royal servant of the Angevin empire; ecclesiastic with allegiances to England, Wales, Rome, and—through his activity in support of the Third Crusade—Jerusalem. As a result, anxieties over his constitutive incongruences circulate throughout Gerald's voluminous writings.

Although he may have felt vast uncertainty about who he was, nonetheless Gerald could confidently declare what he was *not*. Gerald's clerical identity and the specific sexuality attached to it (male celibacy), both steeped in traditions of misogyny, spurred one of the many disidentifications he performed. A primary locus for abjection in Gerald's writing is the female body. Gerald is almost incapable of representing women outside of demonizing, corporeal terms. When the adulteress Nest betrays her son, for example, she deviates "not one whit from her womanly nature" [*mulier muliebri non degenerans a natura*] (*Itinerarium* I.2 90). In Ireland, unlike in Wales, tales of interspecies hybrids (a man-ox, an ox-man, a cow-stag) immediately give rise to anecdotes about women happily having sex with animals. When a goat and a lion copulate with women, both the animal and the woman are, in Gerald's estimation, beasts worthy of death (*O utramque bestiam turpi morte dignissimam!*)[27] Women, like monsters, are a point of ambivalence for Gerald, where "ambivalence" is that which (in Homi Bhabha's formulation) conjoins colonialist attraction to repulsion; like Bhabha, moreover, Gerald refuses to think the gendered component to this desire-disgust.[28] As Gayatri Chakravorty Spivak has observed, the subaltern woman tends to exist in the colonialist imaginary as a muted subject, as a body that produces only through an act of violation.[29]

Postcolonial theory predicts that disidentification based on gender usually will be allied with disidentifications of ethnicity and race, and such proves to be the case with Gerald. Early in his career Gerald learned to allay his ambivalence of origin by becoming an enthusiastic colonizer of Ireland, a place distant enough for him to construct an unambiguous other whose dispossession and eradication allowed him to forget for a while the similarly violent history of colonization that produced him. Both the *Expugnatio Hibernica* and *Topographia Hibernica* are reductive texts that unabashedly glorify the invasion of the island, demonstrating none of the conflicted identifications characteristic of the Welsh texts.

Gerald is fascinated by bodies that cannot choose their allegiances, unassimilated bodies that encode a whole history of conflict and interdependence, bodies that cannot synthesize the differences that they find they enflesh. I have been labeling such corpora with racialized English nouns such as "hybrids," "mixed bloods," "mongrels," "crossbreeds," but we may as well use the word familiar to Gerald to describe flesh that displays constitutive historical differences without a normalizing synthesis: *mixta,* a Latin substantive derived from the verb *miscere* ("to conjoin, intermarry, copulate, confound, disturb"). *Mixta* technically describe paradoxical hybrids and "coincidences of opposites" such as stag-mares, man-cows, and other composite monsters.[30] The grass-eating Welshman suggests the intimacy of Gerald's writing to some of the ideas about mimicry and quiet subversion advanced within recent postcolonial theory. *Mixta* as "conjoined things," however, are uncivil hybrids, confounding monsters. Gilbert Hagurnell and the baby cow that he bore after three years of labor and an unspecified duration of "unnatural vice" figure the boundary-smashing work of medieval hybridity, which crossbreeds exorbitance with intimacy. Read back into their generating historicity, *mixta* do not wholly lose that monstrous alterity that creates in them a point of enjoyment and elicits an intrigued gaze, but neither do they remain wholly abject or wholly other. *Mixta* bridge in their flesh cultures, races, geographies, and temporalities that cannot be assimilated into a coherent totality; *mixta* as monstrous desiring machines embody "incommensurable, competing histories forced together in unnatural unions by colonialism."[31]

Gilbert Hagurnell, the bull, and the calf born of their unsanctioned union are three bodies that in their multiple connections to each other and to the histories and traumas of the land demonstrate how colonialism, sexuality, resistance, submission, and identity are complexly intertwined, and always in danger of going too far, of running amuck. The knight-bull-calf circuit escapes through its sheer excess a capture into the normal, the pure, the dominant. Gilbert, his love, and their progeny are simultaneously utterly condemnable (as monstrous vice, they make no sense to prevailing identity regimes; they are "impossible") and at the same time they embody the limit of what that system can think. Like Michel Foucault's example of the Borgesian encyclopedia that demonstrates "the limitation of our own [system of thought], the stark impossibility of thinking *that,*" this circuit, these *mixta,* are the system's exterior, its inassimilable outside.[32] There is nothing utopian about this man-animal-*mixtum* circuit, but it does demonstrate clearly enough the failings of colonialist epistemologies as well as their embodied anxieties about the irreducibility of those differences, those Others, they hope to assimilate.

Borderland, March, and Middle

William Rufus, second Norman king of England, dreamed of building a bridge to Ireland. In 1097 William penetrated far enough into Wales to glimpse the coast of *Hibernia* and immediately announced: "I will collect a fleet together from my own kingdom and with it make a bridge, so that I can conquer that country" (*Itinerarium* II.1 169).[33] This monumental architecture, Gerald of Wales claims, was to have been constructed near St. David's, that presumed center of Welsh ecclesiastical independence. As the conduit for an invasion force, William's bridge tacitly acknowledges that since Wales has been royally traversed, Ireland will become the next frontier.

William's impossible architecture serves as a useful metaphor for the location of Gerald's South Wales: a middle space that is not fully other, like distant *Hibernia,* nor exactly familiar, like those lands already domesticated into Norman England. Perhaps taking their cue from Caesar, Tacitus, and Bede, contemporary historians repeatedly have described medieval Wales as a frontier, a term that connotes an incipient space awaiting development and populating.[34] A frontier is a temporal and geographic edge where an "advanced" culture is imagined to meet a distant, primitive world in order to begin the process of making the "new" land and its people learn both their backwardness (the frontier is by definition "undeveloped") and their marginality (the center of the world is elsewhere, and so a new cartography of signification, a new way "to divide the world," must be disseminated).[35] William's bridge to Ireland, however, moves southern Wales behind the line of the frontier, but not exactly by assimilating it to Norman England. Wales as bridge to that fantastic elsewhere becomes not an edge but a borderland, an ambiguous middle location caught between a distant, dominant, domestic center and a proximate, absolute, alien outland. By locating the proposed bridge at St. David's, moreover, Gerald illustrates how the overlap of a multiplicity of discourses produce borderlands. St. David's is, for Gerald, a world center. Throughout his work he argues that St. David's is the ancient seat of the archbishopric of Wales, a place owing no allegiance to English Canterbury but rather direct obedience to (and deserving recognition from) distant Rome. Discourses proper to Latin Christianity, Norman-English colonialism, the ambitions of the Marcher lords, and the desires of the native Welsh hybridize at St. David's.

Not a frontier, not an edge, but a middle, a borderland. Gloria Anzaldúa describes the borderland as "a vague and undetermined place created by the emotional residue of an unnatural boundary . . . in a constant state of transition."[36] Borderlands foster "shifting and multiple identity and integrity," since they are home to multiple and "bastard" languages; the borderland is a place of *mestizaje,* of new and impure hybrids, of *los atravesados,* "the squint-eyed, the perverse, the queer, the troublesome, the mongrel, the mulato, the half-breed . . . those who cross over, pass over, or go through the confines of the 'normal.'"[37] Anzaldúa is specifically writing as a conflicted product of numerous cultural forces, as a lesbian feminist with a difficult relationship to her Chicana (white-Mexican-Indian) origin. Her *cultura mestiza* is a historically grounded, queer composite of races, religions, temporalities, sexualities, and species—just like Wales at St. David's, Wales alongside that imaginary bridge.[38]

Anzaldúa figures her "new *mestiza*" as part human, part serpent, as a body that spectacularly displays its constitutive histories of difference, colonialism, and violent struggle without pretending they can be synthesized into some coherent, homogenous, domesticated form.[39] Cyrus Patell has faulted Anzaldua for binaristic thinking, claiming that her hybrids replace the "either/or" of colonialism with a "both/and" that leaves in place an implicit duality.[40] Yet Anzaldua's hybrids are monsters in the medieval sense, conjoined not through a binaristic conjunction but by means of the nontotalizable "and . . . and . . . and . . ." described by Deleuze and Guattari as the schizophrenic, limitless couplings of desiring machines, combining in irreconcilable and impermanent togetherness.[41] The endlessly conjunctive work of monstrous hybridity produces an unbounded middle space, as unstable corporally as it is geographically and temporally. This middle, this bridge conjoining differences, is the borderlands.

The borderlands as a place of monsters is analogous to the Middle Ages as a time of *mixta,* "composites." Unlike Bhabha's unfailingly polite hybrids, whose mimicry may be disconcerting but is in the end familiar, the monsters of Anzaldua and Gerald do not pass between cultures so accommodatingly. Bhabha's hybrids are ultimately reassuring because they arrive from English India, from a moment of colonization that (let's face it) is still being felt in North American university training today. Sly civility is so appealing because it is so literary, so *English. Mixta* as monster is more difficult to accommodate within this paradigm. Although they lack the investment of heroism that Anzaldúa gives to her joyfully contradictory and ambivalent "*raza mestiza*" and to her patron monsters (the Shadow Beast, the serpent-goddesses), Gerald's *mixta* embody an intimate alterity where cultures have crossbred and produced "hybrid progeny, a mutable, more malleable species . . . an 'alien' consciousness."[42] For Gerald, this newness enters the world invested with desire, anxiety, disgust, passion, trepidation—and, when a figure for a wider process of cultural crossfertilization, a certain amount of promise coupled to an Anzaldúa-like "perverse insistence on [historical] specificity," on the embodied materiality of a generative colonialist struggle.[43]

Before the Edwardian conquest, Wales was conceptualized in England as a bifurcated space: *pura Wallia,* the independent land ruled by Welsh princes, and *marchia Wallie,* the "Welsh March" composed of land seized by Norman lords, Gerald's Wales.[44] Rees Davies observes that the use of the term "March" for south Wales was an acknowledgment that "there was a fairly extensive area between native-controlled Wales on the one hand and the kingdom of England on the other which was intermediate in its status, laws, and governance and had its own recognizable habits and institutions."[45] The March was neither Anglo-Norman nor Welsh but an uneasy composite of the two, a borderlands in Anzaldúa's sense, a place where hybrid bodies were revealed through hybrid names (Henri ap Cadwgan ap Bleddyn, Meilir fitz Henry, Maredudd son of Robert fitz Stephen, Gerald of Windsor's daughter and Gerald of Wales's mother Angharad).[46] Linguistically, architecturally, and culturally, the March was a mixed form, a bridge conjoining rather than assimilating differences—*biformis* like a centaur, a minotaur, Janus, a poet, or a man-calf (to cite some classical deployments of this Geraldian adjective).[47] Here a king of England might dream of building a road to Ireland, as if the land he stood upon were safely his; but here also a royal messenger might be forced to eat, seal and all, a letter that displeased the baron to whom it was addressed.[48]

Giraldus Cambrensis is exactly that middle body through which passes *pura Wallia,* Norman visions of colony, conflicting allegiances to church and world and *natio,* a bridge to the new frontier of Ireland. Gerald could have followed his name with "de Barri," as his father and grandfather had done, in order to emphasize an origin in a geographic elsewhere (Barri is an island off the Glamorganshire coast). Instead he emphasized his nativity in Wales by styling himself *Cambrensis,* demonstrating his awareness of this medial position in which established terms fail. Gerald always describes the people from which he partially comes not as *Wallenses* ("foreigners," the English nomination), not as *Britones* (what the people call themselves, in reference to a mythically pure origin), but as *Kambrenses,* "attempting to create a terminology for his own particularly ambiguous ethnic and national position."[49]

This middleness can be found in a point as small as a single man's hybrid body. Keeping in mind its compulsion to local thinking and perspectivism in its specific deployment, this formulation of Geraldian hybridity as Anzalduan *mestizaje* also can be cautiously offered as a possible conjoining truth for much of the medieval period, and not just in Europe: It would be difficult to find a medieval culture that was not in some sense a borderlands, since internal homogeneity may have been an abiding dream, but was almost never a practicable reality. Indeed, Anzaldúa's insight may as well be crossbred with the civil and uncivil hybridity with which this chapter began: Isn't it true that the Middle Ages in their mediacy are a temporal rather than a geographic borderlands, especially in their intimate alterity to the modern, the postmodern, the postcolonial? Can't the Middle Ages as borderland reveal (to use some words meant to describe the work of Gloria Anzaldúa) "the suturing space of multiple oppressions and the potentially liberatory space through which to migrate toward a new subject position"?[50] The study of the Middle Ages then becomes not just a project of recovering neglected pasts but also of opening up a possible future.

Notes

* I would like to thank Glenn Burger, Steven Kruger, Stephen Slemon, and the audience at the Postcolonial Middle Ages workshop (University of Alberta, April 1999) for provocative conversations about this chapter.

1. Robert J. C. Young, *Colonial Desire: Hybridity in Theory, Culture and Race* (New York: Routledge, 1995) p. 26. My discussion of hybridity is indebted to Young's provocative work throughout.

2. At this point the qualifiers "European" and "Western" disappear from my use of "medieval," but I do not wish them to vanish silently: their delimiting force is assumed throughout. This chapter takes as its subject a specifically Anglo-Norman cultural imaginary as it encounters and colonizes differences, as well as how that imaginary looks through the eyes of those it has only partially assimilated.

3. The Normans were only continuing a long tradition of violence against Wales begun in the mid seventh century by the English, first in Mercia and then Wessex (and performed centuries earlier by the Romans). In addition to the writings of Giraldus Cambrensis, my generalizations about medieval Wales are based on the following sources: Robert Bartlett, *Gerald of Wales* (Oxford: Clarendon Press, 1982); A. D. Carr, *Medieval Wales* (New York: St. Martin's Press, 1995); R. R. Davies, *Lordship and Society in the March of Wales* (Oxford: Oxford University Press, 1987) and *Conquest, Coexistence and Change: Wales 1063–1415* (Oxford: Oxford University Press, 1987); Wendy Davies, *Wales in the Early Middle Ages* (Bath: Leicester University Press, 1982); Ralph A. Griffiths, *Conquerors and Conquered in Medieval Wales* (New York: St. Martin's Press, 1994); John Edward Lloyd, *A History of Wales From the Earliest Times to the Edwardian Conquest* (London: Longmans, 1911; reprinted 1967), 2 vols.; Lynn H. Nelson, *The Normans in South Wales, 1070–1171* (Austin: University of Texas Press, 1966); David Walker, *Me-*

dieval Wales (Cambridge: Cambridge University Press, 1990), Gwyn A. Williams, *When Was Wales?* (London: Black Raven Press, 1985).

4. Gerald of Wales, *Itinerarium Kambriae* I.10; v. 6 in J. S. Brewer, J. F. Dimock, and G. F. Warner (eds.), *Giraldi Cambrensis Opera,* 8 vols., *Rerum Britannicarum Medii Aevi Scriptores* ["Rolls Series"] 21 (London: Longmans, 1861–91); *The Journey Through Wales and The Description of Wales,* trans. Lewis Thorpe (London: Penguin Books, 1978), quotation at p. 140. Further citations of the *Itinerarium* appear in text by book and chapter number of the Latin, followed by page number in Thorpe's translation.

5. John Gillingham finds in William of Malmesbury's *Deeds of the English Kings* (1125) the origin for the othering of Celtic peoples; see "The Beginnings of English Imperialism," *Journal of Historical Sociology* 5.4 (1992): 392–409. Even though evidence for such a process is easy enough to find in earlier sources (e.g., Bede), Gillingham's point that the construction of a vast cultural difference between Christians was a particular project of the twelfth century is well taken.

6. Letter 87, *Letters of John of Salisbury, vol. 1, The Early Letters (1153–1161),* ed. W. J. Millor and H. E. Butler, rev. C. N. L. Brooke (London: Thomas Nelson and Sons, 1955), p. 135.

7. *Gesta Stephani,* ed. and trans. K. R. Potter and R. H. C. Davis (Oxford: Oxford University Press, 1976), I.8. Chapters 8 to 11 of the first book of the *Gesta* are dedicated to the Welsh rebellion of 1136 and contain an extended narration of Welsh "bestiality."

8. Chrétien de Troyes famously deploys a version of this ethnic construct in *Le Conte du Graal,* the hero of which is simple Perceval, a backwoods Welshman who cannot tell the difference between an angel descended from heaven and a quotidian knight in armor. Perceval's long process of becoming a Christian *chevalier* is really the long process of losing all signifiers of his ethnicity, striving toward the unmarked body of contemporary French chivalry. *La Queste del Saint Graal* makes the bond between Perceval's Welshness and his initial exclusion from Christianized martial masculinity more explicit by aligning his originary identity with a culture of parricide.

9. Bhabha takes the phrase from a sermon in which Archdeacon Potts complained that recalcitrant "natives" were cleverly agreeing with the truth of Christian theology in order to remain unbaptized: Homi K. Bhabha, "Sly Civility," *The Location of Culture* (New York: Routledge, 1994), pp. 93–101, quotation at p. 99. See also in the same volume the two essays on mimicry: "Of Mimicry and Man: The Ambivalence of Colonial Discourse" (pp. 85–92) and "Signs Taken for Wonders" (pp. 102–22).

10. Stephen Nichols maps these countercurrents in terms of Bakhtinian polyphony in "Fission and Fusion: Mediations of Power in Medieval History and Literature," *Yale French Studies* 70 (1986) : 21–41.

11. *Descriptio Kambriae* II.8, *Giraldi Cambrensis Opera* v.6; *Description of Wales,* trans. Thorpe, p. 267. Further citations appear by book and chapter, followed by page number in English translation.

12. "Nec alia, ut arbitror, gens quam haec Kambrica, aliave lingua, in die districti examinis coram Judice supremo, quicquid de ampliori contingat, pro hoc terrarum angulo respondebit."

13. Bhabha, *Location of Culture* p. 207; see also pp. 112–16.

14. Ibid., p. 112.

15. *Les Grandes Chroniques de France,* ed. Jules Viard (Paris: Librarie Ancienne Édouard Champion, 1923), vol.3; *A Thirteenth-Century Life of Charlemagne,* trans. Robert Levine (New York: Garland Publishing, 1991), quotation at IX 251 (French), p. 115 (English).

16. Ibid., IX 252, p. 115.

17. I do not mean to imply that in Bhabha's formulation "sly civility" and "hybridity" are interchangeable: the former is clearly a special case of the latter. Yet although Bhabha writes that hybridity encompasses the "terrifying, exorbitant object of paranoid classification—a disturbing questioning of the images and presences of authority" (*Location of Culture,* p. 113), the historical and textual examples he theorizes from almost all involve some form of "sly civility," which valorizes cleverness, subtlety, and ironic distance over the "exorbitant" and embodied (see, e.g., the "wily oriental thieves" of Bombay, p. 119).

18. The alteritizing rhetoric of crusade propaganda figured Islam as an inassimilable bodily trauma for *Christianitas.* The Saracen was repeatedly visualized in the act of eviscerating, impaling, or forcefully circumcising Christian bodies, even though the Christians were by their own admission fully committed to just such a program of exorbitant corporeal violence: see Michael Uebel, "Unthinking the Monster: Twelfth-Century Responses to Saracen Alterity" in *Monster Theory: Reading Culture,* ed. Jeffrey Jerome Cohen (Minneapolis: University of Minnesota Press, 1996), pp. 264–91. Geraldine Heng has persuasively argued that romance, the superlative genre of medieval vernacular literature, formed in reaction to the unthinkable events at Ma'arra an-Numan, where crusading Christians cannibalized the corpses of their Muslim enemies; see "Cannibalism, the First Crusade, and the Genesis of Medieval Romance," *differences* 10.1 (1998): 98–174. For a reading of the *Itinerarium* as crusading pilgrimage, see Nichols, "Fission and Fusion."

19. To make matters worse, not only was Gerald forced to undertake the trip with the archbishop of Canterbury, they were joined by Bishop Peter at St. David's in celebrating a mass that performed the obeisance of the Welsh seat to Baldwin. This religious ritual as public theater was surely scripted by the Angevin rulers of England, who saw that the submission of the Welsh church to Canterbury and the submission of the Welsh to the English throne were inextricably linked.

20. For an excellent discussion of the cultural context of Gerald's preaching tour through Wales, see Christopher Tyerman, *England and the Crusades, 1095–1588* (Chicago: University of Chicago Press, 1988) 156.

21. This sexual police work was a specific symptom of Gerald's wider obsession with regularizing the Welsh church. On this point see Davies, *Conquest, Coexistence, and Change,* pp. 176–78. Gerald's uncle David fitz Gerald, bishop of St Davids (1148–76), was among the married clergy.

22. "Argumentum tam hominem, quam animal quodlibet, ab illa, cujus lacte nutritur, naturam contrahere." Gerald is fascinated by such stories. In a later chapter, for example, he tells of a queen who "had a painting of a Negro in her bedroom" and, because she looked at it too much, gave birth to a black baby. Marie-Hélène Huet has studied this visual phenomenon and called it "maternal impression" (*Monstrous Imagination* [Cambridge, MA: Harvard University Press, 1993]), but for Gerald it is more accurately described as *parental* impression: To prove his point, he gives the example of a man who, during intercourse, thought about someone plagued by a nervous tic and engendered a son afflicted by the same bodily contortion (*Itinerarium* II.7 191). Another way of saying this is that for Gerald, hybridity always writes at least two histories across the body.

23. "Miles enim, cui nomen Gillebertus, cognomen vero Hagurnellus, post diutinos continuosque fere triennii languores, et gravissimas tanquam parturientis angustias, demum, videntibus multis, per egestionis fenestram vitulum edidit: novi alicujus et inusitati futuri casus ostentum, aut potius nefandi criminis ultricem declarans indignationem." Although Thorpe's translation does not make this point clear, the gender of *vitulus* can only be masculine ("bull-calf"), so that this is a birth sequence that completely excludes any feminine bodies.

24. More accurately, four of the five sons die upon succeeding to their inheritance; William perished before he could possess the land.

25. "Quia licet gentibus illis per vires nostras magnas injuriam et violentiam irrogemus, nihilominus tamen in terris eisdem jus hereditarium habere noscuntur."

26. Gerald recounts his autobiography in *De Rebus a Se Gestis, Opera* v.1.

27. Yet for all his stated revulsion, Gerald cannot resist visualizing such scenes at length, revealing the investment of desire conjoined to his disgust. Indeed, MS National Library of Ireland 700 illustrates a passionate kiss between each animal and his human lover. The illustrations are clumsily reproduced in *The History and Topography of Ireland,* trans. John J. O'Meara (London: Penguin, 1951). For the Latin, see *Topographia Hibernica* II.23–24, *Opera* v.5.

28. See Bhabha, "Difference, Discrimination, and the Discourse of Colonialism," *The Politics of Theory,* ed. Francis Barker, Peter Hulme, Margaret Iversen and Diana Loxley (Colchester: University of Essex Press, 1983), pp. 194–211, esp. p. 200. On Bhabha's "fastidious" refusal to explore gender, see Anne McClintock, "'No Longer in a Future Heaven': Gender, Race, and Nationalism," in *Dangerous Liaisons: Gender, Nation, and Postcolonial Perspectives,* ed. McClintock, Aamir Mufti, and Ella Shohat (Minneapolis: University of Minnesota Press, 1997), pp. 89–112, esp. 95.

29. See Gayatri Spivak, "Can the Subaltern Speak? Speculations on Widow Sacrifice," *Marxism and the Interpretation of Culture,* ed. Cary Nelson and Lawrence Grossberg (London: Macmillan, 1988) pp. 271–313, esp. p. 295.

30. The gloss "coincidence of opposites" for *mixta* is from Caroline Walker Bynum, "Wonder," *American Historical Review* 102 (February 1997): 1–26, quotation at p. 7.

31. The quotation is Young's gloss on Deleuze and Guattari's desiring machines read through a postcolonial lens in *Colonial Desire,* p. 174.

32. Michel Foucault, *The Order of Things: An Archeology of the Human Sciences* (New York: Vintage Books, 1994), p. xv.

33. "Ad terram istam expugnandam, ex navibus regni mei huc convocatis, pontem adhuc faciam."

34. The "frontier thesis" was famously advanced by Frederick Jackson Turner in 1893 and, although much critiqued, continues to occupy the contemporary historiographic imaginary; "The Significance of the Frontier in American History," in *The Frontier in American History* (New York: Holt, 1947), pp. 1–38. For an overview of the influence of Turner on medieval studies, see the collection of essays edited by Robert Bartlett and Angus MacKay, *Medieval Frontier Societies* (Oxford: Clarendon Press, 1989), especially Robert I. Burns, "The Significance of the Frontier in the Middle Ages," pp. 307–30. For a history of southern Wales heavily invested in the frontier myth, see Nelson, *The Normans in South Wales.* A good recent critique of the frontier which anticipates my argument here is Amy Kaplan, "'Left Alone with America': The Absence of Empire in the Study of American Culture," *Cultures of United States Imperialism,* ed. Kaplan and Donald E. Pease (Durham, NC: Duke University Press, 1993), pp. 3–21.

35. I am thinking here of John Willinsky's linking of education and colonialism in *Learning to Divide the World: Education at Empire's End* (Minneapolis: University of Minnesota Press, 1998).

36. Gloria Anzaldúa, *Borderlands / La Frontera: The New Mestiza* (San Francisco: Aunt Lute Books, 1987), p. 3. For sensitive readings of Anzaldúa's work, see Carlos G. Vélez-Ibáñez, *Border Visions: Mexican Cultures of the Southwest United States* (Tucson: University of Arizona Press, 1996), pp. 216–21, and Robert McRuer, *The Queer Renaissance: Contemporary American Literature and the Reinvention of Lesbian and Gay Identities* (New York: New York University Press, 1997), pp. 116–54. My discussion of Anzaldúa also owes much to conversations with and unpublished presentations by McRuer, to whom I am grateful for inspiration.

37. Quotations from Anzaldúa, *Borderlands / La Frontera,* "Preface" (unpaginated), p. 3, p. 5.

38. Indeed, "bridge" (*puente*) as that which connects both geographies and temporalities is one of Anzaldúa's poetic glosses for "mestiza," as in "Yo soy un puente tendido / del mundo gabacho al del mojado, / lo pasado me estirá pa''trás / y lo presente pa''delante" (ibid., 3). See also "La Prieta," *This Bridge Called My Back: Writings by Radical Women of Color,* ed. Cherríe Mor-

aga and Gloria Anzaldúa, 2nd ed. (New York: Kitchen Table, Women of Color Press, 1983), pp. 198–209; and "Bridge, Drawbridge, Sandbar, or Island: Lesbians-of-Color Hacienda Alianzas," *Bridges of Power: Women's Multicultural Alliances,* ed. Lisa Albrecht and Rose M. Brewer (Philadelphia: New Society, 1990), pp. 216–31.

39. Cf. Robert McRuer, *Queer Renaissance:* "Some overly celebratory understandings of queerness . . . tend to efface the ways in which identities and histories are structured in domination, so that some identities are immobilized while white, male, heterosexual power is able to travel anywhere with ease. Anzaldúa's work undermines this structural domination by insistently foregrounding 'queer *mestiza*' identity." For Anzaldúa, "the border" and "queerness" stand as figures for the failure of easy separation. Rather than establishing two discrete identities, each attempt at separation actually produces (*mestiza*/queer) identities that do not wholly fit in either location" (p.117).

40. Cyrus R. K. Patell, "Comparative American Studies: Hybridty and Beyond," *American Literary History* 11.1 (1999): 166–86, esp. 177–79.

41. On desiring machines, see Gilles Deleuze and Félix Guattari, *L'Anti-Oedipe: Capitalisme et Schizophrénie* (Paris: Éditions de Minuit, 1973), pp. 7–59; *Anti-Oedipus: Capitalism and Schizophrenia,* trans. Robert Hurley, Mark Seem, and Helen R. Lane (Minneapolis: University of Minnesota Press, 1983), pp. 1–50.

42. Anzaldúa, *Borderlands / La Frontera,* p. 77.

43. The quotation is from McRuer's defense of Anzaldúa against Annamarie Jagose's condemnation of her supposed transcendental utopianism; see *Queer Renaissance,* p. 140.

44. On the ambiguities of "Wales" and the fluctuations of its border before 1300, see Davies, *Conquest, Coexistence, and Change,* pp. 4–13. *Pura Wallia* marks the lost dream of the Cambro-Normans to conquer all of Wales (a loss fully approved of by Henry II, who viewed the power of the Marchers with growing suspicion, especially after the campaign in Ireland). Once Henry II reached an accord with the Welsh princelings (1171–72), native Welsh kingdoms regained some of their former vigor and the March became more suspended middle than forward-pushing frontier. Ibid., pp. 53–55, 271–76, 290–91.

45. Rees Davies, "Frontier Arrangements in Fragmented Societies: Ireland and Wales," in *Medieval Frontier Societies,* ed. Robert Bartlett and Angus MacKay (Oxford: Oxford University Press, 1989), pp. 77–100, quotation at p. 81. True to the purpose of the collection of essays for which he writes, Davies here insists on calling Wales a "frontier," even while emphasizing its middleness.

46. On mixed names in the March see Davies, *Conquest, Coexistence, and Change* 102. Davies calls Gerald's Wales a "'middle nation'—a group caught between, and sitting astride, the normal categorizations of race" (p. 103).

47. On literature, architecture, and the mutuality of these transformations, see ibid., pp. 104–107. Gerald often uses *biformis* to describe *mixta,* as in the deer-cow and monkey-puppies of Chester that figure an anxiety about impure national origins (*Itinerarium* II.11 198–99). Horace famously used *biformis* to describe the poet as half man, half swan (*Odes* 2.20.3)

48. The story of how in 1250 Walter Clifford forced a messenger to swallow the king's letter is told in Davies, *Lordship and Society in the March of Wales,* p. 1. Davies, the foremost scholar of the Welsh March, describes the place as a geographically, chronologically, and racially diverse location whose history "seems to disintegrate into plurality and defy the analytical categories of the historian" (p. 8).

49. Bartlett, *Gerald of Wales* p. 185.

50. Sidonie Smith, "The Autobiographical Manifesto: Identities, Temporalities, Politics," *Autobiography and Questions of Gender,* ed. Shirley Neuman (Portland, OR: F. Cass, 1991), pp. 186–212, quotation at p. 200.

CHAPTER 6

TIME BEHIND THE VEIL:
THE MEDIA, THE MIDDLE AGES,
AND ORIENTALISM NOW

Kathleen Davis

This chapter examines the gendered, conflicting, medieval temporalities within the globalizing discourse of contemporary Orientalism. Through close readings of both Chaucer and Said, it argues that medievalists are well positioned to disrupt such temporal oppositions.

Postcolonial time questions the teleological traditions of past and present, and the polarized historicist sensibility of the archaic and the modern.

—Homi Bhabha

In the Autumn of 1996, Diane Sawyer journeyed to Afghanistan for an ABC-TV *20/20* story on the treatment of women under Taliban rule. Sawyer's opening voice-over of *Behind the Veil—A Report on the Woman of Afghanistan* describes this news-gathering venture in terms of travel narrative: "We left New York, heading first to London, then Pakistan, thinking of all we'd heard about the Afghan women, their love of laughter, their fastidious homes, however poor, and their resilience during 18 years of war." This journey from Western metropole to Afghan female domestic space is also figured as time travel (back into the past) as well as dramatic rescue mission of women forced to a return, as the program's title indicates, "behind the veil." The Taliban, Sawyer's voice-over explains, has swept across the country and into the capital with a "fundamentalist iron fist, in effect returning women to the middle ages, while the women of Afghanistan cry out for other women to come help. So we have a plane from the United Nations and it's going to take us about an hour and a half back into the mountains, and from what we've been reading, that's several hundred years in time."[1] Anyone familiar with common tropes of Orientalism and colonial representation will be unsurprised by this image of a modern, technologically efficient Western reporter sweeping across space and back in time to rescue suffering, domesticated, Eastern women (by lifting their veils) from repressive, "third world," reactionary men. Medievalists will be unsurprised by this commonplace, apparently perfunctory association of the Middle Ages with anything labelled inhumane.

The Orientalist polemic of this report, which opposes Afghan and Westernized society in terms of medieval/modern, depraved/righteous, and stagnant/progressive, suggests that the "Woman of Afghanistan" (as her collective singularity here confirms) is not the concern *of,* but rather a signifier *for,* this media production's globally ambitious discourse. Over the past two decades, critical exploration of the entwined significations of time, gender, and sexuality in nationalist projects has demonstrated that in the resolutely heterosexual discourse of nationalism, women bear the burden of representation for the collectivity's identity, particularly as the embodiment of the national, authenticating, past.[2] At stake now, in the struggles of a postcolonial but globalizing world, is the escalating and increasingly violent imposition of signification upon women in supranational cultural confrontations due at least in part to the pressures of Westernization and the aftermath of colonization. The report at hand, designed for an American audience yet casting its mission as fulfillment of a global prerogative ("So we have a plane from the United Nations . . . We left New York, heading first to London, then Pakistan . . ."), participates in a long tradition of violent veiling and unveiling of women in colonial and postcolonial contests between "modern" (Western) and "traditional" (non-Western) societies. Such representations paradoxically reject and redeploy the signifying practices that entrap women: although *Behind the Veil* criticizes the Taliban's veiling of women to signify Afghan society's return to its traditional, fundamental roots, for its own purposes these veiled women signify the moral and cultural superiority of the U.S. and its global allies over "backward" Islamic societies. This report also suggests that U.S. concern, or even force if necessary,[3] bears the global mandate of all morally responsible nations—a mandate that, obviously, intensifies rather than alleviates the signifying burden of women in societies resistant to Western hegemony. My reading of this report as an Orientalist representation, in Said's sense of a production by the West, for the West, should not be taken as a suggestion that Taliban oppression of women does not exist, or that there can be no appropriate intervention. To the contrary, I argue that the intellectual purchase necessary for any helpful action is precluded by such representations, which reinscribe women as signifiers in an even larger conflict.[4]

But what is the role of the Middle Ages in this high-stakes signifying practice? I hope to demonstrate that *Behind the Veil*'s trope of "returning to the Middle Ages" is not simply a generic insult reducible to a residual faith in the myth of progress, but rather that it indicates Orientalism at work. It points to a double reliance by Westenizing/globalizing rhetoric upon the concept of the Middle Ages, which supplies both the image of the common past necessary for a sense of cohesion among modern nations in the present, as well as an alterior, static mode of existence against which claims of modernity can define themselves. Much like the discourse of the modern nation, productions such as *Behind the Veil* ground themselves on a split temporality, paradoxically claiming the Middle Ages as the immature stage from which modernity developed, and as an inert, temporal space incapable of change. Ironically, contemporary critical examination of Orientalism—led by Said's groundbreaking *Orientalism*—reinforces rather than disrupts Westernizing temporal logic by insisting that the Middle Ages provided the textual material for Orientalism and yet was fully prior to any *actual* practice of Orientalism.[5]

If medievalists are to intervene in the discursive traditions of past and present that ground projects of postcolonial imperialism—to question "the polarized historicist *sensibility* of the archaic and the modern," as Bhabha's statement in my epigraph above suggests[6]—then, I believe, we must take on the threefold task of deconstructing the temporalities of today's Orientalism, critiquing the theoretical reproduction of a totalized medieval alterity, and exploring ways that medieval texts and practices can inform (and be elucidated by) the critical apprehension of contemporary Orientalist methodologies. This conviction leads me to design the present essay in three related sections: the first interrogates the gendered temporalities of Orientalist discourses such as *Behind the Veil;* the second traces the logic and implications of the medievalism in Said's *Orientalism;* and the third briefly examines the intersections of the Orientalism in Chaucer's *Man of Law's Tale* with the hegemonic, globalizing strategies at work in Orientalism today.

The Temporalities of the Veil

The Afghan women of *Behind the Veil* bear the burden of signification for two conflicting medieval temporalities. Here, the Middle Ages is both contiguous with modernity (one can move back and forth through a process of repression or progression, for instance); and it is a closed-off, fully anterior, inert space, locked in the grip of the "iron fist" of fundamentalism. The progressive tense of the women's enforced "returning" to the Middle Ages manifests the cultural backsliding of Afghanistan along a contiguous time-line stretching from the medieval to the recognizably modern. Only a month before, we are told, they had been government workers, doctors and teachers; they had performed medicine, even surgery, supported their families, gone to offices, hospitals, and schools, worn Western dress. . . . Now, "doctors, engineers, linguists [are] in virtual house arrest." Their spatial movement, from workplace to home, social productivity to domestication under the body-length bourka, identifies what it means to slide from modernity into the Middle Ages, even as this emerging Middle Ages defines fundamentalist Islam. Despite this suggestion of contiguity between the medieval and the modern, however, the Afghan women's bodies—described as inert, beaten, invisible (one surgeon "in terror would agree only to show us her hands") and lacking individuation (each is fully shrouded under the bourka "to ensure that she presents no temptation, no individuality")—signals their culture's paralysis and absolute disassociation from the modern.

This temporal break between medieval and modern is corroborated by Sawyer's claim to be flying "an hour and a half back into the mountains . . . several hundred years in time," a claim that invokes the concept of what Johannes Fabian has identified as "*spatialized* Time." Evolutionist anthropology, as Fabian has shown, envisioned social progress not as linear but as divergent, and designated for all societies a temporal coordinate on a "stream of Time." Imagining difference as distance, this universalizing strategy, linked to and put in the service of colonialism and imperialism, employed "terms such as primitive, savage (but also tribal, traditional, Third World, or whatever euphemism is current)" as temporal concepts that give meaning "to the distribution of humanity in space."[7] It is no coincidence that *Behind the Veil*'s description of Afghan society neatly corresponds to historicist notions of medieval society as lacking individuation and, as Louise Fradenburg has put it, constituted as "an ideally pure and unchanging object, besieged by a variety of philosophical, political, and sexual perversions."[8] The accuracy with which this media report projects upon Afghanistan the historicized alterity of medieval Europe attests to the continued—I would argue increased—role of "the Middle Ages" in the historicizing projects of Western cultural imperialism, which now confronts peoples who, given their technological threat, can no longer be classified as primitives distanced by many time zones from modernity. According to the temporal logic of *Behind the Veil,* then, Afghanistan's veiled women signify an immoral, inferior culture whose backwardness opposes it not only to the United States, but also to the global community invoked through U.S. association with the United Nations; at the same time, this backwardness represents modernity's common, rejected medieval past, and thus unifies the modern, global community opposed to it. Rescue of these women through their unveiling would signal—and would necessarily require—a return to modernity, defined here as fully coincident with Western economy and mores.

Attempts to unveil women in the name of compassionate modernity have a deep colonial and postcolonial history. Frantz Fanon's "Algeria Unveiled," written during the Algerian revolution, details French efforts to disintegrate "forms of existence likely to evoke a national reality," by concentrating on "the wearing of the veil." The idealizing, moralizing approach of the French procedure as Fanon describes it, as well as its reliance upon an imagined medieval past, bears a remarkable resemblance to the rhetoric of *Behind the Veil:*

> It is the situation of woman that was accordingly taken as the theme of action. The dominant administration solemnly undertook to defend this woman, pictured as humiliated, sequestered, cloistered . . . It described the immense possibilities of woman, unfortunately transformed by the Algerian man into an inert, demonetized, indeed dehumanized object. The behavior of the Algerian was very firmly denounced and described as medieval and barbaric.[9]

Fanon also pinpoints the reactionary intensification of pressure upon women as signifiers of national identity: "To the colonialist offensive against the veil," he observes, "the colonized opposes the cult of the veil."[10] In her analysis of Algerian women's continuing dilemma, Winifred Woodhull observes that the rigid exclusion of women from national political life "increasingly *constitutes* the Algerian nation after independence, just as their veiling—at once a social practice and a powerful symbol—plays a central role in producing and maintaining both Algeria's difference from its colonial oppressor, and the uneasy coalition of heterogeneous and conflicting interests under a single national banner."[11] Events in Iran, where the police squads of Reza Shah once enforced modern Westernization by removing women's veils in public, and where now the revolutionary nationalist regime violently restricts and veils women, offer one more example of the appropriation of women as temporal signifiers in cultural and economic conflicts between East and West.[12] Despite their obviously important political, economic, and cultural differences, each of these struggles over veiling and unveiling women involves constellated national and multinational agendas. Woodhull has rightly called for a feminist analysis that comes to terms with, and begins to dismantle, the embodiment of national conflicts and identity within women. If it is to be successful, however, such an analysis would need to dismantle far more than individual national identities, since the conflicts between the cultural and temporal identities now embodied within women have escalated to global warfare.

The split temporality of identification that I have been examining in *Behind the Veil* has received its most thorough analysis in nationhood studies, prompted largely by Benedict Anderson's investigation of the nation's appeal to the archaic, and Tom Nairn's discussion of the nation as the "modern Janus."[13] The most influential analysis of the nation's "double-time" is undoubtedly Homi Bhabha's essay "DissemiNation," which argues that the figure of the nation-people emerges in the narrative ambivalence between the disjunctive times of the *pedagogical,* "based on the pre-given or constituted historical origin *in the past,"* and the *performative* enunciation of the nation-people as a living principle, "that sign of the *present* through which national life is redeemed and iterated as a reproductive process."[14] Bhabha's interest here is the inevitable split within the "Nation *It/Self,"* and he declines to consider either gender or globalization in this essay. However, the essay upon which he draws heavily for his schematiztion of the nation's double-time, Julia Kristeva's "Woman's Time," is fully invested in problems of gender and globalization. Concerned with the links between political temporalities and female subjectivity, Kristeva outlines the double temporality of national identification under post-war conditions of economic globalization. (She seems to believe, following a Marxist paradigm, that the nation had previously enjoyed a brief essential reality.)[15] In these globalizing circumstances, Kristeva suggests, nations recast their identities to accommodate unity with a multinational grouping, and do so in two conflicting temporal dimensions: the time of linear history, or *cursive time,* within which they imagine their participation in historical and economic progress; and *monumental time,* "the time of another history," within which they forge a deep cultural and religious memory associated with the past of the larger "socio-cultural ensemble." In this process the nation, "far from losing its own traits, rediscovers and accentuates them in a strange temporality, in a kind of 'future perfect', where the most deeply repressed past gives a distinctive character to a logical and sociological distribution of the most modern type." Kristeva notes the traditional linkages of these "times" to gender and sexuality: while linear, historical time is "readily labelled masculine," female subjectivity (encompassing the eternal and cyclic reproduction) is associated with *monumental* time.[16]

In his explanation of the analogy between Kristeva's delineation of a "double temporality" and his own argument for the nation's narrative ambivalence, Bhabha comments: "What is remarkable is her insistence that the gendered sign can hold together such exorbitant historical times."[17] We need to be more attentive than Bhabha, however, to the equally remarkable extent to which the signifiers consistently *are* gendered in the "contest of narrative authority" that he descries in national discourse. Bhabha's double movement of refusing the gendered sign in national discourse and silently eliding Kristeva's discussion of supranational mnemonic processes serves as an indication, I believe, of the complex interrelation of gender, time, and sexuality in global identifications and conflicts. Even if we grant that Kristeva's schema intimates a totalizing system, the reintroduction of the complications of gender and globalization into the theorization of the nation's temporality provides a context for interrogating the conflation of medievalism and violent, gendered signifying practices such as veiling and unveiling women.

The Temporalities of *Orientalism*

Kristeva's suggestion that cultural memory—in the strange temporality of a kind of "future perfect"—organizes the logical and sociological conception of modernity also informs the medieval temporalities in Said's *Orientalism,* which correspond to those I have delineated in *Behind the Veil*. For Said, medieval Orientalism provides the founding schema for Europe's systematic and continuous discourse on the Orient; yet for him the Middle Ages also remains an inert, purely textual space closed off from active, involved, modern Orientalism, which he defines along the Foucauldian divide of the late eighteenth century. The paradigm of Orientalism is Dante's *Inferno,* which, he insists, was corroborated by a "*learned* (and not existential) tradition,"[18] and which time and again illustrates the "schematization" of a system that has remained unchanged in its essential "character" until today.[19] As Kathleen Biddick observes in her chapter in this volume, "Dante, in effect, provided Said with an originary moment for Orientalism perfectable in the 'secularizing elements in eighteenth-century European culture.'" Said's insistence upon a purely textual medieval Orientalism untainted by any experiential intercourse with the East safeguards one of the major arguments of his book: that European Orientalist representations had no basis in a "real" Orient. Even though he stipulates that both Orient and Occident are historically constructed, and even though he rehearses the poststructuralist understanding of representation as necessarily a displacement, rather than the deliverance of any *real thing,* Said must further remove the Orient from the Orientalist.[20] Robert Young explains the theoretical conflict within which Said purifies medieval Orientalism of any "reality":

... on the one hand he suggests that Orientalism merely consists of a representation that has nothing to do with the "'real" Orient', denying any correspondence between Orientalism and the Orient ... while on the other hand he argues that its knowledge was put in the service of colonial conquest, occupation, and administration. . . . How then can Said argue that the 'Orient' is just a representation, if he also wants to claim that 'Orientalism' provided the necessary knowledge for actual colonial conquest?[21]

The polarized nature of Said's argument requires extremes: the more he wishes to claim that modern Orientalist knowledge participated in the activity of colonialism, the more he must disassociate the medieval foundation of Orientalism from any hint of actuality. This emptying out of the Middle Ages as a category with its own history participates in a strategy with a long modern and imperial genealogy: it paradoxically claims the Middle Ages as both the origin of a progressive history and as an inert, sealed off space *before* the movement of history. Said's own explanation of this temporal relation demonstrates with remarkable clarity the performance of the Middle Ages as a kind of "future perfect" for modernity:

> My thesis is that the essential aspects of modern Orientalist theory and praxis (from which present-day Orientalism derives) can be understood, not as a sudden access of objective knowledge about the Orient, but as a set of structures inherited from the past, secularized, redisposed, and re-formed by such disciplines as philology, which in turn were naturalized, modernized, and laicized substitutes for (or versions of) Christian supernaturalism.[22]

The Middle Ages provides the structure that already will have been, and is thus always ready for modern realization.

Said's grounding of Orientalism in the Middle Ages has another, so far overlooked, function: it rationalizes his often criticized choice of limiting his analysis almost exclusively to the Arab Middle East and to British, French, and more recently, American practice.[23] As Said explains it, in attempting to find a point of departure and a logical way to reduce "a very fat archive to manageable dimensions," he chose to limit his "set of questions to the Anglo-French-American experience of the Arabs and Islam, which for almost a thousand years together stood for the Orient."[24] Said credits this strain of Orientalism with the production of "Europe" itself. Through its encounter with Islam, Europe "strengthened [its] system of representing the Orient, and . . . turned Islam into the very epitome of an outsider against which the whole of European civilization from the Middle Ages on was founded."[25] Thus, Said bases the scope and shape of *Orientalism,* and Orientalism (indeed the "whole of European civilization"), on his delineation of a cohesive discourse grounded in the European Middle Ages.

Even though Said distorts and over-generalizes the history of medieval Orientalism—he virtually ignores the complex engagement with Jewishness, for instance[26]—he is certainly right that Christian Europe's encounter with Islam performed a crucial role in its identification processes, and that the vitriolic stereotypes in medieval representations of Islam have close counterparts in Orientalism today. My goal in challenging the antiempirical and "closed system" of Orientalism that Said discovers in the Middle Ages is not, as Shelia Delany puts it, to "claim" active Orientalism for the fourteenth century, even though I thoroughly agree with her argument that medieval Orientalism, including Chaucer's, entailed material and institutional praxis.[27] I want rather to interrogate Said's dichotomy, particularly because I believe it instates a core "reality" that privileges and solidifies the very discourse he critiques. If we grant with Said that medieval Europe's system of representing Islam is purely antiempirical, based not on any experience with Islam but only on a fully closed, self-generated tradition, then we privilege Europe as an absolutely self-constituting object. This assumption not only undermines Said's work, but is complicit with 20/20's contemporary Orientalism, which likewise invokes a medieval past for a shared, enclosed "first world" identity that can be turned against Othered, "backward" societies. The task of disrupting this temporal opposition falls to medievalists. With that in mind, I turn to Chaucer's Man of Law's Tale, which brings gender, time, and Orientalism together with "England."

The Temporalities of Custance

The Man of Law's Tale reaches back to the sixth century in order to tell a story of England's Christianization and inclusion within the political domain of Europe. Like Behind the Veil, it writes this identity process on a female body, and like the Orientalism described by Said, it relies upon an image of Islam as an outsider, against which an English and a European identity emerges. Chaucer's Orientalism certainly did not represent a "real" Orient; nonetheless, I will argue that actual experience with the Near East played an important role in shaping the identities retrospectively narrated in Chaucer's tale. Sheila Delany has documented the military, economic, social, and political presence of the Orient in late fourteenth-century Europe, particularly as it pertained to Chaucer's experience in England. She notes that the rich import/export trade that flowed through Mediterranean ports brought valued commodities and luxuries as well as hard currency to European markets and interests, as did, of course, the lucrative pilgrimage business. Throughout the second half of the century, various European clashes with Turks and Muslims, such as the 1365 attack

on Alexandria commemorated in *La Prise d'Alexandrie* by Chaucer's re-
spected contemporary Guillaume de Machaut, gained widespread attention. Likewise, intermittent but intense lobbying and fund-raising for
crusades kept the ideals as well as reports of this practice in the foreground.
For instance, the relentless effort of Phillipe de Mézières, who founded an
Order for the purpose of regaining Jerusalem, eventually involved
Chaucer's friend and fellow-diplomat Lewis Clifford. As the records of the
Scrope-Grosvenor trial indicate, Chaucer was familiar with the exploits, if
not the participants, of Crusades from Egypt to Lithuania.[28]

In her analysis of the Orientalism in the *Man of Law's Tale,* Susan
Schibanoff attends to what she terms "the rhetoric of proximity" in medieval Orientalism. This rhetoric, she explains, troped the familiarity of
Islam (which was intensified by its threatening geographical proximity)
"not to mute the threat of the new religion to Europe, but to intensify it,
to increase rather than reduce the 'pressure' it created in the occidental
mind." To this end, she argues, many scholars, most notably Peter the Venerable, figured Islam as an insidious heresy—an *in*fectious *in*filtrator—
rather than as a less threatening, exterior, infidel religion.[29] The
characterizations that Schibanoff delineates eventuated, at least in part,
from serious (although rarely benign) study and translation of Islamic
texts—with an intense concern about Islam's relation and similarity to
Christianity—especially during the twelfth and thirteenth centuries, the
high point of both the crusades and intellectual exchange with Arab scholarship. European intellectual life was, of course, heavily indebted to this
scholarship, and in that sense its literary tradition was already fully inhabited by "the Orient."[30] For those experienced in trade and international
affairs, as was Chaucer, Europe existed in a system of interchange with a
Near Eastern culture of undeniable wealth, formidable military and intellectual power, and a menacing religion. Such an interchange does not suggest that the Orientalism of the *Man of Law's Tale* represented a "real"
Orient, but rather that its representations are responses, both to the stereotypes of literary tradition and to an intricate, problematic relation with the
Near East, particularly Islam. If we recognize this literary relation, then we
can also recognize that the Euro-Christian national identities shaped and
authenticated through medieval literary tradition are already inhabited by
an "Oriental" presence—a presence not generated solely by a European
imagination, but also by Islamic cultures that shared Europe's history.

The opening of *The Man of Law's Tale* gives us Rome and Europe
through the eyes of Syrian merchants who are honest and wealthy, and
who circulate the renown of the Emperor's daughter Custance across the
border, just as they circulate their merchandise. As Schibanoff notes,
Chaucer's presentation of these merchants as positive characters, familiar

with European language and culture, is a departure from his sources, which emphasize their foreignness.[31] Custance is certainly a representative of "Europe" (over which she is fit to be "queene"[32]) in this tale, but while she is still in Rome, the distinction between Europe and the Islamic East is not clear. Not only does her father approve her marriage to the Sultan, but the Pope expresses confidence that the promised conversions of the Syrians will increase the jurisdiction of "Christes lawe" (233–41). The Sultan's apparently sincere conversion and his ideal romance-hero behavior further suggest significant compatibility between nations and cultures.[33] This proposed Christianization and political marriage-alliance with the "Barbre nacioun" of Syria (281) must necessarily fail, as the Man of Law, speaking after all hope of "reclaiming" the Holy Land had waned, well knows. More importantly, however, his tale retrospectively defines the terms of success and failure for attaining an identity within the European system from the perspective of fourteenth-century England. How and why the Syrian marriage alliance fails, despite the proximity as well as the cultural and economic compatibility of Syria and Rome, will define how and why far-off England came to be encompassed within Europe's borders instead.

The political border between Europe and the Orient materializes clearly only as Custance crosses into Syria. The Man of Law's comment on the grief at her departure associates it with a violent breaking of political boundaries:

> I trowe at Troye, whan Pirrus brak the wal
> or Ilion brende, at Thebes the citee,
> N'at Rome, for the harm thurgh Hanybal
> That Romayns hath venquysshed tymes thre,
> Nas herd swich tendre wepyng for pitee
> As in the chambre was for hire departynge. (288–93)

Because the "Imprudent Emperour of Rome" cannot know the future (309–15), and cannot comprehend the distinctions between Europe and the "strange nacioun" of Syria, he has endangered Rome itself. In the idiom of the "exchange of women," and as these disastrous political defeats suggest, the "vanquishing" (or "breaking the wall") of the Emperor's daughter in an inappropriate marriage alliance can only bring grief and tragically shattered boundaries.[34]

The consequent violence emerges, unsurprisingly, embodied within a woman. The pattern of antifeminism in this tale has been frequently studied, and placed in context with Orientalism by Schibanoff, who argues that through the two discourses of antifeminism and Orientalism the tale creates two "outsiders," the oriental and woman, in order to motivate "the sense of a common vested interest among English men."[35] I agree with Schibanoff's detection of an English identity-formation in this tale, but suggest that its Orientalist discourse works *through,* rather than in addition to, its discourse on women. The contrast between Custance, who is the paragon of female virtue—passive, static, and servile—and the Sultaness, who is the ultimate evil—"Virago," usurper of male power, and cause of damnation—not only defines "woman" in the tale, but, in the sense that women serve as "symbolic bearers of the collectivity's identity," it defines their cultures as well.[36] Unlike the somewhat European Sultan, who like the Emperor is fully engrossed in the contemporary (linear time) activities that mutually involve and sustain their polities, the Sultaness rejects this "newe lawe" (337), and vows to uphold her culture's traditions and religion. Her credo to Mohammed and to the past manifests the essence of her culture, and suddenly makes the shared incidentals of Roman and Syrian economies and etiquette seem inconsequential. Despite her apparent agency, the Sultaness functions here as a sign for the East and its essential difference from Europe; her successful destruction of the Christian alliance writes an Isalmic past necessary to late medieval European historiography, which must remember Islam as murderous and so incapable of eradicating its error that contact with it spawns only violence and death, rather than the shared life of spiritual conversion or human progeny.

The border between Europe and the East, which emerged as Custance crossed into Syria, becomes absolute as she floats back out to sea, her marriage unconsummated. There can be no political/blood alliance, no meaningful exchange between these now clearly delimited political/religious communities. Such religious and political identities did not exist in the sixth century when the tale is set, of course (Mohammed died in 632). This anachronism does not indicate historical naivete, but rather the nature of the mythmaking at work here: this tale produces a historically constructed *past* for Europe that defines and validates its existence *in the present.* For the fourteenth-century writer who is busily thinking and writing a European identity, Europe *becomes* Europe over and against an Islamic East because it is Christian, an identity effected only through the refusal of the cultural ambivalence prompted by the clearly admirable learning and material resources of the Orient, attributes evident in this tale and inescapable to the late medieval Christian. Thus, as Said suggests, Europe founds its identity here against an Islamic East, but this identity is far from pure representation divorced from experience. In this tale, Europe is forced to designate a narrow Christian identity for itself precisely because it has encountered the East.

The terms of European identity formulated through Custance's experience in Syria provide the basis for writing an English European identity. She arrives in England, as in Syria, still a virgin, "constant" bearer of Euro-

Christianity, and her approach again produces a sense of political borders: she is driven, the Man of Law narrates, into "oure occian," "oure wilde see" (505–06).[37] Anonymous and timeless, Custance functions as the repository of cultural memory—through her England will remember itself within Europe. The events in England in many ways repeat her experiences in Syria, but the crucial difference of the English response to Custance and Christianity is comprehensible only inasmuch as the Syrian episode confers its meaning. The English conversion, for instance, proceeds not from rational calculation or sexual desire, but through divine revelation. The miraculous punishment of the knight who had falsely accused Custance signals God's attention to the English, and effects their permanent entrance into the Christian community. England, unlike Syria, successfully kills the threatening aspect of its past—the mother-in-law who would reject the new power alignment—and thus clears the way for a successful union between now fully compatible cultures. The legitimacy of this union is corroborated by the successful sexual union of Aella and Custance (to which the Man of Law devotes unusual attention). Custance's journey with her son back to Rome, her reunion there with Aella, their son Maurice's designation as heir to the Empire, their travel back to England and hers back again to Rome—all signal the success and legitimacy of this blood alliance, and circumscribe Europe, which now includes England, as the proper space of Christian circulation and exchange. *The Man of Law's Tale* does, as Schibanoff argues, "provide an etiology of British Christianity"; it also creates a bond among English men—in the fourteenth century *and* today— and "locates its historical origin in the Saxon past of Aella's Northumberland."[38] But this origin, and Saxon Northumberland insofar as it locates a Christian English past, is cut through with an "Oriental" presence that defines the very terms of its identity. If England or Europe seem whole, it is because Custance is there, eternal memory but irrevocably past, bearing the sign of its identity.

Conclusion

The significations so violently imposed upon women in contemporary political and cultural struggles cannot be adequately theorized without specific attention to the reliance of national and supranational identities upon "the Middle Ages." In turn, as long as postcolonial critique reproduces the terms through which imperial logic grounded itself upon the Middle Ages, this theorization cannot even begin. Refusing the historical significance of medieval Orientalism such as that wrought upon the bodies of Custance and her mothers-in-law guarantees the continuing reproduction of these patterns of violence. If we are to come to terms with and begin to dismantle the embodiment of national and supranational conflicts within women, then we must, I suggest, also dismantle prevailing historical conceptions of time. In his Sixteenth Thesis on the Philosophy of History, Walter Benjamin imagines a historical materialist writing history. I have never seen this thesis cited, perhaps because it has been overshadowed by the "Angel of Progress" in the Ninth Thesis, or perhaps because it is so misogynist. Here it is in part:

> Historicism gives the "eternal" image of the past; historical materialism supplies a unique experience with the past. The historical materialist leaves it to others to be drained by the whore called "Once upon a time" in historicism's bordello. He remains in control of his powers, man enough to blast open the continuum of history.[39]

He is right about the whore of course. The "eternal" image of the past is written on a woman and everyone has used her. So, according to the system Benjamin uses here, the one doing the writing, and the blasting, must be a "man." But I wonder, if we medievalists blast open the "times" of history, we won't blast away its genders too.

Notes

I am extremely greatful to Susan Crane and John Rickard for their helpful comments on earlier versions of this essay.

1. *Behind The Veil—A Report on the Woman of Afghanistan, 20/20,* American Broadcasting Companies, Inc. November 1, 1996 (transcript unpaginated). As I was finishing this essay, Diane Sawyer appeared in another *20/20* report, "Honor Killing" (January 22, 1999), which targeted all societies labeled "traditional" (but gave examples only from the Middle East), and persistently employed the rhetorical question, "Do you know how this looks to the rest of the world?" My use of the term Orientalism here refers to Edward Said's critique in his *Orientalism* (reprint, with new Afterword, New York: Vintage, 1994), as well as to his application of that term to American media practices in *Covering Islam: How the Media and the Experts Determine How We See the Rest of the World* (reprint, New York: Vintage Books, 1997).

2. For some of the important critical work on gender, time and nation, see Anne McClintock, *Imperial Leather: Race, Gender and Sexuality in the Colonial Contest* (New York: Routledge, 1995); *Nationalisms and Sexualities,* ed. A. Parker, M. Russo, D. Sommer and P. Yaegger (New York: Routledge, 1992); *Woman—Nation—State,* ed. Nira Yuval-Davis and Floya Anthias (London: Macmillan, 1989); Carol Pateman, *The Sexual Contract* (Cambridge: Polity, 1988); Etienne Balibar and Immanuel Wallerstein, *Race, Nation, Class: Ambiguous Identities,* trans. Chris Turner (London: Verso, 1991); *Social Text* (special issue on "Queer

Transexions of Race, Nation, and Gender") 52–53 (1997). Nira Yuval-Davis gives an encyclopedic overview of many of the pertinent issues in *Gender and Nation* (London: Sage, 1997).

3. At the show's closing, in response to Barbara Walters' question, "Would pressure from this country make a difference?" Sawyer remarks, "Pressure probably would. I think the U.S. is regrouping now trying to decide what to do . . . we can only hope that the Taliban know that the U.S. is watching on these women and they'd better be safe."

4. In *Gender and Nation,* Nira Yuval-Davis discusses the difficulties of addressing women's problems in different cultures, an issue which is often trapped in either "universal" or "relativist" arguments. The former (of which *Behind the Veil* is an example) imposes one cultural position on all cultures; the latter homogenizes the difference of other cultures without allowing for the women's dissidence within their cultures. Yuval-Davis argues for what she calls "transversal" politics, which replaces perceived unity and homogeneity "by dialogues which give recognition to the specific positionings of those who participate in them as well as to the 'unfinished knowledge' that each such situated positioning can offer" (p. 131). See generally her chapter 6. Gayatri Spivak has consistently critiqued a feminist politics that imposes homogeneous ideals and goals upon "Woman." See especially "Bonding in Difference," in *An Other Tongue: Nation and Ethnicity in the Linguistic Borderlands,* ed. Alfred Arteaga (Durham, NC: Duke University Press, 1994), pp. 273–85.

5. Contemporary critical analysis of Orientalism shares this tendency with contemporary nationhood theory, which uncritically reproduces imperial representations of the Middle Ages. I discuss the rhetorical positioning of the Middle Ages in both national discourse and contemporary theories of the nation in "National Writing in the Ninth Century: A Reminder for Postcolonial Thinking About the Nation," *Journal for Medieval and Early Modern Studies* 28:3 (1998): 611–37. For discussions of the role of the Middle Ages in writing modern history, see Lee Patterson, *Negotiating the Past: The Historical Understanding of Medieval Literature* (Madison: University of Wisconsin Press, 1987); Louise O. Fradenburg, "Voice Memorial": Loss and Reparation in Chaucer's Poetry," *Exemplaria* 2:1 (1990): 169–202. For the importance of medievalism and medieval studies to English colonial projects, see Kathleen Biddick, *The Shock of Medievalism* (Durham, NC: Duke University Press, 1998); and Allen Frantzen, *Desire for Origins: New Language, Old English, and Teaching the Tradition* (New Brunswick, NJ: Rutgers University Press, 1990). For discussion of American uses of European Middle Ages, see Gabrielle M. Spiegel, "Medievalisms Old and New: The Rediscovery of Alterity in North American Medieval Studies," *American Historical Review* 103 (1998): 677–704.

6. Homi Bhabha, "DissemiNation: Time, Narrative, and the Margins of the Modern Nation," in *The Location of Culture* (London: Routledge, 1994), p. 153 (emphasis in original).

7. Johannes Fabian, *Time and the Other: How Anthropology Makes Its Object* (New York: Columbia University Press, 1983), pp. 15, 17–18, 25.

8. Louise Fradenburg, "Voice Memorial," 173.

9. Frantz Fanon, "Algeria Unveiled," in *A Dying Colonialism,* trans. Haakon Chevalier (New York: Grove Press, 1965), pp. 37–38. Ellipsis in original.

10. Fanon, "Algeria Unveiled," p. 47.

11. Winifred Woodhull, "Unveiling Algeria," *Genders* 10 (1991): 114 (emphasis in original). Woodhull rightly criticizes some of Fanon's blind spots to Algerian repression of women, as does Anne McClintock in *Imperial Leather,* pp. 365–67.

12. Nayereh Tohidi, "Gender and Islamic Fundamentalism: Feminist Politics in Iran," in *Third World Women and the Politics of Feminism,* ed. Chandra Talpade Mohanty, Ann Russo, and Lourdes Torres (Bloomington: Indiana University Press, 1991), pp. 252–53. Tohidi's essay details the complex interactions of gender, class, religion, and politics in the Iranian case (as Woodhull's essay does for the Algerian situation), which I do not have space to recount here.

13. Benedict Anderson, *Imagined Communities: Reflections on the Origin and Spread of Nationalism* (London: Verso, 1983, revised edition, 1991); Tom Nairn, *The Break-Up of Britain* (London: Verso, 1977). For a discussion of the development of the idea of the nation's contradictory times, see McClintock, *Imperial Leather,* pp. 358–60.

14. Bhabha, "DissemiNation," p. 145, emphasis in original. For further discussion of the implications of the nation's split temporality for postcolonial studies, see Gyan Prakash, "The Modern Nation's Return in the Archaic," *Critical Inquiry* 23 (1997): 536–56.

15. Julia Kristeva, "Women's Time," in *The Kristeva Reader,* ed. Toril Moi (New York: Columbia University Press, 1986), pp. 188–192. This essay was first published in 1979, and translated into English in 1981 (*Signs* 7:1). Kristeva discusses the nation as the "dream and reality of the nineteenth century," and its essence, defined by Marx, as "economic homogeneity, historical tradition and linguistic unity," p. 188.

16. Kristeva, "Woman's Time," pp. 188–193. Kristeva has sometimes been criticized for essentializing assumptions about certain, especially non-European, cultures. See Lisa Lowe, *Critical Terrains: French and British Orientalisms* (Ithaca and London: Cornell University Press, 1991).

17. Bhabha, "DissemiNation," p. 153. For a critique of Bhabha's dismissal of gender in a different context, see McClintock, *Imperial Leather,* pp. 362–63.

18. Said, *Orientalism,* pp. 247, 211 (emphasis in original). Said does not claim that medieval Europe had no experience with the Orient, of course, and several times catalogues those experiences (pp. 59, 74). His argument is that medieval Orientalist representations had no basis in these experiences, but were informed *only* by textual tradition.

19. Said, *Orientalism,* pp. 68, 62. For Said's use of Dante as the exemplar of Orientalism's system, see also pp. 69, 71, 72, 95. For his statements on the consistent character of Orientalism since the Middle Ages, see also pp. 287, 243.

20. Said, *Orientalism* pp. 21–22. Clifford notes that "Said's discourse analysis does not itself escape the all inclusive 'Occidentalism' he specifically rejects as an alternative to Orientalism":"On Orientalism," *The Predicament of Culture* (Cambridge, MA: Harvard University Press, 1988), p. 271.

21. Robert Young, *White Mythologies: Writing History and the West* (London and New York: Routledge, 1990), p. 129.

22. Said, *Orientalism,* p. 122.

23. For discussion of the problems Said's selectivity entails for his book, see James Clifford's "On Orientalism."

24. Said, *Orientalism,* pp. 16–17.

25. Said, *Orientalism,* p. 70.

26. For a discussion of the complexity of Europe's interrelation with Eastern cultures, as well as a critique of Said's use of the past, see Thierry Hentsch, *Imagining the Middle East,* trans. Fred A. Reed (Montreal, New York: Black Rose Books, 1992), especially chapter one. I am grateful to Sylvia Tomasch for recommending this reference. For a brilliant analysis of the Jewish presence at the center of Dante's *Divine Comedy,* see Tomasch's "Judecca, Dante's Satan, and the *Dis*-placed Jew" in *Text and Territory: Geographical Imagination in the European Middle Ages,* ed. Tomasch and Sealy Gilles (Philadelphia: University of Pennsylvania Press, 1998), pp. 247–67.

27. Sheila Delany, *The Naked Text: Chaucer's Legend of Good Women* (Berkeley: University of California Press, 1994), pp. 165, 166–73.

28. Delany, *The Naked Text,* pp. 166–170.

29. Susan Schibanoff, "Worlds Apart: Orientalism, Antifeminism, and Heresy in Chaucer's *Man of Law's Tale.*" *Exemplaria* 8.1 (1996): 70, 62, 71–73.

30. For detailed accounts of European Christian study of Islam, as well as intellectual exchange, see Norman Daniel, *Islam and the West: The Making of an Image* (Edinburgh: Edinburgh University Press, 1960); Dorothee Metlitzki, *The Matter of Araby in Medieval England* (New Haven: Yale University Press, 1977); and R. W. Southern, *Western Views of Islam in the Middle Ages* (Cambridge, MA: Harvard University Press, 1962).

31. Schibanoff, p. 78. Chaucer's primary source is Nicholas Trevet's Anglo-Norman *Chronicles,* and he may also have relied on Gower's analogue in *Confessio Amantis.* For a bibliography of comparisons between Chaucer's tale and its analogues, see David Raybin, "Custance and History: Woman as Outsider in Chaucer's *Man of Law's Tale*" *Studies in the Age of Chaucer* 12 (1990): 72 n.19. While Schibanoff argues that Chaucer sets up the familiarity of the Syrians in order to intensify the proximate threat of Islam, I want to point out that "Europe" emerges in this tale only through its border-relation to the "Barbre nacioun" (p. 281) of Syria.

32. *Man of Law's Tale,* 161. All citations of Chaucer are by line number from *The Riverside Chaucer,* ed. Larry D. Benson (Boston: Houghton Mifflin, 1987).

33. For the Sultan's character, see Delany, "Womanliness in the *Man of Law's Tale,*" in *Writing Woman: Women Writers and Women in Literature Medieval to Modern* (New York: Schocken, 1983), p. 39.

34. For a detailed discussion of the operation of the "exchange of women" in this tale, see Carolyn Dinshaw, "The Law of Man and Its 'Abhomyna-cions,'" *Exemplaria* 1:1 (1989): 117–148.

35. Schibanoff, p. 94. In addition, see Shelia Delany, "Womanliness in *The Man of Law's Tale*," pp. 36–46; and Raybin, "Custance and History."

36. Yuval-Davis, *Gender and Nation* (London: Sage Publications, 1997), p. 45.

37. In his essay on "Custance and History," David Raybin observes that the unchanging Custance is "timeless," aligned with the eternal, and "outside history," which progresses according to masculine values, a formulation that recalls Kristeva's discussion of *monumental time*. Raybin, "Custance and History," pp. 68–71.

38. Schibanoff, "Worlds Apart," pp. 83, 94.

39. Walter Benjamin, *Theses on the Philosophy of History,* in *Illuminations,* ed. Hannah Arendt, trans. Harry Zohn (Schocken Books, 1968), p. 262.

CHAPTER 7

NATIVE STUDIES:
ORIENTALISM AND MEDIEVALISM

John M. Ganim

> *Starting in the sixteenth century, the Middle Ages reveal an identity crisis: Sometimes the medieval is the starting point of Western European cultural self-consciousness, at other times the forms of medieval culture are defined as foreign, especially Eastern, in origin. Orientalism and Nativism are inextricably intertwined within the "Medieval."*

In the climactic scene of *The Book of Saladin,* the liberator of Jerusalem accepts the surrender of the city from its Christian garrison:

> "Tell your people," Salah al-Din told him, "that we shall not treat them as your forebears treated us when they first took this city. As a child I was told of what Godfrey and Tancredi did to our people. Remind these frightened Christians of what Believers and Jews suffered ninety years ago. The heads of our children were displayed on pikes. Old men and women of all ages were tortured and burnt. These streets were washed in blood, Balian. Some of the emirs would like to wash them again, but this time in your blood. They remind me that we all believe in an eye for an eye and a tooth for a tooth."[1]

Saladin appears here simultaneously as an opposite figure of the fanatical crusaders, as the enlightened exception found in Western accounts themselves, and as the legendary military hero of Islam. In passage after passage, the projections of Western Christianity are revealed as projections: It is the

West that is intolerant, fanatical, millenialist, and vengeful. The West is represented by traitors, anti-Semitic fanatics, sociopaths, and a few enlightened individuals who dimly perceive the more powerful truths of Islam. The East is represented by subtle and complex thinkers, profoundly human military and political leaders and enormously complex national and ethnic identities. It is the East that reminds the West what its highest ideals should be, it is the East that defines the West. *The Book of Saladin,* that is, reverses the structures of Orientalism at their point of origin.[2]

The Book of Saladin is, of course, not a medieval narrative at all, but a late-twentieth-century novel published in 1998 and written by the British Pakistani author, producer, and activist Tariq Ali. As such, it is not only an account of Salah-ud-Din's life, fully aware of medieval Arabic and other chronicles as well as Western sources, but also a meditation on politics, both of the Western and international left, and probably also something of a *roman à clef.* Written in a Britain transformed by both the 1960s, postimperial immigration, and Thatcherism, it is replete with modern and postmodern subplots. Salah-ud-Din was a Kurdish warrior, and his minority status is an important part of the story (as indeed it was historically) and of his self-consciousness. The fiction of the novel is that the story of the Kurdish hero is being narrated to a Jewish scribe. The chief romantic relationship in the novel is a lesbian affair between the principal Sultana and another member of the harem. Homosexual relationships are smilingly accepted in the Moslem camp, secretly and furtively destructive in the Christian camps. Eunuchs (mostly enslaved choirboys) turn out to be only partly incapacitated. Even heroic leadership itself is represented ironically, since Salah-ud-Din is often ill, uncertain, and politic in his exercise of military and political power through caution and calculation rather than charisma and dynamism. Although Jerusalem is recaptured, the "Franj" are not entirely expelled, and the campaign ends with a negotiated settlement (as indeed it did).

Indeed, at times the novel reads like an allegory of negotiation, cultural, political, and personal. *The Book of Saladin* and its author are intensely aware of the postcolonial condition. The crusaders have occupied the eastern Mediterranean coast for centuries. Their presence divides rather than unifies the forces of Islam, torn apart by their own conflicting political goals. At the same time, the confluence of Christian, Islamic, and Jewish ideas and practices results in a crossfertilization and alliances often confusing even to its participants. The form *The Book of Saladin* takes, as much of the historical romance as of the historical novel, is a form with a hybridized origin. Like the novel itself, it is a form that is most Western when it seems most Eastern, most Eastern when it seems most Western, most historicized when it seems most modern and most modern when it seems to be recreating the past. Its tone is as much elegaic as heroic, and it imagines an orientalized "Middle Ages" as both origin and point of decline.[3]

If *The Book of Saladin* reverses the categories of Otherness as they articulated themselves in the later Middle Ages, it should remind us that some crucially dominant ideas about the Middle Ages in the West, especially as the West discovers its own modernity (which involved the very nomenclature of the "Middle Ages"), depended on a geographic as well as a historical distinction. The aim of this chapter is to point out that the idea of the Middle Ages as it developed from its earliest formulations in the historical self-consciousness of Western Europe is part of what we used to call an identity crisis, a deeply uncertain sense of what the West is and should be. The idea of the Middle Ages as a pure Europe (or England or France or Germany) both rests on and reacts to an uncomfortable sense of instability about origins, about what the West is and from where it came. The definition of medieval culture, especially literature and architecture, from its earliest formulation in the Renaissance to the twentieth century, has been a site of a contest over the idea of the West and, by definition, that which is non-Western.[4] In the sixteenth and seventeeth centuries, the condemnation of the Gothic and the defense of neoclassical models and the anxiety over the formlessness of medieval narrative was expressed in a rhetoric of foreignness, citing the sources of medieval forms in "Saracen" and Eastern cultures. This is especially true of genres and forms that later medievalisms interpret as metonymically medieval, such as Gothic architecture and medieval romance. Gothic architecture was interpreted at times as deeply native, as when the interior roof vaulting of Gothic was thought to imitate the trees of the northern forests inhabited by the "Goths," but even that emphasis was unflattering, meant to suggest a certain crudeness and barbarism. At other times, however, the pointed Gothic arch was ascribed to Eastern, usually "Saracen" influence. John Evelyn in his *Account of Architects and Architecture* (1707) regards the development of the Gothic as inseparable from racial invasion: "It was after the Irruption, and Swarmes of those Truculent Peoples from the North; the Moors and Arabs from the South and East, over-running the Civiliz'd World; that wherever they fixed themselves, they soon began to debauch this Noble and Useful Art."[5] The "Noble and Useful Art" is of course architecture in the Vitruvian, neoclassical mode. The architect Christopher Wren, in defending his own classicism, denigrates "the Saracen mode of building, seen in the East, soon spread over Europe, and particularly in France."[6] Wren's phrasing repeats an English trope of French capitulation, even France as a source of foreign ideas. The Orient, as it was later said, begins at Calais.

Medieval literature, or at least medieval romance, also was regarded, even by its earliest defenders, as a record of a national past but also as foreign, and particularly Eastern, in conception. The eighteenth century, which defends and even invents medieval romance, is obsessed with its non-Western origins. To defend Romance, for its eighteenth-century champions, was to defend fiction itself, to defend the validity of imagination.[7] Such potentially uncontrollable wildness is ascribed to an otherness both within and without, to the West's barbaric past on one hand and to the model of Eastern literatures on the other. The metaphor of the earliest studies of medieval romance is one of miscegenation. In contrast to the condemnation of the uncertain parentage of medieval cultural forms as expressed by Renaissance writers, eighteenth-century scholars were in fact attracted to the possibility of cultural mixture. Thomas Warton's *History of English Poetry* opens with an argument that medieval romance, and fiction in general, is virtually created by the meeting of Saracen and crusader. At roughly the same time, the French scholar Pierre-Daniel Huet's essay on romance was translated into English, repeating the speculation that romance has its origins in Moorish influence on Spain. Huet describes fiction itself, with its layers of allegory and rhetoric, as originating in the East, insinuating into the West through various routes.[8] Arguments were mounted on both sides of the question of origins, most pointedly by the generally dismissive Joseph Ritson, but throughout the long period of relatively amateur and preacademic reconstruction of medieval literary history, the triad of Romance, Fiction, and the East is a constant theme.[9] In the eighteenth century, enthusiasm for these forms resulted in a celebration of the very exoticism that the Renaissance had condemned. The antiquarianism of that century was inseparably linked in its sensibility with the fascination with oriental exoticism and the wonders of the primitive world. Bishop Percy, William Hurd, and Warton constructed a medieval world that was both a native past and an exotic otherness.[10]

By the late eighteenth century, this dual understanding of the medieval as embodying the imaginative and creative abilities of an East imbued with the gift of fantasy as well as the primal record of historical origins is complicated by the reality of mercantile expansion and the beginnings of the imperial project, with its concomitant intellectual apparatus, an apparatus that begins at least with a positive and celebratory attitude toward its object of study. In the wake of Sir William Jones' establishment of the Asiatick Society of Bengal and his thesis that the classical languages of the West and Sanskrit were descended from a common source, a phase of celebration of all things Indian ran through German Romanticism.[11] Jones thought that these cultures shared not only language but religious myths, that their common polytheism was a degeneration from an original monotheism. This enthusiasm ignited both Friedrich and August Schlegel's original interest in Sanskrit. An Indian Golden Age was imagined as an earlier form of a spiritually unified Middle Ages. This idealism did not last too long into the early nineteenth century, when evidence began to weigh against some of Jones's assumptions, but a general notion that European civilizations shared with Indian and other civilizations a common source, that all people, or some of us, were branches from a common tree, remained the controlling explanation for the striking new evidence of a shared linguistic source.

With the inclusion of India into the empire after the mid-nineteenth century, however, and the newly powerful influence of race as a defining factor in history and the dual linkage of civilization and progress as concepts, the egalitarianism and prelapsarianism of Romantic orientalism was replaced by a historiography of conquest. How could the evidence of the great Indian past be reconciled with the colonial challenge of governing an inferior people and a decadent civilization? The high moment of Indian civilization was imagined as the result of conquest and control of a higher "Aryan" civilization over a lower and not coincidentally darker and more southerly "Dravidian" civilization. Again, the Middle Ages turned out to be a useful metaphor. The deep layers of Indian civilization and its hidden affinities with the West were again imagined as medieval, as in the Victorian legal scholar Henry Maine's parallel of the Anglo-Saxon and Indian village. (Indeed, even the plural nomenclature of medievalism in English, partly historically responsible and partly a matter of national self-definition based on the conquest, turns out to be usefully employed, refining the singular Middle Age of German or French scholarly language.[12]) Maine attempted to justify the British modernization of India by claiming it was an inevitable indigenous development, and he did so, remarkably enough, by analogy to the Middle Ages. According to Savigny, the imposition of Roman law on Germanic village organization transformed village custom into the basis of the modern nation-state. Maine appropriated from Kemble, the great Anglo-Saxonist, an idealization of the Anglo-Saxon village and pointed to similarities with the Indian village. Where the English were in the Middle Ages, so was India in the mid-nineteenth century.[13]

The largely structural suppositions of the earlier model of Aryan dispersal was replaced from the mid-nineteenth century on by evolutionary, and often Social Darwinist, premises. The obvious political and imperial assumption of European racial superiority at the same time was a problem for the image of the Middle Ages. Earlier Enlightenment and Whig notions of progress always had denigrated the Dark Ages, but the rise of anthropology and its unstable ideological affinity with colonialism also had an impact on the study and popular conception of the medieval, which now began to be regarded with a combination of fascination and condescension. In the early nineteenth century, Romantic national self-definition had rewritten the medieval past as a site of origin and indigenous essence, but by the middle and late years of that century the security of this site becomes less certain. As anthropology developed a way of understanding the alien objects of empire, its techniques also could always be applied to the alterity of our own history, of the customs of the colonizers themselves in an earlier stage of development.

Academic anthropology, with its emphasis on fieldwork, would eventually question crudely Social Darwinist assumptions, and would also reject the armchair anthropology of writers like J. G. Frazer, whose *The Golden Bough* described the magical outlook of the mind of prescientific cultures. Frazer makes a surprising number of allusions to medieval European culture, as if that culture could be analogous to the archaic worlds it seeks to describe.[14] But the full expression of Frazerian anthropology appears shortly after the turn of the century in E. K. Chambers' *The Mediaeval Stage*. Chambers describes classical culture in racialized terms: "The mimetic instinct, which no race of mankind is wholly without, appears to have been unusually strong amongst the peoples of the Mediterranean stock" (1), but the Romans, "athletic rather than mimetic," highlight the spectacular, a tendency exaggerated by "slaves and foreigners" (3). But Chambers's heart is in folk drama. He imagines a parallel agriculture folk culture, responding only to seasonal change, carrying on its practices under the surface veneer of Christianity. Fragments of the old religion attach themselves to the church calendar. Fertility rites are disguised as village festivity: maypoles and the village maying; garlands and garlanding customs; rain charms and sun charms; bonfires and other holiday fires; animal and cereal sacrifices, many echoes of the Frazerian dying and reborn god. For Chambers even games and other ludic forms are remnants of earlier agricultural and fertility rituals, such as races, wrestling matches, tug-of-wars, charivari, hock-tide capture, and ransom of men by women. Because of our own interest in the mystery plays, we have emphasized this part of Chambers's history, but his most characteristic arguments are articulated in terms of these folk forms and other plays, such as the Robin Hood plays, mummers' plays, and sword dances that owe strong allegiances to folk customs.

A little known by-product of this anthropological medievalism is its representation at international exhibitions, which in the nineteenth and early twentieth century become almost a minor industry themselves. From the middle of the nineteenth through the early twentieth centuries, the great European powers mounted enormous international exhibitions, displaying both their technological and economic power and their newly acquired colonial possessions.[15] The fairs justified themselves by comparison with medieval trade fairs, as did the Crystal Palace Great Exhibition of 1851. Indeed, at the Exhibition of Ancient and Medieval Art of 1850, me-

dieval artifacts were shown as a Ruskinian inspiration to modern manu-
facturers to higher standards of design and craftsmanship.[16] At the Crystal
Palace, one of the most popular exhibits was the India section. Still informed by the notion of Aryan origins, and before the absorption of India
into the empire, that section emphasized luxury and undirected wealth. Interestingly, however, there was also a "medieval" section, which seemed to
have been mostly a display of metallurgy, particularly armor. "We enter the
western division of the nave," says the illustrated catalog. "We have here the
Indian Court, Africa . . . the West Indies, the Cape of Good Hope, the Medieval Court. . . . The long avenue leading from the Medieval Court to the
end of the building is devoted to general hardware . . . of all kinds."[17] The
Crystal Palace sheltered all its exhibits under one roof, but by the 1867 International Exhibition in Paris, colonial and exotic pavilions created a park
around the central and featured roofed area. This created a model in which
scholarly anthropological displays, pavilions of exotic foreign cultures, and
circuslike entertainment was grouped together away from the exhibits of
the technological and scientific achievements of the imperial powers.[18] At
the 1886 Colonial and Indian Exhibition in London, the intent was to suggest an analogy between the temporal present in the colonies and the medieval past of the home country. Among the displays of Southeast Asian
artifacts, flora, and fauna, England itself is represented by an "Old London"
street, constructed of a pastiche of pre–Great Fire London.[19] The Eiffel
Tower, at the 1889 International Exhibition in Paris, was originally surrounded by such "villages." The central exhibition of modern technology
was approached through exotic cultural displays, including Old Paris and
Old Vienna, both of which lumped together medieval and Renaissance details to equate the "old" with pre-Enlightenment cultures, whether European or not. In International Exhibitions and World's Fairs, medieval
"villages" are associated with colonial and imperial displays in a complex
representation of history as geography. While such structures could easily
be dismissed precisely as curiosities, in the context of the ideology of
world's fairs, they present the Middle Ages as both domestic and foreign.

   This almost physical marginalization of the Middle Ages suggests the
diminishment of the importance of medieval culture as an ideal model as
the twentieth century began. As a result, the image of the Middle Ages as
foreign and marginal had to be countered by twentieth-century medievalism. Attempts to recover medieval imagery in Progressive America, for instance, from Henry Adams (who never mentions these historical theme
villages in his famous description of—and medieval retreat from—the
Paris 1900 Exhibition) through Woodrow Wilson, are marked by an association of medieval ideals with lost civic virtues. Such an association, however, cannot overcome an increasing sense of the Middle Ages as an

irrelevant and dated avocation. Even the Renaissance of medieval studies in 1920s America and the founding of the Medieval Academy emphasized how the Middle Ages was really, well, the Renaissance, the real origin of modern society. Just as Progressivism was a political means of maintaining the ideals of a genteel Protestant America facing the challenge of immigration and rapid change, for much of the twentieth century scholarship on medieval literature tended to emphasize its sophistication, its intellectual framework, and its structural and ideological coherence (notwithstanding the fact that the vehicle of that coherence was the church). The positivist achievement of this perspective was huge, but it is interesting to note how, until recently, its mandarinism has had to exclude or anathematize positions that might undermine respectability.

Two of the most controversially heterodox scholarly positions of the early to mid-twentieth century, for instance, were the theory of the Celtic origins of Arthurian literature and the theory of the Arabic origins of courtly love. The scholarly literature surrounding these positions has been enormous and deeply contested, too vast to summarize here. French scholarship from the 1920s on, including such widely read scholars as the approving Denomy and the disapproving de Rougemont, ascribed the major themes and sources of late-medieval love literature to sources in Arabic and Mozarabic poetry.[20] The thesis is arguable on questions of historical evidence and direct transmission, but the circumstantial evidence is powerful. The possibility, even the likelihood, of cross-cultural influence and literary revisionism has disappeared from the scholarly radar screen, largely because Anglo-American scholarship has more or less made courtly love itself disappear, dismissing it as a neoromantic historical fantasy or explaining it as a transmutation of a European tradition of erotic poetry descending from Ovid.

The relation of Arthurian romance to Celtic myth is widely known through the literature of high modernism, the most notorious being T. S. Eliot's footnotes to *From Ritual to Romance* in *The Waste Land* and, in fact, *The Waste Land* itself. This approach to Arthurian romance was born in the "Cambridge School" interpretation of Greek drama as displaced ritual and was fostered by the enormous influence of Frazer's *The Golden Bough,* central to Eliot's own reading. But the scholarly project is carried out in greatest detail by R. S. Loomis and his collaborators.[21] Loomis traced as many possible conceivable details of Arthurian romance back to Celtic myth and moved the debate from the Frazerian association of previous scholars to a question of precedent. In Loomis, even Celtic myth is described as if it were a literary tradition, rendering it to some extent palatable to progressive (and positivist) medievalism. Loomis's ability to combine anthropology and literary history renders his enterprise still useful. But what is especially interesting is the withering barrage of his opponents, both of his Celticism and of his mythic priorities. By emphasizing the British origins of Arthurian legend, Loomis drew the wrath of a French Arthurian establishment. Of course, the Celtic thesis, once a strong position particularly in the United States, is now the province largely of popular medievalism and a somewhat worn Jungianism. If the generally anthropological approach to Arthurian romance has its roots in the colonial projects of the nineteenth century as I have described them, at the same time the lack of serious consideration of the subordinate sources of British culture is also problematic. In the English fairs I mentioned, Ireland and Scotland were typically depicted in terms of their romantic "medieval" past, complete with hand-weaving demonstrations and folk singing, while England was symbolized by manufacturing and science, representing the Celtic parts of Britain as if colonies within.

It is unlikely that these fringe theses will be revived in anything resembling their earlier form, but more recently anthropology, although drastically redefined, has been revived as an approach to medieval and early modern texts through the New Historicism and the sporadic impact of the ideas of M. M. Bakhtin.[22] This is also true of the nonliterary scholarship to which much current medieval literary study is indebted. Historians such as Natalie Davis in the United States, Carlo Ginzburg in Italy, Aron Gurevich in Russia, Peter Burke in Great Britain, and the turn toward the history of mentalité among the Annales school infused what used to be the province of folklore and anthropology with renewed importance for other disciplines, albeit in a much more rationalized and less romantic mode.[23] Moreover, the internal critique of anthropology by Marshall Sahlins and Clifford Geertz, and the interest in medieval ritual by Victor Turner has moved medieval studies as much toward anthropology as history. In so doing, we have moved towards an admission of the anthropological status of the Middle Ages from its earliest formulations as a category of knowledge.[24] Beneath its apparent stability as an idea, the Middle Ages repeatedly has been represented as both domestic and foreign, as both historical origin and historical rupture, as both native and "native."

Notes

1. Tariq Ali, *The Book of Salidin* (London: Verso, 1998). Edward Said contributed a blurb to the publication of the novel. See, of course, Edward Said, *Orientalism* (New York: Pantheon, 1978).
2. For an important, but very different, association of orientalism and "anglo-saxonism," see Allen J. Frantzen, *Desire for Origins: New Language, Old Eng-*

lish and Teaching the Tradition (New Brunswick, NJ: Rutgers University Press, 1990).

3. For an analysis of the instability of categories within Orientalist discourse, see Lisa Lowe, *Critical Terrains: French and British Orientalisms* (Ithaca: Cornell University Press, 1991).

4. On the suppression of Arabic sources from the history of medieval literature, see Maria Rose Menocal, *The Arabic Role in Medieval Literary History* (Philadelphia: University of Pennsylvania press, 1987) and Menocal, *Shards of Love: Exile and the Origins of Lyric* (Durham, NC: Duke University Press, 1994).

5. Roland Freart, *A Parallel of the Antient Architecture With the Modern . . . To Which Is Added An Account of Architects and Architecture,* 3rd. ed., trans. John Evelyn (London: T. Browne, 1723), p. 9.

6. Christopher Wren, "On the State of Westminster Abbey," in *Memoires of the Life of Sir Christopher Wren,* ed. James Elmes (London: Priestley and Weale, 1823), p. 110. Molière praised the paintings of his friend Pierre Mignard at Val-de-Grâce, which contrasted with "du fade goût des ornements gothiques,/ Ces monstres odieux des siècles ignorants." *Oevres complètes de Molière,* ed. Eugène Despois and Paul Mesnard (Paris: Hachette, 1886) vol. 9, p. 541.

7. The best guide to the rediscovery of romance in the eighteenth century remains Arthur Johnston, *Enchanted Ground* (London: Athlone, 1964). For a larger framework behind these literary ideas, see René Wellek, *The Rise of English Literary History* (Chapel Hill: University of North Carolina Press, 1941) and *A History of Modern Criticism: 1750–1950,* vol. I: *The Later Eighteenth Century* (New Haven, CT: Yale University Press, 1955). See John M. Ganim, "The Myth of Medieval Romance" in *Medievalism and the Modernist Temper,* ed. R. Howard Bloch and Stephen G. Nichols (Baltimore: Johns Hopkins University Press, 1996), pp. 148–67.

8. Pierre Daniel Huet, *A Treatise of Romances and Their Original* (London: T. Battersby for S. Heyrick, 1672).

9. Joseph Ritson, *Ancient Engleish Metrical Romanceës,* 3 vols. (London: W. Nicol, 1803), p. xxviii.

10. See Richard Hurd, *Hurd's Letters on Chivalry and Romance, with the Third Elizabethan Dialogue,* ed. Edith J. Morley (London: Frowde, 1911), p. 154.

11. George W. Stocking, Jr., *Victorian Anthropology* (New York: Free Press, 1987), p. 23; Thomas Trautmann, *Aryans and British India* (Berkeley: University of California Press, 1997).

12. See R. J. Smith, *The Gothic Bequest: Medieval Institutions in British Thought* (Cambridge: Cambridge University Press, 1987), especially on the politics of the "Norman Yoke" suppressing an essential Anglo-Saxon Englishness and its use as a way of justifying parliamentary power.

13. Stocking, *Victorian Anthropology* is the best study of its subject. See also his *After Tylor: British Social Anthropology 1988–1951* (Madison: University of Wisconsin Press, 1995).

14. Sir James Frazer, *The Golden Bough: A Study of Magic and Religion,* 3rd ed. (New York: St. Martin's Press, 1966).

15. For heavily illustrated studies of international exhibitions and world's fairs in general, see John Allwood, *The Great Exhibitions* (London: Studio Vista, 1977) and Wolfgang Friebe, *Buildings of the World Exhibitions* (Leipzig: Edition Leipzig, 1985). For an extended analysis of the relation of world's fairs to imperial politics, see the important study by Paul Greenhalgh, *Ephemeral Vistas: The Expositions Universelles, Great Exhibitions and World's Fairs, 1851–1939* (Manchester: Manchester University Press, 1988). Approaching American fairs from a similar perspective is Robert Rydell, *All the World's a Fair: Visions of Empire at American International Exhibitions* (Chicago: University of Chicago Press, 1984). The literature on individual world's fairs and international exhibitions is too extensive to list here.

16. Yvonne French, *The Great Exhibition: 1851* (London: Harvill, 1940), remains a good account of the development of the exhibition.

17. *Illustrated Catalogue of the Great Exhibition of 1851* (London: The Art Journal, 1851).

18. An interesting prehistory of the ethnic displays of the international exhibitions can be found in the standard study by Richard D. Altick, *The Shows of London* (Cambridge, MA: Harvard University Press, 1978), esp. pp. 268–301.

19. See *Reminiscences of the Colonial and Indian Exhibition,* ed. Frank Cundall (London: William Clowes, 1886), and E.-T. Hamy, *Études Ethnographiques et Archéologiques sur L'Exposition Coloniale et Indienne de Londres* (Paris: Ernest Leroux, 1887).

20. See Menocal, *Arabic Role.*

21. Roger Sherman Loomis, *Celtic Myth and Arthurian Romance* (New York: Haskell House, 1927); *Arthurian Literature in the Middle Ages: A Collaborative History,* ed. Roger Sherman Loomis (Oxford: Clarendon, 1961).

22. On the ironic Orientalism of Bakhtin's ideas, see John M. Ganim, "Medieval Literature as Monster: The Grotesque Before and After Bakhtin," *Exemplaria* 7 (1995): 27–40.

23. See Traian Stoianovich, *French Historical Method: The* Annales *Paradigm* (Ithaca, NY: Cornell University Press, 1976); John M. Ganim, "The Literary Uses of the New History," in *The Idea of Medieval Literature: New Essays on Chaucer and Medieval Culture in Honor of Donald R. Howard,* ed. James M. Dean and Christian K. Zacher (Newark: University of Delaware Press, 1992), pp. 209–26. For Gurevich, see Aron Gurevich, *Categories of Medieval Culture,* trans. G. L. Campbell (London: Routledge, 1985); *Historical Anthropology of the Middle Ages,* ed. Jana Howlett (Chicago: University of Chicago Press, 1992); *Medieval Popular Culture,* trans. Janos M. Bak and Paul A. Hollingsworth (Cambridge: Cambridge University Press, 1988; for Ginzburg, see Carlo Ginzburg, *The Cheese and the Worms: The Cosmos of a Sixteenth Century Miller,* trans. John and Anne Tedeschi (Baltimore: Johns

Hopkins University Press, 1980); for Davis, see Natalie Zemon Davis, *Society and Culture in Early Modern France* (Stanford, CA: Stanford University Press, 1975); for Sahlins, see Marshall Sahlins, *Islands of History* (Chicago: University of Chicago Press, 1985).

24. On Turner, see the excellent volume edited by Kathleen M. Ashley, *Victor Turner and the Construction of Cultural Criticism* (Bloomington: Indiana University Press, 1990).

CHAPTER 8

THE ROMANCE OF ENGLAND:
RICHARD COER DE LYON, SARACENS, JEWS,
AND THE POLITICS OF RACE AND NATION*

Geraldine Heng

> *This chapter examines how popular romance organizes the emergence of the medieval nation, by manipulating racializing discourses through the circuit of an aggressive, cannibalistic joke.*

> It took considerable efforts of distortion to shape both the land and the people into a vision of a single community.
>
> —Thorlac Turville-Petre, *England the Nation: Language, Literature, and National Identity, 1290–1340*

At the heart of one version of the thirteenth/fourteenth/fifteenth century romance, *Richard Coer de Lyon (RCL)*[1]—whose Middle English texts recount, in romance mode, the putative history of the Third Crusade of Latin Christendom against the Islamic empire of Saladin in the Levant—is a spectacular story of cannibalism performed by the king of England, Richard I. During his siege of the Muslim-occupied city of Acre, the story goes, Richard falls ill from the travails of his sea journey to Syria, the unnatural cold and heat of the local climate, and the unsuitable "mete and drynk" that his body endures on campaign (3043–48). Richard's illness is historically documented; but what follows as cure is purest romance.

In his malady, Richard yearns for pork—animal flesh, I have suggested elsewhere, that in medieval culture symbolically distinguishes Christians from Muslims, who are prohibited by religious orthodoxy from the consumption of swine's flesh. Since they are in Syria, Richard's men discover no pork anywhere to be had, but an "old knyȝt" fashions an ingenious substitute: at the knight's detailed instructions and unbeknownst to Richard, the steward has a young, fat Saracen killed, opened up, and flayed; boiled with saffron and other spices, the freshly killed corpse is turned into a broth for the king's delectation. The dish is simultaneously offered as a tempting delicacy to lure back the king's appetite and for the food's specially curative, medicinal properties; once supped, the king will sleep and sweat off his fever and awaken restored, whole again (3077–3102). Not only does the planned cure perform with remarkable success, but Richard devours his meal with greedy relish, eating faster than his carver is able to carve the human flesh for him (3110), gnawing at the bones of his Saracen victim, and washing the whole down with plentiful drink (3111–12). Richard's folk are delighted at their kindly, healthful, and private joke at the King's expense—"His people turned themselves away and laugh" [Hys ffolk hem tournyd away and lowȝ,] (3114)—a collective prank that mightily restores the king's vitality; and Richard's people duly give thanks to "Jesus and Mary" for their help (3122–23).

Shortly after boisterously returning to skirmish with the Saracens, Richard demands at supper "the head of that same swine of which I ate" (3198–99), because, he says, he feels faint and fears the return of his malady. The cook at first resists, but, threatened with the loss of his own head, returns on his knees with the black, grinning head of the dead (and eaten) Saracen, in a scene that triumphantly stages the horror of the head, its racial difference, and its inhuman, devilish nature. Narrative attention zeroes in on the black face and black beard of the detached head, set off against white teeth that are bared by widely grinning lips (3211–13). Richard's response ("What devil is this?" 3214) is extravagant laughter. He had not known before, he exclaims, that Saracen flesh was this delicious: now his army would never lack for food, since they were able, in any assault, to slay Saracens and take their flesh to boil, roast, or bake, gnawing the flesh to the bones; never again would he and his men fear hunger in their campaign of conquest in the Levant (3216–3226).

What is extraordinary about this bizarre performance of cannibalism by a celebrated English king is less the cannibalism itself than the depiction of cannibalism *as a joke in a popular romance*—a joke that, like romance itself, has healing and aggressive properties; that is to say, a properly romantic kind of joke. Pointedly, the joke here is attached to a historical English king to announce and embellish, not to condemn, his legend: Richard I, one of the most admired of Christian warriors, crusaders, and medieval English monarchs, is a magnificent cannibal of a gloriously unapologetic, aggressive kind.[2] The selection of Richard is an inspired decision: among medieval kings, Richard's personal magnetism, his aura as a crusading leader of Christendom, and his legend as a military genius, are unmatched.[3] Richard is the ideal symbol to figure a magnitude of cultural drives pulsing through the long centuries of this romance's formation: aggressive territorial ambitions, the consumption and discipline of alien communities, and the nascent, overarching impulse toward the formation of the medieval nation.[4]

The Thirteenth Century and Beyond:
Nation and Romance in the Epistemic Crucible

The thirteenth century—the period in which *RCL* was first begun, according to the text's editorial traditions—is not only that century in which inscriptions of medieval nationalism begin to call attention to themselves in a pronounced fashion in the cultural documents of England. I will argue, here, that the thirteenth century is an extraordinary period in medieval history that positions an epistemic break, and witnesses the rise of a new epistemic formation in medieval culture: a formation in which institutions of control are innovatively expanded, intensified, and refined through instruments of inquisition, regulation, and discipline that continue through the later centuries of the Middle Ages. A symbolic moment of this new episteme is constituted by the Fourth Lateran Council under the presiding genius of Pope Innocent III in 1215, a council that generated *seventy* canons—more than double the number issued by any of the three previous Laterans of the preceding century, and more than triple those of Lateran I—and representing a massive codification of rules on a vast array of subjects. There are canons setting out the doctrinal basis upon which heresy would henceforth be relentlessly prosecuted; canons mandating and schematizing the internal examination of the individual Christian through confession (after Lateran IV, it is often noted, confessional manuals proliferate); canons governing marriage, excommunication, and the sacraments; canons instructing on the payment of tithes and taxes and the making of contracts; canons detailing the governance of clergy and clerical conduct, benefices, and parishes; even canons specifying conditions of appearance, dress, and distinguishing badges for racial and religious minorities living throughout Christendom.

If Lateran IV furnished the ideological basis for disciplining the individual by searching out the secrets of conscience hidden within the body, the thirteenth century also infamously witnessed the rise and proliferation of another panopticonic institution aimed at viewing, examining, and controlling the insides of persons: the inquisition, whose methods of interrogation scrutinized the interior, even as its methods of evidence disciplined the exterior by mapping the body's extensive geographies of pain.[5] Close attention to the human microcosm was paired with concomitant attention to the macrocosm of Christendom-at-large. The early century saw an ominous expansion of the uses of the crusade—that military arm of Latin Christendom, comprising the combined might and armies of Europe—an institution originally designed by Pope Urban II a century before to pull together centrifugal forces in the *congregatio fidelium*. In the thirteenth century the crusade was for the first time turned *against* internal members of the *congregatio fidelium* itself: in 1204 the Fourth Crusade captured and eviscerated Constantinople, occupying Greek Christian territory for more than half a century afterward, and irreparably destroying thereafter the capacity of Eastern Christianity to continue in its centuries-long role as a bulwark against Islam in the Mediterranean; from 1208 to 1229 the bloody, relentless persecution and massacre of Albigensians in southern France under the rubric of crusade was inaugurated. Just as the thirteenth century witnessed the church's campaign against so-called schismatics and heretics crystallize in doctrinally and militarily innovative ways, it also witnessed efforts to contain and limit potential deviance by extending the umbra of the church, as the rise of the mendicant orders in the first half of the century attests. The mendicants—a mobile, spiritual army of friars-at-large, undertaking the new, as well as older, religious duties—function, then, as a missionary presence of the church in the field and an essential component of enforcement and ideological reproduction. Answering directly to the pope, the orders supplied the ranks of papal inquisitors admirably: unlike older dispensations, their mobility in ferreting out heresy and heretics everywhere meant an efficient deployment to new tasks. In philosophy and cultural work, the impulse toward containment, assimilation, and regulation finds the century engaged in producing *summae*—vast compendia of knowledge aggregatively systematized; refining the procedures, interrogatory methods, and evidential system of scholasticism; and amassing encyclopedia-like literary compilations, such as the interminable Old French Vulgate cycle of prose Arthurian romances.

It is not a coincidence, then, that a century that saw interiors turned inside out for inspection, and internal partitionings and divisions enacted in Christendom (a logical if ironic consequence of the church's will-to-power and centralizing initiatives) should also witness a fractionalizing, partitioning drive at work in the European polity that powered nascent nationalisms. The rise of medieval nationalism in the crucible of epistemic change is not, I argue, merely conjunctural or accidental. In the thirteenth

century, nationalism in England has at hand examples, ideas, agents, and in-
strumentalities only vestigially (if at all) available earlier. Among the
regimes that develop in the episteme of the thirteenth century and after, I
contend, is *a racializing discourse* posited on religion, color, and bodily difference, the intense and searching examination of which—close attention
to distinguishing details that putatively mark off essences—sets the later
Middle Ages apart from the earlier Middle Ages. Although part of a transformational grammar of race that extends beyond the Middle Ages, the
emergence of a distinctive racializing discourse in the later medieval period specifically attests the instrumentality of racialized categories in the
formation of a medieval nation. That nation is not, of course, a modern
state: among the distinguishing properties of the medieval nation—always
a community of the realm, *communitas regni*—is the symbolizing potential
of the king, whose figural status allows leveling discourses and an expressive vocabulary of unity, cohesion, and stability to be imagined, in a language functioning as the linguistic equivalent of the nation's incipient
modernity.

My discussion of *RCL* as an exemplar of nationalist romance in England from the thirteenth through fifteenth centuries thus has a number of
moments. I begin from the critical commonplace that war, in medieval history as in medieval romance, is a productive channel for nationalism; and
religious war—the crusade—is the productive channel for a nationalism
that, in the Middle Ages, is always and fundamentally traversed, determined, and articulated by religious investments: a specificity of medieval
nationalism. My discussion of a racializing discourse in England that answers to the interests of nation-formation thus follows the example of
RCL by always reading racial difference, including depictions of skin color
and bodily markers, as intersecting with religious difference: with Islam
and Judaism. My selection of an English romance contends, moreover, that
the use of English in medieval England is a bid for a linguistic modernity
and a linguistic nationalism that parallels and articulates the rise of the medieval nation. Finally, the choice of a *popular* romance as an exemplar—
RCL survives in seven manuscripts and two printed editions, and its
narrative is traversed by utopian fictions of class unity and justice—intimates the work of popular literary productions, and popular romances, in
particular, in the discursive work of imagining the nation. For it is in popular, not chivalric, romance that the impetus toward nation formation can
be readily read: chivalric productions being, above all, the ideological property of elites whose class interests are typically overriding, and whose class
culture constitutes chivalry as an international formation whose loyalties
exceed the merely local or national. Although popular romance utilizes
conventions and topoi made conveniently familiar to all audiences by

older modalities of romance, the determinations of popular romance, I suggest, lie elsewhere, and allow the channeling of broader, deeper, and new *national* currents, forms of address, and experimentation.

Black Humor, or the Color Politics of a Cannibalistic Joke: Nationalism, Colonization, History

A joke that works begs to be told more than once, and the romance of Richard/England shows what can be gained when a successful joke is craftily repeated. With Richard's delighted discovery that Muslims can simultaneously be conquered and eaten in military assault (3220–25)—territorial digestion felicitously accompanying alimentary digestion—a *second* episode of cannibalism naturally follows. This second cannibalism is designed as a diplomatic exercise, carefully staged to bring home the full, intimidatory power of Christian military-gustatory aggression to Saladin's aged, aristocratic ambassadors. Richard invites the ambassadors to a state dinner. As the meal's first course, Richard, who happens to have in captivity the sons of the kings of Niniveh, Persia, Samaria, Egypt, and Africa (3598–3603), has these scions beheaded, and their shaven and plucked, cooked heads are set before the Saracen diners who are their kinsmen. Each head arrives on a platter, piping hot, and is arranged so that the face looks upward, with bared, grinning teeth like before, and bears the name of the decapitated prince and his lineage labeled on its brow (3428–30)— every dish being set between two diners, in the grand style of royal and state dinners in medieval literature and history. As the horrified relatives weep over the beardless, hairless heads of their slain family members (3466) and grow terrified for their lives, Richard's own dish of Saracen's head, complete with label, is carved up for him by the royal carver; and, before the horrified eyes of all, Richard the Lionheart devours the flesh with "herte good" (3481)—with a hearty, lion-size appetite. Lest the meaning of this sublimely diabolical performance be lost on the beholder, Richard commands the ambassadors to return to their master, Saladin, with the message that he and his men plan to eat every living Saracen in Saladin's lands, and will not return again to England until every Muslim inhabitant has been eaten (3555–62).

This time around the king of England emphasizes to the Muslim dignitaries that his gustatory practices are not unique to himself, but will be the routine, identifying practice of a generalized commonality of peoples: Englishmen. To an English Christian subject, Richard announces, there is no flesh so nourishing as the flesh of a Saracen ("þer is no fflesch so norysschaunt / Vnto an Ynglyssche Cristen-man . . . As þe flesshe of a Sarazyn," 3548–52): in fact, what defines the Englishman—the national subject—is his delight in eating up the natives in his march of conquest into foreign—international—territory. As Richard gleefully mimes that foreign aggression through a cannibalistic joke, he thus perceptibly conjures up a national collectivity of souls, materializes a unity of Christian Englishmen. The joke, meanwhile, taps conventions of humor that make the transgression of taboos acceptable, narratable: Richard's barbarism in territorial and gustatory arenas can be overlooked, even admired, in the English king's skillful manipulation of a joke's trajectory in overpowering limits of permission, in the push for the punchline; so that the aggressive, nationalistic pleasure can be enjoyed with the full approval of conscience. (It's only a joke, after all.) The meaning of Richard's grisly joke is not, of course, lost on the graybeard ambassadors, whose powerlessness and feebleness are silently echoed in the demasculinized, plucked heads of their murdered kinsmen. In their subsequent report to Saladin—a report that, in a double narration, performatively keeps the shocking scene before our eyes after the actual event has passed—the ambassadors speak directly to the territorial implications of a communalized English, Christian nationalism-cannibalism: now that Richard has won Acre, they urge, he means to go forth to conquer lands east, west, south, and north—the entire Islamic world—and eat their children and themselves (3666–69). In devouring the heirs of Muslim kings and princes of the Orient (3658–61), English Christians will swallow up lineages and sweep away succession, consuming the future itself, in world domination.

A nationalistic joke, of course, is ideal for expressing international aggression, since aggression is precisely the point of its humor. A joke, as Freud once pointed out, cannily taps sources of aggressive pleasure when directed against others; a collective joke, moreover, bribes an audience "into taking sides . . . without any very close investigation" and works to draw "the laughers" over to one's side ("die Lacher auf seine Seite ziehen"), instantly uniting the collectivity of those who laugh and share the joke.[6] Thanks to the circuit of the joke in this romance, nationalist and colonial ambitions are exemplified as continuous—logically partnered with each other in the discourse of war and power. In service to the community of those who would laugh, and share the joke, Richard's act superbly demonstrates ideological mastery by deftly turning an originally affectionate joke against the king, in the first cannibalism, into a collective hostile joke against the enemy, in the second cannibalism: extrapolating, in the process, a community called "England," made up of "good," "English," "Christian men" who are defined by their appetite for Muslims. Before that moment where the collectivity of Englishmen is magically constituted in Richard's speech, however, another defining instant is first necessary: a key genetic recognition when what is *not, and can never be,* English is conclusively identified. The basis of a communal English identity rests on that prior identification when Richard grasps for the first time that he has committed cannibalism: in the shock when the black face of the Saracen head, produced by the terrified cook, stares at him. Richard's gaze instantly takes in, and establishes beyond question, the evidence of cannibalism and the evidence of racial-religious difference, in what is undeniably a racial recognition: the instant in which the darkness of Saracen skin—a biological, genetic marker of racial difference—pulls into stark focus the Islamic otherness of the enemy, in opposition to English Christians. Next comes the Saracen's black beard, a sign of cultural difference—masculinity defined by religion and ethnicity—but a cultural alterity that signally acts to confirm the essential biological nature announced by the skin.[7] So important is this seemingly casual presentation that color is the first thing that we, and Richard, are forced to see, in acknowledging the victim: for the black face ("swarte vys," 3211), "blacke berd," and "whyte teeþ" (3212), and widely grinning lips ("lyppys grennyd wyde," 3213) definitively establish the dead Saracen (and not the cannibalistic Christian king) as the "devil" ("deuyl," 3214) that Richard immediately designates him. Invisibly, via the visible intelligibility of color, a racializing discourse has surfaced alongside the discourse of nationalism and colonization with which it is blended through humor—the racialized humor of the collective national joke.[8]

"There Be Jews Here":
Or, How One Community Consumes
Another in Nationalist Romance

Yet there is one more, important target of the cannibalistic joke lying hidden behind the target of the Saracen head—another racial-religious community of swarthy, bearded Levantines who are also imagined in medieval culture, particularly from the thirteenth century, as devilish, inimically hostile to Christians, and deserving death or a fate worse than death: the Jews. If Richard's demand for a head on a platter seems uncannily to resemble typological revenge for the biblical decapitation of the forerunner and cousin of Christ, we recall that the killing of Jews was an integral part of crusade history as well as of Richard's ascension to the throne of England. The so-called Popular Crusade of 1096, erupting after Urban II's rousing exhortations at Clermont, showed how easily medieval modalities of thought made it possible to slide ideologically from one religious target to another—from the projected massacres of Muslims in the East, the enemy outside Western Europe, to immediate massacres of Jewish communities in the Rhineland, the enemy within Europe itself.[9] The very coronation of

the famed English crusader-king in 1189 occasioned a slaughter of Jews at
Westminster and London that spread to Lynn in Norfolk, Norwich, Stamford, and York—events celebrated by some twelfth century chroniclers
with as much relish as the slaughter of that other infidel enemy in
Richard's campaigns.[10]

The political implications of the medieval capacity to think analogically
are starkly visible in persecutory movements in which the targets of violence shift, spread, and stretch across a spectrum of nonidentical communities. David Nirenberg's discussion of the Shepherds' and Cowherds'
crusades of 1320–21 shows how violence detours beyond its initial targets
to absorb other targets and communities, finally subsuming Muslims, Jews,
lepers, practitioners of sorcery, whose unlikeness and nonidentity are easily bridged by habits of analogical thinking that catch at the underlying resemblance of these targets by virtue of the targets' alterity, their difference
from cultural normativity: a thinking that enables targets to shift, substitute,
and stand in for one another.[11] We should not be surprised, then, to find
Muslims acting strangely like Jews in *RCL*. The historical anti-Jewish libel
of well poisoning, a libel that takes root in Chinon in 1320–21 and infamously recurs in Europe during the Black Death, is attributed here to Saladin, as if Jews and Muslims were identical:

> He leet taken alle þe cors,
> Boþe off dede men, and off hors,
> And caste into þe watyr off oure welle
> Vs to poysoun and to quelle;
> Dede he neuerre a wers dede
> To Crystene-men ffor no nede.
> For þorw3 þat poysoun, and that brethe,
> Ffourty þousand toke her dethe. (2749–56)

This depiction of Muslims as virtual Jews in the calumny of well poisoning is part of *RCL*'s narrative from at least the earliest surviving manuscript of the text, the fragment in the Auchinleck, dated circa
1330—about a generation after the expulsion of Jews from England in
1290, and the nearly simultaneous loss of the last crusader colony, Acre, to
Muslims in 1291. Significantly, although awash with Saracens, *RCL* is ignorant about medieval Muslims and their religion: Islam is not a
monotheism prohibiting deistic representation; rather, Saracen idols, gods,
and temples abound; "heathen" and "pagan" are interchangeable synonyms; and the Islamic "gods"—Mahoun (Mohammad), Termagant, Ap-
polyn (Apollo), Jupiter—are mere conventions familiarized by the
chansons de geste. Richard, a home-grown hero, resembles the Richard of

medieval chronicles, but Saladin is a mere *chanson* villain. If this romance written in England is unfamiliar with the foreign enemies of Christendom it describes in Outremer, what other enemies of Christendom might it be more familiar with, closer to home in England, who might come to mind in conceiving threats to *communitas Christiana* and English interests?

Despite the early Augustinian tradition of relative tolerance toward Jews in Christian communities, and protections occasionally extended by pope, ecclesiastic, and emperor, Christian polemicists from the twelfth century on increasingly accumulated arguments that positioned Jewish institutions, traditions, and practices as cornerstones upon which the consolidation of Christian doctrine and principles might be established. The rhetorical strategies of Odo of Cambrai, Guibert of Nogent, Rupert of Deutz, Petrus Alphonsi, Peter Abelard, and Peter the Venerable variously represented Jews as the antithesis of Christians, depicting Jewish rejection of the Incarnation as evidence of a literality—an incapacity for allegorical and metaphoric thinking—that rendered the Jew subhuman, animal-like, through a lack in the faculty of reason (Abulafia). In the thirteenth century, the ideological reduction of Jews to animality found hideous expression in the *Judensau,* the conflation of Jews with swine, tabooed animals in Judaism as much as Islam, in "portrayals of Jews sucking at the teats of a sow."[12] Also from the thirteenth century come confirmed blood libels against Jewish communities—the calumny that Jews murdered Christians, especially children, because Christian blood was consumed in Passover rituals—a thinly disguised accusation of vampiric cannibalism. A period of special epistemic virulence toward Jews, the thirteenth century issued the libel of Jewish Host-desecration—a libel that freshened the old tradition that Jews were the killers of Christ, by insinuating that Christ's deicide at Jewish hands was not only conscious, but repeated *post mortem* through Jewish torture and destruction of the Eucharist. A twelfth-century polemicist like Rupert of Deutz may have considered Jews rather than Muslims the antithesis of Christians, but the thirteenth century witnessed the consolidation of Jews as the standard by which contempt for enemies could be measured and fittingly expressed: Robert de Clari's chronicle on the Fourth Crusade's annexation of Constantinople reports that the bishops of Soissons, Troyes, and Halberstadt and the abbot of Loos vindicated Latin Christendom's attack on Greek Christendom as righteous by decisively dismissing the Byzantine victims as "worse than Jews."[13]

In the new episteme, then, *RCL*'s two cannibalisms seem to serve up a special kind of punishment, and English Christendom's communal narration on what kind of justice Jews, as much as Saracens, deserve. For the killers of Christ who cannibalistically require Christian blood, what better desert could there be than the answer of Semitic heads on a platter, to be cannibalistically consumed in turn by Christian Englishmen? Moreover, the covert, second meaning of the cannibalistic scenes must be arrived at— can only be read—*allegorically,* since the decapitated heads in the foreground are ostensibly Saracen ones: through allegory, then, a race believed incapable of grasping allegory—their defining difference from Christians, who are expert exegetical readers and manipulators of biblical allegory— may be fittingly humiliated. The polemical equation of Jews with carnality, animal senses, and the body, and the *Judensau's* conflation of Jews with swine make Richard's desire for swine's flesh, and his eating of humans as if they were animals, grotesquely meaningful. Even the image of the grinning maws of Richard's victims has a counterpart in the *adversus Judaeos* tradition: Guibert de Nogent, for example, counterposes a polemic around the "filthy gaping jaws" of the Jews, the "mouths which . . . mock the life-giving sacraments," mouths that are forever closed by their tortuous passage through Richard's purposeful joke.[14]

That Jews, as much as Muslims, are the targets in *RCL*'s two scenes of cannibalism is aided by medieval Christendom's understanding that Jews collaborated with Muslims in Islamic invasions of Europe and Jerusalem. Oppressed Jews in Visigothic Spain were believed to have conspired with, invited, and assisted Arab and Berber invaders from the Mahgreb against the Visigothic Catholic monarch, Roderick, in the second decade of the eighth century, a consequence of the fact that in Visigothic Spain after 589, Jews were persecuted, exiled, or forced to convert.[15] Several thousand Jews were reputed to have fought alongside Abd-al Rahman and 10,000 Berbers against Charles Martel at Poitiers in 732. Closer to the crusades, "Adhemar of Chabannes (c. 1028) and the Cluniac Ralph Glaber (c. 1044) testify to the belief, widespread among the Christians of France, that the Jews were in league with the Muslims and that the destruction of the Holy Sepulchre in 1009 by the Fatimid caliph of Egypt, al-Hakim, was a product of a joint Islamo/Judaic conspiracy."[16] In Saladin's time, the closeness between Muslims and Jews was suggestively expressed when the Kurdish emperor, upon recapturing Jerusalem, brought in Jews to resettle the holy city.[17] The imagined co-identity of Christendom's enemies is symbolically rendered in Lateran IV's Canon 68, which assigns a distinction in clothing to mark off Jews and Saracens alike, collectively and together, from Christians, as if the two infidel nations were halves of a single body of aliens.

If the medieval ideological mind is able to confuse Jews with Muslims, *RCL*'s obsessive description of the forcible mass conversions of Saracens can be seen as more than just a simple fantasy. With seeming ahistoricity, *RCL* offers conversion as a major objective of crusader colonization: mass conversion follows the conquest of Niniveh (5370–71) and Babylon (5881–82); the crusaders demand conversion at Ebedy (4421–25); and in a declaration of crusade policy, Richard orders Philip Augustus to put to the sword everyone he finds in "Toun, cytee, and castel" who will not convert (3821–28), an imperative Richard repeats to his own army (3965–70). In *RCL,* territorial annexation is synonymous with forcible conversion, and the alternative to conversion is death. History, by contrast, shows Muslim conversion to Christianity in the Levant as infrequent and sporadic; enough of a novelty for it to be noticed, commented on, and recorded when it happened; and overwhelmingly dictated by the self-interest or faith of each individual.[18] Indeed, medieval history shows that it is *Jews in Europe* who are forced to undergo conversion, or suffer death at the hands of Christians, more than Muslims in the Holy Land: forcible conversion or death is a choice repeatedly offered to Jewries in medieval England, France, Spain, and Germany. In playing thus with historical conditions that seem to vanish in medieval romance only to reappear, transformed, *RCL* hints at a curious parallel when it elects to articulate its theme of (Muslim) conversion with its theme of territorial dispossession and repossession in the Holy Land. For not only are Jews the most prominent alien community in England denied ownership of land in fee while subject to periodic eruptions of forcible conversion or death, but an accident of economic history also made landless English Jews "the vehicle" and visible medium for the transfer of land ownership in England of the twelfth and thirteenth centuries—and thus a figure of territorial dispossession and repossession in the home country of this romance.[19]

RCL's spectacles of conversion also eloquently speak to a history of conversion enacted in the English homeland. While inducements to convert to Christianity were sporadic in twelfth-century England—typically the spillovers of mob violence—in the thirteenth century, under repeated papal and ecclesiastical attentions, the discourse of conversion systematized into formal institutions of recruitment that received the endorsement of English kings; English kings even "began to confiscate Jewish synagogues and turn them into churches." In 1232 Henry III formally established a "Domus Conversorum" for Jewish converts to Christianity, and baptisms of converted Jews were enacted before the king, "who took evident pleasure in naming the new converts."[20] Proselytization "was henceforth carried on more and more systematically"; by the 1240s and 1250s Jewish converts to Christianity "may have numbered as many as 300 in a total Jewish population that did not exceed 5,000 and that may have been as low as 3,000."[21] By 1280 Edward I required all Jews to attend conversionist sermons preached at them during Lent to turn them from Judaism, "in accordance with the Papal Bull *Vineam Sore* of the previous year."[22]

The presence of a visible, economically active Jewish community in England living "cheek by jowl" with Christians[23]—a presence especially

prominent in major cities like London and York, and in eastern and southeastern England—must have been troubling, because communal identity
is defined not only *against* but also always *in terms of* the other. English
Christians depended on Jews for the support of economic life, religious
crusades, and transactions of knowledge, culture, and doctrinal theology.
And unlike national rivals across the sea or ethnic antagonists sharing a
border with the English polity—the French, Irish, Welsh, Scots—Jews
constituted a prominent resident alien community *within* England itself,
as England was consolidating as a nation; an alien community whose existence and daily activities were intimately bound up with the economic
and social life of the dominant community but from which, nonetheless,
it necessarily remained apart, by virtue of fundamental differences of race-
religion. That the status of Jews is an obsessive target of attention for a medieval English society in transition, for English kings enlarging their fiscal
and ideological resources, and for prelates consolidating Christian doctrine is attested to by the panopticonic gaze witnessed in a series of ever-
changing statutes, provisions, and obsessions that met at the locus of
Jewish identity.

English economic dependence on Jewish mediation in finance, and the
crown's dependence on tallages levied on English Jewry (after Henry II
dispensed with loans in favor of straightforward methods of fiscal extrac-
tion), meant that the association of Jews with profit drew as much inquis-
itive scrutiny as the threat of race-and-religion that Jews, as domestic
aliens, were able to figure for the polity. Documents of debt to Jews and
excitement over putative Jewish wealth featured prominently in anti-Jewish attacks, along with forced conversions. Not surprisingly, thus, profit and
conversion are linked themes in *RCL*. Richard warns Philip Augustus not
to accept bribes of "gold, syluer" or any reward (3824) offered by desperate infidels: historically apt counsel to the king of France, since French
Jewries may have escaped the conversions or death suffered by their coreligionists in the Rhineland in 1096 by buying off crusaders with large
bribes. Richard's own practices show how the fiscal resources of his victims could profit Christians, so that "Earl, baron, knight, commoner/Had
as much as they wanted" (5891–92), a haunting reminder of how attacks
against Jews in the wake of Richard's ascension festivities in England also
profited the Christian benefactors of violence, especially would-be, self-
described crusaders. Roger of Howden tells of failed bribery, plunder, the
killing of Jews, and the burning of records of debt to Jews at York; Roger
of Wendover recounts the slaying of Jews at Norwich, Stamford, and St.
Edmunds by crusaders, and plunder and the burning of debt papers at
York; William of Newburgh describes plunder at Lynn, plunder and killing
at Stamford by crusaders for the expenses of Richard's crusade, and even

more massive plunder by crusaders for the same purpose at York, along with forcible and failed conversions and mass slaughter.[24]

Other foreign themes in *RCL* are also acted out by domestic subjects in English history. At *RCL*'s romance banquet, Saracen guests are conspicuously present, and princely Saracen victims are killed at Richard's command. Historically, Jews were conspicuously required to be *absent* from Richard's coronation banquet, although they were soon also killed, it is thought, by the king's command. Two of the Jews persecuted at the time of the banquet and shortly after—Benedict and Joceus of York—are likened by medieval chroniclers to princes who live in near-regal luxury, in homes likened to palaces.[25] Benedict was immortalized in chronicles as the Jew who was converted to Christianity during the attacks at Richard's coronation, and who subsequently reconverted to Judaism.[26] Benedict's trajectory—from Judaism to Judaism, with a temporary detour through Christianity—thus queerly mimes the trajectory of the renegade at Orgulous, in *RCL,* who proceeds from Christianity to Christianity, with a temporary detour through Islam (4076ff, 4215–25). Even the labels on the Saracen heads at Richard's banquet, functioning as badges of identity for the victims, seem queerly to reproduce the Jewish "badges of shame" that also proclaimed identity and filiation (and that, as specified by the Statute of Jewry of 1275 were as large as labels: six inches long by three inches wide).[27] Finally, if the romance Richard treats his Saracen victims as if they were not fully and autonomously human, and little more than chattel, we note that the historical Richard, the king of England, possessed English Jews by right, customarily, from the time of Edward the Confessor on, as legally the property or chattel of the crown.

Although Canons 67 through 70 of Lateran IV furnished an ideological guide of general principles for containment, specifying conditions under which Jews were required to tender tithes, refrain from public appearance on certain days of Holy Week, be prohibited public office, and exhibit differences of dress from Christians, thirteenth-century England took the policing, marking, and scrutiny of Jewish activity and bodies to enthusiastic lengths. A scant three years after Lateran IV, English Jews had to wear that infamous badge which publicly marked off their difference. In 1222 the demand for Jewish self-identification was repeated at the Council of Oxford, which specified the size of the badge for Jews of both sexes. In 1253 Henry III ordered the badge to be worn in a prominent position on the breast, and in 1275 Edward I's *Statutum de Judeismo* increased the badge's size, demanded that it be exhibited prominently over the heart, specified color, and ordered all Jewish *children* above the age of seven to display the badge. If a whiff of communal hysteria seems to touch the obsession over the size, color, placement, prominence, and universality of the

Jewish badge, we understand that the manipulation of domestic minorities is a formative moment in the self-construction of national majorities. Knowing who and what a religious-racial minority is, is an essential stage in knowing who and what a national majority is, and is not: the stable, legible categories of the one fiction enabling and stabilizing the categories of the other. Getting the lineaments of the two communities inhabiting the homeland fixed, visible, and clear is thus a project of some urgency, and in 1287 the Diocesan Synod of Exeter accordingly forbade Jews to employ Christian servants, hold public office, feast with Christians, attend Christians in the capacity of physicians, venture into churches, leave houses or even keep windows open at Eastertide, withhold tithes, or omit the wearing of the Jewish badge: prohibitions that ruminated on and ramified the prescriptive strictures of Lateran IV.[28] Even as these prohibitions advertise the fears of religious authority, they also tellingly announce English Christian dependence on and intimacy with English Jews—a comingling in private and public life that disturbed the project of stable, known, and separate identities within England's borders.[29]

The expulsion of the Jews from England in 1290 by Edward can thus be viewed as a social as well as an economic phenomenon. In economic terms, the expulsion has been rightly read as the culminating logic of a long process of systematic exactions that depleted the Jews' financial resources, with profit accruing to the crown also from the expulsion. In social terms, the eviction is legible as part of a processional logic of national consolidation that occurred in thirteenth-century England, a logic that renders the inassimilable aliens who are too intimately interwoven into the life of the Christian communal body to be useful through the very process of their excision from that body. At least one scholar has demonstrated how the removal of the Jewish community in England—an inconveniently present "Israel of the flesh"—facilitated the substitution of the *English themselves* as the new chosen community of God—an "Israel of the spirit"—as an emerging nationalist idea: a substitution that witnesses the cultural colonization of an old, familiar biblical topos for new, secular, and nationalist purposes, once Jews themselves, the old chosen people of God, were no longer present in the flesh to hinder imaginative reconfiguration in the nation's interest.[30] In the context of that cultural logic, the fate of the *Domus Conversorum,* home for converts from Judaism, seems highly symbolic, and even ironically inevitable. After the Jewish expulsion, in the last decade of the thirteenth century the *Domus* was converted into a residence for clerks of Chancery conducting government business; it then became, in the fourteenth century, "the recognized center for Chancery business, called the . . . Rolls House until the Public Record Office was built on the same site in 1845 and 1895."[31]

With eloquence, the home where once-Jews were found became the site where the business of the new nation of England was recorded and kept, the official repository of England itself, once Jews were evicted from the national homeland: a potent symbol of the consolidation of the nation on the cornerstone of minority identity.

In English history, the alien infidels at home ultimately prove indigestible, and are expelled from England. In English romance, the alien infidels safely at a distance across the sea prove eminently digestible, and become a welcome part of the English diet of jokes, into which they are then incorporated. Romance, of course, is skilled at offering presence in the place of absence, a vocabulary for speaking difference differently, and for magical transformations: like the *Domus Conversorum*, romance is the perfect site for multiple conversions, in the making of a nation.

A Matter of England:
Nation, Christendom, Language,
"Class," and Other Romance Matters

Against contemporary theorization in the Western academy that locates the emergence of nations and nationalisms in modern, postmedieval periods of history—usually the eighteenth and nineteenth centuries—medievalists have struggled in recent years to outline specifically medieval forms of the nation, and of nationalist feeling and identification, even arguing for the rise of the nation-*state* and statism during the European Middle Ages itself. Although the arguments are multifarious and undeniably *en procès,* a consensus has emerged that discourses of the nation in the medieval period, like nationalist discourses of the eighteenth and nineteenth centuries, hinge on Ben Anderson's formulation of the nation as an "imagined (political) community" while departing in other details—cultural, social, political, economic—from nationalist formations in postmedieval centuries. Key to the notion of an imagined community, medievalist scholarship decides, is self-identification by a national grouping, especially in defining one's national community against large communities of others in oppositional confrontations over territory, political jurisdiction, and dominion, and in warfare. Part of that self-identification involves a recognizably national form of address perceptible in the literary, historical, and cultural documents of a country at various stages of medieval nationalist discourse. Equally distinctive is the production of a symbolic system that uniquely signals and presents a nation as occupying different cultural and symbolic space from others within transnational groupings such as Western Christendom. Finally, the role of language, geographical boundedness, and ideologies of solidarity that cut across competing, antagonistic interests among the social and economic groups in feudal society are indispensable components of the nation-in-progress.

Medievalists agree that from the thirteenth century onward, discourses of the nation are visible and can be read with ease in medieval England, aided by the boundedness of insular geography and despite (or because of) holdings in France by the English monarch and barony and England's annexations of territorially contiguous neighbors.[32] Indeed, chronicle histories display a nascent sense of an "English" identity among Anglo-Normans from the end of the twelfth century—or even, as John Gillingham has argued, from as early as the mid-twelfth century.[33] English military confrontations with the Welsh, Irish, Scots, and French in the twelfth and thirteenth centuries—when "English power . . . was institutionalised in Wales and Ireland"—deepened an emerging national community's projection of its difference from its contingent enemies: we are reminded that "the Magna Carta revolt as it appears from an English perspective, was also a war of . . . the French, the Welsh, and the Scots against the English—and was so perceived at the time," while Henry III's struggles against Louis VIII of France "polarized the difference between English and French interests and encouraged a sense of apartness on both sides of the Channel"[34] For Matthew Paris, the great nationalist historian, the struggles between England and France in the early thirteenth century assume the proportions of a contest between nations; it is he who, in the thirteenth century, renders England as a territorially distinct and bounded political and symbolic entity in his detailed maps of England, which produce the nation as a mappable collectivity with a known geography, occupying a distinctive, separate space of its own.[35] Despite the truism that "'The nation . . . is an abstraction, an allegory, a myth that does not correspond to a reality that can be scientifically defined,'" the medieval cartographer's projection of a geopolitical category—territorial space coincident with the name of the nation, uniquely shaped and set off—is a powerfully performative moment, a moment that enacts and points to the performativity of nationalist discourse, and the power of such discourse to bring nations into being: "a dry, rancorous political fact" of national history is that "'Nationalism is not the awakening of nations to self-consciousness; [nationalism] *invents* nations where they do not exist.'"[36] By the late thirteenth century, the anonymous author of the *Cursor Mundi* easily names "ingland the nacione" and specifies the "Englis tong" as a unifying "speche" possessed by "englijs men in comune."[37]

In the fourteenth century, Edward III's assertion of sovereignty over France and his claim to the French throne over the Valois monarch's—the pretext that inaugurates the so-called Anglo-French war of a hundred years—merely brings to dramatic culmination, then, a long process of nationalist self-assertion at the expense of England's territorial enemies. Fortuitously, for a popular English romance that would articulate its nationalism through the crusader rivalry of an English king, Richard I, and a French king, Philip II, the war in the later fourteenth century once more pitted an English Richard (Richard II) against a hated French Philip (Philip VI), in a richly symbolic coincidence: Richard's father, Edward III, had even suggested to Philip another joint crusading enterprise of English and French armies against the Saracens.

One necessary instrumentality is a vocabulary of symbols that underpin the imagining of a national totality. Among *RCL's* contributions is the spinning of a national insult into a shared communal badge with a touch of pride for Englishmen: the romance makes the rude folk epithet, *caudatus anglicus* (tailed English) hurled by enemies at Richard's men into a unifying resource to describe the English community's vaunt that they make their French counterparts turn tail in war (2016). The bandying-about of the epithet in strategic contexts produces a badge of identity that horizontally knits together the English "taylardes" (tailed ones) of high, low, and middling degrees into community under a single, homogenized, and witty rubric.[38] Another emblem is Richard's axe "that was wrought in England" (6802). That terrifying weapon, used only by the English king in *RCL,* was a favorite of Anglo-Saxon warriors: both housecarls, the elite professional guard of the thegn's *domus,* and the fyrd, or army of conscripts, are depicted in the Bayeux Tapestry as wielding the battle-ax at Hastings; even the Anglo-Saxons of the Byzantine emperor's Varangian guard legendarily wielded the weapon. The Tapestry also depicts Duke William using the battle-ax, which Anglo-Normans continued to employ after Hastings. Economically, Richard's ax unites two opposing military and political lineages, signaling their combination in the now-English king who deftly handles a cultural icon common to both.[39] Richard's use of bees to attack Saracens (2905ff) has equally resonant symbolism, since honey was to Western European domestic production what sugar was to the export culture of the Levant. Egypt and Syria—Saladin's empire and the domicile of *RCL's* Saracens—were great producers of sugar through the Middle Ages (even during the economic decline of the Levantine sugar industry in the fifteenth century) and supplied Western Europe's demand for sugar long after the last crusader state had vanished;[40] by contrast, honey is Europe's export to Egypt and Syria.[41] The visibility of sugar as an export of the East guarantees that bees, honey, and hives would constitute an excellent symbolic marker for domestic culture in the West: when the king of England has hives hurled into Acre, then, and the bees stingingly harass the Saracens, a defiant statement of economic and ideological superiority is made of a distinctly vengeful kind—a thumbnail sketch of *translatio imperii,* the

West's ascension to economic and cultural hegemony over the East, bit-ingly expressed. In case we miss the point, Christians themselves are later likened to swarming bees (5793–94). Richard's spectacular windmill that seems to grind men's bones instead of wheat or barley is an ideological boast of the same kind (2656–82), a hyperbolic reminder of English tech-nological superiority: the first attested windmill in Europe is found in Yorkshire in 1185, and according to Ambroise's eyewitness account of Richard's crusade, crusaders constructed the first windmill ever known in Syria (3227–29).[42]

It is important to remember that the form of the English nation, dur-ing the long period of *RCL's* making, is that of the *communitas regni*. Eng-land is an imagined political *community of the realm*—a medieval nation-as-kingdom, with the ruler at its apex—rather than a constitution-ally driven modern nation-state, with state apparatuses—although a me-dieval nation that is undeniably possessed of a nascent impetus toward horizontal leveling. In the drive of nationalist discourses toward horizon-tal linkages—solidarities with the vital "ability to rouse unlike peoples in dramatically unlike conditions in an impassioned chorus of voluntary co-operation and sacrifice"[43]—Christianity itself has traditionally furnished exploitable ideological resources. Clearly visible in *RCL,* a text that nar-rates nationalism in tandem with militant Christianity, is what might be called *a class dissimulation,* a projective discourse of baronial and monarchic subscription to equitable distributions of compensation for military labor. According to this popular romance, the English king and his knights are committed to the fair distribution of wealth among all Christian men, in-cluding commoners, boys, and servants: Richard, as the king who repre-sents the community, sets the example by sharing "gret tresour" (5889) with all—"the high and the low" (6527)—so that each had as much as he wished to have (5892), an example also scrupulously adhered to by Richard's lieutenants, Fouk Doyly at Ebedy (4605–8, 4676–77) and Sir Thomas of Multoun at Castle Orgulous (4287–94). It is commonality of membership in the Christian community—and masculine military labor—that drives the utopian fiction that fair distribution is possible in feudal cul-ture. Rewriting the history of the First Crusade, when the Christian poor died in droves during famine at the siege of Antioch, the rich of the Third Crusade in this romance charitably share their wealth during famine at the siege of Acre, so that the plight of both greater and lesser Christian folk (2873) is ameliorated. Revealingly, as the crusaders are sharing in the spoils of their military labor, it is specifically only *English* Christians who are de-picted as receiving their share of spoils—not French, Greek, or other Christians. In demonstrating how membership in an overarching Christ-ian community can subserve, rather than subtract from, nationalist impulses and discourses, *RCL* identifies the enabling possibilities of ideological manipulation in wielding religion as an expressly *national* resource.[44]

But the fair distribution of wealth set in motion by the English king also strongly suggests a *secular* fiction of utopian justice at work in this romance: a broadly national utopianism that exercises a broadly populist kind of justice. Richard's distribution of "great treasure" to all, both high and low, represents the medieval king as *directly* accountable to his populace—thus subverting the imported Norman-Angevin-Plantagenet feudal system in which the king had no direct political access to the population at large, but only an access governed by and mediated through innumerable layers of subinfeudation. By representing the medieval monarch as accountable directly to all his men, the class dissimulation in this popular romance slyly undercuts feudal modalities of hierarchy and the fossilized stratifications of power typical in feudalism—a dissimulation no doubt especially attractive in fourteenth- and fifteenth-century England, when social mobility is a channel of hope and opportunity for all but the *haute* nobility. This populist representation is strategically aided by nostalgic echoes from an Anglo-Saxon past before the advent of Norman feudalism, a nostalgia located, for instance, in Richard's preference for Anglo-Saxon toasts("Wesseyl," 6816). Of course, nationalist manipulations of this kind are still marked by the discourse of rampant militarism: in the same narrative breath that describes the sharing of wealth, we are told of the dispossession of the Islamic inhabitants of the Levant, as English crusaders are given Muslim property, lands, cities, and homes (4602–4, 4660–63, 4295–99) and the conquered territories of the East are repopulated by the English Christians of the West, who readily celebrate their triumphant share in colonization and empire formation. We are reminded, in *RCL's* discourse of nationalism, that a nation secures its borders and identity in part by the aggressive outward extension and consolidation of borders: the romance example thus evocatively anticipates the postmedieval historical example of Victorian and modern imperial England.

In the discourse of the nation, Middle English romances form a special category of cultural articulation, though an equally privileged literature is also, of course, that genre of English chronicle histories of England/Britain called the *Brut,* spawned from Geoffrey of Monmouth's Latin *Historia Regum Britannie* and its French vernacular derivatives. By contrast, the epic, according to Diane Speed, is the one narrative genre that runs counter to nationalist discourse (because the "chain-reaction of destruction" in epic thematizes social disorder, chaos, and extralegality, all antithetical to national formations). Speed and others insist that the medieval English romance constitutes a literature ideally consonant with and fully of "a type with the discourse of the nation": "It is immediately clear, merely from the overt

subject matter, that a number of these romances belong in the discourse of
the nation, that they have as a primary function a construction of England
that articulates the partially conceptualized impulses observable in the new
English-language writing of the preceding century."[45] Because the narrative
address of large numbers of English romances seem to be distinctively popular or national, or both, and to share a coherency of assumptions, conventions, and mutuality of reference, scholars have argued that English
romances, despite French counterparts or originals, effectively comprise a
textual community of their own.[46] The sine qua non of their textual com-
munality is, of course, that the romances are written in *English*—not French
or Latin, transregional or international languages. The choice of English was
a choice in favor of exclusivity, since English ensured that the romances addressed only an insular audience, eschewing the outside, and all possibility
of international reception: "the very act of writing in English," as Turville-
Petre puts it, "is a statement about belonging," about making a literature
available only to a national audience in England.[47]

RCL, which begins by announcing its decision to narrate its tale in
English because scarcely one among a hundred nonlearned men can understand the tale in French (21–24), represents its choice of English as a
populist move, a bid for the broadest possible address. To insist on a world
of difference between English and French, this romance claims English as
the language used by Richard and his knights: when a knight brings good
news about an unguarded gate that will give the siege army unresisted
entry into Messina, he emphatically brings the news to Richard as "Tales
in Englyssh, stoute and bolde" (1916). Good news comes in English—not
French—and no doubt this romance itself, dramatically also a tale in English, stout and bold, is part of the corpus of good news. Nationalist consciousness requires that the romance Richard *has* English, unlike the
French-speaking historical Richard, a king notorious for having spent a
mere six months in England in his decade-long reign, and his disloyal joke
that he would have sold off London itself, had he been able to find a buyer.

The Plantagent king linked to the earliest public communication in
English is not, of course, Richard, but John's son, Henry III, whose confirmation of the Provisions of Oxford in 1258 was issued in English in "the
month of October in the two-and-fortieth year of our reign." By pro-
claiming his confirmation not only in French, the language of his baronial
elites who had coerced Henry into the Provisions, but also in English, the
language of the other social classes of his realm, Henry's act affords a
glimpse of how English, in the mid-thirteenth century, arcs across divisions
of class and power and reaches into "every . . . shire over all the kingdom
in England."[48] After Henry, the romance Richard's association with English, not French, is perhaps meant to recall Edward I, who, "facing the

French attack in 1295, accused the French of trying to exterminate the English language"[49]—a vilification that underscores the unifying possibilities of linguistic nationalism. The contention, in the parliaments of 1295, 1344, 1346, and 1376, that French victory in the Anglo-French wars would "annihilate the English language"[50] argues that English, by the fact that it was not the lingua franca of England's hostile continental competitor and enemy, came to be associated with the nation itself.

RCL's Richard at Jaffa even launches his attack against his foes with an English joke, when he announces that he has come to drink to his foes' health: "Wesseyl j schal drynke ȝow too!" (6816). "Wesseyl," which descends from the Anglo-Saxon "wæs-hæil," is a greeting and toast unforgettably depicted in Geoffrey's *Historia* as offered by Renwein, daughter of Hengist (chief among the Saxon invaders of Britain), to the British king Vortigern ("Lauerd king, Waesseil!")[51] to seduce him and begin the Saxon settlement of Britain. The romance Richard not only knows his British history but represents himself, in a word, as aligned with Anglo-Saxon English and England. Deliberately, in *RCL,* a linguistic and political history is retrieved that ignores the Norman conquest of 1066 and French rule.

In arcing back centuries to a language that is a momento of preconquest England, the romance breaks with the more recent, French-dominated past: a break that is necessary in articulating both national identification and a paradoxical modernity for English society. Nationalist identification, it has been said, requires a strategic act of forgetting: "Forgetting . . . is a crucial factor in the creation of a nation," especially the willed forgetting of a minus-in-the-origin, the "deeds of violence which took place at the origin of all political formations."[52] One strategy in the *communitas regni* is to forget Richard's continental descent through his parents Henry II and Eleanor of Aquitaine, his grandparents Geoffrey of Anjou and the Empress Matilda, and his great-grandfather Henry I's parent, William of Normandy, the invader of England: and to remember, instead, Richard's Anglo-Saxon heritage through his great-grandmother Matilda, Henry I's wife—a woman "descended from the stock of King Alfred"[53] and "a kinswoman of King Edward [the Confessor]" (Anglo-Saxon Chronicle s.a. 1100), whose own mother Margaret had been the great-granddaughter of Edmund Ironside. A royal genealogy traced through the Saxon female line bypasses the Norman invasion, and represents the imagined political community as newly remade from the shards of an older past nostalgically retrievable in an array of linguistic and narrative artifacts, from weapons, to lineages, to toasts.[54]

In the fourteenth and fifteenth centuries, a bid for English is also a bid for a linguistic modernity from the languages available in England. In that contest of languages, Latin—magisterial, scholarly, statutory, ecclesiastical—was irredeemably bound to ancient history and church power, just as French—still preferred by the great nobles (as supposedly represented in their library collections) and the language of law, government, and diplomacy—was bound to the history of an elite minority and insular colonization.[55] Anglo-French, moreover, had increasingly assumed the status of a provincial dialect, a medium whose pastness was emphasized by the fact that the centers of French linguistic authority and vigor lay elsewhere, on the continent. By contrast, English, without the burden of association with French dominion, and derived from a pre-Norman era before the fall into French feudalism, could—in a period that was soon to exhaust feudalism—fortuitously be reinvested as the language most paradoxically allied to the modern and the new: the language with the greatest potential for articulating new, broad-based currents of transformation channeling through English society. Froissart's contention that "in about 1337 Edward III ordered the gentry and bourgeoisie of England to teach their children French 'so that they would become better able and qualified for their wars'"[56] expresses the common notion that it was English which was the normative, everyday language of the commons: of bourgeoisie and gentry, social groups whose ambitions, capital accumulation, and mobility were busily disrupting feudal certitudes and categories, and powering the engine of England's economic modernity in the late Middle Ages. English was the language of an emerging new literature catering to these urban interests and social classes—a linguistic community ably tapped by Chaucer—and the tongue of a heterogenous collectivity of peoples that was assuming the proportions of a national formation. The very diversity and proliferation of English dialects in the fourteenth and fifteenth centuries, so memorably captured in Chaucer's rueful fretting over his text ("ther is so gret diversite / In Englissh and in writyng of oure tonge" [*Troilus* 1793–94]), testifies to the health and sheer vitality of English, a language vigorously expanding its range and usages and active in its growth, resources, and dispersal. Significantly, Caxton, England's first commercial print publisher (a man with a "sure sense of the public's tastes, many parts of which he may well have solidified"[57]) used the new, modern print technology for issuing books almost exclusively in English, himself translating works from Latin and French into English.

In 1362, as John Fisher points out, Parliament admitted for the first time that it was addressed in English, and passed a statute for court proceedings henceforth to be "conducted in English because the litigants could not understand French"; and "the parliaments of 1363, 1364, and 1381 were opened in English."[58] Fisher persuasively argues that early in the fifteenth century, Henry V saw that in English lay the linguistic future of the nation, and, from 1417 until his death in 1422, used English "in nearly all his correspondence with the government and the citizens of London and other English cities," setting an example followed by literary authors and "establishing English as the national language of England."[59]

Among texts exercising the discourse of the nation, *RCL* ranks as one of the most popular of English romances in terms of manuscript survival, tying in a dead heat with *Bevis of Hampton* and the *Siege of Jerusalem*.[60] After the advent of print technology, *RCL* continued to be chosen for publication: Wynkyn de Worde, Caxton's commercially minded successor after 1491 at the Westminster press, included *RCL* among his offerings in 1509 and 1528; John Purfoot, a later publisher, secured a license for reissuing *RCL* in 1568–69, and manuscript copies of *RCL* still circulated in the sixteenth century (a copy being owned by "a certain James Haword" in 1562).[61] The popularity of *RCL* may owe something to the romance's strategy of interpellating an especially broad range of constituents as an internal narrative constituency along with the mandatory constituents of king, courtiers, and knights: thus it is that servant boys (5891) receive ample compensation for military labor alongside the barony and knights (5891); and when the English king summons a parliament, together with the barons, knights, and ecclesiastics who attend, come also servants (1267) and burgesses (1266). That both "the high and the low" (6527) feature in the romance partially explains how *RCL* can describe the noble art of war traditionally associated only with the military estate of king, barony, and knights as a "mystere" (3860)—a word denoting a craft or trade practiced by merchants/artisans/craftsfolk/tradesmen, and the specialized organizations ("guilds") that sponsored their membership to the freedom of cities like London, and city citizenship, with attendant rights and duties, as well as regulated training for apprentices, market monopolies, and financing for industries and community culture. Provocatively, at the micrological level of vocabulary, the service obligations of an older, traditional estate are assimilated to the commerce-craftsmanship of the emergent bourgeoisie powering the engine of civic authority in English cities. It would seem that *RCL* found an audience across socioeconomic classes and constituents in Anglophone England during its long textual history: or at least that a linguistic cooptation of this kind, in which the noble art of war can be rubricated as commercial craft—marking a class capture, in language—would afford pleasure to some of this popular romance's audience communities.

Scholarship believes, in main, that medieval romances in English were read or listened to by a wide social spectrum, ranging from lower nobility and gentry to mercers and burgesses; and the Auchinleck manuscript in which *RCL* appears may have constituted a single-volume library of texts for an owner or owners possessing something like mercantile status.[62] Thrupp estimates, from the evidence of male witnesses in a consistory court of Edward IV, that 50 percent of male Londoners of mercantile-craftsmen rank might be able to read English in the mid-fifteenth century; and among "the twenty odd books contained in sixteen bequests made between the years 1403 and 1483" in this class, are included a Brut and two copies of a *Polychronicon,* testifying, perhaps, to a class interest in the history of the nation.[63] More than one scholar has argued that in late medieval England, the cheap paper quartos of printed copies "in which appeared such romances as . . . *Richard Coeur de Lion,* were undoubtedly meant . . . to circulate widely among a somewhat humbler public. Many of them were probably sold to country readers; peddled about by traveling booksellers, they were the true precursors of the chapbooks of the seventeenth century."[64] The limitations of documentary evidence mean that arguments on the audience of Middle English romances remain necessarily circumstantial; nonetheless, *RCL*'s internal narrative evidence plainly suggests that the *fiction* of broad-based appeal is a useful construction.

Furthermore, although I describe *RCL*'s utopian narrative premise of transclass solidarity in war as an idealized dissimulation that subserves the overarching interests of a community in the grip of nationalization, late medieval English history in fact witnesses spontaneous occasions of contingent collaboration across social classes to meet military exigencies that threaten the formative nation. Thus at the battle of Neville's Cross, "a hastily assembled body" of peasants, clerics, and knights fought side by side; and, in the south, merchants and churchmen spontaneously organized alongside knights "when the enemy suddenly appeared before Winchelsea, Rye, or Southampton." Indeed, concern "for England's security" would appear to have been an interest that traversed all social classes in the crucible of a nationalizing culture. A sense of national responsibility would appear to fuel the sentiments of "Kentish peasants during the revolt of 1381" when, at "an assembly held at Dartford it was decided that 'no one who lived within twelve leagues of the sea should go with them, but should guard the coasts against enemies.'"[65]

A context of spontaneous mobilizations organized around national rather than class interests imparts, then, some intelligibility to an extraordinary incident narrated in *RCL.* One of *RCL*'s innovations is a startling rescripting of a historical incident of enmity that erupted between Richard and Duke Leopold of Austria. In chronicle accounts, Richard earns Leopold's hostility by gratuitously casting down the duke's banners from the walls of Acre, where the banners of the triumphant crusading leaders are displayed after the city's capture.[66] *RCL,* which has the confrontation occur at "Chaloyn" (5951), does not have Richard gratuitously insult Leopold by an arrogant act but assigns Leopold responsibility for the hatred that, historically, results in Richard's postcrusade capture in Europe by

the duke and lengthy incarceration. Unlike every single "king and emperor" present at "Chaloyn," who contributes to the collective labor of re-
building the protective walls around the city by cooperatively and
democratically hauling stones or mortar (5969–70), the duke of Austria refuses to sully his hands with manual labor, haughtily declaring "my father
was not a mason or a carpenter, and even if your walls all utterly shake to
pieces, I shall never help to make them" (5978–80). With purest fury,
Richard then assaults the duke, hurling Leopold's banner in the river. The
English king is fully justified, we are to understand, because of the duke's
avowal of allegiance to his class, his boastful class insult, and his arrogant
refusal to perform menial labor that he sees as beneath his class position.
Remarkably, in order for Richard's indignation and retaliation to be received as just, the audience for this romance must be willing to accept the
fiction that manual labor is appropriate activity for dukes, kings, and emperors when an act of solidarity requires communal cooperation that cuts
across all lines of social and economic division. In a culture where Froissart can suggest that one of Edward III's knights who is "a paragon of
chivalric skill, valor, and beauty" would never be "accepted as a gentleman"
because he had been the son of a mason, and where "occupations were
considered 'vile' if they involved manual labor or menial service,"[67] the fiction of class solidarity through combined physical labor is a bold and daring one indeed.[68]

Indeed, bold and daring fictions, I have suggested, are the specialty of
this romance, with its many experiments in service to the discourse of the
nation. The nation itself—an experiment that has not yet seen its conclusion, despite twenty-first century transnationalism and the movement and
reach of global capital—is perhaps the boldest and most daring medieval
fiction of all. The production of "England" in English romances, literature,
and culture, in the episteme of the thirteenth century and after, is a cat-
achresis so bold that it must infinitely, repeatedly, be defended, managed,
argued, explored, and reperformed. That a celebrated English monarch and
his crusade, cannibalism and conquest, war and jokes, Saracens, Jews, and
the English language and its fictions of class and identity, should all be part
of the arsenal of defense and argument, explanation and performance,
merely suggests that romance is, in fact, a genre of the nation: a genre *about*
the nation, and for the nation's important fictions.

Notes

★ "The Romance of England" is extracted from a chapter of a book-in-
progress, *Empire of Magic: Medieval Romance and the Politics of Cultural Fan-*

tasy. It is minimally annotated here to honor length requirements; a full documentary apparatus accompanies the full chapter. Portions of this chapter were presented to audiences at the Center for Cultural Studies, University of California at Santa Cruz, and the Middle English division of the Modern Language Association, in 1998.

1. *RCL* survives in seven manuscripts and two early printings. Brunner's edition traces two lines of descent, "A" and "B" versions, with the oldest extant mss—the Auchinleck and Egerton, from the early and later fourteenth century—represented in B: *Richard Coer de Lyon. Der Mittelenglische Versroman Richard Löwenherz,* ed. Karl Brunner (Wien: Wilhelm Braumüller, 1913). Scholars have sometimes argued that B is "closest to the 'original'": John Finlayson, "*Richard, Coer de Lyon:* Romance, History, or Something in Between?" *Studies in Philology* 87 (1990): 156–80, 179; a lost Anglo-Norman ur-text from the thirteenth century: "Entstehungszeit der Dichtung ist . . . das 13. Jahrhundert anzusetzen": Brunner, ed. *Richard Coer de Lyon,* p. 11. I follow editorial tradition in reading the romance as emerging in the thirteenth century (while bracketing the existence of a French original whose contents are irretrievable, despite the lure of an occasional narrative hint or fiction), but whose text required the next centuries of collective authorship by copyists, redactors, and editors to complete. Lineation and numbering are Brunner's. The first cannibalism is not in all the mss (the text in the Auchinleck is a mere fragment); the second cannibalism is in the Egerton and both versions of narrative descent; the well poisoning is represented also in A and B. The long period of *RCL*'s compilation means that the work must be read as a repository of patterns, investments, and obsessions inscribed over centuries and aggregated through the hands and intelligences that compiled its dual textual traditions. To read *RCL* is thus truly to read the sedimented locations of culture and history: This most medieval of romances richly exemplifies medieval textual culture and the community of producers at work on a text, whose completed personality is then necessarily a corporate one, of many parts, over time.

2. I have argued elsewhere that historical cannibalism committed by Latin Christians on Turkish cadavers during the First Crusade functions as the anacrusis for the emergence of medieval romance and the King Arthur legend in Geoffrey of Monmouth's *Historia Regum Britannie,* in early twelfth-century Anglo-Norman England, an argument too complex to rehearse here. (See Geraldine Heng, "Cannibalism, the First Crusade, and the Genesis of Medieval Romance," *differences* 10.1 (1998): 98–174.) No sufficient discourse on cannibalism by Latin Christians existed in late eleventh-/early twelfth-century Europe, when Geoffrey's *Historia* exorcised the trauma of crusader cannibalism, with its horrors of infernal pollution, through the transformations and celebration magically afforded by romance: By contrast, the much-later *RCL* is able to perform crusader cannibalism as a joke precisely *because* a discourse on cannibalism has coalesced in the interval, a discourse in which Geoffrey's *Historia* played no small part

in a literary genealogy that makes possible the production of *this* cannibalism, in the later Middle Ages, as a joke.

3. Even Richard's supple facility with jokes is attested by various sources. William of Newburgh recounts Richard's famous joke on his willingness to sell off London, if he could only find a buyer: see William of Newburgh, *Historia Rerum Anglicarum, Chronicles of the Reigns of Stephen, Henry II, and Richard I,* vol 1, ed. Richard Howlett (London: Longman, 1884), p. 306. William of Newburg also cites Richard's celebrated jest that he had made a new earl out of an old bishop, after inducing Hugh, bishop of Durham, to purchase the earldom of Northumberland from the crown, I:305; also Roger of Wendover, *Rogeri de Wendover Liber qui dicitur Flores Historiarum ab Anno Domini MCLIV annoque Henrici Anglorum regis secundi primo,* ed. Henry G. Hewlett, Chronicles and Memorials of Great Britain and Ireland during the Middle Ages, no. 84 (London: Longman, 1886–89), I:168. A joke expressing Richard's crafty diplomacy is recorded by Saladin's biographer, the imam Baha' ad-Din. To drive a wedge between Saladin and his younger brother and trusted lieutenant, Al-Adil, Richard provocatively suggests to Al-Adil that Al-Adil should marry Joanna, Richard's widowed sister, the former queen of William II of Sicily, and that the conjugal couple be given Jerusalem to govern, by Saladin, as king and queen, together with the territory commanded by Latins and Muslims on the Levantine coast and in the interior. That Saladin recognized Richard's trick is borne out by the emir's ready acquiescence to the unthinkable match and his certainty that the English king had no intention of carrying out his proposal: Beha' ed-Din, *Saladin, or What Befell Sultan Yusuf* (1137–1193) (Lahore: Islamic Book Service, 1976), pp. 310–311; *Arab Historians of the Crusades,* ed. and trans. Francesco Gabrieli, vol. 3 (London: Routledge, 1969), p. 227; Steven Runciman, *A History of the Crusades,* vol. 3 (Cambridge: Cambridge University Press, 1951), pp. 59–60.

4. The choice of Richard as an organizing figure for the imagined community of the realm is not unproblematic, given hints of sexual irregularity in Richard's history and the medieval epistemic tendency to equate sodomy with heresy, etc. (The chronicler, Roger of Howden, for example, recognizes notable, repeating instances of what looks like the sin of sodomy in Richard's chequered life: *Chronica Magistri Rogeri de Houedene,* ed. William Stubbs, Chronicles and Memorials of Great Britain and Ireland during the Middle Ages, no. 51, 4 vols. [London: Longman, 1868–71] II:318, III:288–89.) My chapter's section on sodomy shows how humor, puns, jokes, and the manipulation of English-language resources produce a brilliant romance solution in *RCL* that advances *RCL*'s nationalist discourse.

5. Some of the impulses I identify as characterizing epistemic beginnings in the "thirteenth century" may of course be nascent in the twelfth century as well, history producing jagged rather than neat epistemic edges.

6. Sigmund Freud, *The Standard Edition of the Complete Psychological Works of Sigmund Freud,* ed. and trans. James Strachey, 24 vols. (London: Hogarth, 1960) 8:103.

7. The late medieval European discourse on color is, of course, unstable and riven with contradictions; however, the point to be made is that blackness is *not neutral,* but negatively valenced, in the epistemic formation I describe. That a racializing discourse exists in which color is positioned instrumentally, from the thirteenth century onward, is inescapable: The attention given to blackness and variations on blackness, in cultural texts ranging from romances like the *King of Tars, Moriaen,* and *Parzival,* to the statuary of St. Maurice, and visual representations of Lady Fortune (in which characters are black, piebald, mottled, split into black-and-white halves, etc.) suggests a discursive system in place to guide responses to characters and fictions from cues supplied by color. Nonetheless, the prime role of religion in the medieval period means that certain essentialisms can be trumped in appropriate contexts: In literature, for instance, baptism often whitens the skin color of blacks and partial blacks, indicating that the spiritual essence conferred by religion can have priority over the genetic essence conferred by the biologism of color. A black St. Maurice, moreover, is also patently acceptable. That religion might be understood to impart an essence is a special feature of the medieval moment in the transformational grammar of race: a grammar yet to be fully plotted, since cultural theory currently overconcentrates on postmedieval racial discourses. But to grasp that religion locates an essence is to grasp only partially the specificities of the medieval racializing apparatus. Disbelief and suspicion toward Jewish *conversos* in the period suggests that even after conversion, something is felt to continue, as a remainder—a core essence—within the once Judaic body, that religious conversion, however essential, cannot erase: a remainder that can only be racially named. My article in progress, "Race and Nation in Epistemic Change: Jews and Medieval England," further theorizes the cultural politics of medieval racializing discourses.

8. Historical moments gleam through the two cannibalisms in *RCL:* Richard is, in fact, recorded by chroniclers as recovering rather suddenly from his illness at Acre, after sweating off his malady: Richard of Devizes, *Cronicon Richardi Divisensis De Tempore Regis Richardi Primi,* ed. John T. Appleby (Toronto and NY: Thomas Nelson, 1963), p. 81; the English king does take enemy heads for trophies: *Itinerarium Peregrinorum et Gesta Regis Ricardi,* ed. William Stubbs (London: Longman, 1864), p. 251; and has the beards of antagonists who capitulate shaven off: *Itinerarium,* p. 201; Ambroise, *L'Estoire de la Guerre Sainte,* ed. Gaston Paris (Paris: Imprimerie Nationale, 1897), 1948. The blackness of Saracen skin, as a visible marker of the devilishness and otherness of the enemy, is also historically remarked on: *Itinerarium,* p. 262; Ambroise places on record the loathly blackness of Saracens but omits devilishness (*L'Estoire,* 6215–18); and dead Turks are desecrated

by deliberately mingling and confusing their corpses with swine's flesh/pigs' carcasses: Ambroise, *L'Estoire,* 11285–6; *Itinerarium,* p. 412.

9. Jewish chronicles document pogroms at Mainz, Worms, Speyer, Cologne, Regensburg and elsewhere during the Popular Crusade; the Second Crusade also occasioned the sacrifice of medieval Jewries: see *The Jews and the Crusaders: The Hebrew Chronicles of the First and Second Crusades,* ed. and trans. Shlomo Eidelberg (Madison: University of Wisconsin Press, 1977). Crusades are linked to the punishment of Jews also through legalized fiscal extortions: Peter the Venerable suggested that Jews should be made to finance the cost of the Second Crusade (Anna Sapia Abulafia, "Bodies in the Jewish-Christian Debate," in *Framing Medieval Bodies,* ed. Sarah Kay and Miri Rubin [New York: Manchester University Press, 1994], p. 130); and English monarchs plundered Jews through tallages during the many crusades declared in the twelfth and thirteenth centuries (Cecil Roth, *A History of the Jews in England* [Oxford: Clarendon, 1941], pp. 17 n.2, 44, 46, 67; H. G. Richardson, *The English Jewry under Angevin Kings* [London: Methuen, 1960], pp. 162, 163, 214; Christopher Tyerman, *England and the Crusades 1095–1588* [Chicago: University of Chicago Press, 1988], p. 79).

10. E.g., Richard of Devizes, *Cronicon Richardi,* 3–4; William of Newburgh, *Historia Rerum,* I: 294–99, I: 308–22; cf. Roger of Wendover, *Flores Historiarum,* I:166–67, 176–77.

11. John Boswell notes, e.g., that in the thirteenth and fourteenth centuries, Jews, Muslims, heretics, traitors, "sodomites," tended to be lumped together by association, as were lepers, Jews, and witches, although each group was "disliked by the majority for entirely different reasons. . . . There was certainly no single cause for such varied expressions of public hostility, but it is difficult to view them as wholly unrelated. However different the immediate circumstances . . . they all drew support from widespread fears of alien and disruptive social elements, fears which could easily be focused on vulnerable or little-understood minority groups": *Christianity, Social Tolerance, and Homosexuality: Gay People in Western Europe from the Beginning of the Christian Era to the Fourteenth Century* (Chicago: University of Chicago Press, 1980), p. 272. Vern Bullogh traces ideological constructions linking together homosexuality-heresy-witchcraft/sorcery-transvestism: "Heresy, Witchcraft, and Sexuality," *Journal of Homosexuality* 1:2 (1976): 183–201. Analogical thinking is quickly reinforced, of course, when contingent collusions among enemy (or outcast) communities historically seem, however contentiously, to occur. (The historicity of some putative collusions continues to be debated, including that of the so-called Lepers' plot of projected well poisoning, which in 1321 conveniently attaches lepers to Jews at the instigation of Granada.) See Sophia Menache, "Faith, Myth, and Politics: The Stereotype of the Jews and Their Expulsion from England and France," *The Jewish Quarterly Review* 75: 4 (1985): 369–70; cf. David Nirenberg, *Communities of Violence: Persecution of Minorities in the Middle Ages* (Princeton, NJ: Princeton University Press, 1996).

12. Jeremy Cohen, *The Friars and the Jews: The Evolution of Medieval Anti-Judaism* (Ithaca, NY: Cornell University Press, 1982), p. 244.

13. Robert de Clari, *La Conquête de Constantinople,* ed. Philippe Lauer (Paris: Champion, 1956), p. 72.

14. Anna Sapia Abulafia, "Christian Imagery of Jews in the Twelfth Century: A Look at Odo of Cambrai and Guibert of Nogent," *Theoretische Geschiedenis* 16 (1989): 387.

15. See W. Montgomery Watt and Pierre Cachia, *A History of Islamic Spain* (Edinburgh: Edinburgh University Press, 1965), pp. 12, 14, 32; Allan Harris Cutler and Helen Elmquist Cutler, *The Jew as Ally of the Muslim: Medieval Roots of Anti-Semitism* (Notre Dame, IN: University of Notre Dame Press, 1986), p. 93.

16. Cutler and Cutler, *Jew as Ally,* p. 87. " . . . that the Fatimid caliphs of Egypt employed Jewish viziers in the second half of the tenth century may have contributed to the fact that the Jews of Western Europe were blamed when the Fatimid caliph destroyed the Holy Sepulchre in Jerusalem" (p. 93). In the medieval association of Jews with Muslims, emphasis need only fall, of course, on Christian *perceptions* of collusion: "there is . . . an eleventh-century tradition that the Jews betrayed Toulouse to the Arabs circa 756–788. . . . Toulouse never fell to the Arabs; rather, it fell to the Normans in 848. This tradition that the Jews betrayed Toulouse may reflect an earlier ninth- or tenth-century . . . charge that the Jews betrayed Marseilles to the Arabs in 848" (p. 91).

17. Runciman, *Crusades,* II:467.

18. "Muslim conversion was not a mass phenomenon in the Crusading Kingdom": Benjamin Z. Kedar, *Crusade and Mission: European Approaches toward the Muslims* (Princeton, NJ: Princeton University Press, 1984), p. 82. Indeed, Levantine lore documents the *prevention* of conversion: A famous incident describes how the Templars undermined intended mass conversion by the Batinis (the Shi'ite Muslim group popularly known as the Assassins) to ensure that the tax paid to their order by these Muslims inhabiting Templar-controlled territory would continue to furnish Templar revenues—a revealing fiscal explanation for why conversion should *not* take place in Christian-dominated Levantine territory. William of Tyre also records how, in 1154, when the fugitive son of an Egyptian vizier fell into Templar hands and asked to convert, even learning Latin, the Templars handed back the would-be convert to the Egyptians instead for 60,000 pieces of gold (Kedar, *Crusade and Mission,* p. 82 n.112). Historically, Richard of England and Philip Augustus acted to *end* Muslim conversions after their conquest of Acre, when the crusader kings discovered that the new Christians, on receiving freedom with Christianity, simply absconded for Saladin's camp (p. 83).

19. Harold Pollins, *Economic History of the Jews in England* (East Brunswick, NJ: Associated University Presses, 1982), p. 17. Social historians argue that Jewish moneylenders in England became associated with land, by serving as

the medium through which encumbered estates passing as security through Jewish hands might be acquired by religious houses, secular groups, or great magnates with ambitions to extend wealth or status through property holdings. In the twelfth and thirteenth centuries, Cistercian and Augustinian houses (Meaux Abbey, Malton Priory, Fountains Abbey, Waltham Abbey, Kirkstead, Biddlesden, Holy Trinity, Aldgate, and Healaugh Park), Premonstratensians, Gilbertines, Cluniacs, and Benedictines acquired mortgaged properties through Jewish financiers: Richardson, *English Jewry,* pp. 90–103. The transactional system encompassed "so wide a geographical range and so many religious orders" (p. 99) that it ultimately acted as a "solvent which broke down the apparent rigidity of the structure of feudal land tenure and facilitated the transfer of estates" (p. 94) as "'land is . . . brought to the market and feudal rights are . . . capitalized'": Robin R. Mundill, *England's Jewish Solution: Experiment and Expulsion, 1262–1290* (Cambridge: Cambridge University Press, 1998), p. 37. By the reign of Henry III, cumulative land transfer through Jewish intermediaries had produced sufficient consequences in the loss of feudal dues and military service, and had so concentrated estates and military power in the hands of great landowners as to subtract from the prerogatives of the crown: Roth, *History,* p. 64. The Provisions of Jewry enacted by Henry III in 1269 specifically declared that "No debts whatsoever might be contracted in future with Jews on the security of lands held in fee" and "all obligations of the sort already registered were cancelled": p. 65; "the right to make loans on the security of real estate was from this period progressively restricted": p. 108.

20. Robert C. Stacey, "The Conversion of Jews to Christianity in Thirteenth-Century England," *Speculum* 67:2 (April 1992): 265, 269.

21. Roth, *History,* p. 43; Stacey, "Conversion of Jews," p. 269.

22. Roth, *History,* p. 79; see also Stacey, "Conversion of Jews," p. 267.

23. Stacey, "Conversion of Jews," p. 264.

24. Roger of Howden, *Chronica Magistri,* III: 33–34; Roger of Wendover, *Flores Historiarum,* I: 176–7; William of Newburgh, *Historia Rerum,* I: 308–310, 564–5; 566–71.

25. William of Newburgh, *Historia Rerum,* I: 294–5, 312–313.

26. Roger of Howden, *Chronica Magistri,* III: 12–13; William of Newburgh, *Historia Rerum,* I: 295.

27. James Parkes, *The Jew in the Medieval Community* (New York: Hermon, 1976), p. 395.

28. Roth, *History,* pp. 76, 95–96, 78.

29. "What was remarkable about a Jewish *commune* was that it existed within, and yet apart from, an urban *commune:* in the words of a royal letter of 1218, the Jews were accustomed to have *communam inter Christianos* or, as it is elsewhere expressed, *communam cum eis*": Richardson, *English Jewry,* p. 134. Mundill notes: "Jews lived in 'open' rather than 'closed' Jewries. There were no ghettos in England" (*Jewish Solution,* p.

33). Cecil Roth, *The Jews of Medieval Oxford* (Oxford: Clarendon, 1951) and Vivian D. Lipman, *The Jews of Medieval Norwich* (London: Jewish Historical Society of England, 1967), document the lived intimacy of particular Jewish and Christian communities. Unsurprisingly, a thirteenth-century legal text specified that those who had sexual intercourse with Jews were to be buried alive: Boswell, *Christianity, Social Tolerance and Homosexuality,* p. 292.

30. Menache, "Faith, Myth, and Politics," pp. 360–63.

31. John H. Fisher, "Chancery and the Emergence of Standard Written English in the Fifteenth Century," *Speculum* 52 (1977): 874.

32. "The sea defined the nation's territory": Turville-Petre, *England the Nation,* p. 4.

33. John Gillingham, "Foundations of a Disunited Kingdom," in *Uniting the Kingdom? The Making of British History,* eds. Alexander Grant and Keith J. Stringer (New York: Routledge, 1995), p. 54 *passim.* By "the end of the twelfth century the Normans had been absorbed by intermarriage. This is specifically stated in the *Dialogue of the Exchequer* and it is also indicated by the way charters are no longer addressed to both French and English but simply to all faithful persons . . . nationalist [feeling] is explicit even in an official document from 1217, which looks forward to the 'English' *(Anglici)* recovering their lands in Normandy": M. T. Clanchy, *England and Its Rulers 1066–1272: Foreign Lordship and National Identity* (Oxford: Blackwell, 1983), p. 252. Ernest Renan's classic essay describes the "fusion of . . . component populations" as an essential stage of nation-formation: "What Is a Nation?" in *Nation and Narration,* ed. Homi K. Bhabha (New York: Routledge, 1990), pp. 8–22, 10. R. R. Davies makes the difficult "maximum case" for an English nation-*state* as existing from as early as the mid-11th century: "Good Order and 'Sweet Civility': The Cultural Parameters of the Medieval English State," Plenary address, Annual Meeting of the Medieval Academy of America, March 27, 1998.

34. Robin Frame, "Overlordship and Reaction, c.1200–c.1450," in *Uniting the Kingdom,* p. 83; Gillingham, "Foundations," p. 63; Clanchy, *England and its Rulers,* p. 204.

35. Clanchy, *England and its Rulers,* p. 204; Turville-Petre, *England the Nation,* p. 3. "In all the maps Scotland and Wales are included, but are at the same time distinguished with rubrics describing their peoples as different in origin and character": Turville-Petre, p. 2. Clanchy adds that "in the thirteenth century . . . England became territorially distinct from Scotland and Wales because they too were developing into nation states" (p. 249).

36. Timothy Brennan, "The National Longing for Form," in *Nation and Narration,* ed. Bhabha, pp. 44–49.

37. John Barnie, *War in Medieval English Society: Social Values in the Hundred Years War 1337–99* (Ithaca, NY: Cornell University Press, 1974), p. 101.

38. I discuss this particular "badge" of English identity in detail in my book chapter.

39. Kelly De Vries, *Medieval Military Technology* (Lewiston, NY: Broadview, 1992), pp. 17–18.

40. William D. Phillips, Jr., "Sugar Production and Trade in the Mediterranean at the Time of the Crusades," in *The Meeting of Two Worlds: Cultural Exchange between East and West during the Period of the Crusades,* ed. Vladimir P. Goss and Christine Verzár Bornstein, Studies in Medieval Culture, vol. 21 (Kalamazoo, MI: Medieval Institute, 1986), p. 397; Janet Abu-Llughod, *Before European Hegemony: The World System A.D. 1250–1350* (Oxford: Oxford University Press, 1989), p. 232; Eliyahu Ashtor, *Levant Trade in the Later Middle Ages.* (Princeton, NJ: Princeton University Press, 1983), pp. 15, 206–8 *passim*).

41. Ashtor, *Levant Trade,* pp. 17, 23, 146, 160, 161 *passim*. Like other crusaders, Fulcher of Chartres in the First (Phillips, "Sugar Production and Trade," p. 395) and Oliver of Paderborn in the Fifth Crusade remark on the presence of the "honey cane" and its amazing sweetness. The crusader states and Cyprus later began sugarcane plantations; Spain, Crete, and eventually, Sicily, were also sugar producers. Phillips reads "the transmission to the West of the techniques of cultivation, production, and refining of sugar" (p. 393) as an example of how *translatio imperii* functioned, as "the West wrested economic ascendancy from the East" (p. 403), a point implicit also in Ashtor (*Levant Trade,* pp. 206–8). Interestingly, beehives symbolize the English polity in "Mum and the Sothsegger." On the subject of nationalist emblems in *RCL,* Finlayson points out that even Richard's siege engine, the Mategriffin, is "made out of 'embre of Englonde' (1850)" (p. 171). R. S. Loomis observes that the Auchinleck ms even has an illustration of Richard with a large axe in his hands (folio 326), and identifying insignia on his surcoat: "*Richard Coeur de Lion* and the *Pas Saladin* in Medieval Art," *PMLA* 30 (1915): 509–28, 523.

42. Lynn White, Jr., *Medieval Technology and Social Change* (Oxford: Oxford University Press, 1962), p. 87.

43. Brennan, "National Longing for Form," p. 45.

44. "It is precisely during the thirteenth century that scholars discern the first appearance of nationalism and patriotism in Western Europe, in the law and the propaganda of the period. By the end of the century . . . *patria* denoted specific national entities like England and France. Yet the notion of the *patria* and devotion thereto (patriotism) had always constituted important motifs in the theology of the Church . . . the emergence of feelings of patriotism on behalf of one's polity also derived from the current tendency to view Christendom as a corporate *corpus mysticum*": Cohen, *Friars,* p. 254. On the church's implicit grasp of, and ability to tap, impulses and momentum that also drive nationalist modalities, symbolizations, and unificatory practices, see Robert Bartlett, *The Making of Europe: Conquest, Colonization, and Cultural Change, 950–1350* (Princeton, NJ: Princeton University Press, 1993). Menache sees "the Biblical heritage, so deeply rooted in the medieval mentality" as "an important propaganda tool in

molding . . . national consciousness," so that eventually, useful biblical topoi of community, like an "Israel of the spirit," are secularized by nationalizing discourses: "Faith, Myth, and Politics," p. 374.

45. Diane Speed, "The Construction of the Nation in Middle English Romance," in *Readings in Medieval English Romance,* ed. Carol M. Meale (Cambridge: D. S. Brewer, 1994), pp. 146, 145.

46. "It seems to have been understood virtually from the beginning that these poems constituted a distinct corpus: there is substantial intertextuality amongst the various romances, frequently involving the recurrent use of generic conventions, sometimes apparent borrowing from one work to another, and explicit reference" (Meale, "Nation" p. 144). The case for a textual community of romances in England performing cultural work specific to the land, and distinguishable from the work of romance on the continent, is first made by Susan Crane, whose important argument on behalf of an "insular" group of Anglo-Norman and Middle English romances critically facilitates the later arguments of Turville-Petre, Speed, and others, on the distinctive commonality of the ME romances. Susan Crane, *Insular Romance: Politics, Faith, and Culture in Anglo-Norman and Middle English Literature* (Berkeley: University of California Press, 1986).

47. Turville-Petre, *England the Nation,* p. 11.

48. "þe Monþe of Octobr' Inþe Twoandfowertrþʒe ʒeare of vre cruninge" (Patent Roll, 43 Henry III. m.15., n.40), *The Only English Proclamation of Henry III,* ed. Alexander J. Ellis (London: Transactions of the Philological Society, 1868), pp. 19, 23.

49. Turville-Petre, *England the Nation,* p. 9.

50. John H. Fisher, "A Language Policy for Lancastrian England," *PMLA* 107 (1992): 1169.

51. Geoffrey of Monmouth, *The Historia Regum Britannie of Geoffrey of Monmouth I. Bern, Burgerbibliothek, MS 568,* ed. Neil Wright (Cambridge: D. S. Brewer, 1985), p. 67.

52. Renan, "What is a Nation?" p. 11.

53. Orderic Vitalis, *The Ecclesiastical History of Ordericus Vitalis,* ed. Marjorie Chibnall, 6 vols. (Oxford: Clarendon, 1969–1980), V: 298–99.

54. The Norman invasion is also the occasion of Jewish migration to England: William I invited Jews from Rouen in the late eleventh century, and English Jews, like the Anglo-French elites with whom they were associated by provenance, used French as well as Latin and Hebrew. French was perhaps even their "preferred . . . everyday language" (Mundill, *England's Jewish Solution,* p. 28). The desire to forget the Norman invasion is thus an overdetermined species of nationalistic desire.

55. See Timothy A. Shonk, "A Study of the Auchinleck Manuscript: Bookmen and Bookmaking in the Early Fourteenth Century," *Speculum* 60 (1985): 71–91, 89; Laura Hibbard Loomis, "The Auchinleck Manuscript and a Possible London Bookshop of 1330–1340," in *Adventures in the Middle Ages: A*

Memorial Collection of Essays and Studies (New York: Burt Franklin, 1962), p. 155.

56. Barnie, *War in Medieval English Society,* p. 98. Barnie quotes Froissart's observation that in the peace negotiations of 1393, the leaders of the English embassy were painfully conscious that "the French which they had learnt at home during their childhood was not of the same nature and condition as that of France," and had to ask for clarification "of any language that was obscure and hard or difficult for them to understand" in the written French of the proposals the English received. Noting that "such eminent princes" as the dukes of Gloucester and Lancaster were the leaders of the English embassy, Barnie extrapolates the likely humiliation among the *haute* nobility of "speaking an uncouth provincial dialect" (p. 100). The "forgetting" Renan finds essential for the "creation of a nation" (p. 11) notably includes the ironic "forgetting, by the conquerors, of their own language" ("What is a Nation?" p. 10).

57. Velma Bourgeois Richmond, *The Popularity of Middle English Romance* (Bowling Green, OH: Bowling Green University Popular Press, 1975), p. 7.

58. Fisher, "Chancery," pp. 879, 880.

59. Fisher, "Language Policy," p. 171.

60. A necessary if not sufficient benchmark of a romance's popularity is, of course, its number of surviving manuscripts: Derek Pearsall, who lists *RCL* as one of the top eight most popular Middle English romances out of about ninety-five surviving verse romances (by his count), considers "5 or more" mss an indication of popularity: "The English Romance in the Fifteenth Century," in *Essays and Studies 1976,* ed. E. Talbot Donaldson (London: John Murray, 1976), pp. 56–83, 58. *RCL, Bevis,* and *Siege* each has seven mss. Harriet Hudson, who counts more than 120 surviving ME romances, also seconds Brewer's observation "that for each remaining copy, there were once at least five more" copies of a medieval text: Hudson, "Toward a Theory of Popular Literature: The Case of the Middle English Romances," *Journal of Popular Culture* 23:3 (Winter 1989): 31–50; "Introduction" x. A "popular" medieval audience might include knights, esquires, petty aristocrats, gentry, civil servants and administrators, burgesses, *haute et petite bourgeoisie,* and a wide variety of townspeople and others who might listen to the reading or narration of a romance, as well as a wide range of reading publics. Recent scholarship (e.g., Justice's *Writing and Rebellion,* on the peasant revolt of 1381) has suggested that literacy in late medieval England was more widespread than formerly supposed. Indeed, only royalty and *haute* nobility of magnatial rank, whose library holdings seem to indicate a preference for Latin and Anglo-French rather than English texts, have been excluded from considerations of possible reading audiences, although obviously not from audiences for recitation in English, if Chaucer's and Gower's experience offers ground for extrapolation. The two print copies of *RCL,* from 1509 and 1528, were published by Wynkyn de Worde, who "saw the future of commercial printing" in

markets of increasingly "larger and less exclusive" audiences (Pearsall, "Fifteenth Century," p. 83).

61. Brunner, *RCL*, p. 7; Ronald S. Crane, *The Vogue of Medieval Chivalric Romance During the English Renaissance* (Menasha, WI: George Banta, 1919), p. 7.

62. See Shonk, "Auchinleck Manuscript," Pearsall, "Fifteenth Century," H. Loomis, "Possible London Bookshop," Richmond, *Popularity of Middle English Romance, et al.*

63. Sylvia Thrupp, *The Merchant Class of Medieval London 1300–1500* (Chicago: University of Chicago Press, 1948), pp. 158, 162–63.

64. R. Crane, *Vogue of Medieval Chivalric Romance*, pp. 9–10.

65. Barnie, *War in Medieval English Society*, pp. 106, 107, 108.

66. Richard of Devizes, *Cronicon Richardi*, pp. 46–47.

67. Thrupp, *Merchant Class*, pp. 309–10, 306.

68. In one complaint in Chancery a clerical schoolmaster was accused of offending "a draper's apprentice by sending him into the kitchen 'to washe pottes pannes disshes and to dighte mete'" (Thrupp, *Merchant Class*, p. 159).

CHAPTER 9

MARKING TIME:
BRANWEN, DAUGHTER OF LLYR
AND THE COLONIAL REFRAIN

Patricia Clare Ingham

> *This chapter explores the work that "Time" performs both inside and outside the colonialist imaginary, finding in a Welsh text a compelling argument against the "natural" loss of the past.*

> The very first thing that strikes one in reading the "Mabinogion" is how evidently the medieval story-teller is pillaging an antiquity of which he does not fully possess the secret; he is like a peasant building his hut on the site of Halicarnassus or Ephesus; he builds, but what he builds is full of materials of which he knows not the history, or knows by a glimmering tradition merely—stones "not of this building," but of an older architecture, greater, cunninger, more majestical.
>
> —*Matthew Arnold,* On the Study of Celtic Literature

If Matthew Arnold's writings on culture are among his best-known works, his appreciation of Welsh language and literature, while less well known, may be only marginally less influential. Arnold's *On the Study of Celtic Literature,* following Ernest Renan's 1854 *Essai sur la Poesie des Races Celtiques* (both of which followed Lady Charlotte Guest's publication of *The Mabinogion,* beginning in 1835) focused well-deserved attention, both scholarly and popular, on the *Mabinogi* and on Welsh literary texts more generally.[1] The authority of Arnold's opinion has been important to Welsh scholars, a fact evidenced by the frequency with which the passage cited as epigraph appears in scholarly accounts. C. W. Sullivan calls Arnold "the godfather" of the "search for sources," a scholarly pursuit that "was to guide *Mabinogi* criticism for almost 100 years" (xvii). Preeminent Celticist Rachel Bromwich identifies Arnold with "inaugurat[ing] . . . a dispassionate and scholarly attitude towards Celtic Studies which made possible their acceptance . . . as a serious academic discipline."[2] Indeed, Arnold's appreciation of the importance of Celtic literatures to what he called "the English spirit" led him to push for the establishment of a chair of Celtic at Oxford, a chair that remains today in the faculty of Medieval and Modern European Languages.[3]

Arnold's sponsorship of Celtic studies deserves analysis, especially in light of the provocative imagery used in the passage just cited. In Arnold's formulation the Welsh artist appears not as a conscious cultural agent intervening in his own historical moment but as an accidental tourist only dimly aware of the "glimmering tradition" with which he works. "Like a peasant building his hut," the Welsh writer crafts a rustic, unrefined text from the remains of a "greater, cunninger, more majestical" tradition. Welsh medieval literary endeavor is always already imbued with the most incalculable of losses. Its once-majestic tradition recurs, but only in broken fragments. For all his romantic delectation of the lost majesty of Welsh art, Arnold offers no testimony to the specific history, or to the agents, of its destruction. Nor does he attend to the poignant details of the *Mabinogi* writer's historical moment. The force to which Welsh literature submits seems here the disembodied, yet irresistible, passage of Time itself. In a formulation that both alludes to a history of conquest and represses it, the Welsh writer "pillages an antiquity" that is apparently not his own. This image of a literary past lost not through acts of conquest but through the ravages of Time testifies to melancholy loss; yet it also hides the particular losses suffered by Welsh victims in the dim mists of an archaic, irrecoverable past. Conquest is recast as cultural decline.

As his role in the establishment of Celtic studies makes clear, Arnold was passionately interested in mediating the loss of medieval Welsh texts. He argued for a recovery of the "roots" of "Celtic Literature" through the "science of philology," bringing "the Celt and sound criticism together . . . almost for the first time in their lives." Robert J. C. Young's postcolonial reading of Arnold's cultural theories suggests that the latter's recommendation of philology as a "disinterested, positive, and constructive criticism" was not itself historically disinterested.[4] On one hand, Arnold's account of the instrumentality of Celtic literatures to English culture challenged more deeply racist beliefs of the time, beliefs that the "Celts" were an illegitimate and disordered race who deserved to be, in the words of Robert Knox, "forced from the soil."[5] Yet Arnold's appreciation of Welsh language did not extend to contemporary, or political, uses of it; he actively opposed Welsh as the language of instruction in Welsh schools. *On the Study of Celtic Literature,* moreover, argues for the preservation of Celtic culture not as "an active, living, force" but as "an object of academic study, the museum relic of an extinct culture."[6] Arnold's account, Young argues, remains structured by a colonialist desire:

> The Celtic spirit can be released into English culture by turning it into an academic subject, so that it becomes part of English culture just as the Celt is, Arnold claims, part of the English race. Never was the colonial relation to other cultures in the 19th century more clearly stated: the force of "modern civilization" destroys the last vestiges of a vanquished culture to turn it into an object of academic study, with its own university chair.[7]

Celtic studies developed through a genealogy rife with colonial consolidations. Very old texts, like "primitive" peoples, offer a site wherein the power of "modernity"—its putatively "dispassionate" and "scientific" methods—pierces secrets, transforming the unknowable into categories for study. This history is not, of course, unique to Celtic studies. Postcolonial theorists remind us that the disciplines of British literature, positivist history, and evolutionary science, to name only a few, are similarly implicated in the production of colonialist knowledge systems. Postcolonial cultural studies (particularly that branch called colonial-discourse analysis, identified with the work of Edward Said, Gayatri Spivak, and Homi Bhabha) suggests that, in addition to the annexation of land, the commodification of marketable resources and objects, the disruption of "native" ruling structures and "native" cultural productions, colonialism "permeated forms of knowledge," even the very structures through which we may "try to understand colonialism itself."[8] First identified with Edward Said's *Orientalism,* this insight has led Homi Bhabha to call for a "critical ethnography of the West," that is, an examination of the structures of Western knowledge systems as products of colonial desire and colonialist politics.

It is from this vantage that I wish to reconsider the colonial implications of the archaic past offered by one of the four "branches" of the *Mabinogi,* "Branwen, Daughter of Llyr." It is from this view, moreover, that I wish to rethink Arnold's role in a history whereby as Rachel Bromwich puts it, "a dispassionate and scholarly attitude . . . made possible [the] acceptance" of Celtic studies "as a serious academic discipline."[9] I begin with a more detailed, if necessarily brief, explication of the archaic past, its loss and recovery in *On the Study of Celtic Literatures*. Next I read "Branwen, Daughter of Llyr," for its depiction of loss and change and for what it offers for a postcolonial view of the archaic. In the discussion that follows I hope to refute the persistent misapprehension that the object of study for medievalists is the time "before" colonialism, or the implication that historical specificity of medieval colonial relations means that they have little in common with later affairs. Instead, I will offer a view of how colonialism repeats and recurs in some habits and assumptions important to medieval studies, and suggest that medievalists might contribute to the "discourse of oppositionality" postcolonial cultural studies demands.[10]

In my attention to the colonial history particular to Celtic studies I do not wish to isolate this important field or to suggest it be discarded as a vestige of colonial contamination. My intention is quite the opposite, and my reading of "Branwen" is possible only because of the important, difficult work done by specialists in Welsh history, language, and literature. Yet I do hope to show that all our dreamings of the Middle Ages must confront the possibility that colonialist desires and demands are embedded in our view of time, in the "science" of our methodologies, and in the "dispassionate" truths structuring our histories.

Past Times

Matthew Arnold identifies an English-speaking consolidation "of all the inhabitants of these islands" with the "real and legitimate force" of "modern civilization."[11] This is, for Arnold, "a mere affair of time,"

> of what is called modern civilisation, and modern civilisation is a real, legitimate force; the change must come and its accomplishment is a mere affair of time. The sooner the Welsh language disappears as an instrument of the practical, political, and social life of Wales, the better; the better for England, the better for Wales itself. . . . The moment [the Welsh author] has anything of real importance to say, anything the world will the least care to hear, he must speak English. . . . For all modern purposes, I repeat, let us all as soon as possible be one people; let the Welshman speak English and, if he is an author, let him write English.[12]

On their face, Arnold's words imply the loss of a Welsh linguistic future as a progressivist fait accompli. The putatively civilizing influence of English figures as a corollary not to colonial relations, but to the irresistible passage of time. Progress, change, and "modernity" become the demand to which Welsh literati must submit, at least if they have anything important to say that the world will want to hear. Yet Arnold's self-conscious repetition of the force of modern English betrays an anxious concern with Welsh resistance. What begins as a passionate praise of modernity becomes finally a plea that the Welsh writer change to accommodate English linguistic nationalism. Arnold's description of the relentless demands of modernity thus displays, through its repetition and its anxiety, a tendentious colonial demand. Definitions of a progressive modernity converge with desires to annihilate the "prodigiously living" aspect of Welsh linguistic difference.[13] In Arnold's view, resistance to English linguistic hegemony figures simultaneously as regressive, narrow, and, perhaps worst of all, trivial.

Anne McClintock argues that notions of modernity like Arnold's consolidate imperial authority. In this trope of time, "colonized people do not inhabit history proper but exist in a permanently anterior time within the geographic space of the modern empire as anachronistic humans, atavistic, irrational, bereft of human agency—the living embodiment of the archaic 'primitive.'"[14] Tropes of the archaic persist throughout *On the Study of Celtic Literature;* Wales stands not as a modern, literate, civilization but, like the *Mabinogi* itself, as "a perfect treasure house of mysterious ruins."[15] This may be precisely why the study of premodern Welsh literature becomes, for Arnold, a crucial avenue for cultural recovery. Welsh linguistic culture remains legitimated so long as it offers a purchase on a past archaic richness, removed from any political and historical context. Arnold's essay displays the richness of Welsh cultural difference without implying that such diversities deserve a political future.

Yet the question of a future remains important to Arnold, who imagines a happier insular future through the "scientific" study of philology, a "dispassionate" approach that can reach beyond the prejudices of his time. Philology "carries us toward ideas of affinity of race" with the ambitious hopes that the "gentle ministrations of science" might deliver "a message of peace to Ireland."[16] Arnold's recommendation of the legitimate study of past Welsh literature through the disinterested "science of philology" was designed in part to disable late-Victorian racism, offering a crucial alternative to the standard English opinion of the time. Yet it also rendered illegitimate the passionate efforts of Welsh linguistic resistance.[17] So long as the dispassionate method of science defines the serious, legitimate, and scholarly approach, any interested, passionate response to the particular history of Welsh losses, and any passionate resistance to an "English-only" future, becomes as illegitimate (and as irrational) as anti-Welsh racism. Arguments about the progressive import of a linguistic scientific method ensure that the study of Welsh literature invigorates a totalizing English modernity. A linguistic past devoid of the materiality of its politics consolidates the loss of the modern Welsh language in the service of an "English-speaking" insular whole. There is, moreover, a larger racial politics here, for

Arnold praises ancient Welsh literature in the service of insular unity while England annexes the Indian subcontinent. An independent India will be the next "archaic" culture lost to an English view of "progress."

Evidence from Arnold's essay corroborates the insistence in postcolonial cultural studies that our commitment to progressive chronologies remains a legacy of colonialism. Arnold's account of progress replaces the opposition of English to Welsh with the opposition of science to passion. Yet his putatively inclusive, broad-minded scientific method fronts the narrow interests of English culture and renders Welsh linguistic partisanship as the vestige of an archaic insular fragmentation.[18] To what extent, we must ask, does Arnold's nineteenth-century colonial view still haunt these methods? How frequently does source study or philology encourage scholars to treat the traditional texts of linguistic minorities as repositories of archaic fragments, or as linguistic treasure houses, rather than to examine what Patrick Ford calls the "integrity of their texts"?[19] To what extent do these methods underemphasize the linguistic and cultural agency of authors working with oral formulaic motifs? I ask these questions not to suggest we eschew philology or source study as hopelessly contaminated methods, but to remind us of their politically interested implications. Embedded in the assumption that the scientific truth of philology is superior to the passions of politics is a politicized history that enshrines English modernity as progressive by locating a polyglot, fragmented insular culture in a lost medieval past.

Like Arnold's essay, "Branwen, Daughter of Llyr" depicts Welsh culture amid loss. Yet unlike Arnold's work, "Branwen" shows us that loss results from a specific set of geopolitical and historical actions rather than from the irresistible, disembodied passage of time. The author/redactor of "Branwen" imagines a future edged with poignant images of guilt and desolation; this text testifies not to "a mysterious treasure house of riches" but to the complex agency of an author on the border between a native, oral past and a colonized, textual future. "Branwen" tells this story through a fragmentary and allusive narrative, and I will read this tale through a history of colonial relations despite the fact that it offers no sequential, explicit chronology of colonization. Instead of a linear history of imperial origin, we find a repetitive and fragmented account of the doubleness of loss and survival, told through a complicated memoir of inner-Celtic affections and aggressions. This is a story about Welsh survival despite disastrous loss and despite the failed alliance between two "Celtic" cultures. The double, and dissipated, logic of this tale—its use of archaic time—eludes a colonial gaze that views the archaic and the fragmentary only as regressive preconditions for modernity and civilization. In "Branwen, Daughter of Llyr," archaic fragmentation comes as the denouement to colonial complications, and it speaks of inconsolable loss.

Border Voices: Branwen and Colonial Loss

By all accounts "Branwen, Daughter of Llyr" travels well through time.[20] Most scholars agree, moreover, that "Branwen" has important historicist ambitions of its own. Historical approaches have been important to *Mabinogi* scholarship, originally through source study. Attention to the texts' aesthetic strengths later augmented source study, and recent readings examine the social and political contexts, often through a comparative literary method.[21] This scholarly genealogy implicitly positions the *Mabinogi* on a set of frontiers—some temporal, like the shift from oral tradition to manuscript culture, others territorial, as in the consideration of the texts' "Celtic," "European," or English concerns. Borders, and the cultural losses and survivals produced at such places and during such times, are thus implicitly important to scholarship; yet they remain undeveloped for a reading of the texts themselves.

In the second "branch" of the *Mabinogi,* the border position of the texts resonates with the figure of Branwen. Through her marriage to the Irish king Matholwch, Branwen inhabits the border between two warring neighbors as kin of both; eventually she becomes the proximate cause of their conflict, a relationship she attempts to rectify by forging peace between them. But the assignment of dual loyalties within the story's complex network of relationships backfires, resulting in the almost total annihilation of one people and the near destruction of the other.[22] The tale complicates Branwen's intercultural relation early on when it describes her marriage with Matholwch as a means to "Ymrwymaw Ynys Y Kedeirn ac Iwerdon y gyt, ual y bydynt gadarnach" [to bind the Isle of the Mighty with Ireland so that together (they) will be mightier].[23] Apparently the political and military fortunes of both Ireland and Wales need strengthening, and the existence of a common enemy whose imperialistic ambitions might inspire such an alliance is thus both implied and repressed.[24]

A view to the periods with which this text is identified proves instructive here. England's aggressions toward Wales and Ireland intensified in both centuries identified with this text's emergence, the twelfth and the fourteenth. When viewed from the perspective of England's colonial aggressions vis-à-vis the so-called Celtic Fringe, the "Red Book" manuscript becomes politically provocative. Within it we read both the tale of "Branwen," a text that can only allude to the political context of English imperialism, alongside explicit historical accounts of England's imperialistic encroachment upon Wales and Ireland. That codex includes, for example, a version of the *Brut y Tywysogyon* (Chronicle of Princes), which tells of Henry II's journey through Wales on his way to Ireland in 1171.[25] Historians expand on primary source testimony describing the structural upheaval accompanying the social, political, and economic devastation during the period.[26] The late fourteenth century (the date of the Red Book) is famous for both the Glyn Dwr rebellion and the racism of English anti-Welsh Penal Laws; and prophecies of a "Celtic Federation" uniting to throw off the yoke of the English were in the air.[27]

But how does the story of an Irish/Welsh alliance pertain to Welsh anxieties vis-à-vis the English? We still need to explore the significance of the tale's specifically Irish/Welsh rivalry. The network of Irish/Welsh relationships in both the narrative and in late-medieval history proves to be quite complex. The alliance Branwen embodies becomes so problematic for both parties that neither becomes stronger; in fact, Celtic "inner" rivalries become the central conflict, emerging when Branwen's stepbrother, Efnisien, insults the Irish. His act of purported political and cultural loyalty to the Welsh suggests a split in the "Welsh" position—although Efnisien is present at the forging of the Irish/Welsh alliance in the tale's opening moments, he nonetheless nearly succeeds in destroying it. His actions foreground the uneasy nature of an Irish/Welsh union, eventually shattering the delicate balance of Branwen's position as "foreign" queen.

Bran redresses Efnisien's affront, but Irish grumbling recurs when, years after the wedding, Matholoch's familiars demand that Branwen be held guilty, by kinship association, of Efnisien's insult. This puzzling return of an insult already remedied drives the remainder of the tale. It poignantly depicts trauma's repetition, showing how past losses and aggressions erupt to disrupt the present, a point to which I will eventually return. As a result of this disruption Branwen becomes a political prisoner of the Irish court. She is now a victim of "foreign" oppression, and here the role of Ireland in the tale, and in the political context that surrounds it, seems to shift.[28] Ireland moves from ally to enemy of the Welsh, rejecting and imprisoning that bond intended to make both kingdoms "mightier."

Ambivalence toward Ireland resonates with historical testimony about Irish/Welsh relations throughout the medieval period. Although there were times when Welsh nobles fled to Ireland in search of sanctuary from the Anglo-Normans, in the past Dublin had launched invasions across the Irish sea. Wales was positioned defensively on all sides, and historical records evidence the rivalries among precisely those countries that many imagine as a romantically unified "Celtic Federation." Given the vulnerability of Welsh geopolitical fortunes, cultural safety could exist only within Welsh borders. If we add to this the larger context of English aggression toward both Celtic lands, we may arrive at some sense of the ambivalence with which the Welsh might have perceived their Irish neighbors and their potential as allies. Indeed, as I shall argue later, the issue of cultural loyalty to a Welsh people becomes the central problem the tale of "Branwen" at-

tempts to resolve, a problem raised early on in Efnisien's refusal to acqui-
esce to Bran's decision for Irish alliance. And despite the fact that the tale
seems well aware of Branwen's persistent good faith and ingenuity under
very difficult circumstances, her explicit position in between Ireland and
Wales makes *her* activity, rather than Efnisien's, the focus for anxieties about
group loyalty.

The difficulties of Branwen's border position, moreover, are linked with
her facility with speech and texts. While a prisoner of the Irish, Branwen
"speaks" for the first time. Her speech is not traditionally linguistic, nor is
it immediately directed toward a human being. Over a period of years,
Branwen "Meithryn ederyn drydwen a wnæth hitheu ar dal y noe gyt a
hi, a dyscu ieith idi, a menegi y'r ederyn y ryw wr oed brawt" [nourished
a starling, on the edge of her kneading-trough, she did teach it speech, and
tell the bird the kind of man her brother was].[29] Branwen's relationship
with the starling places her again on a cultural border, one linked specifically to linguistic technologies: the oral, prelinguistic, "natural" world of
the bird and the textual, symbolic world of political action. Hence her
message to her brother Bran (who, apparently, is literate, as is she) is written that he might understand it. Branwen does not expect Bran to speak
to the bird, nor does the bird use spoken language to communicate Branwen's pleas for help, despite the fact that she has taught it "ieith," speech.
Branwen's use of written text is superfluous given the bird's learned facility with speech; yet she can speak the language of both bird and text, and
by her "bilingual" position gains a temporary liberation. Informing her
family of Irish insults against her, Branwen invites military intervention on
her behalf. Yet, tragically, her return to her Welsh "roots" for rescue ushers
in devastating destruction for both Celtic cultures.

Branwen's position on a linguistic border has particular resonances for
the cultural agency of the Welsh author/compiler. The tale's emphasis on
the bilingual nature of Branwen's act (and the repetition of the starling's
link to technologies both of speech and of texts) marks Branwen as a displaced figure of bardic power; in the rest of the tale, as we will see, Branwen's desolate end helps contain and control scribal anxieties about
linguistic and textual change, anxieties that allude to the problems of colonial accommodation. The textual inscription of an oral tradition like the
Mabinogi would require the same sort of "bilingual" facility on the part of
a scribe/redactor that Branwen herself deploys. Steeped in an older, native,
oral tradition, anxious about its survival, Welsh authors may have felt themselves trapped and desperate in much the same way as Branwen, with their
only hope of preserving their traditional oral culture resting on their ability to translate it into a new language: the language of texts. In the more
textually based imperialistic culture of England, Welsh bards must plant

their feet in the same two worlds as Branwen, remembering the old ways and accommodating themselves to textual innovations.

Evidence suggests that both the compiler of the *Mabinogi* and the professional scribes of the Red Book coped with changes in textual production. Proinsias Mac Cana implicitly positions the *Mabinogi* writer on an oral/textual border when he describes his prose as "consciously wrought from a judicious blend of colloquial and learned techniques," yet "a talent more at home with Latin manuscript texts than with the oral telling of myth."[30] While offering important objections to Mac Cana's approach, Patrick Ford links narrative changes with both "textual integrity" and with a community's preservation of its cultural traditions. Following Susan Wittig's account of the narrative structure of Middle English romance, Ford links narrative "structural shifts" with the "reinforcement and perpetuation of certain social and political beliefs held by the community."[31] Gifford Charles-Edwards, moreover, identifies the period of the Red Book's production, following the decline of monastic scriptoria, with the emergence of Oxford-educated, professional, secular scribes in Wales.[32] Crafting a manuscript of Welsh cultural "riches" like that of the Red Book of Hergest offers a method for preserving a tradition under siege while accommodating a textual technology important to colonial governments and in a book hand learned at an English cultural center. Loss infuses such moments of cultural change.[33]

Branwen's ultimate fate at the hands of the compiler or scribe expresses the experience of this kind of loss, the inevitability of which is evident when her "bilingual" act results in a war between the two "allies" with Branwen's son Gwern, the incarnation of the Irish/Welsh alliance, at its center. The question of Gwern's ability to be loyal to his Welsh relatives, having been fostered "in the best place for men in Ireland," disturbs Efnisien, who, rather than risk an "unbalanced" union, destroys both the boy and the relationship. The resulting battle kills all the Irish lords and all but seven of the Welsh. The issue of orality recurs at this point in the "cauldron of rebirth" episode, a moment often viewed as a particularly awkward interpolation of an oral, folkloric motif. Efnisien catches and kills Irish warriors whose speech reveals their hiding places; these once-dead warriors emerge from this cauldron magically resurrected yet mute. Ford suggests that this image of a military force without the facility of speech resonates with a cultural concern over the disruptive and violent power of warriors. Yet since it is a warrior's verbosity that emerges as dangerous and deservedly lost, I would argue that the text is emphasizing orality here, within the context of war. Orality proves dangerous in times of war, an image that resonates with the disruptive consequence of Branwen's earlier bilingual powers. Here orality links with the Irish as enemies of the Welsh;

the loss of orality constitutes one step in the triumph of the Welsh over them. And this loss comes not through an irresistible, disembodied passage of time but as the result of a particular, and particularly complicated, battle. The implications of this for the position of the author/compiler will be clearer in a moment.

Branwen's border position appears more complicated than that of the loose-lipped Irish warriors. Her response to her son Gwern contrasts with Efnisien's, and I turn for a moment to the question of Branwen's loyalties. She attempts to save her son's life not out of some transcendent principle of right or duty to a people but out of her maternal tie to a particular individual, what the story would have us see as a poignant, if selfish, fixation with a particular relationship. Her refusal to forgo the particularities of her maternal relationship ultimately results in her death, once she returns to Wales. But why does the tale finally shift from Branwen's doubled role as a mediator between two cultures to her position as mother and to her maternal desire to rescue the particular life of her son? And why does Bran, who restrains her from saving Gwern's life, come to represent the communal "good" of the Welsh "people" rather than the particularity of Welsh interests vis-à-vis the Irish? Why does Branwen finally figure herself, in contrast to Efnisien, as the selfish destroyer of both peoples whose alliance she earlier embodied?

Branwen banishes Welsh fear over a loss of cultural sovereignty. If the compiler/scribe can contain the dangerous aspects of his own border position within the person of Branwen, he can control his fear and imagine a different ending. This "different" ending for Wales appears in the "head of the king" motif, where the remnant Welsh community, once Branwen is dead, maintains its tie to its cultural past by creating a new court centered on the severed "head" of Bran. This head protects the community from the dangers of assimilation and grants it prosperity and happiness as it rebuilds itself. The transcendental community lives on for many years, protected, indeed nurtured, by the transcendental "Father."

In contrast to Bran's magical power to recover the fortunes of his troubled community beyond death, Branwen holds herself responsible for bringing death to her two families: "Alas, son of God," she says as she dies, "woe that I was ever born, for two good islands were destroyed because of me" ["Oy a uab Duw," heb hi, "guae ui o'm ganedigaeth. Ys da dwy ynys a diffeithwyt o'm achaws I"].[34] Why must Branwen bear this grief? And why must her grief kill her? These questions point to the apotropaic fantasies provided by gender. It is not incidental that it is Branwen's accommodationist position as mother which "compromises" her clan loyalties. This narrative implies that there is danger in mothers and their particularities. Maternal loyalties such as Branwen's might compromise the military

fortunes of a people at war, and this tale reminds mothers that clan obligations should outrank their particular maternal bonds. Branwen, as woman
and mother, is the bearer of the individuality that threatens the fiction of
the transcendent clan community, while Bran acts as guardian of this
group, one that is understood to exist beyond the specificities of individual lives.[35]

The doubleness of ideology at work here connects Branwen's character
with the tale's double-edged construction of the Irish, just as Branwen and
the Irish warriors were both connected to orality. On one hand, the Welsh
scribe/redactor cautions against a too-rigid identification with a Celtic
past. When, despite their perfidy, Branwen remains faithful to the Irish,
steadfastly protecting the alliance with them, even pleading the Irish cause
before her brother, the redactor seems to imply that her loyalty to this
Celtic identity is overly rigid and that such rigidity can endanger Welsh
cultural sovereignty, and even their existence. But the Irish also play the
role of foreign power. They are the "foreigners" who imprison Branwen
despite an alliance with them. They use her wisdom and double-cross her.
The tale implicitly cautions against a naiveté in such intercultural affairs.
Choose your loyalties wisely, the redactor seems to say, lest they destroy the
very thing you hope to gain. Thus, this tale implicitly argues for a way of
negotiating the border position of both Branwen and the Welsh author.
On the border between its Welsh, oral past and English, textual future,
Welsh culture must carefully prepare for innovations (in language and textuality) without losing its identity with the transcendental, transhistorical
community it expresses. Within such a difficult position individual loyalties to the "ideal" group are especially vulnerable and particularities of loyalty are especially to be feared.

Branwen's death, while not altogether suicidal, is imbued with a self-ha-
tred that refigures the guilt of the scribe who adopts an accommodationist
position similar to her own. And Branwen's melancholic passing carries the
pain and loss of those particular historical moments wherein English annexation eroded Welsh culture step by step. The transcendental "head of the
king" motif protects Welsh compilers and professional scribes from coping
with the losses that accompanied the accommodations demanded by empire. Branwen was sacrificed to the trauma of those accommodations.[36]

Survival, Loss, and the Colonial Refrain

"The constant concern of the author of the Four Branches," writes J. K.
Bollard, "is the modes of personal conduct which are necessary for society
to survive and progress."[37] Yet the poignant attention in "Branwen, Daughter of Llyr" to cultural survival returns us not to progress but to the archaic

images of Welsh sovereignty through the figures of Bran and Branwen, figures imbued with loss. When it does, "Branwen" makes legible the archaic as an image of both cultural trauma and cultural survival. Unlike the opposition of an archaic past to a progressive future we read in Arnold's account, the archaic sovereignty to which "Branwen" returns suggests that the simultaneity of loss and survival haunts the accommodations of a colonial scene.

Postcolonial accounts of culture sever the links between survival and progress. They suggest, as do recent analyses of trauma and history, that repetitive and recurring fragments from the past might be read as evidence not of a regressive interest in trivia but of the intransigence of traumatic histories. Arnold's condescension toward the "residual" or "fragmented" character of medieval Welsh narratives obscures this particular traumatic history. Yet the "fragments" encoded in "Branwen" still can offer a reading of the compiler's efforts to preserve vestiges of an oral culture while accommodating the innovative literary technologies, the textual methods respected by imperial governments. That constitutes not a pillaging of antiquity so much as a response to a difficult moment of cultural transition.

When the memory of Efnisien's insult to the Irish inexplicably erupts years later to disrupt Branwen's marriage, we see a past pain that refuses redress, a loss that survives to return again. Linking survival with loss rather than with progress resonates with the postcolonial insistence that we eschew a progressive chronology.[38] And the tale, with its patchwork of fragments, its return to archaic images of the magical Bran and the desolate Branwen, marks the time of the colonial encounter not chronologically but contrapuntally: Loss and survival, Irish and Welsh and English, play over and through one another, simultaneous, distinct, yet related, of varying degrees of intensity at various times. Gilles Deleuze and Félix Guattari recently have offered a way of thinking about contrapuntal and repetitive timing in what they call "the refrain," a notion indebted to musical time and birdsong.[39] The "refrain" is expressive and territorial, marking time through a repetition of sounds. Just as music takes over the space it spills into, with strains of varying intensity and endurance (louder here, fainter there), the refrain takes up space in time; it thus helps us think about time and space together. The notion of the "refrain" might help us think about the recurrence of the colonial scene in various times and places: in the eleventh and fourteenth centuries; in Matthew Arnold's nineteenth century; or in modern scholarly methods that continue to treat texts like the *Mabinogi* as residual vestiges of some vague archaic past. Such a notion might replace a chronological view of progress so as to cope with the repetitive compulsions of colonial culture.

If we hope to battle the recapitulation of the colonial demand in our own day, we need careful accounts of categories like archaic fragmentation, accounts that consider alternative histories and alternative uses of those imaginary structures. A postcolonial view of archaic fragmentation might even inspire sympathy for the apparent guilt of accommodationism, especially if, as in Branwen's case, it comes from a poignant desire to rescue another life. In its final episodes the tale of Branwen can, moreover, remind us the value of the particular, and the poignancy of its loss. It can suggest that when we hold particular desires and particular lives to be of less value than large, communal, cultural identities, we collude with the empire's insistence that parts are nothing but broken fragments, trivial details, expressing only narrow interests. "Branwen" can remind us that particular lives and particular acts do not deserve to be sacrificed to larger cultural or national wholes. We might recover Branwen's story so as to mark our time not with the lethal victimizations and the guilt she was made to suffer but with her ingenuity and courage in the hope of a more compassionate postcolonial future.

Notes

1. For an account of the reception of the texts of the *Mabinogi* following the "Romantic Revival" at the end of the eighteenth century, and for an account of Lady Charlotte's role in the publication of these texts, see Rachel Bromwich, "The Mabinogion and Lady Charlotte Guest," in *The Mabinogi: A Book of Essays,* ed. C. W. Sullivan III (New York: Garland, 1996), pp. 3–18.

2. Mention occurs in John Rhys, "Introduction," to diplomatics edition of *The Red Book of Hergest* (Oxford: Clarendon, 1887), ix–x; and in Proinsias Mac Cana, *The Mabinogi* (Cardiff: University of Wales Press, 1992), p. 51. See C. W. Sullivan, "Introduction," in *The Mabinogi,* xvii; Rachel Bromwich, *Matthew Arnold and Celtic Literature: A Retrospect: 1865–1965* (Oxford: Clarendon, 1965), p. 1. Patrick K. Ford has noted that "the notion of an antiquity pillaged has been more or less pervasive in Welsh scholarship" (p. 199), and he has been a staunch opponent of the implications of Arnold's view. See "Prolegomena to a Reading of the Mabinogi," reprinted in *The Mabinogi,* ed. Sullivan, pp. 197–216. On larger questions of how medieval studies recapitulates colonial disavowals, see Kathleen Biddick, *The Shock of Medievalism* (Durham, NC: Duke University Press, 1998).

3. Welsh scholars emphasize the primacy of Wales's relations to European culture as a whole; in their view emphasizing English relations can constitute another colonizing gesture, reductively viewing Welsh culture as derivative of its relations with England. I am grateful to Stephen Knight who first pointed this out to me. The European connection is, of course, also important to Renan's "Essai sur le Poésie des Races Celtiques." As my read-

ing of "Branwen" will make clearer, I am interested in the colonial relations vis-à-vis Wales as part of a larger intercultural scene. Welsh/English
relations need not be opposed to attention to a larger context. For a comparative analysis of the Welsh poet Dafydd ap Gwilym and his near-con-
temporary Chaucer that suggests the European character of medieval
Welsh poetry, see Stephen Knight "Chaucer's British Rival," *Leeds Studies
in English* 20 (1989): 21–98.

4. These pertain to Arnold's more widely read *Culture and Anarchy*. My con-
   sideration of *On Celtic Literature* is everywhere endebted to Young's work.
   See Robert J. C. Young, *Colonial Desire: Hybridity in Theory, Culture and Race*
   (New York: Routledge, 1995), particularly pp. 55–89.

5. Robert Knox, *The Races of Man*, p. 379, as cited by Young, *Colonial Desire*,
   p. 72. As Young puts it: "In the 1860s anti-Irish prejudice was still rife in
   Britain, so [for Arnold] to advocate the accommodation of Celtic culture
   in any form was a radical move" (p. 72).

6. Young, *Colonial Desire*, p. 71.

7. Ibid.

8. Ibid., p. 163. See Edward Said, *Orientalism* (New York: Vintage Books,
   1978); Homi K. Bhabha, "Of Mimicry and Man: The Ambivalence of
   Colonial Discourse," *October* 28 (1984): 125–33, and "DissemiNation:
   Time, Narrative, and the Margins of the Modern Nation," in *Nation and
   Narration*, ed. Bhabha (New York: Routledge, 1990); Gayatri Spivak, "Can
   the Subaltern Speak?" in *Marxism and the Interpretation of Culture*, ed. Cary
   Nelson and Lawrence Grossberg (Urbana: University of Illinois, 1988), pp.
   271–313, and *In Other Worlds: Essays in Cultural Politics* (New York: Rout-
   ledge, 1987). This approach has been challenged by Benita Parry and
   Chandra Talpade Mohanty for what they consider is a lack of concern for
   more materialist oppositional historical inquiry. See Benita Parry, "Problems in Current Theories of Colonial Discourse," in *The Post-Colonial
   Studies Reader*, ed. Bill Ashcroft, Gareth Griffiths, and Helen Tiffin (New
   York: Routledge, 1997), pp. 36–44. Young sees their critique as "a form of
   category mistake": *Colonial Desire*, p. 163.

9. Rachel Bromwich, *Matthew Arnold*, p. 1.

10. I borrow this phrase from Ashcroft, Griffiths, and Tiffin, editors of *The Post-
    Colonial Studies Reader*, who write "Post-colonial does not mean 'post-in-
    dependence,' or 'after colonialism,' for this would be to falsely ascribe an
    end to the colonial process. . . . 'Post-colonialism' begins from the very first
    moment of colonial contact. It is the discourse of oppositionality which
    colonialism brings into being": p. 117.

11. Arnold, *Celtic Literature*, p. 296.

12. Ibid., pp. 296–7.

13. Bhabha points to the prodigiously living aspects of a "national people":
    "DissemiNation," p. 297.

14. Anne McClintock, *Imperial Leather: Race, Gender, and Sexuality in the Colo-
    nial Conquest* (New York: Routledge, 1995), p. 40.

15. Arnold, *Celtic Literature,* p. 322.

16. Ibid., pp. 335, 386.

17. Indeed Arnold explicitly criticized the modern Welsh literary competition the *Eisteddfod* for its "literary cultivation of Welsh as an instrument of living literature," as "a fantastic and mischief-working delusion" (*Celtic Literature,* p. 297). Welsh writers have, to be sure, remained unconvinced by this aspect of Arnold's essay; the *Eisteddfod* continues to the present day.

18. The image of a fragmented Welsh will haunt the historiography of medieval Wales up until, at least, World War II. R.R. Davies has written "the basic presuppositions of English historiography, notably its . . . bias (all the stronger for being unspoken and unexamined) in favor of strong government, legal uniformity, and direct and clear lines of command and authority. Such a historiography finds it difficult to come to terms with societies which are institutionally fragmented, fluid in their frontiers, multiple in their loyalties, cultures, and laws." Yet "such," Davies writes, "are most medieval frontier societies": R. R. Davies, "Frontier Arrangements in Fragmented Societies: Ireland and Wales," in *Medieval Frontier Societies,* ed. Robert Bartlett and Angus Mackay (Oxford: Clarendon, 1989), pp. 78–100.

19. Patrick Ford, "Prolegomena," p. 215.

20. The Red Book ms. dates from the early fourteenth century; based on philological evidence, the text itself has been dated from the mid-eleventh or late twelfth centuries. For the debate on dating, see T. M. Charles-Edwards, "The Date of the Four Branches of the Mabinogi," in *The Mabinogi,* ed. Sullivan, pp. 19–78.

21. For example, Juliette Wood, "The Calumniated Wife in Medieval Welsh Literature," Catherine A. McKenna, "The Theme of Sovereignty in Pwyll," Patrick K. Ford, "Branwen: A Study of Celtic Affinities," Andrew Welsh, "*Manawydan fab Llyr:* Wales, England, and the "New Man," all reprinted in *The Mabinogi,* ed. Sullivan. For a review of the pertinent scholarship on Branwen, see Mac Cana, *The Mabinogi,* pp. 129–32, n 24.

22. Andrew Welsh reads the figure of Branwen as a "peace-weaving queen"; Patrick Ford suggests that questions of militarism are important to this text. Andrew Welsh, "Branwen, Beowulf and the Tragic Peaceweaving Tale," *Viator* 22 (1991): 1–13; Ford, "Celtic Affinities," p. 111.

23. The Welsh text is taken from Derick S. Thomson, ed. *Branwen Uerch Lyr,* Mediaeval and Modern Welsh Series, vol. 2 (Dublin: Dublin Institute of Advanced Studies, 1961); quotation at p.2. Translations are based on Gwyn Jones and Thomas Jones, *The Mabinogion* (London: Everyman, 1979; reprinted 1989).

24. Saunders Lewis identifies a triangulation of Irish, Welsh, and English concerns in the text. He identifies "British" interests with Anglo-Norman ones, reading Bran as a kind of double for Henry II. Lewis' concern with establishing the *Mabinogi*'s Welsh credentials (contra Morgan Watkins's *La civilisation francaise dans les Mabinogion*) contributes to his argument (as do

his political positions on Welsh nationalism). His argument has been supplanted by T. M. Charles-Edwards' position ("Date," pp. 19–78). However, I agree with Lewis that this moment in the text positions Welsh sovereignty defensively, although I think it alludes to England as a common enemy of both Ireland and Wales. Lewis, "Branwen," *Ysgrifau Beirniadol* 5 (1970): 30–43. The implications of this for questions of cultural change will be clearer in a moment.

25. Edwardian conquest was to prove equally devastating; chronicle entries narrate territorial and economic losses suffered at the hands of Edward's "hosts" of military troops. See *Brut Y Tywysogyon, Red Book of Hergest Version,* ed. Thomas Jones (Cardiff: University of Wales Press, 1955).

26. For example, R. R. Davies, *Conquest, Coexistence and Change: Wales 1063–1415* (Oxford: Oxford University Press, 1987); David Walker, *Medieval Wales,* Cambridge Medieval Textbooks (Cambridge: Cambridge University Press, 1990); Glyn Roberts, "Wales and England: Antipathy and Sympathy 1282–1485," *Welsh History Review* 1 (1966): 375–96.

27. Pertinent histories include R. R. Davies, "The English State and the 'Celtic' Peoples, 1100–1400," *Journal of Historical Sociology* 6 (1993); and his *Conquest, Coexistance, and Change;* David Johnson, "Iolo Goch and the English: Welsh Poetry and Politics in the Fourteenth Century," *Cambridge Medieval Celtic Studies* 12 (1986): 73–98.

28. Juliette Wood calls Branwen victimization a result of "xenophobia," (p. 65) and reads the calumniated wife motif in "Branwen" (a "folk motif incorporated into a literary work") in relation to the history of the treatment of foreigners: "Calumniated Wife," pp. 65–75.

29. *Branwen Uerch Lyr* p.9.

30. Mac Cana, *The Mabinogi,* pp. 44, 45.

31. The words are Wittig's as cited by Ford, "Celtic Affinities," p. 118, n. 33: Susan Wittig, *Stylistic and Narrative Structure in the Middle English Romances* (Austin: University of Texas Press, 1978). Ford disagrees with Mac Cana's reading of the fragmentary nature of the uses of Irish "sources" in Branwen; he argues that scholars must "begin with the principle of the integrity of the text" (p. 118, n 33). My reading attempts to link textual integrity to cultural innovations, and I would suggest that Mac Cana's discomfort with what he terms the text's "residual" character betrays Matthew Arnold's influence. See Mac Cana, *The Mabinogion,* pp. 50–51.

32. Grifford Charles-Edwards, "The Scribes of the Red Book of Hergest," *The National Library of Wales Journal* 21 (1980): 246–56.

33. From this view we could consider the "branch" "Manawydan, son of Llyr" for its explicit attention to innovation and an English locale. See Welsh, "Manawydan."

34. *Branwen Uerch Lyr* p. 15.

35. Maurice Bloch's anthropological account of Merina society argues that "traditional" (hierarchical) cultures cope with loss through a double figuration of death. The threat of decay of physical death poses to community

is split from death as a transcendent union beyond the grave. Bloch argues that women's cultural association with physical birth grounds their identification, in these societies, with physical death and bodily decay; this frees men to remain linked to transcendence, both "spiritual" birth and transcendent unions beyond such loss: "Death, Women, Power," in *Death and the Regeneration of Life,* ed. Maurice Bloch and Jonathan Parry (Cambridge: Cambridge University Press, 1982), pp. 211–30. Julia Kristeva's identification of the "death bearing woman" with separation from the mother and with subjectivity in language suggests the implications of this for authorship: *Black Sun: Melancholia and Depression,* trans. Leon S. Roudiez (New York: Columbia University Press, 1989). Klaus Theweleit describes as "orphic [literary] production" a male author's need to imagine his own future as a continuation of the past while accommodating cultural, and technological, change. In this structure, the woman, like Eurydice, is sacrificed so that the male, like Orpheo, can accommodate innovation and, through the memory of his beloved, retain a coherent link to his past. Theweleit shows, through the history of Gottfried Benn, how such authorial structures desire and produce dead female bodies: "The Politics of Orpheus: Between Women, Hades, Political Power and the Media," *New German Critique* 36 (1985): 133–56. A more patient explication of these theories must be deferred at present.

36. Ford points to the possibility that Branwen and Bendigeidfran might be "one and the same name," although Branwen is clearly "the feminine form" while Bran clearly is "conceived as a male deity in Welsh": "Celtic Affinities," p. 105. We might thus read Bran and Branwen as a doubled figure for Welsh sovereignty, suggesting that the text's final split between Branwen's loss and Bran's recovery negotiates losses and recoveries for cultural sovereignty.

37. J. K. Bollard, "The Structure of the Four Branches of the *Mabinogi,*" in *The Mabinogi,* ed. Sullivan, pp. 165–96, quotation at p. 167.

38. Sara Suleri argues that colonial intimacies "dissipate the logic of origins, or the rational framework of chronologies," implying that if we are to read the historical thicknesses of a colonial past we may need access to fragments, and to apparently irrational models of time (p. 9). See her "Introduction" to *The Rhetoric of English India* (Chicago: University of Chicago Press, 1990), pp. 1–23. Anne McClintock argues that while "a good deal of postcolonial studies has set itself against the imperial idea of linear time," "the term postcolonial . . . is haunted by the very figure of linear development that it sets out to dismantle. . . . Metaphorically, the term postcolonialism marks history as a series of stages along an epochal road from "the precolonial," to "the colonial," to "the postcolonial"—an unbidden, if disavowed commitment to linear time and the idea of development" (*Imperial Leather,* p. 10). For a postcolonial reading of the timing of the "medieval" and the nation, see Kathleen Davis, "National Writing in the

Ninth Century: A Reminder for Postcolonial Thinking about the Nation," *Journal of Medieval and Early Modern Studies* 28 (1998): 611–37.

39. Gilles Deleuze and Félix Guattari, *A Thousand Plateaus: Capitalism and Schizophrenia* (Minneapolis: University of Minnesota Press, 1987); see especially "Of the Refrain," pp. 310–50.

CHAPTER 10

FETISHISM, 1927, 1614, 1461*

Steven F. Kruger

> *This chapter considers part of the history and prehistory of the fetish in order to call attention to the ways in which a certain fetishistic logic—a simultaneous denial and recognition—characterizes the development of interlocking Western discourses of sexual perversion, religious/racial distinction, and historical periodization.*

This chapter attempts an (admittedly oblique) approach to the question of how modern postcolonial narratives (for instance, of sexuality) might be useful for reading the Middle Ages, and, inversely, of how the medieval might be implicated in an understanding of modern (post)colonial dynamics. I look first to Freud's writing on fetishism as providing a useful if problematic way of conceiving not just sexuality but also the unequal and violent interracial, interreligious contacts of both colonial and medieval moments. Freud's theory, however, cannot be seen as just a modern (and hence neutral and objective) analytical tool for understanding psychic and social relations.[1] Looking backward from the Freudian moment to its early modern prehistory, we can see that the Freudian and post-Freudian treatment of fetishism is indelibly marked by an earlier, racialized discourse of the fetish. That discourse haunts Freud's treatment of the "perversions," which might indeed be seen—if only in part—as continuing that classification of human subspecies and races that accelerated with the "age of discovery." But the early modern discourse of the fetish also has its prehistories, and I conclude by considering how, in a certain fetishistic movement, that discourse both depends on and denies the medieval.

The main promise of psychoanalytic thinking on the fetish lies in its capacity for calling into question the normality and centrality of heterosexuality. Freud posits a developmental route for fetishism ("the fetish is a substitute for the woman's [mother's] phallus which the little boy once believed in and does not wish to forego") and details the ambivalent mental process that route enables: "In the world of psychical reality the woman still has a penis in spite of all, but this penis is no longer the same as it once was. Something else has taken its place, has been appointed its successor, so to speak, and now absorbs all the interest which formerly belonged to the penis." Freud goes on to suggest that his "solution" to the problem of fetishism is valuable not just in itself but because the processes here analyzed are more generally operative in sexual development: "Probably no male human being is spared the terrifying shock of threatened castration at the sight of the female genitals. We cannot explain why it is that some of them become homosexual in consequence of this experience, others ward it off by creating a fetish, and the great majority overcome it."[2] There are, of course, deep problems with such formulations, not the least of which is the assumption of a male position as the starting point for the theory of sexuality and the consequent privileging of castration, and therefore lack, in the etiology of desire.[3] Yet Freud's placing the three possible outcomes of male sexuality on a more or less equal footing suggests a strong and admirable impulse toward depathologizing nonmajority sexualities.[4]

Elsewhere, however, Freud's work on fetishism and the other "perversions" participates, like earlier sexological writing, in an opposite movement, one that is not inaccurately described in Michel Foucault's words as "an *incorporation of perversions* and a new *specification of individuals.*"[5] Richard von Krafft-Ebing, in his *Psychopathia Sexualis,* connects fetishism to the development of "normal" love: "The germ of sexual love is probably to be found in the individual charm (*fetich*) with which persons of opposite sex sway each other."[6] But the classificatory and pathologizing impulses in Krafft-Ebing are strong: "The body-fetishist is not to be regarded as a monster by virtue of his or her excesses, like the sadist or masochist, but rather by virtue of his or her deficiencies."[7] Havelock Ellis approaches fetishism within his treatment of "erotic symbolism," and, as with Krafft-Ebing and Freud, there is a certain impulse toward normalization. At the same time, Ellis moves to associate the "perversions" with "primitive" cultures. Thus, for Ellis, foot fetishism represents a "re-emergence, by a pseudo-atavism or arrest of development, of a mental or emotional impulse which was probably experienced by our forefathers, and is often traceable among young children today."[8] A certain kinship with Freud's ideas about the relation between civilizational and individual development is apparent here. In their detailing of fetishism, all three of these sexological discourses share (to return to Foucault) a focus "on this whole alien strain [that] did not aim to suppress it, but rather to give it an analytical, visible, and permanent reality: it was implanted in bodies, slipped in beneath modes of conduct, made into a principle of classification and intelligibility, established as a *raison d'être* and a natural order of disorder."[9] Yet even Foucault's work, while it recognizes in the "deployment of sexuality" an implication in the development of modern "racism," often does not take into account how colonial histories mark the new regimes of sexuality.[10] Such a marking, however, is evident in Freud's popularizing lecture on "The Sexual Life of Man": even as he is concerned to argue that an understanding of the "normal" depends on its relation to "morbid forms of sexuality," Freud orders the "perversions" along a clearly pathologizing, zoological "scale" of being, thus following a "scientific" procedure akin to the hierarchized ranking of "the races of man" that characterized European colonial experience:

> These perverts [i.e., inverts] do at least seek to achieve very much the same ends with the objects of their desires as normal people do with theirs. But after them comes a long series of abnormal types, in whom the sexual activities become increasingly further removed from anything which appears attractive to a reasonable being. In their manifold variety and their strangeness these types may be compared to the grotesque monstrosities painted by P. Brueghel to represent the temptation of St. Anthony. The chaotic assembly calls out for classification if it is not to bewilder us completely.

Freud lists a variety of "perverse" types, including "the fetishists," who directly precede necrophiliacs and Freud's concluding exclamation, "But enough of these horrors!"[11]

We might recognize Freud's ambivalent stance toward the "perversions" as itself fetishistic in structure. While, on one hand, the analysis of the *dynamic* of fetishism allows for the insight that there is no ideal sexuality based in *presence,* all sexuality, even that "*known as* normal sexual life,"[12] being founded on a certain lack or absence; on the other hand, the hypostasization of sexual types in a "scale" of being covers over, denies, that radical insight, asserting on the contrary a certain fullness to that "normal" sexuality "attractive to a reasonable being," a fullness indeed compared to the metaphysical security of the Christian saint over against "grotesque monstrosities." While "these mad, extraordinary and horrible things" that are the "perversions" call into question the "normal"—"play[ing] the same part in their lives as normal sexual satisfaction plays in ours"—they also allow for the firm distinction between "*their* lives" and "*ours,*" between debased, arrested sexual development and full, adult sexuality.[13]

The prehistory and origin of the word "fetish" have been traced in some detail by William Pietz.[14] Michael Taussig provides a convenient summary of this account:

> Bill Pietz has presented us with a genealogy of the *fetish* that grounds this eminently strange word in the practice of *making,* rooted in strategic social relations of trade, religion, slaving, and modern science. To this end, he discusses certain social practices in the commerce of ancient Rome (separating natural products from *factitious,* artificially cultivated, ones), in early Roman Christianity (with God making man in his image, but man denied, therefore, similar sorts of making), the "bad making" of the *maleficium* of the magic of the Middle Ages, the notion of the fetish or *fetisso* in the Portuguese pidgin trading language of the West African slave routes, and finally, the positivist rendering of fetishism as the sheen or mystical counterpart to their virtual worship of objectness.[15]

As Pietz emphasizes, the word "fetish" has a history intimately linked to the late-sixteenth and early-seventeenth-century European exploitation of Africa and in particular of the "Guinea" "gold," "ivory," and "slave" coasts.[16] While the earliest form of the word, Portuguese "feitiço," literally "something made" and hence a "charm," seems to have emerged in the late Middle Ages to refer to sorcery and magic, the word's much broader sixteenth-century currency—along with the emergence of a new form, "fetisso"—is clearly linked to colonialism.[17] The word was quickly borrowed into Italian, and, in the first fifteen years of the seventeenth century, it gained a remarkable trans-European dissemination: Its first attested use in Dutch was in 1602, in French in 1605, in German in 1606, in English in 1613.[18] Spanish, despite the presence of a cognate form "hechizo," meaning "artificial, false," also adopted "fetiche" (though I have not been able to date the adoption).[19] The history of forms of the word—where earlier forms based on the Portuguese, like the English "fetisso," were replaced by ones based on the French "fétiche," a movement that occurred in Portuguese itself[20]—emphasizes the initially transnational situation of the word. Indeed, the conflicting etymological theories about the early years of "fetish" and its derivatives all suggest that it, like the merchandise of the Guinea coast to whose culture it was first firmly attached, was subject to a vigorous international "trade." Pietz would firmly attach the development of "pidgin 'fetisso'" to "the complex intercultural world" of "the German coast," "crossed by many different African and European languages but with no language of its own."[21] One etymology of later European forms traces the word from Portuguese, through "a Portuguese creole dialect of the African coast," to French and then the other European languages.[22] Another, noting "that the Italian *feticcio* appeared already in translations from the Portuguese . . . in 1562 and 1586," suggests that "from the Portuguese, [fetish] passed to the Italian, . . . from the Italian to the French; and from there to the Castilian and other European languages."[23] The *Grande Larousse,* etymologizing "féticheur," proposes a route from Portuguese to Dutch to French.[24]

By the time of its earliest appearance in English, in *Purchas his Pilgrimage,* "fetish" (in the older form "fetisso") already had a relatively wide range of meanings, all attached to a description of the culture of "Guinea."[25] The "Fetisso" is a whole set of religious objects—ranging from "the highest tree in the Toune" to which the king "prayeth and sacrificeth"; to the "strawen Rings, called *Fetissos* or *Gods*" that receive sacrifices of "Wheat, with Water and Oyle"; to similar "straw-Fetissos" worn copiously "about their feet" and arms, and on their "garment[s]," and that are similarly the object of sacrifice. "Fetisso" is also the name for the god to whom all these actions are directed, and the religious cult is presided over by a priest named the "Fetissero." "Fetisso" is shown to take its place at all stages of the life of the people, from birth to death: It protects babies from demonic abduction and from "vomiting," "falling," "bleeding," sleeplessness, "wild beasts"; it presides over eating and drinking, grants protection against the native "Deitie" or "Deuill," makes the fishing industry prosper, provides a test in cases of "criminall accusation," and takes a central place in funeral rites. The "Fetisso" is also importantly wrapped up with sexuality. Its first mention comes in reference to marriage customs: "If the husband suspects his wife, hee makes triall of her honestie, by causing her to eat salt with divers Fetisso ceremonies hereafter mentioned, the feare whereof makes her confesse. They haue many wiues, if they can buy and keepe them." The proliferation of "fetissos" in Purchas serves to emphasize that these are, as he says, "superstitious fancies," and to make clear that African society and culture are permeated by such "superstition."[26]

By 1704, when William [Willem] Bosman's Dutch *A New and Accurate Description of the Coast of Guinea, Divided into The Gold, The Slave, and The Ivory Coasts* was published, the European treatment of African "fetishistic" religion had become standardized.[27] "Fetiche" in Bosman is again connected to idol worship, to the magic injury of enemies, to the trial of criminals, to the making of oaths. Bosman repeats the idea found in Purchas that "Fetiche" provides a means for finding out a woman's adultery, and he adds that the "Negroes'" wished-for "Rewards consist in the Multiplicity of Wives and Slaves, and their Punishments in the want of them." He also includes a meaning for "Fetiche" not found in Purchas, but one that anticipates later economic uses of the term: "Fetiches" are a kind of "false" gold commonly used in trading:

the Gold it self is indeed very little worth . . . and yet it passes currant all over the Coast. . . . [T]he *Negroes* . . . mix[] it with other Gold [and] bring it to us . . . and as soon as received, the Clerks are ordered to pick it out of the other with which it is mixed; so that this Stuff seems to pass backward and forward without the least diminution, notwithstanding large quantities of it are annually sent to *Europe* by the *French* and *Portugueze,* besides what we our selves spend: But the *Negroes* making them faster than we export them, they are like to continue long enough.[28]

Just as the religious fetish represents a debased version of "true" (Christian) religion—in Bosman's words, "How their Gods are represented to them, or what Idea they form of them, I never yet could learn, because indeed they do not know themselves"—the monetary fetish represents an empty, profitless version of "true," productive—that is, European—commerce.

Bosman's and Purchas's accounts stand within a whole, trans-European set of texts that provide a certain prehistory not just for Freud but also for Karl Marx's reenvisioning of European commerce in the terms of a "primitive" (and implicitly racialized) "commodity fetishism." One of Marx's great innovations, after all, was to make "modern" capitalism and bourgeois society themselves part of "the prehistoric stage of human society."[29] As Anne McClintock notes, "Both psychoanalysis and Marxism took shape around the idea of fetishism as a primitive regression and the disavowal of the social value of domestic work."[30]

So far as I have discovered, in his writings on sexual fetishism Freud refers directly only once to the anthropological/religious meaning of "fetish" that, in the late nineteenth and early twentieth centuries was still its main denotation:[31] "Such substitutes [for the sexual object] are with some justice likened to the fetishes in which savages believe that their gods are embodied."[32] Conversely, in his work on the origins of religion, Freud only rarely refers to fetishistic religious practices, preferring instead to base his theory on an analysis of totemism.[33] One might say that, in instituting the psychoanalytic theory of the fetish, Freud largely "represses" an earlier, and at the time still dominant, discourse. But that discourse "returns" as the classificatory strain of Freudian thinking about the "perversions"—that is, as a racializing treatment of sexual types that diverge, more or less radically, from a position of metaphysical fullness identified with the "normal."

The extent to which, in fact, post-Freudian discourses on sexual fetishism have remained enmeshed in a racializing attribution to the fetishist of a "superstitious" (Purchas) distance from the real thing, from the "Idea" (Bosman) of (hetero)sexuality, is suggested by the route one coun-

terdiscourse takes in its "celebration of leathersexuality." Here are the
opening words of Geoff Mains's 1984 liberationist *Urban Aboriginals:*

> This book is a journey into the aboriginal soul. . . . It is a journey marked
> by fetish and mana, shaman, ritual and trance. Here, men partake of a very
> real magic. They are men among whom danger, fear and new hope have
> broken many of the misconceptions upon which western civilization fal-
> ters. These are men not apart from but of the very blood of that civiliza-
> tion. Urbane and savage in the same breath, they are animal and human in
> the same stroke. Of Caliban, Prospero admits: "This thing of darkness I ac-
> knowledge mine."[34]

Mains here recognizes the stigmatizing attribution of something racially
"primitive" or "savage" to (fetishistic) leathersex: rather than disavow that
attribution, he embraces it, making access to the "aboriginal soul" a necessity for the self-understanding of an endangered "western civilization."

The Freudian idea of the fetish "travels" with some ease to the context of
medieval religious controversy. To take just one, relatively familiar, late-medieval example, the *Croxton Play of the Sacrament* (which dates the events it
claims to depict to 1461), we might read the play's expressed Jewish skepti-
cism about the Host as demonstrating a certain antifetishistic logic. As the
leader of the Jews, Jonathas, might say, the ideology of the Eucharist is a
Christian ploy for covering over the emptiness of their God, an emptiness
that will easily be shown through the dismantling of the fetish object.[35] But
already in the ambivalence of their initial attitude toward the Host—they
wish both to prove the falseness of Christian doctrine about the Eucharist
and to torture the Host as if it were indeed a sentient being—the Jews show
themselves susceptible to the power of the object they attack, and they
demonstrate precisely a fetishistic logic. In their actions—they torture the
Host to prove its nonidentity with the tortured Christ—they simultaneously disavow and acknowledge the reality of transubstantiation. The play's
Christian author turns the Jewish attack on Christian fetishism back against
the Jews, who are shown finally to be the "true," self-deceiving fetishists.
Where the Host remains intact, demonstrating its fullness and plenitude—
its real divinity—the Jews, trusting in themselves and the strength of their
own bodies, trusting that these will provide them an access to "truth," literally disintegrate. The Host sticks to Jonathas's hand; nailing the Host (and
hence his own hand) to a post in an attempt to separate the hand from the
Host, Jonathas instead succeeds in separating his arm from his body. Jewish
rather than Christian belief is shown to be the empty cover, and the Jews'
only way out of their emptiness is conversion—an embracing of the object

they originally attacked, seeing and now believing in its powerful plenitude. Indeed, conversion allows the miraculous reintegration of Jonathas's fragmented body.

We can recognize here at work not just the play of partiality and fullness that Freud's theory of fetishism points us toward but also—in the Christian author's demonstration of the *superiority* of the objects of Christian faith—a move not unlike Freud's privileging of certain kinds of sexuality over others. Just as Freudian discourse on the fetish remains enmeshed in a racializing hierarchization of sexuality, so the "fetish accusations" of medieval religious controversy attempt to institute a violent hierarchy. The radical potential of Freud's theory lies in its enabling us to recognize how the claim to religious fullness, like the claim to the fullness of "normal" sexuality, itself rests on a fetishistic logic. The interplay of the miraculously intact Eucharist and the miraculously dis- and reintegrated Jewish body on one hand disavows lack (the Jewish belief in the emptiness of Christian incarnational doctrine) but on the other calls our attention to it—in the Christian anxiety provoked by Jewish disbelief and in the (anxious) attempt to counter that disbelief. To quote Freud one last time: "On the one hand, with the help of certain mechanisms [the child] rejects reality and refuses to accept any prohibition; on the other hand, in the same breath he recognizes the danger of reality, takes over the fear of that danger as a symptom and tries subsequently to divest himself of the fear."[36]

The medieval history of Western European religious controversy might productively be read via the fetish: Debates within Christianity, and among Christianity, Judaism, and Islam, consistently focus on questions of presence and absence, and they consistently contain avowals of plenitude that are simultaneously disavowals of a feared emptiness. Knowing something of this history, one might wonder why, in the sixteenth and seventeenth centuries, a new term, "fetisso"/"fetish," was felt to be necessary to describe the new cultures encountered, and actively exploited, in Africa. The Middle Ages had, in the contacts and conflicts among Islam, Christianity, and Judaism, evolved a complex and flexible language of blame, involving attacks on both the rationality and the body of the other and ontological distinctions between the human (and chosen) self and the not-quite-human other. What necessitated the early modern transformation of such medieval discourses?

Of course, as Pietz suggests, "fetish" is not a wholly new coinage; via Portuguese "feitiço" there is a clear link to medieval religious controversy, especially orthodox Christian attacks on magical, "superstitious" practices associated with witches, heretics, and women.[37] But Pietz himself sees a radical discontinuity between such medieval uses and "the novel idea of the fetish on the West African coast" which he regards as an expression of "a new historical problematic outside the horizon of Christian thought."[38] The new forms of "feitiço"—"fetisso" and "fétiche"/"fetish"—and the rapid development of new words based on such forms in most European languages suggest as well a certain discontinuity. While it is clear, in authors like Purchas and Bosman, that "fetisso"/"fetish" is not a *necessary* coinage— "gods," "idols," "straw rings" all provide synonyms—the repetition of the new word, in its many different senses, in the many situations in which it is said to apply, and the immediate coinage of derivative forms—"fetissero," "fetissan," "feticheer"—create a strangeness effect that both authors seem to cultivate. It is as if only a new word, multiply and shiftingly defined and deployed, can adequately capture the otherness of this situation. The Africans of the "Guinea" coast are part of what is being actively constructed as a *new* experience, suddenly central to European enterprise, and "fetish" serves as one of the tools not just for describing that experience but for making it *new.*

More specifically, the early modern deployment of "fetish" reveals two significant differences from the situation that conditioned medieval religious polemic. The first is internal to Europe and reflects the deep rivenness of Christianity in the wake of the Reformation. Purchas likens "Fetissos" "to the Popish praying-Beads."[39] Bosman compares fetish poisonings to "the Art of poisoning . . . peculiar to the *Italians,*" and he likens the power of the African priest to that of "the Papacy." In commenting on the possible susceptibility of Africans to conversion, he says: "If it was possible to convert the *Negroes* to the Christian Religion, the *Roman*-Catholicks would succeed better than we should, because they already agree in several particulars, especially in their ridiculous Ceremonies."[40] I do not yet know if Catholic writers make similar anti-Protestant use of the fetish, but clearly, at least on the Protestant side, the discourse about Africa serves the purposes of intra-European religious polemic.[41]

At the same time that Europe is religiously split, however, the economic fortunes of its component parts are becoming increasingly interdependent, and dependent especially on trade in the newfound wealth of the Americas, Asia, and Africa.[42] "Fetish" is part of a discourse that moves to bolster all of Europe against its others, and here specifically Africa, an other that is not just being economically exploited but whose people have been made into commodities. We might recognize a variety of ways in which that commodification is justified by Europeans—for instance, in accounts of how easily the natives sell each other as slaves—and the invention of the fetish participates in such justifications; from Voltaire's *Candide:* "when my mother sold me for ten patacóns on the Guinea coast, she said to me: 'My dear child, bless our fetishes, worship them always, they will make you live happily; you have the honor to be a slave to our lords the whites, and thereby you are making the Fortune of your father and mother.'"[43] In descriptions like Purchas's and Bosman's, sprinkled with "fetissos" and "fetiches," the people merge with their "superstitious" trappings, trappings that are indeed, in Bosman, equivalent to a kind of debased currency. People themselves, in such "ethnographic" accounts, show themselves always to be already a kind of "fetishized" merchandise, like gold or ivory having their own peculiar "coast," and ready for trade.

But if "fetish" and its dissemination indeed respond to early modern religious and commercial situations in a way significantly different from their medieval predecessors, they also serve (fetishistically) to cover over certain historical continuities. The split within Western Christianity repeats, although of course with differences, the split of Eastern and Western churches and various medieval schisms and conflicts within the Western church itself. The early modern consolidation of Europe in contradistinction to Asia and Africa continues certain complex medieval movements associated with the Crusades, with the politics of Iberia and of the Mediterranean more generally. The slave trade itself, associated so strongly with the "modern" discovery of a "New World," continues (again, with differences) an active medieval (especially Mediterranean) slave trade.[44] If we are to understand both the medieval and early modern, we must attend not only to the latter's self-construction over against the former but also to the ways in which that self-construction enacts the logic of the fetish—asserting difference at least in part to deny what is simultaneously recognized, the ways in which that which is *not* "modern" not only *survives into* but *constitutively shapes* "modernity."

Notes

*This essay was originally presented at the Modern Language Association convention on a panel organized by Kathy Lavezzo including papers by Kathleen Biddick and Andrew Taylor and a response by Laurie Finke. I thank the various members of that panel for their helpful comments; I am also indebted to Ron Scapp and John Weir, who listened to early versions, and to Glenn Burger, who read it in its later stages.

1. See Bruno Latour, *We Have Never Been Modern,* trans. Catherine Porter (Cambridge, MA: Harvard University Press, 1993), on the construction of a "modern critical stance" that "would establish a partition between a natural world that has always been there, a society with predictable and stable interests and stakes, and a discourse that is independent of both reference and society" (p. 11).

2. Sigmund Freud, "Fetishism" [1927], in *Sigmund Freud: Sexuality and the Psychology of Love,* ed. Philip Rieff, trans. Joan Riviere [1928] (New York: Collier/Macmillan, 1963), pp. 204–9, quotation at pp. 205–6.

3. For two important critiques of the Freudian starting point and its consequences, see Gilles Deleuze and Félix Guattari, *Anti-Oedipus: Capitalism and Schizophrenia,* trans. Robert Hurley, Mark Seem, and Helen R. Lane (Minneapolis: University of Minnesota Press, 1983), and Luce Irigaray, *Speculum of the Other Woman,* trans. Gillian C. Gill (Ithaca, NY: Cornell University Press, 1985).

4. Also see the similar passage at the end of "The Sexual Aberrations," in Freud's *Three Essays on the Theory of Sexuality,* trans. James Strachey (New York: Avon, 1962): "By demonstrating the part played by perverse impulses in the formation of symptoms in the psychoneuroses, we have quite remarkably increased the number of people who might be regarded as perverts. It is not only that neurotics in themselves constitute a very numerous class, but it must also be considered that an unbroken chain bridges the gap between the neuroses in all their manifestations and normality. . . . [T]he extraordinarily wide dissemination of the perversions forces us to suppose that the disposition to perversions is itself of no great rarity but must form a part of what passes as the normal constitution. . . . What is in question are the innate constitutional roots of the sexual instinct. In one class of cases (the perversions) these roots may grow into the actual vehicles of sexual activity; in others they may be submitted to an insufficient suppression (repression) and thus be able in a roundabout way to attract a considerable proportion of sexual energy to themselves as symptoms; while in the most favourable cases, which lie between these two extremes, they may by means of effective restriction and other kinds of modification bring about what is known as normal sexual life" (pp. 63–64).

5. Michel Foucault, *The History of Sexuality, Volume I: An Introduction,* trans. Robert Hurley (New York: Random House, 1978), pp. 42–43.

6. Richard von Krafft-Ebing, *Psychopathia Sexualis, with Especial Reference to the Antipathic Sexual Instinct: A Medico-Forensic Study,* trans. Franklin S. Klaf [from the twelfth German ed.] (New York: Stein and Day, 1965), p. 11.

7. Ibid., p. 144.

8. Havelock Ellis, *Studies in the Psychology of Sex,* 2 vols. (New York: Random House, 1936), vol. 2, pt. 1 [III.1], p. 27.

9. Foucault, *History of Sexuality,* p. 44.

10. For an analysis that addresses this lack, see Ann Laura Stoler, *Race and the Education of Desire: Foucault's History of Sexuality and the Colonial Order of Things* (Durham, NC: Duke University Press, 1995).

11. Sigmund Freud, *A General Introduction to Psychoanalysis,* trans. Joan Riviere (New York: Pocket Books, 1953), pp. 314–16.

12. Freud, *Three Essays,* p. 64; my emphasis.

13. Freud, *General Introduction,* p. 315.

14. "The Problem of the Fetish, I," *Res* 9 (Spring 1985): 5–17, and "The Problem of the Fetish, II: The Origin of the Fetish," *Res* 13 (Spring 1987): 23–45.

15. Michael Taussig, "*Maleficium:* State Fetishism," in *Fetishism as Cultural Discourse,* ed. Emily Apter and William Pietz (Ithaca, NY: Cornell University Press, 1993), pp. 217–47, quotation at pp. 224–25.

16. On "Enlightenment Europe's image of 'Guinea,'" see William Pietz, "The Problem of the Fetish, IIIa: Bosman's Guinea and the Enlightenment Theory of Fetishism," *Res* 16 (Autumn 1998): 105–23, at 105–6.

17. See Pietz, "Problem of the Fetish, II," and the discussion of "fetishism and imperialism," indebted to Pietz, in Anne McClintock, *Imperial Leather: Race, Gender and Sexuality in the Colonial Contest* (New York: Routledge, 1995), pp. 185–89. Also see Bruno Migliorini, *Lingua d'oggi e di ieri* (Caltanissetta-Roma: Sciascia, 1973): "Il portoghese *feitiço,* da cui *feticcio,* come nome dell'"idolo" fatto da mano umana, opera di fattucchieria, implica quella che era la concezione dei colonizzatori cristiani del Cinquecento" [The Portuguese *feitiço,* from which *feticcio* derives, as the name of an "idol" made by human hands, the work of sorcery, implies that this was the conception of the Christian colonizers of the sixteenth century] (p. 15; my translation). Consult, as well, Jose Pedro Machado, *Dicionário etimológico da língua portuguesa* (Lisbon: Editorial Confluencia, 1956–59).

18. For the Italian instance, see Enrico Zaccaria, *L'elemento iberico nella lingua italiana* (Bologna: C. Cappelli, 1927), p. 470, correcting p. 171; Zaccaria's information is interpreted in Joan Corominas, *Diccionario crítico etimológico castellano e hispánico* (Madrid: Gredos, 1980–91), s.v. "hacer"; see also Manlio Cortelazzo and Paolo Zolli, *Dizionario etimologico della lingua italiana* (Bologna: Zanichelli, 1979–85), and Salvatore Battaglia, *Grande dizionario della lingua italiana* (Turin: Unione tipografico-editrice torinese, 1961-). For the Dutch instance, I take the date provided by the *Grande Larousse de la langue française* (Paris: Librairie Larousse, 1971–78), s.v. "féticheur": "récits de voyageurs néerlandais, comme Marees, 1602"; see also C. Kruyskamp, *Groot woordenboek der nederlandse taal* ('s Gravenhage: Martinus Nijhoff, 1961). On Pieter de Marees's 1602 *Beschryvinghe ende Historische Verhael van het Gout Koninckrijck van Gunea,* see Pietz, "Problem of the Fetish, II,": "It was Marees's text that introduced the term 'Fetisso' into the languages of northern Europe" (p. 39). The *Grande Larousse* supplies information on the first French use; see also Émile Littré, *Dictionnaire de la langue française* (Paris: Gallimard, 1964–65). For the German instance, see Friedrich Kluge, *Etymologisches Wörterbuch der deutschen Sprache* (Berlin: de Gruyter, 1967). For the English instance, see J. A. Simpson and E. S. C. Weiner, *Oxford English Dictionary,* second ed. (New York: Oxford University Press, 1989).

19. See Corominas, *Diccionario crítico etimológico,* s.v. "hacer," and the discussion in Pietz, "Problem of the Fetish, II," of the development of Spanish forms "*hechizo, hechicero,* and *hechiceria*" (p. 34). The word also appears in Danish

("fetisch"), Norwegian ("fetisj") and Swedish ("fetisch"); see J. Kaper, *Dansk-Norsk—Tysk Haand-Ordbog* (Copenhagen: Gyldendalske Boghandels Forlag [F. Hegel & Son]/Graebes Bogtrykkeri, 1889); Theodor Gleditsch, *English-Norwegian Dictionary* (London: Allen & Unwin, 1950); and Bertil Molde, *Illustrerad Svensk Ordbok* (Stockholm: Natur och kultur, 1964). It does not, however, appear in Icelandic, where native words for magic and idolatry are used to translate "fetish" and its derivatives: for fetish, "töfragripur" (magic thing/animal), "goth" (god), and "dyrkun" (worship); for fetishism, "trú á töfragrip" (belief in a magic thing), "skurthgothadyrkun" (idol god worship), "blótskapur" (a disposition toward idolatrous sacrifice [blót]); for fetishist, "skurthgothadyrkari" (idol god worshipper). See Sigurthur Örn Bogason, *Ensk-Islensk Orthabók* (Reykjavik: Utgafandi Isafoldarprentsmithja, 1976).

20. See Machado, *Dicionário etimológico.*
21. Pietz, "Problem of the Fetish, II," p. 39.
22. Corominas, *Diccionario crítico etimológico,* s.v. "hacer"; my translation.
23. Ibid., my translation. The original discussion of etymology in Corominas reads:"De una alteración de *feitiço,* en la pronunciación de un dialecto portugués criollo de la costa africana, dialectos que confunden *s* con _, pudo tomarse el fr.*fétiche*'fetiche' . . . que despues pasó al cast.*fetiche*. . . . Sin embargo el heche de que el it. *feticcio* aparezca ya en traducciones del portugués, publicadas en 1562 y 1586 . . . sugiere otra explicación preferible: del portugués pasó al italiano, . . . del italiano, al francés; y de éste al castellano y demás lenguas europeas."
24. The original reads: "*féticheur* . . . (adaptation de *fétichère* . . . néerl. *feticheer,* lui-même empr. d'un dér. portug. de *feitiço* . . . [*fetisser* . . . est une francisation de *fetissero* . . . repris au portug. par l'intermédiaire de récits de voyageurs néerlandais, comme Marees, 1602]).
25. *Purchas his Pilgrimage* was first printed in 1613; I have had access to a copy dated 1614. Samuel Purchas, *Purchas his Pilgrimage or Relations of the World and the religions observed in all ages and Places discovered from the Creation unto this Present* (London: Printed by William Stansby for Henrie Fetherstone, and are to be sold at his Shop in Pauls Church-yard at the Signe of the Rose, 1614), Book 6, chap. 15. Purchas invokes a Dutch "Description of Guinea" of 1600 (perhaps Marees's 1602 text)as his source. (Pietz, however, claims that "the English translation [of Marees] in Purchase [*sic*] did not appear until 1625," "Problem of the Fetish, II," p. 39.)
26. Purchas, *Purchas his Pilgrimage,* pp. 649–53.
27. William Bosman, *A New and Accurate Description of the Coast of Guinea, Divided into The Gold, The Slave, and The Ivory Coasts* (London: Printed for James Knapton, at the Crown, and Dan. Midwinter, at the Rose and Crown, in St. Paul's Church-Yard, 1705), ed. with intro. John Ralph Willis (New York: Barnes & Noble, 1967). The original title is *Nauwkeri Beschrving van de Guinese goudtand en slaven-Kust* (Utrecht, 1704; Amsterdam, 1709). A French version was published in Utrecht in 1705, the English

translation that same year, and a German translation of the French a year later (Hamburg, 1706). An Italian version followed at midcentury (Venice, 1752–54). See Bosman, *New and Accurate Description,* p. xix. As Pietz notes, Bosman's text "provided the image and conception of fetishes on which Enlightenment intellectuals based their elaboration of the notion into a general theory primitive religion" ("Problem of the fetish, I," p. 5); see especially Pietz's discussion of Bosman in "Problem of the Fetish, IIIa."

28. Bosman, *New and Accurate Description,* pp. 147–49, 150, 155, 81, 82.

29. On commodity fetishism, see Karl Marx, *Capital,* vol. 1, trans. Ben Fowkes (New York: Vintage/Random House, 1977), pp. 163–77. For the phrase cited, see Marx's *A Contribution to the Critique of Political Economy* (1859) as excerpted in *Marx and Engels on Economics, Politics, and Society: Essential Readings with Editorial Commentary,* ed. John E. Elliott (Santa Monica: Goodyear Publishing Co., 1981), p. 4.

30. McClintock, *Imperial Leather,* p. 138. For wide-ranging considerations of some of the intersections of psychoanalytic and Marxist accounts of fetishism, see the essays collected by Apter and Pietz in *Fetishism as Cultural Discourse.*

31. The *Oxford English Dictionary* and the other dictionaries cited above testify to the continued use of "fetish" in its explicitly racialized senses.

32. Freud, *Three Essays,* p. 42. Compare Krafft-Ebing, *Psychopathia Sexualis:* "*Religious* fetichism finds its original motive in the delusion that its object, *i.e.,* the idol is not a mere symbol, but possesses divine attributes, and ascribes to it peculiar wonder-working (relics) or protective (amulets) virtues. . . . Analogies [of erotic fetichism] with religious fetichism are always discernible; for, in the latter, the most insignificant objects (hair, nails, bones, etc.) become at times fetiches which produce feelings of delight and even ecstasy" (p. 11); "I have called [this] 'fetichism' because this enthusiasm for certain portions of the body (or even articles of attire) and the worship of them, in obedience to sexual impulses, frequently call to mind the reverence for relics, holy objects, etc., in religious cults" (p. 143).

33. In doing so, Freud chooses to see religion as "neurotic" in structure rather than "perverse." That is, his theory rests on the belief in an originary moment of strong patriarchal authority broken by the murder of the father, which is repressed but which returns, neurotically, as the figure of the totem and, later, the figure of a monotheistic god. See Freud, *Totem and Taboo: Resemblances between the Psychic Lives of Savages and Neurotics,* trans. A. A. Brill (New York: Vintage/Random House, 1946; *The Future of an Illusion,* trans. James Strachey (based on W. D. Robson-Scott's translation [1928]) (New York: Norton, 1961; and *Moses and Monotheism,* trans. Katherine Jones (New York: Vintage/Random House, 1967). An alternative, "perverse" history of religion might begin with the recognition of a *lack* of transcendent presence that must be denied and hence covered over by the fetish, which replaces that lack with a presence that, nonetheless, always carries with it a recognition of the original lack.

For one of Freud's rare references to fetishistic religion, see *Civilization and Its Discontents,* trans. James Strachey (based on Joan Riviere's translation [1930]) (New York: Norton, 1961): "It is remarkable how differently a primitive man behaves. If he has met with a misfortune, he does not throw the blame on himself but on his fetish, which has obviously not done its duty, and he gives it a thrashing instead of punishing himself" (p. 88).

34. Geoff Mains, *Urban Aboriginals: A Celebration of Leathersexuality* (San Francisco: Gay Sunshine Press, 1984), p. 9. Mains was a biologist, author of *The Oxygen Revolution* (Newton Abbot, United Kingdom: David & Charles, 1972) and the novel *Gentle Warriors* (Stamford, CT: Knights Press, 1989). His life is briefly discussed in Mark Thompson, ed., *Leatherfolk: Radical Sex, People, Politics, and Practice* (Boston: Alyson, 1991), pp. 239–42, which also includes some of Mains's writing about leather. I discuss *Gentle Warriors* at length in *AIDS Narratives: Gender and Sexuality, Fiction and Science* (New York: Garland Publishing, 1996), pp. 205–57.

35. I have used the text of the *Croxton Play of the Sacrament* in *Medieval Drama,* ed. David Bevington (Boston: Houghton Mifflin, 1975).

36. Freud, "Splitting of the Ego in the Defensive Process" [1938], in *Sigmund Freud: Sexuality and the Psychology of Love,* ed. Philip Rieff, trans. James Strachey (New York: Collier/Macmillan, 1963), pp. 210–13, quotation at p. 211.

37. See Carlo Ginzburg, *Ecstasies: Deciphering the Witches' Sabbath,* trans. Raymond Rosenthal (New York: Pantheon, 1991), for a wide-ranging argument about continuities between medieval persecution of Jews and heretics and the early modern fascination with witches.

38. Pietz, "Problem of the Fetish, II," p. 36; see also in the same essay Pietz's claim that "[t]he novel idea of the Fetisso that emerged out of cross-cultural interaction on the West African coast was utterly alien to the ideas of the Christian theory of idolatry" (p. 45).

39. Purchas, *Purchas his Pilgrimage,* p. 652.

40. Bosman, *New and Accurate Description,* pp. 148, 149, 154. Here Bosman observes religious practices that anthropologists (and Freud) would call "totemic": "The *Romanists* have their allotted times for eating peculiar sorts of Food, or perhaps wholly abstaining from it, in which the *Negroes* out-do them; for each Person here is forbidden the eating of one sort of Flesh or other; one eats no Mutton, another no Goats-Flesh, Beef, Swines-Flesh, Wild-Fowl, Cocks, with white Feathers, &c. This Restraint is not laid upon them for a limited time, but for their whole Lives: And if the *Romanists* brag of the Antiquities of their Ecclesiastical Commands; so if you ask the *Negroes* why they do this, they will readily tell you, because their Ancestors did so from the beginning of the World, and it hath been handed down from one Age to another by Tradition. The Son never eats what the Father is restrained from, as the Daughter herein follows the Mother's Example; and this Rule is so strictly observed amongst them, that 'tis impossible to perswade them to the contrary" (pp. 154–55).

41. For further consideration of Protestant analogies between Catholicism and fetishism, see Pietz, "Problem of the Fetish, I," p. 14 and "Problem of the Fetish, II," pp. 39–40.

42. For one treatment of the complex developments in Europe during this period, see Fernand Braudel, *Civilization and Capitalism: 15th–18th Century:* vol. 1, *The Structures of Everyday Life,* trans. Miriam Kochan, revised Siân Reynolds; vol. 2, *The Wheels of Commerce;* vol. 3, *The Perspectives of the World;* vols. 2–3, trans. Siân Reynolds (New York: Harper & Row, 1981–84).

43. Voltaire, *Candide,* trans. Donald M. Frame (New York: NAL/Signet, 1961), pp. 60–61. Voltaire goes on to use "fetish attribution" also to attack a hypocritical Christianity complicit with the slave trade: "Alas! I don't know if I made their fortune, but they didn't make mine. Dogs, monkeys, parrots are a thousand times less miserable than we are. The Dutch fetishes who converted me tell me every Sunday that we are all, whites and blacks, children of Adam. I am no genealogist, but if those preachers are telling the truth, we are all second cousins. Now you must admit that no one would treat his relatives in a more horrible way" (p. 61).

44. My thinking here has been influenced by Kathleen Biddick, "Translating the Foreskin," in *Queering the Middle Ages/Historicizing Postmodernity,* ed. Glenn Burger and Steven F. Kruger (Minneapolis: University of Minnesota Press, forthcoming).

CHAPTER 11

COMMON LANGUAGE AND COMMON PROFIT

Kellie Robertson

> *Late medieval attempts to control mercantile trade and individual spirituality employed a similar rhetoric of identity regulation, a vocabulary that asserted absolute value. This chapter looks at the relationship between two sites where such control was resisted: the marketplace and the growing body of vernacular theological literature funded by it.*

Still everyone would gladly receive a Bible. And why? That he may store it up as a curiosity; sell it for a few pice; or use it for waste paper. . . . Some have been bartered in the markets. . . . If these remarks are at all warranted then an indiscriminate distribution of the scriptures, to everyone who may say he wants a Bible, can be little less than a waste of time, a waste of money and a waste of expectations.

—*Missionary's Register, May 1817*

The gospel, which Christ gave to the clergy and the doctors of the church, that they might administer it to the laity and to weaker brethren, according to the demands of the time and the needs of the individual, as a sweet food for the mind, that Master John Wyclif translated from Latin into the language not of angels but of Englishmen, so that he made that common and open to the laity, and to women who were able to read, which used to be for literate and perceptive clerks and spread the Evangelists' pearls to be trampled by swine. And thus that which was dear to the clergy and the laity alike became as it were a jest common to both, and the clerks' jewels became the playthings of laymen, that the laity might enjoy now forever what had once been the clergy's talent from on high.

—*Henry Knighton, Knighton's Chronicle, 1337–96, ca.1390*

A nineteenth-century missionary objects to the Bible being sold in an Indian marketplace; a fourteenth-century chronicler objects to its degradation at the hands of the common people. Both writers express anxiety over how the English Bible is to be valued, over its potential to be placed in an everyday nexus of exchange. Homi Bhabha has argued that it is the presence of the English book—particularly the English Bible—that creates the "agonistic colonial space" in nineteenth-century narrative, whether novels or missionary writings.[1] Bhabha shows how the mystified power of the English book, while intended to "fix" colonial subjects in a Western scheme of representation, instead ultimately calls into question (through processes of differentiation and discrimination) its own twin discourses of linguistic and national authority. But how did the English book come to occupy this position of authority in the first place? How do we begin to account for the distance between the twelfth-century Middle English whose prestige was defined by the farmhands who spoke it, and present-day standard English, the international "default" language of global capitalism and, hence, translation? As the theoretical paradigm best equipped to situate the social, cultural, and political commitments of modern global English, postcolonial theory offers an appropriate position from which to analyze how English began to assert itself as a fit medium for intellectual work in late medieval Britain. This chapter argues that one of the ways the English book gained its presence was by laying claim to the public space through an alignment with the "common profit," a term that was itself being redefined in relation to the marketplace at this time. To this end, I read controversy over vernacular translation against contemporary debate over trade, exploring how the same questions of authority and ambivalence that surrounded the reception of the English book in nineteenth-century India also marked its emergence in medieval Britain.

If the changing fortunes of English were clearly implicated in the changing economic conditions of late medieval London, historians and literary scholars have traditionally assumed that their relation was an unproblematically causal one: The growth of trade bred a new class of wealthy merchants who created a market for English books, particularly vernacular translations of Latin texts.[2] While this reading of these phenomena has a compelling explanatory power, the mechanics of this proposed relation have remained vague, and the unspoken, essentially Marxist teleology of production that underlies it has gone largely unchallenged. This model also fails to address the fact that translation and trade were both suspect activities in the eyes of late-fourteenth-century ecclesiastics. The translation of the Bible into English, initially associated with the heresiarch John Wyclif and later with the Lollards, elicited the church's censure and subsequently aroused suspicions about vernacular texts in general; critiques of mercan-

tile trade, traditionally built on a biblical basis of camels and needles, came
to occupy a disproportionately large place in the estates literature of the
time.[3] Recent postcolonial work on issues of language difference and
translation allows us to nuance the perceived economic determinism that
underlies the simultaneous "rise" of both the English language and mercantile trade, asking us to view this relation as a potentially cognate (rather
than exclusively causal) one. In encouraging us to understand these phenomena as the result of shared social stimuli (rather than as teleological imperative), the work of critics like Bhabha, Talal Asad, and Tejaswini
Niranjana also provide a framework for explaining why justifications of
English at the end of the fourteenth century were primarily associated
with dissenting social positions.[4]

Common Profit and the
Commodification of Scripture

When thinking about the controversy generated by translation at the end
of the fourteenth century, it is important to remember that the Bible had
been translated into other European vernaculars without causing the out-
cry that it did in late medieval Britain.[5] Debate over scriptural translation
was brought to a close in 1407 when Archbishop Thomas Arundel prohibited the ownership or production of unlicensed English Bibles, a prohibition that would remain in effect up until the Reformation.[6] While debate
over Bible translation had ostensibly revolved around whether it was possible to produce a faithful translation of the Vulgate, translation opponents
often shifted the terms of the argument to focus on the immorality of both
the undertaking and the persons associated with it. The translator of the
Wycliffite Bible counters such arguments by reminding his critics that they
lack the divine perspective necessary to pass judgment on the morality of
those men currently undertaking the translation, concluding

> lete hem [opponents of translation] neuere dampne a þing þat mai be don
> lefulli bi Goddis lawe, as weeryng of a good cloþ for a tyme, eitþer riding
> on an hors for a greet iourney, whanne þei witen not wherfore it is don; for
> such þingis moun be don of symple men, wiþ as greet charite and uertu as
> summe, þat holden hem greete and wise, kunnen ride in a gilt sadil, eiþer
> vse cuyssyns and beddis and cloþis of gold and of silk wiþ oþere vanitees of
> þe world. God graunte pite, merci and charite and loue of comoun profyt,
> and putte awei suche foli domis þat ben aȝens resoun and charite.[7]

The Wycliffite writer here shifts the discussion away from the theological
and moral propriety of translation onto the ground of its civic utility; he

explicitly positions ecclesiastics who object to the translation of the Bible as working against the "common profit," a charge that is repeated throughout the prologue.[8] The Middle English variants of "common profit" (including *comoun profyt* and *commune profit*) were the usual translation of *bonum commune,* itself an extension of the classical concept of *res publica* that viewed the public good as a function of an individual's responsibility to society. A plastic term, the *bonum commune* of late antiquity referred to those mechanisms that guaranteed the public peace; in a Christian theological context it came to be viewed as the rationale for every Christian's duty to one another.[9] In justifying translation in the name of common profit, the Wycliffite translator changes the rhetorical valences of the term. His usage pits the public good against the closed interpretative community of the church: Those who oppose English translation oppose the common welfare. When invoked by Wycliffite translation partisans, the common profit comes to be associated with the development of a lay (vernacular) hermeneutics, one developed in opposition to clerical Latin exegesis. In this view, translation serves the common profit by bringing the Bible into the public square, redefining the dynamic of public and private space as knowledge moves from the cloister to the marketplace.

In his discussion of cultural translation in social anthropology, Talal Asad has asserted that asymmetries in language use demand an investigation into the social implications of the inequality of languages at any given moment.[10] In the passage quoted earlier, the Wycliffite Bible translator demonstrates that translation has affinities with other activities viewed as socially transgressive—such as common people wearing clothes made of expensive material or riding on horses—activities that contravened estates expectations and the sumptuary laws that codified them.[11] The translator also distinguishes between God's law and man's law, concluding through analogy that prohibitions against translation fall under the latter rubric. From the translator's perspective, knowledge of the Bible is seen to be a social regulator that functions to enforce estates difference (just as sumptuary laws do). In this way, the passage exposes the performative practices of cultural authority, revealing how language privilege functions both mimetically and constitutively with regard to ecclesiastical authority.

The Wycliffite Bible translator was intent on showing that the mechanisms controlling the circulation of knowledge were contingent and socially constructed rather than immutable, natural, and divinely ordained; similarly, other Lollard writers revealed how the availability of biblical knowledge underwrote estates divisions. A contemporary Lollard sermon responds to charges that English scripture would lead to social strife and potentially even political rebellion by reminding listeners that this was precisely the argument made to Pilate by the Pharisees in order to convince him that Christ should be put to death. After advocating the availability of scripture in the "modyr tonge," the writer criticizes the church's resistance to the dissemination of sacred knowledge in terms borrowed from the Gospel of Matthew, troping contemporary English ecclesiastics as the watchers over Christ's tomb sent by Pilate:

> And þus doon owre hyȝe preestis and oure newe religiows: þei dreedon hem þat Godis lawe schal qwikon aftur þis, and herfore þei make statutes stable as stoon, and geton graunt of knytes to confermen hem, and þese þei marken wel wiþ witnesse of lordis, leste þat trewþe of Godis lawe hid in þe sepulchre berste owt to knowyng of comun puple. O Crist! þi lawe is hyd ȝeet; whanne wolt þow sende þin aungel to remeue þis stoon and schewe þi trewþe to þi folc? Wel I wot þat knytes taken gold in þis caas to helpe þat þi lawe be hyd and þin ordynaunce cese.[12]

When the efficacy of translation is described in terms of the power of the resurrected Christ, the Latin of the ecclesiastic becomes the tomb of meaning and the act of translation, its savior. This passage not only tropes English scripture in christological terms, it also makes explicit the social inequalities that, according to Asad, always inform such controversy: The circulation of knowledge is regulated not only by the church in its role as guardian of Latin textual culture but by the lords and knights who attempt to reinforce this prerogative with (presumably) parliamentary statutes. Linguistic difference is here underwritten by estates difference: The writer implies that those who pray and those who fight collude to keep knowledge from those who work (the "comun puple"). Truth is not only hidden by the church, it is effectively commodified by the knights who sell knowledge that is not theirs to sell, since the scriptures should be (at least in the Lollard view) common property.

If Lollard writers object to what they see as insider trading of biblical knowledge, this does not mean that they object to the commodification of scripture per se; it is rather a question of who is to be the merchant. The Wycliffite Bible translator responsible for the epilogue to the Gospel of Matthew finds trade and translation to be analogous activities. He closes his comments on the difficulties involved in interpretation and translation with a series of apostrophes exhorting first Christ and then all good Christians to defend the studying and teaching of English scripture, asking his audience why they allow worldly priests to rob them first of the Bible and then of their worldly goods, "by vertu of deed leed or rotun wex, getun thorou symonye." The writer then encourages his audience to seek the words of the gospel from "trewe prestis, as ye seken worldly goodis of wordly men."[13] This analogy not only equates biblical knowledge with worldly goods, it also turns all priests into merchants, differentiating between those who engage in legitimate trade and those who do not. The latter prevent the faithful access to English scripture, offering to show them relics and to sell them pardons instead. The Lollard writer implies that the good Christian is a savvy shopper who recognizes a bad bargain when he sees it. Asad's insight into how linguistic inequality reflects social inequality allows us to situate more fully the multiple vectors of critique at work in all of these Lollard comparisons where translation of the Bible is envisioned as a way to blur not only the line between "lered" and "lewed"—between those with Latin and those without—but also the lines between the estates (e.g., between merchants and ecclesiastics). In all of these passages, economic exchange is presented as the subtext of linguistic exchange. Similarly, all raise questions about the authenticity of valuation in these exchanges: legitimate trade in English scripture brings about the greater circulation of sacred knowledge, while illegitimate trade in scripture by knights and "high priests" keeps this knowledge out of the marketplace.

This overlap between the discourses of trade and translation is significant since at this time the marketplace (like the English language) was also being redefined in relation to the common profit. The church had long mistrusted those who spent their lives engaged in trade, yet the increasing centrality of this activity to medieval economic life forced ecclesiastical writers to address the possibility of being both a good merchant and a good Christian. Whether it was licit for a merchant to buy goods cheaply and then to sell them dearly was a problem that had preoccupied the church fathers and medieval theologians in turn. From an early date, the church had deemed the activity illicit, disapproving of a trade whose impetus was greed, whose unscrupulous means nearly always involved the merchant in sin, and whose end gave the merchant an inappropriate control over the necessities of life, particularly in times of scarcity. And yet by the end of the fourteenth century, the church found itself called upon to accommodate the lives of parishoners increasingly defined by monetary transactions and markets.[14]

The merchant's problematic theological situation can be seen in the uneasy position he occupies in William Langland's *Piers Plowman*. When Truth offers a general pardon to those who work well, the merchants are initially excluded, only to have salvation promised to them contingently based on whether or not they spend their profits on the common welfare: contributing to hospitals, fixing bridges, and helping the poor.[15] Mercantile trade is here justified on the basis of its utility to the common profit. While the spiritually marginal position of merchants in the eyes of the church is figured by their marginal position in Truth's pardon, it is only the merchant's salvation that is explicitly portrayed in comforting detail: "And y shal sende ȝow mysulue seynt Mihel myn angel/ That no deuel shal ȝow dere ne despeyre in ȝoure deynge/ And sethe sende ȝoure soules þer y mysulue dwelle/ And abyde þer in my blisse, body and soule for euere."[16] Like the Wycliffite Bible translators, Langland solves a theological problem ("how is a merchant to be saved?") through recourse to the social ("a merchant is saved through civic service").

Hybridity, Exchange, and Common Estimation

While Langland mitigates the church's traditional opposition to trade, the language in which he does so did not originate with him. Medieval ecclesiastical writers often used the classical notion of common profit to underwrite the division of labor in Christian society: If each estate works well, the community prospers. Since this division of labor was seen to be divinely ordained, the common profit was one of the ways in which the doctrine of social difference was naturalized. If these divisions could not be effectively coordinated by the church and the king, then the social fabric of the community would be at risk. This view of the common profit topos, while popular in sermon literature, finds its most enthusiastic and coherent articulation in John Gower's *Mirour de l'Omme* (ca. 1377) which argues that every class of society had failed to ensure the proper maintenance of the common profit. Gower particularly objects to the mercantile mores that he blames for destroying London:

> In Florence and in Venice Fraud has his fortress and his license, and at Bruges and Ghent likewise. Under his care also is placed the noble city on the Thames which Brutus founded; but Fraud is bringing it to ruin; he is clipping away the possessions of his neighbors, for he cares not in what guise (whether behind or before) he seeks his own lucre, disdaining the profit of the community [*le commun proufit*].[17]

It was not just merchants, however, but knights, lawyers, craftsmen, and clergy—members of all estates—who put their individual welfare ahead of the common good and thus shared responsibility for the social disorder afflicting England in the 1370s. According to Gower, the common profit was the absolute standard against which the faults of each class could be calibrated; it was also the instrument best suited to restoring moral standards to models of mercantile exchange whose mechanisms of valuation had become problematic.

It was precisely this idea of the common profit as an inherent measure of value (and thus an effective means of social regulation) that would get revised in the controversy over trade and translation. The process through which the common profit gets appropriated to justify suspect activities such as trade and translation can be read as one of "hybridization." According to Bhabha, hybridization is

> the name for the strategic reversal of the process of domination through disavowal (that is, the production of discriminatory identities that secures the pure and original identity of authority). . . . It displays the necessary deformation and displacement of all sites of discrimination and domination.[18]

If authority constitutes its identity through discrimination (self/other, subject/object), the hybrid object resists authority by reflecting back a deformed or distorted image of the authoritative subject to itself. Debates over trade and the translation of the Bible were two sites of discrimination where English ecclesiastical authority was staged in the fourteenth century. These debates acted as constitutive places of difference where the church attempted to create its own image along the divide of *literati/illiterati,* good Christian/bad Christian, orthodox/heretical. When fourteenth-century writers began to justify the English language and mercantile trade through recourse to the common profit, it became increasingly more difficult for the church to define itself in these oppositional ways. English translations and merchants can be seen as hybrid objects of ecclesiastical discourse insofar as hybridity functions by repeating (or mimicking) the terms through which the governing power rules, in this case, the language of common profit. When merchants began to be defended on the grounds of social utility, the church could no longer unproblematically affirm the pursuit of the common as opposed to the individual profit. When translation advocates defended vernacular translation on the grounds that the Vulgate was itself a translation, the church saw this argument as a threat to the myth of plenitude (or full presence) enjoyed by the Vulgate; the English Bible became a sign of the Vulgate's belatedness, its lack of originary authority. "Faced with the hybridity of its objects," Bhabha writes, "the *presence* of power is revealed as something other than what its rules of recognition assert."[19] Likewise, trade and translation as sites of exchange are hybrid to the extent that they destabilize the church's own discourse of a theologically and socially conservative notion of the common profit.

One symptom of this hybridity was the increasing importance of common valuation in both economic and linguistic thought. If the church preached the good of the common profit, it was a common profit whose parameters were determined by the church; when this term gets refigured in debates over trade and translation, the good of the common profit comes to be determined by common, rather than ecclesiastical, estimation.

This emphasis on common estimation was first given voice in the scholastic commentaries on Aristotle's *Nichomachean Ethics* produced during the thirteenth century. Aristotle saw justice in exchange as the end of trade, arguing that the value of a commodity should be based primarily on an individual's need for that commodity.[20] While scholastic commentators like Albertus Magnus agreed with the basic tenets guiding Aristotle's search for the just price, they modified his view by asserting that common rather than individual utility determined value. Value should be based to a greater degree on factors like the labor involved in finding and transporting merchandise and the expenses incurred en route. According to this view, it was legitimate for the merchant to include a percentage of profit in the selling price, since he was making otherwise unavailable goods available to the public.[21] These insights into the importance of common valuation formed the basis for later, more vigorous justifications of the merchant's profit (a profit that Aristotle had unequivocally condemned). Over the course of the fourteenth century, first economic and then theological treatises elaborated how profits gained from trade were justified if they benefited the public good rather than just the merchant's private good.[22] In the wake of neo-Aristotelian reformulations of exchange, value was seen to be based more on market conditions and less on an inherent cost of production or an individual need; value was seen to be differential rather than absolute. Common estimation had succeeded in relativizing notions of the common profit since market experience showed that there was no such thing as essential or "natural" commodity value.

Appeals to common estimation also began to exert a stronger influence on views of linguistic exchange at this time. By the end of the fourteenth century, there were several competing answers to the question of how equity in linguistic exchange was to be achieved between languages. Some writers found that parity between languages was achieved by translating in a literal, word-for-word manner; others felt that an idiomatic translation (with its acknowledgement of common usage) was the "more equal." Jerome had advocated translating "non verbum de verbo, sed sensum exprimere de sensu" [not word for word but rather according to the sense] except in the case of the Bible, where he concluded that the very word order was part of the divine plan.[23] This latter model of literal translation still found advocates in the late fourteenth century: In the *De Contrarietate Duorum Dominorum,* Wyclif describes language as a *habitus,* or garment, for meaning, with the implication that meaning stands and only the "outer layer" is transformed when texts move from one language to another.[24] This view of translation (based as it is on a strain of semantic essentialism) is the linguistic corollary of the original Aristotelian model of economic exchange: Words have natural or essential meanings that can be exchanged for other words in a directly proportional way. Wyclif's belief in the radical exchangeability of signs across languages was put into practice in the early versions of the Wycliffite Bible where the translators adhered to the original syntax—a word-for-word translation of the Word—and thus produced a "translation" that was virtually unreadable without the Latin alongside it.

This problem with the method of translation began to be recognized as the Wycliffite Bible underwent further revision, and by the mid-to-late 1380s the translators' practice had shifted to a more idiomatic rendering, one that the laity could understand (even if it was farther away from the exact wording of the Latin). This preference for idiomatic translation can be seen in the prologue attached to many versions of the Wycliffite Bible where the translator claims that idiomatic translation (unlike literal) can result in meaning that is closer to divine intention rather than farther from it, language that is "more true" and "more open" than its Latin original.[25] Ecclesiastical opponents of the vernacular Bible criticized this model of translation on the basis of fidelity, arguing that *translatio* here functioned as *interpretatio,* a pessimistic view of the unavoidable slippage between languages. The Wycliffite Bible translators, on the other hand, not only acknowledged the potential for surplus semantic value in language, the impossibility of exact linguistic exchange, but valorized it as productive.

While the Wycliffite translators explicitly addressed the conflict between these two methods of translating in the Bible's prologue, their contemporary Geoffrey Chaucer staged this conflict in his poem *Troilus and Criseyde* where the narrator vacillates between two models of translation, precisely the same two models currently at the heart of debates over the viability of Bible translation. Written in the late 1380s, Chaucer's poem explores the difference between idiomatic and literal translation in language that linked linguistic to economic exchange. The Proem to Book II of *Troilus and Criseyde* sets out a linguistic cambio that reflected Chaucer's understanding of the fourteenth-century marketplace. The narrator begins by reaffirming his desire to translate literally: "as myn auctour seyde, so sey I," but he then proceeds to instruct his audience in the kinds of linguistic change that render literal translation problematic:

> Ye knowe ek that in forme of speche is chaunge
> Withinne a thousand yeer, and wordes tho
> That hadden pris, now wonder nyce and straunge
> Us thinketh hem, and yet thei spake hem so,
> And spedde as wel in love as men now do;
> Ek for to wynnen love in sondry ages
> In sondry londes, sondry ben usages.[26]

He describes an economy of linguistic transformation where individual words have a certain "pris," or value, that allows men to "spe[d]e" and ultimately to win the commodity of love. He then warns any lovers in his audience who may be tempted to judge Troilus' language and to conclude "so nold I nat love purchase" to remember that "ecch contree hath his lawes." By figuring his translation project in terms of trade, Chaucer reminds us that agreements between buyers and sellers find analogs in the contracts established between readers and writers to minimize (but not wholly eliminate) the inherent indeterminacy of meaning. The author describes the effects of both linguistic inflation (where words within a single tongue potentially lose their value over time) and cultural (or geographical) difference on idiom. Chaucer saw linguistic and economic exchange as not only commensurate but mutually illuminating: A translator's job was to recognize that semantic value is based on a fluctuating standard of common usage and then to negotiate rates of exchange between languages. It is the specificities of the marketplace, the exigencies of time and place, and most of all common utility that determine what will sell, whether goods, words, or love. Chaucer appeals to a model of semantic relativism that reinforces the need for idiomatic translation since linguistic usage depends on what a given market will bear. By the end of his discussion in the Proem to Book II, Chaucer's narrator has revised his initial embrace of literal translation and can now only conclude "myn auctour shal I folwen, if I konne."[27]

The theory of translation explored by Chaucer and embraced by the Wycliffite Bible translators acknowledged that there was not one-to-one correspondence between languages, that semantic value was indeed relative. The growing fourteenth-century recognition that meaning was neither essential nor God-given but was rather agreed upon in common by the users of the language parallels the growing recognition in the economic sphere that value was man-made, a product "of common judgement expressed in a market price that naturally varied according to time and place."[28] In translation, as in trade, there are no essences. Debates over linguistic and economic exchange were not just over how one substitutes words in order to render an exact biblical meaning or money for commodities but about the very process of exchange that engenders conditions of relative value and substitutability. Bible translation was opposed not only because it was associated with the heterodox theological and social program put forward by Wyclif and implemented by his followers, but because the project of idiomatic translation, like mercantile trade, threatened a worldview that saw value as inherent in both words and objects. Neo-Aristotelian ideas of common estimation began to influence the existing notion of the common good and, consequently, to loosen the church's hold on a theologically conservative model of common profit. Both merchants and English books reflected back a notion of the common profit that challenged rather than affirmed the church's hierarchical social vision. Such hybrids, as Bhabha reminds us, were capable of posing questions about authority that the authorities themselves could not answer.

London Merchants and "Common Profit" Books

If late fourteenth-century debates about translation and trade raised similar questions about authenticity in value, I want to end by looking at how this language of public utility and common profit influenced the production of actual English books (and how the modern reception of these books raises similar questions about authenticity). The material fallout of these debates can be seen in the production of "common profit" books in the early years of the fifteenth century. This designation describes several manuscripts commissioned for London merchants that all contain English theological treatises and that all share a colophon specifying how the book is intended to circulate. An example of one such manuscript is Cambridge University Library, Ff. 6. 31, a collection of English tracts that includes several pieces in favor of translating English scripture. An inscription on the last folio describes the motivation for assembling these tracts and gives instructions for its future use:

> This booke was made of þe goodis of John Collopp for a comyn profite that þat persoone þat hath þis booke committid to him of þe persoone þat haþ þeroweth to committe it: haue þe use þerof þe turme of his lyf prayyng for þe soule of þe seid john. and þat he þat haþ þe forseid use of comyssion whanne he occupieth it not: committe it for a tyme to sum oþer persoone and also þat persoone to whom it was committid for þe turme of lyf. under þe forseid condicions delyuer it to anoþer persoone þe turme of his lyf and so be it delyuered and committid fro persoone to persoone man or woman as longe as þe booke endureth (f. 162).

This colophon sets out in precisely contractual language how the book was produced and how it should be passed freely around a community of male and female readers. The same colophon is found almost verbatim in at least four other manuscripts.[29]

The assertion that the books circulate freely for the good of the common profit raises several related questions: What is the effect of a bookseller starting to produce books for free, books that would circulate in opposition to the for-profit book trade that constituted his livelihood? What does producing English books in the name of the "common profit" mean in this instance? How we answer these questions tells us as much about modern desires to define ourselves against a univocal past as it does about late medieval modes of exchange. Many theories of economic, and hence social, valuation posit the Middle Ages as a site of "authentic" exchange, particularly those influenced by a humanist-inflected strain of Marxism.[30] Such a view would understand the colophon's invocation of the common profit to exclude motives of individual profit or gain. Production of these books would thus reflect a purely theological utility; they would be seen to endorse vernacular literacy as a way of uniting the laboring classes of the third estate in opposition to a perceived clerical stranglehold on sacred knowledge. A second (and largely antithetical) way of viewing these common profit books would be to emphasize their place in the rise of English translations from the fourteenth century onward, a phenomenon seen as the direct result of the rise of a "new" monied merchant class with a desire to imitate its betters by commissioning such manuscripts. This view (more characteristic of so-called structural Marxism) would read the apparent contradictions in the production of these manuscripts as evidence of a merchant oligarchy using book production and vernacular literacy to identify with the secular clergy and nobility, tacitly distancing itself from the (presumably) illiterate and bookless manual laboring classes. The production of these books would then be seen as a proleptic moment of merchants trying to differentiate themselves from other laboring estates, of a search for "culture" (in our modern sense of that term) at the expense of the *culturis,* an attempt to appropriate the notion of "common profit" by one particular segment of the commons. What both of these readings share, however, is a desire to measure the authenticity of motivation behind the production of these books. The first model rejects capitalist modes of valuation and exchange while the second model discerns a proto-bourgeois mentality in the commissioning of these works. Both analyses look to these books as evidence in determining the point at which medieval society stops being shaped by integrated, cohesive, and "authentic" exchange (a feudal model) and starts being shaped by conscious mechanisms of exchange (a proto-capitalist one).

In her discussion of the place of translation in the colonial context of nineteenth-century India, Tejaswini Niranjana asserts that debates over translated texts are never just about the possibility or impossibility of linguistic fidelity; instead arguments over translation should be read as sites of cultural representation.[31] We can apply Niranjana's insight to help us out of the authentic/inauthentic binary with regard to these common profit books. Instead of reading them as documents in the transition from the "feudalism" to "capitalism" debate, we can read them as places where several systems of exchange—economic, theological, linguistic—overlap. As theological texts in the vernacular, they challenge traditional avenues for the circulation of knowledge, complicating the church's ability to draw the dividing line between "lered" (clerical) and "lewed" (lay). As mercantile-financed expressions of piety, these manuscripts problematize easy assumptions about the necessary sin involved in trade. These books also challenge modern theoretical views that tend to privilege the circumstances of production over consumption.[32] Indeed, it is the consumption of these books (how they circulate in order to knit together a community of Christian readers) that legitimates their production. One cannot be considered independently from the other: "this book was made from the goods of John Collop for the common profit." The individual profit, accrued in the book trade, is what makes possible the free circulation of these books in the name of the common good, and that circulation retrospectively legitimates the pursuit of the individual profit in the first place. In this way, common profit books can be seen as the merchant's answer to the church's traditional opposition to trade.

As a type of cultural production, these manuscripts appear as the result of a necessary differentiation of labor rather than as simply the by-product of capitalist modes of exchange breeding a cynical class consciousness. They are less the product of a conscious decision on the part of merchants to separate themselves from others who labor than a response to a theological difficulty not faced by, say, agricultural laborers, the value of whose work was self-evident. The production of these books can be seen as a way of legitimating the profits of their trade (as articulated in passus 9 of *Piers Plowman*) while simultaneously resisting the church's representation of merchants as innately sinful. The search for individual profit through trade thus somewhat paradoxically necessitated a more cogent theorization of common profit. While these two concepts appear to oppose one another from a modern standpoint, in medieval mercantile practice the pursuit of the common profit was not experienced as distinguishable from the search for individual profit. These manuscripts conflate material profit (the goods of the merchant), social profit (circulation of English books), and theological profit (the salvation of John Collop and other readers) in a way that is difficult to explain in terms set forth by postindustrial theorizations of value. Just as medieval merchants and the translated Bible refused to reflect back a neat image of the church, so too these vernacular manuscripts produced by merchants refuse to offer us an unproblematic space on which to posit the origins of our own modern capitalist identity.

By looking at one of the ways in which English began to assert itself as a public language (through equation with the common profit), we can see that its "rise" cannot be explained solely in terms of economic determinism or through recourse to totalizing notions of medieval lay piety. It was the result of neither unfettered agency on the part of its speakers nor a merchant class trying to separate itself from the rest of those who labor. Instead, some of the earliest examples of English books circulating in public are the result of mercantile hybridity, of booksellers living "in translation." Instead of assuming that these manuscripts are simultaneously evidence for and the result of the rise of mercantile trade and the increase in vernacular translation that it engendered, it is more useful to explore (as current postcolonial critics encourage us to do) the interplay of social pressures that shaped these phenomena simultaneously. In these terms, trade and translation both bear the marks of ecclesiastical discrimination on the one hand, and neo-Aristotelian views of exchange that shifted notions of authentic value on the other. English achieved its public role in part through an increasing acceptance of relative notions of value in exchange, both linguistic and economic. If some modern critics (literary, economic, or social) desire to locate an "authentic" site of exchange in the Middle Ages, it is important to remember that it was precisely these questions of how value was to be determined that were at the heart of the most controversial issues of the day.

Notes

1. Bhabha argues that the English book is a site where the colonial power authorizes itself through difference, not an absolute difference, however, but a continually renegotiated line between true and false: "it is precisely to intervene in such a battle for the *status* of the truth that it becomes crucial to examine the *presence* of the English book. For it is this *surface* that stabilizes the agonistic colonial space; it is its *appearance* that regulates the ambivalence between origin and *Entstellung*, discipline and desire, mimesis and repetition." "Signs Taken for Wonders: Questions of Ambivalence and Authority under a Tree Outside Delhi, May 1817" *Critical Inquiry* 12 (1985): 152.

2. This view is the basis for M. B. Parkes's much-cited article "The Literacy of the Laity," where he puts forward the case for "the emergence of this rising middle class as a class of cultivated readers": in *The Medieval World*, ed. David Daiches and Anthony Thorlby (London: Aldus Books, 1973), p. 562. Parkes argues that the literacy of "the increasing bourgeoisie," while originally pragmatic in the sense that it arose out of the world of commercial transactions, quickly led to the growth of an organized book trade in London. In a similar vein, Carol Meale recently has argued that "the combination of ever-cheapening methods of manufacture and an increase in disposable income among the middle classes led the way towards an expansion of the manuscript book-trade upon which the eventual viability of printing in England . . . was directly dependent": "Patrons, Buyers and Owners: Book Production and Social Status," in *Book Production and Publishing in Britain,*

1375–1475, ed. Jeremy Griffiths and Derek Pearsall (Cambridge: Cambridge University Press, 1989), p. 201. Meale discusses why the English middle classes played a much greater part in book production than their continental counterparts, attributing this active participation to both a lack of insular royal patronage and to the social pretentions of the merchant classes who saw books as signs of the wealth and prestige. The final part of this chapter suggests another explanation for mercantile participation in book production.

3. On the connection between heresy and Bible translation, see Anne Hudson, *The Premature Reformation: Wycliffite Texts and Lollard History* (Oxford: Clarendon Press, 1988). The foundational scholarship on Lollard interest in Bible translation is to be found in the work of Margaret Deanesley, *The Lollard Bible* (Cambridge: Cambridge University Press, 1920). G. R. Owst discusses the condemnation of the merchant in late-fourteenth-century preaching literature: *Literature and Pulpit in Medieval England* (Cambridge: Cambridge University Press, 1933), pp. 352–61. The church's attitude toward trade is neatly encapsulated in a fourteenth-century sermon *exemplum* (discussed by Alan J. Fletcher) which illustrates that "the three estates are God's handiwork, but the devil has to take credit for the bourgeoisie": *Preaching, Politics and Poetry in Late-Medieval England* (Dublin: Four Courts Press, 1998), p. 231 n66. Lester K. Little argues that the increase in pictorial representations of avarice (as opposed to pride) in ecclesiastical art of the late thirteenth and fourteenth centuries corresponds to the increase in mercantile activity: "Pride goes Before Avarice: Social Change and the Vices in Latin Christendom," *American Historical Review* 76 (1971): 16–49, esp. 38–39. The situation of mercantile trade in late medieval Britain is discussed further below.

4. Issues of translation as cultural representation are explored in Tejaswini Niranjana, *Siting Translation: History, Post-structuralism, and the Colonial Context* (Berkeley: University of California Press, 1992), and Talal Asad, *Genealogies of Religion* (Baltimore: Johns Hopkins University Press, 1993). Ruth Evans has insightfully discussed how the application of postcolonial theory to medieval translations serves to redress a tendency, prevalent in both medieval studies and modern translation studies, to focus on whether a translation is "good" or "bad" at the expense of thinking critically about the social significance of a given translation practice: "Translating Past Cultures?" in *The Medieval Translator IV,* ed. Roger Ellis and Ruth Evans (Exeter: University of Exeter Press, 1994), pp. 20–45.

5. Pro-translation partisans call on these vernacular precedents as well as earlier Anglo-Saxon ones to justify their practice; see, for example, the prolific translator John Trevisa's "Dialogue between a Lord and a Clerk on Translation" (ll. 128–44 in Ronald Waldron, "Trevisa's Original Prefaces on Translation: A Critical Edition" in *Medieval English Studies Presented to George Kane,* ed. Edward Donald Kennedy et al. (Cambridge: D. S. Brewer, 1988), pp. 285–99); and also the Prologue to the Wycliffite Bible, repro-

duced in *Selections from English Wycliffite Writings,* ed. Anne Hudson (Cambridge: Cambridge University Press, 1978), p. 70–71, ll. 134–72.

6. For details of this proscription, see Anne Hudson, "The Debate on Bible Translation, Oxford 1401," *English Historical Review* 90 (1975): 1–18; and Nicholas Watson, "Censorship and Cultural Change in Late Medieval England: Vernacular Theology, the Oxford Translation Debate, and Arundel's Constitutions of 1409," *Speculum* 70 (1995): 822–64.

7. Wycliffite Bible Prologue, pp. 122–30.

8. The translator announces at the beginning of the prologue that he has undertaken his translation "wiþ comune charite" to aid in the salvation of all those Christians in England whom God desired to be saved (ll. 24–26); elsewhere the author asks that those who would fault his translation amend it "for charite and for comoun profyt of cristne soulis" (ll. 69–70).

9. By the fourteenth century, "common profit" had become a synonym for "Christian charity" in sermon literature; see, for example, John Bromyard's *Summa Praedicantium* (Venice: D. Nicolinum, 1586), I:155. In addition to its theological uses, the term also had developed specific political uses (e.g., as a ground on which to oppose tyranny); for the reception of the term from late antiquity through the European Middle Ages, see *The Cambridge History of Medieval Political Thought,* ed. J. H. Burns (Cambridge: Cambridge University Press, 1988). These related uses of the term "common profit" arose from a desire to calibrate a single individual's behavior against the larger needs of the society: a merchant's good against that of the Christian community or a king's interests in relation to those of his subjects. Interest in this question was a product of its cultural moment insofar as it can be linked to an increased interest in the mechanics of associational forms, including the rise and incorporation of guilds and questions concerning the proper role of parliamentary legislatures in relation to the monarchy. On the relation of guilds to the common profit, see Anthony Black, *Guilds and Civil Society in European Political Thought from the Twelfth Century to the Present* (London: Methuen, 1984), esp. pp. 24–28 and 70–71. On questions of rulership in fourteenth-century England, see Richard H. Jones, "Absolutism and the Common Good," in *The Royal Policy of Richard II* (Oxford: Basil Blackwell, 1968), pp. 145–163.

10. Asad, *Genealogies,* pp. 189–93.

11. For a discussion of similar breaches of these codes, see Jill Mann, *Chaucer and Medieval Estates Satire* (Cambridge: Cambridge University Press, 1973).

12. Sermon 45 in *English Wycliffite Sermons,* vol. 1, ed. Anne Hudson (Oxford: Clarendon Press, 1983), p. 426, ll. 44–53.

13. Deanesley, *Lollard Bible,* p. 461.

14. James Masschaele charts the phenomenal rise in English markets during the thirteenth and fourteenth centuries, noting that more than 1,000 were created between 1200 and 1350: *Peasants, Merchants, and Markets: Inland Trade in Medieval England, 1150–1350* (New York: St. Martin's Press, 1997), esp. pp. 57–72. Pamela Nightingale discusses the factors that lead to the

rapid growth of the urban merchant class during the second half of the fourteenth century: *A Medieval Mercantile Community: The Grocer's Company and the Politics and Trade of London, 1000–1485* (New Haven, CT:Yale University Press, 1995). The economic and social position of merchants at this time is discussed by Sylvia Thrupp, *The Merchant Class of Medieval London, 1300–1500* (Ann Arbor: University of Michigan Press, 1948). For the church's traditional suspicions toward trade, see John W. Baldwin, *The Medieval Theories of the Just Price: Romanists, Canonists, and Theologians in the Twelfth and Thirteenth Centuries* (Philadelphia: Transactions of the American Historical Society, 49, pt. 4, 1959), pp. 14–15.

15. "Ac vnder his secrete seal Treuthe sente hem a lettre/ That bad hem bugge boldly what hem best likede/ And sethe sullen hit aȝeyn and saue þe wynnynges,/ Amende meson-dewes þerwith and myseyse men fynde/ And wyckede wayes with here goed amende/ And brugges tobrokene by the heye wayes/ Amende in som manere wyse and maydones helpe,/ Pore peple bedredene and prisones in stokkes/ Fynde hem for godes loue, and fauntkynes to scole,/ Releue religion and renten hem bettere": *Piers Plowman by William Langland: An Edition of the C-Text,* ed. Derek Pearsall (Berkeley: University of California Press, 1978), 9. 27–36. Further citations to *Piers Plowman* refer to this edition.

16. Ibid. C.9. 38–42.

17. John Gower, *Mirour de l'Omme,* trans. William Burton Wilson (East Lansing, MI: Colleagues Press, 1992), p. 331, §25249.

18. Bhabha, "Signs," p. 154.

19. Ibid.

20. My discussion of the medieval reception of Aristotle is primarily indebted to Baldwin, *Medieval Theories of the Just Price* and Joel Kaye, *Economy and Nature in the Fourteenth Century: Money, Market Exchange and the Emergence of Scientific Thought* (Cambridge: Cambridge University Press, 1998). The Aristotelian view of trade is succinctly summarized by Kaye: "In contrast to the theories of classical economists and to our modern understanding of economic motivation, in both Aristotelian and scholastic economic theory, not profit and the desire for gain but the establishment of equality is the proper motive and end of exchange. . . . Equality was not only the proper end of exchange, it also governed the entire process. In Aristotle's view, commodity equalization was a natural process, set in motion by naturally existing inequalities in the distribution of resources. The possibility of reestablishing equality was the necessary precondition of all exchange" (p. 45).

21. Kaye discusses this shift of emphasis in the medieval reception of Aristotle, concluding: "Where in Aristotle's scheme it is the usefulness to the individual that determines an artifact's value, in Albert's thought, it is the artifact's common utility that determines its value. Where Aristotle considered value in the context of individual exchange, Albert considered its formation in the context of a supra-personal marketplace": *Economy and Nature,*

p. 74. Baldwin also explores the neo-Aristotelian innovations of Thomas Aquinas and Albertus Magnus in *Medieval Theories of the Just Price,* esp. pp. 74–75.

22. Kaye, *Economy and Nature,* p. 157.

23. Rita Copeland discusses Jerome's views on translation in the context of classical rhetorical theory in *Rhetoric, Hermeneutics and Translation in the Late Middle Ages: Academic Traditions and Vernacular Texts* (Cambridge: Cambridge University Press, 1991), pp. 45–55. Brenda Deen Schildgen evaluates the influence of Jerome's views in the late fourteenth century: "Jerome's *Prefatory Epistles* to the Bible and *The Canterbury Tales,*" *Studies in the Age of Chaucer* 15 (1993): 111–30.

24. Anne Hudson discusses this passage in "Wyclif and the English Language," in *Wyclif in His Times,* ed. Anthony Kenny (Oxford: Clarendon Press, 1986), p. 90. For a more general discussion of Wyclif's views on English, see Margaret Aston's "Wyclif and the Vernacular," in *From Ockham to Wyclif,* ed. Anne Hudson and Michael Wilks, Studies in Church History, Subsidia vol. 5 (Cambridge: Basil Blackwell, 1987), pp. 281–330.

25. "First it is to knowe þat þe beste translating is, out of Latyn into English, to translate aftir þe sentence and not oneli aftir þe wordis, *so þat þe sentence be as opin eiþer openere in English as in Latyn,* and go not fer fro þe lettre; and if þe lettre mai not be suid in þe translating, let þe sentence euere be hool and open, for þe wordis owen to serue to þe entent and sentence, and ellis þe wordis ben superflu eiþer false" (ll. 36–41, emphasis mine). A few lines later the translator reasserts that his purpose was to make the meaning "as trewe and open in English as it is in Latyn, eiþer more trewe and more open þan it is in Latyn" (ll. 67–69). In these passages, the act of translation generates a semantic openness that valorizes the vernacular as a "truer" medium than Latin.

26. All citations of Chaucer are taken from *The Riverside Chaucer,* 3rd ed., ed. Larry D. Benson (Boston: Houghton Mifflin, 1987), quotations at II.18, II.22–28.

27. Ibid. II.49.

28. Kaye, *Economy and Nature,* p. 111.

29. Two manuscripts of vernacular theological treatises found in the British Library have the same inscription except one substitutes the name "John Gamalin" (MS Harley 2336) while the other substitutes "Robert Holond" (MS Harley 993). Lambeth Palace 472 (a copy of Hilton's *Scale of Perfection*) has the name "Jon Killum" at this point, while the colophon attached to Bodleian Library, MS Douce 25 (a translation of the *Speculum Ecclesie*) asserts that the book was made of the goods of "a certain person." On the relations among these manuscripts, see Michael Sargent, "Walter Hilton's Scale of Perfection: the London Manuscript Group Reconsidered," *Medium Aevum* 52 (1983): 205–6. A discussion of the dating of these books is found in A. I. Doyle's unpublished dissertation, "A Survey of the Origins and Circulation of Theological Writings in English in the 14th, 15th, and

early 16th Centuries with Special Consideration of the Part of the Clergy Therein" (Ph.D. diss., University of Cambridge, 1953), II.208–14. Wendy Scase has discussed these manuscripts in the context of testamentary charity and the London book trade: "Reginald Pecock, John Carpenter and John Colop's 'Common-Profit' Books: Aspects of Book Ownership and Circulation in Fifteenth-Century London," *Medium Aevum* 61 (1992): 261–74.

30. I am thinking particularly of Raymond Williams's brand of cultural materialism: see, for instance, his *Sociology of Culture* (Chicago: University of Chicago Press, 1981), where he attempts to extend discussion of the literary producer's relation to culture back beyond the market economy by introducing the Celtic bard as a model of medieval poetic production. Williams differentiates the work of the bard as institutionalized cultural production where, in his words, "exchange factors [were] fully integrated and in that sense coherent" from later medieval patronage systems defined by "social relations of conscious exchange" (p. 39); these are in turn differentiated from later systems of explicitly monetary exchange. While Williams introduces early medieval models in order to disrupt a received Marxist teleology of reflective art, he ends up substituting another strain of teleological thinking: one that still relies on the representation of early societies as "more culturally integrated" than later ones whose cultural pluralism makes possible a dissenting art in the face of centralized social institutions. This formulation merely shifts the locus of an essential, positive value in exchange back one notch on the medieval time line: If Marxist theories of cultural production used to depend on the analogies medieval: Renaissance as feudal: capitalist, Williams introduces a Celtic, primitive icon to pull a tour of duty as the former term while promoting "late medieval" to the latter position.

31. Niranjana, *Siting Translation,* pp. 3–4.

32. A point made by Jean Baudrillard about Marxist models of economy and culture in general: "The Concept of Labor," in *The Mirror of Production,* trans. Mark Postner (St. Louis: Telos Press, 1975), pp. 21–51.

CHAPTER 12

ALIEN NATION: LONDON'S ALIENS AND LYDGATE'S MUMMINGS FOR THE MERCERS AND GOLDSMITHS

Claire Sponsler

> *The two mummings John Lydgate wrote for the winter festivities of 1429 reimagine the "problem" of alien tradesmen—a persistent concern for fifteenth-century Londoners—by turning unwelcome competitors into beneficent gift-givers. Replacing xenophobia with allophila and protectionism with openness, the mummings fantasize a new metropolis in which aliens join natives in endorsing existing structures for the benefit of all.*

In the winter of 1429, John Lydgate wrote two mummings for the entertainment of London guildsmen during their holiday revels. The *Mumming for the Mercers* was written for Twelfth Night, the feast on the eve of Epiphany on January 6, 1429, and was performed by the mercers' guild to entertain William Estfeld, Lord Mayor of London, who was a member of their company. The mumming begins with a long introductory speech by a presenter, possibly Lydgate himself, disguised as a herald from Jupiter who recounts his journey across Africa and Europe before his final arrival on the Thames. The herald then apparently ushers three ships into the hall from which mummers descend to greet the mayor. (They were probably dressed as Oriental merchants bringing him gifts of silk.) The *Mumming for the Goldsmiths* was performed a month later, on Candlemas Eve (February 2) by the goldsmiths' guild, also for Mayor Estfeld. In this mumming, Fortune acts as a messenger who delivers to the mayor a letter containing news that David and the twelve tribes of Israel have come to visit him and present gifts. A procession of Old Testament figures appears, bringing the Ark of the Covenant and announcing that London will be blessed so long as the Ark is safeguarded at the mayor's house. A group of Levites is then called on to sing a song of praise.[1]

These mummings, with their beckoning gestures of welcome to foreigners and their construction of London as a trading mecca, provide a useful avenue for an investigation of the interlocking and at times competing discourses of colony, empire, and nativism within Lancastrian England. Performed at the height of nationalist fervor in the midst of the English-French campaigns of 1428–29, not long before the young Henry VI was crowned king of England and France (on November 6, 1429, and December 16, 1430, respectively), as England attempted to throw off its own centuries-long colonial status and turn the tables on its former occupiers, these mummings are striking for the way they rework the threat of invasion as invited visit, thus transforming enemies into guests. The mummings similarly reimagine the problem of alien merchants and tradesmen, which for much of the fifteenth century was a pressing concern for London guilds, by turning unwelcome competitors into beneficent gift-givers and supporters, not underminers, of the mayor's authority. In these ways, Lydgate's two mummings can be read as revisionist performances whose ideological work is geared toward reinventing native and foreign relations within the charged space of polyglot, ethnically diverse, socially divisive, and economically competitive London. By imagining the happy inscription of foreign merchants into the space of London trading relations, even if only temporarily and under the guise of holiday gift-giving and entertainment, these mummings offered their guildsmen audiences the chance to construct an alternate set of social and economic relations with the colonies of foreigners living among them, a set of relations that does not so much exile aliens as recolonize them on terms most favorable to the native citizens of London.

In the remainder of this chapter, I consider these seldom-discussed performances in the context of London's mercantile communities.[2] By reading Lydgate's mummings alongside what we know about the London companies' conflicted attitudes toward alien merchants—attitudes that ranged from xenophobia and protectionism on one hand to admission of foreigners into full guild membership on the other—it is possible to trace the negotiation of ethnic and national differences in the late medieval metropolis.

Strangers in the Metropolis

Late medieval London was a cosmopolitan city whose 50,000 or so residents were linguistically and ethnically diverse. Unique among English cities, London recruited its residents from every region of England and expanded its population each year. To give a sense of the numbers involved for just one guild, in the years from 1404 to 1442, some 578 apprentices were admitted to the Goldsmiths' Company, an average of 17 per year. Where they came from is not known, but of the 14 admitted in 1407, the only year in which details are given, only 1 was from London; all the rest were from other parts of the country.[3] In addition to the constant influx of new residents from the surrounding countryside and farther afield in England, individuals and even communities from various countries on the continent also lived in the city or its suburbs, especially Westminster and Southwark. Colonies of foreign merchants had been established in London at least from the early fourteenth century on. Most came from the Low Countries, the Rhineland, and the ports of the Baltic coast from Lübeck to Danzig, with a few from central Germany and France as well as Italy, Spain, and Greece.[4] Lombard Street had an Italian community of long standing, and the Hanseatic merchants even had a guildhall in London (the *gildhalla Theutonicorum*) in Thames Street next to the Steelyard allotted the merchants of Cologne. Some of these foreigners, like the Hansards, had well-established rights and immunities—including the right to hold property and sell retail. Others depended more tenuously on royal or civic tolerance and could be easy scapegoats in times of economic stress.[5]

Although London's population was much more diverse than that of most English towns, there was a fairly rigid differentiation among its various residents, especially as they were slotted into the broad categories of citizens, foreigners, and aliens. The term "foreigners" was used for the English-born unenfranchised, that is, those who were not "citizens" who had sworn loyalty to the city government and who promised to bear their share of taxation and civic duty; local birth was no assurance of citizenship, since even people native to London might be called foreigners if they were not enfranchised. Those born overseas were referred to as "aliens," or sometimes "strangers" or "Dutchmen," a generic term often applied to anyone from outside England. "Citizen," "foreigner," and "alien" were legal terms, since only citizens were legally entitled to buy in the city with the intent to resell and to keep shops for the purpose of retailing merchandise.[6] To be anything but a citizen, then, meant exclusion from the full rights and privileges of enfranchisement, but also, so long as one could avoid detection, freedom from taxation, trade regulations, and various civic responsibilities.

As the Flemish merchants murdered in the riots of 1381 attest, aliens were not always welcomed into the city and were frequent targets during times of social, economic, religious, or political discontent. While Jews offer the best-known example of racial and religious others purged from England, other groups, while allowed temporary residence within the country, were also on occasion vilified and made vulnerable to physical attack. Particularly as English nationalism grew during the course of the fifteenth century, foreigners faced increased antagonism. In a flare-up of antiforeigner sentiment in 1406, Parliament ordered many aliens to leave England; seven were goldsmiths in London who paid the Exchequer for the right to stay.[7] The insular hostility expressed in the *Libelle of English Polycye* (1436) and in various protectionist trade and sumptuary statutes was echoed in the riots of 1456 and 1457 against the presence of aliens in London, especially Italian and Lombard merchants.[8] Closer to the time when Lydgate's mummings were being performed, in a widely reported incident of 1429 a Breton servant and alleged spy, who had been accused of murdering a widow, was being escorted into exile by parish constables when he was overtaken by a crowd of women who snatched him from the constables and stoned him to death; presumably his nationality was part of what incited the attack.[9]

This antipathy toward outsiders was mirrored in the London guild system, which tended to exclude aliens, as well as "foreigners" from the countryside, in most cases forbidding them to be enrolled as apprentices or to set up shop.[10] Despite these attempts at exclusion, the economic advantages of working and trading in London were such that aliens persisted in finding ways of infiltrating the city's commercial system; as a result, for most of the fifteenth century London's guilds grappled with the problem of alien merchants who openly or covertly sought work in the city or just outside it. Records show goldsmiths authorizing wardens and officers to conduct searches, probably quarterly, to find alien goldsmiths, especially in Foster Lane and Lombard Street, which housed most of the craft; the wardens also seem to have searched Southwark—a favorite of alien goldsmiths—for "false boys" (i.e., foreign or alien apprentices) or "untrue workers," often pursuing their quarry with vigor, to judge by the fines levied.[11] In 1424 ten "Dutchmen" were fined for "misworking," and in 1434 the "Ordinance of Dutchmen" forbade the employment of aliens, except for certain persons.[12] Although earlier in the century the Goldsmiths' Company had granted some aliens licenses to work, by midcentury attitudes were hardening against the presence of aliens.[13] An ordinance of 1469 attempted to correct the past practice of allowing foreign goldsmiths to set up working houses and chambers of goldsmithry and to keep apprentices by specifying that all foreign goldsmiths living in London, Southwark, or Westminster for at least five years be permitted to hold working houses and chambers of goldsmithry, but forbidding new arrivals to do the same until they had been resident for five years.[14] And a statute of 1477–78 reiterated that alien and stranger goldsmiths within the city and within two miles outside were to be subject to the wardens of the Goldsmiths' Company.

Despite these proscriptions, earlier in the century numbers of aliens had found admission to London's guilds. To cite just two examples, in 1428 the alien John Coster paid 10 marks for a license to work in his chamber for life and swore to keep the craft's secrets; in 1434 a Parisian goldsmith named Raymond Wachter paid 20 marks for a license to work with his four servants and later that year paid 40 pounds to be admitted as a freeman of the Goldsmiths' Company.[15] There were apparently enough alien goldsmiths living in London that they had a fraternity of St. Eloi, named after the goldsmith who in the seventh century became bishop of Noyon and was adopted as patron saint of goldsmiths in many European countries. Some aliens also managed to purchase admission to guilds, as Gisbert van Diste did in 1431 when he bought admission to the Goldsmiths' Company.[16] The extent to which aliens had infiltrated guilds is suggested by records for the Goldsmiths' Company indicating that in 1444 the total full plus pensioned members as approximately 140, which probably included proportions similar to those in 1477, when the 180 members included 57 wardens, assistants, and liveried members; 62 young men; 19 official and pensioners; plus 23 aliens living in the city and 18 in Westminster and Southwark. Aliens who had paid for full membership of the company were eligible for alms and in 1476 Gerard Haverbeke was granted 1 shilling 2 pence per week.[17]

Whatever degree of success individual aliens had in becoming members of Londons companies, nativist animosities lingered. Part of the guilds' hostility toward alien practitioners of crafts had to do with the desire to maintain standards, to regulate prices, and to lessen competition. But another part arose out of nativist biases against outsiders. A good example of the latter sentiment can be found in a wager that took place at the Pope's Head Tavern in Cornhill during the fourth year of Edward IV's reign. The wager involved a test of skill between one Oliver Davy, a citizen and goldsmith of London, and White Johnson, an "Alicant strangioure goldsmyth of the same citie," designed to see whether native or foreign goldsmiths were more adept at their craft. Perhaps not surprisingly, the wager was judged in favor of the Englishman.[18] What this test of skill suggests is a continuing rivalry between native-born citizens and aliens, a rivalry that intensified the differences between the groups.

The Mummings

Lydgate's mummings can be seen as festive interventions in this complex set of relations between natives and foreigners, citizens of London and aliens. In both mummings, alien merchants are freely "admitted" into the fellowship, as the guildsmen enjoy the spectacle of their company members dressed up as Jews or merchants from the East, irresistibly drawn to London in homage to Mayor Estfeld. Ideological conflicts animating the polemics of the late 1420s are submerged under a glowing patina of openness, amiability, and generosity—sentiments in short supply on the streets of London outside the mercers' and goldsmiths' halls. But if in these mummings alien merchants are welcomed into the guilds, they are at the same placed in a clearly subordinate position of submission, as gift-bearers come to pay tribute to the crowning symbol of London's power. In addition, their otherness is made less threatening through the use of various distancing mechanisms.

The *Mumming for the Mercers,* with its extensive classical allusions, its conceit of Jupiter's herald being sent as an envoy to the mayor, and its mixing of real and mythic geographies, manages to distance its alien merchants from any association with the actual aliens working in London, some of whom might have been present in the mercers' hall in Cheapside on this very occasion. The mumming's fifteen Chaucerian stanzas sketch an expansive and somewhat jumbled geographic panopticon, beginning with the Euphrates and Jerusalem, then moving over Libya, Ethiopia, India, Mt. Parnassus, Syria, the Tagus River, and on to Europe, Egypt, the Red Sea, Morocco, Spain, Calais, the Thames, St. Paul's, and finally "Londones tovne," where the herald lands. Although various gods and goddesses— Mars, Venus, the muses—as well as illustrious authors—Macrobius, Ovid, Virgil, Petrarch, Boccaccio—are invoked, the mumming's emphasis is strongly mercantile, as the mention of Calais suggests. As he approaches London, the herald encounters three ships, each with lettering on its side. The first ship, from which a man fishes but brings up empty nets, has on one side the words "grande travayle" and on the other "nulle avayle," underscoring the fisherman's fruitless labor. The second ship, which he encounters as it is unloading, has a cabin gaily painted with flowers and the words "Taunt haut et bas que homme soyt, / Touz ioures regracyer dieux doyt," which stress the need to be thankful for whatever fortune brings. The third ship holds another fisherman with overflowing nets—"so gret plentee, he nyst what til do"—and is painted with the words "grande peyne" and "grande gayne." This progression from dearth to prosperity as the herald nears London sets the stage for the final set of ships he encounters, which are anchored on the Thames "Hem to refresshe and to taken ayr" and from which "Certein estates" have descended to visit and see "the noble Mayr."[19]

These "Certein estates," which are described as those who "purveye and provyde," were probably members of the Mercers' Company, costumed as Oriental merchants, bringing to the mayor gifts of silk, one of the commodities the mercers traded in. As Glynne Wickham observes, Lydgate here combines the tradition of the visit of the Magi, associated with the feast of Epiphany on January 6, with the miraculous draught of fishes as a way of enhancing the mummers' own gift-giving.[20] In its basic dynamic, this mumming was not unlike the mumming for Richard II in 1377, when London's civic authorities rode to the palace of Kensington at night disguised as a pope, emperor, cardinals, knights, and African or Eastern ambassadors. When they arrived they dismounted and carried three gifts for the king into the hall—a bowl, a cup, and a ring of gold—with several smaller gifts for the queen mother and other family members. After dancing the mummers played a dice game with loaded dice to be sure Richard would win the gifts.[21] In both instances, the performance functioned as a reminder of the mutual obligations of ruler and ruled, with the mummers' gifts not only honoring the mayor or king but also underscoring his responsibility to his subjects. The giving and receiving of the gifts, including the gift of the performance itself, symbolized a reciprocal relationship premised on loyal service on the part of the subordinates and beneficent paternalism on the part of the ruler. Such gift-giving was well suited to the feast of Epiphany when the Magi presented gifts to the infant Jesus as a sign of obeisance and humility. The liturgical message of Epiphany could be readily appropriated within the context of a guildhall performance to reaffirm structures of authority and patterns of obligation linking mayor and merchants.[22] One function of the aliens in this ceremony of mutual duty might have been to provide assurance that even the most unruly of the mayor's subjects could be envisioned as firmly under his command.

The *Mumming for the Goldsmiths,* which consists of fourteen Chaucerian stanzas, makes a similar point. The mumming is a conventional mixture of homage, praise, veiled advice, and wishful thinking offered by subjects to their sovereign. It was performed, John Shirley's headnote claims, after supper on Candlemas night, a festival in honor of the presentation of the infant Jesus in the temple and the purification of the Virgin Mary. Although for fifteenth-century Londoners, the Israelites accompanying David would have seemed exotic and unknown, given that Jews were virtually nonexistent in England since their expulsion in the thirteenth century, the mumming's mention of Jesse, David, and the twelve tribes of Israel are traditional and expected themes in relation to the Virgin Mary, emphasizing as they do the lineage of Jesus. What is more unusual is that David and the Levites would be bringing gifts "boþe hevenly and moral, / Apperteyning vn-to good gouuernuance" to the mayor. Specifically, they bring the "arke of God," which will ensure that "grace and good eure and long prosperitee" will long abide in the city and will protect "þe Meyre, þe citeseyns, þe comunes of þis tovne," keeping the city perpetually "at rest."[23] As the latter claim implies, one of the assets of the ark is its peacekeeping propensities, which promise to settle urban unrest once and for all.

A larger concern of the mumming, however, has to do with good leadership, which is linked to the virtue of humility and the exclusion of "al veyne ambycyoun." The ark contains three gifts for the mayor—"konnyng, grace and might"—which are designed to help him govern with "wisdome, pees and right" and to ordain just laws about which no man will complain. Inside the ark, in addition, there is a writ that specifies what the mayor should punish and what he should spare, as well as how his mercy ought to modify his rigor. So long as the ark stays with the mayor, the presenter promises, adversity will be banished and "pees and rest, welfare and vnytee" will reign througout the city.[24] The not-so-hidden message in these lines is that the goldsmiths expect the mayor to exercise his office effectively and fairly, assuring the smooth running of the city and therefore the continued profitability of its mercantile communities. Disorder, unrest, and lawlessness must be cast out in order for the city's commercial enterprises to thrive. Along with its gifts to the mayor, the mumming offers, then, a pointed reminder of his responsibilities as the city's chief authority as well as a reiteration of the importance of maintaining social order to ensure economic prosperity.

Imagined Communities

Given the two mummings' ritual emphasis on strengthening bonds of obligation and on the duties of mayoralty, what meaning might the inscription of alien merchants have had? What cultural attitudes allowed these London merchants to revel in the sight of their fellow guildsmen costumed as alien others? What is suggested by each mumming's figuration of London as a trading mecca, the center to which exotic outsiders are drawn? How, if public sentiment ran high against foreigners and if guild regulations excluded aliens, could the mercers and goldsmiths so comfortably "admit" foreigners into their fellowship as they do in these plays?

Benedict Anderson has proposed that nations be thought of as imagined communities. They are *imagined,* he argues, because the members of even the smallest nation will never know most of their fellow members yet will carry in their minds an image of their unity; they are imagined as *communities* because each nation-state is conceived as "a deep, horizontal comradeship."[25] London's guilds can be thought of similarly. Like nations, they were imagined communities created out of a collectively shared image of themselves as a fellowship, however stratified and unequal that fellowship might have been in practice. Within the imagined community of the guild, Lydgate's mummings were performances whose at least partial effect was to reproduce the specific kind of community the mercers and goldsmiths took themselves to be.

Cultural theory since Michel Foucault has stressed that cultural productions are grounded in specific interests and power relations. As Foucault has argued, everything from prisons, asylums, and town planning, to knowledge, language, and narratives are produced within existing power structures and serve in turn to reproduce and maintain systems of dominance. In short, cultural productions are forms of governmentality no less potent than political organizations and legislative bodies. At the same time, it is important to recognize that in the Foucaultian view power is often only partial and heterogeneous and does not unilaterally dominate but rather is revalued, critiqued, and placed at risk by being enacted and experienced. In these enactments, struggle, misrecognition, and disingenuous adaptation can all be part of the processes whereby hegemony is challenged, however temporarily and contingently. Within London mercantile culture, ceremonial occasions, including feasts and seasonal entertainments like Lydgate's mummings, provided arenas for the working through of such challenges, fostering a creative refashioning of recalcitrant and unpleasant socioeconomic realities.[26]

The need for such refashioning arose from the peculiar predicament of London's commercial communities. The late medieval city was, as David Harris Sacks reminds us, "not only a stronghold, marked by a jurisdictional as well as a physical boundary that distinguished its inhabitants from their fellow Englishmen, but a passage point for people and commodities." Because urban society was fashioned from the diverse socioeconomic activities of a relatively dense and compacted population, its social order was, in Sacks' words, "always vulnerable to regional, national, and even international economic developments beyond the political control of its inhabitants." Despite strong impulses of corporate solidarity and a propensity for collective action made possible only by the city's self-enclosure separating its citizens from the surrounding countryside, the city could not fence itself off entirely. A city like London was instead a shifting mix of what Sacks describes as "openness to the world of commerce and industry and closeness behind protective walls." Although urban structures like the guild system sought to impose an orderly grid on urban life, lines of demarcation were often unclear, with overlapping markets and levels of authority and with people and goods passing into and out of the city. The result, Sacks claims, was that individuals and groups within the city were "free to form differing relationships to this wider context of action."[27] Thus, how to hold the city and its overlapping communities together in the face of inevitable conflicts in the communities was an important concern of urban life.

From a Foucaultian perspective acknowledging the vulnerability of power, the alien merchants welcomed into the mercers' and goldsmiths' halls can be seen as placing at risk the imagined community of these London guildsmen. By explicitly permitting nonmembers to invade the inner sanctum of the guildhall, the mummings presented their spectators with an image of their communities as more open than closed and of their socioeconomic boundaries as more permeable than intact. In these ways, the mummings entertained the possibility of a different construction of their respective groupings, a construction in which the distinction between Us and Them was to some extent undermined.

But at least two things worked to contain and resolve the risks the mummings took. First of all, through its heightening of the notion of "alien," the exotic otherness of these gift-bearing merchants from distant and unknown lands masks the threat of actual outsiders to London's commercial interests. It would have been relatively easy to imagine the incorporation of distanced and highly exotic, not to mention quasi-mythic, strangers whose resemblance to aliens and foreigners closer to home—in northern Europe or in the countryside just beyond London—was not so obvious. Moreover, because the Israelites and merchants from the East probably were impersonated by fellow guildsmen, while they momentarily offer images of alterity and resistance to authority—images most commonly associated with alien merchants resident in London—they also figure the careful inscription of that alerity into the corporate body via the very bodies of the guildsmen playing the parts. The mummings set up the Orient "as a sort of surrogate and even underground self" against which European culture defines itself, as Edward Said argues occurs so often in Western appropriations of the East.[28] But they do so in a fairly safe and readily assimilable way. So the specific kind of otherness the mummings model worked to neutralize the ideological risks these performances took.

Second, although the mummings introduce an element of disorder and misrule into the guildhall's inner sanctum, they did so within a context that also contained and neutralized that disorder. On one hand, allowing alien merchants to invade the guildhall during these performances confronted the assembled mercers and goldsmiths with the vision of outsiders penetrating the socioeconomic boundaries that for the most part excluded outsiders from full participation in the symbolic and material advantages offered by membership in a guild. At some level, this penetration by outsiders must be read as the enactment of what from the viewpoint of many "citizens" would have been a highly undesirable event, with potentially severe consequences for their economic well-being. On the other hand, the festive occasion worked to contain that threat and defuse the latent danger of welcoming aliens fully into the corporate body. The plot of each mumming furthers this neutralizing of potential threats by clearly subordinating the outsiders to the authority of the mayor to whom they freely bring their wealth and fealty. In this way the mummings are consistent with the generally conservative nature of most festive misrule, which, as Michael Bristol has argued, is at heart reactionary because it "seeks to restrain and limit all radicalisation from below in the form of individual deviation from socially accepted norms, and all radicalisation from above in the form of departures from traditional and customarily tolerated patterns of governance."[29]

In the end, then, what Lydgate offered the London mercers and goldsmiths who watched these holiday entertainments was a fantasy of easy solutions to the complex problems facing urban manufacturing and trading communities. Fully aware of the advantages of maintaining tightly policed corporate boundaries, in order to facilitate the regulation of production, the setting of prices, and control over the flow of goods, London's corporations could hardly be blamed for seeking to protect these beneficial features of urban life. At the same time, widening markets were recognized as keys to continued profits, and thus the necessity of aliens as conduits for imports and exports could not be completely denied. Moreover, trade was already dependent on aliens: Eileen Power and Michael Postan have estimated that in the fifteenth century, 55 percent of the export trade in broad cloths was in the hands of Englishmen, 21 percent in the hands of Hansards, and 24 percent in the hands of other aliens.[30] The different strata of the city and of the guilds probably would have experienced the relative desirability of aliens differently. Wealthier and more powerful groups could more easily view the presence of aliens as further opportunity for profit, while for apprentices and those lower on the socioeconomic scale, aliens represented greater competition for scarcer resources—in the riots of 1457, for example, it was an alliance of servants and apprentices who conspired to massacre the Lombard colony in Bread Street.[31] So the reactions among the spectators at the mummings for Mayor Estfeld might have been varied.[32] But it is plausible to assume that all members of the companies, whether those for whom aliens represented increased opportunities for profit or those for whom they were impediments to employment and financial gain, might have found reason to be comforted by the image of alien merchants bringing gifts and paying homage to the mayor.

Lydgate's mummings seem calibrated to meet the desire of mercantile fellowships inclined to see themselves not just as citizens of an exclusively English community but also as members of a cosmopolitan trading group, yet who also, fearing losses of privileges attendant on the maintenance of limited and exclusive commercial communities, found it appealing to construct an image of English centrality to the mercantile world. At a time when the borders of the trading community were quickly expanding, trade guilds could no longer remain unwavering bastions of traditional values; instead they faced pressures to evolve in response to new economic and social changes. Already by the late 1420s, London's livery companies were metropolitan and their membership was diverse in attitudes, interests, and experiences. While alien merchants in the city and its suburbs remained in some ways a threat, not just the real presence but also the considerable potential value of such aliens had to be reckoned with. Lydgate's mummings can be seen as attempts to resolve this conflict, offering a consoling image of how London's companies might best meet the challenge of growing internationalism. Replacing xenophobia with allophilia and protectionism with openness, the mummings for the mercers and goldsmiths fantasized a new metropolis in which aliens joined natives in endorsing existing structures of rule for the profit of all. As such, Lydgate's mummings stand as early instances of the kind of wishful thinking that would continue to haunt narratives of invasion and displacement for many years to come.

Notes

1. The mummings survive in a single manuscript, MS Trinity College Cambridge. R.3.20, with rubrics by John Shirley, printed in Henry N. McCracken, *The Minor Poems of John Lydgate,* 2 vols., EETS OS 192 (London: Oxford University Press, 1934), 2:695–701; for commentary, see 1:201–3.

2. For discussions of these mummings, see Derek Pearsall, *John Lydgate* (Charlottesville: University of Virginia Press, 1970), pp. 73, 185; and Walter F. Schirmer, *John Lydgate: A Study in the Culture of the Fifteenth Century,* trans. Ann E. Keep (London: Methuen, 1961), pp. 100–08.

3. See T. F. Reddaway, *The Early History of the Goldsmiths' Company, 1327–1509* (London: Edward Arnold, 1975), p. 107.

4. See Sylvia L. Thrupp, "Aliens in and Around London in the Fifteenth Century," in *Studies in London History,* ed. A. E. J. Hollaender and W. Kellaway (London: Hodder and Stoughton, 1969), p. 120.

5. E. F. Jacob, *The Fifteenth Century, 1399–1485* (Oxford: Clarendon, 1961), p. 357. Edward III actively encouraged alien merchants, sending emissaries to Flanders to entice Flemish weavers to England and subsequently protecting aliens against the hostilities of native clothworkers; see May McKisack, *The Fourteenth Century, 1307–1399* (Oxford: Clarendon, 1959), pp. 367–68.

6. For a succinct discussion of these terms, see Sylvia L. Thrupp, *The Merchant Class of Medieval London, 1300–1500* (Chicago: University of Chicago Press, 1948), p. 2–3.

7. See *Rotuli Parliamentorum* (London, 1783), 3:578b.

8. The privileges enjoyed by Italians in the wool trade, with agents riding around the Cotswolds competing with English buyers for the best crop,

was a source of insular hostility, in part responsible for the riots of the mid-1450s that caused many Italians to leave London for Southampton and Winchester: see Jacob, *Fifteenth Century,* pp. 352–55.

9. For a discussion of the stoning, which is described in the contemporary *Brut,* see Ralph A. Griffiths, "A Breton Spy in London, 1425–29," in his *King and Country: England and Wales in the Fifteenth Century* (London: Hambledon Press, 1991), pp. 222–23.

10. See McKisack, *Fourteenth Century,* pp. 359, 378.

11. Worshipful Company of Goldsmiths, Minute Book A a, 165; cited in Reddaway, *Early History of the Goldsmiths' Company,* pp. 108–9.

12. Minute Book A a, 155; cited in ibid., pp. 123–24.

13. Marian Campbell, "English Goldsmiths in the Fifteenth Century," in *England in the Fifteenth Century,* ed. Daniel Williams (Woodbridge, Suffolk: Boydell, 1987), pp. 43–52, esp. p. 44.

14. Reddaway, *Goldsmiths' Company,* p. 263.

15. Ibid., pp. 122, 107–08.

16. For a discussion of both the fraternity of St. Eloi and the admission of aliens to corporations, see ibid., p. 129.

17. See Minute Book A, 201–220 and 190, respectively; cited in ibid., pp. 138 and 148.

18. The wager is described in William Herbert, *The History of the Twelve Great Livery Companies of London,* 2 vols. (London, 1834 & 1837; repr. New York: Augustus M. Kelley, 1968), 2:197.

19. Lydgate, *Mumming for the Mercers,* in McCracken, *Minor Poems of John Lydgate,* pp. 695–98.

20. A mercer was a merchant trading in small wares and by 1429 would have been emphasizing wool, cloth, and luxury fabrics such as silk. Glynne Wickham, *Early English Stages, 1300 to 1600,* 3 vols. (London: Routledge & Kegan Paul, 1981), 3:48–49, states definitively that the three ships are ushered into the hall with merchants from the East on board, although the text of the mumming only suggests that merchants costumed in Oriental fashion might have on board.

21. See the discussion of the mumming for Richard II in Wickham, *Early English Stages,* 3:49.

22. For a useful discussion of the social and political uses of Epiphany performances, see Peter H. Greenfield, "Festive Drama at Christmas in Aristocratic Households," in *Festive Drama,* ed. Meg Twycross (Woodbridge, Suffolk: D. S. Brewer, 1996), pp. 34–40, esp. p. 36.

23. Lydgate, *Mumming for the Goldsmiths,* pp. 698–701.

24. Ibid.

25. Benedict Anderson, *Imagined Communities: Reflections on the Origin and Spread of Nationalism* (London: Verso, 1983), pp. 15–16.

26. For a useful discussion of mercantile literary culture in London, including guild dramas, see Carol M. Meale, "*The Libelle of Englyshe Polycye* and Mercantile Literary Culture in Late-Medieval London," in *London and Europe*

in the Later Middle Ages, ed. Julia Boffey and Pamela King (London: Center for Medieval and Renaissance Studies, 1995), pp. 181–227.

27. David Harris Sacks, *The Widening Gate: Bristol and the Atlantic Economy, 1450–1700* (Berkeley: University of California Press, 1991), pp. 4, 10.

28. Edward Said, *Orientalism* (New York: Random House, 1978), p. 3.

29. Michael D. Bristol, *Carnival and Theatre: Plebeian Culture and the Structure of Authority in Renaissance England* (London: Methuen, 1985), p. 52.

30. Eileen E. Power and Michael M. Postan, *Studies in English Trade in the Fifteenth Century* (London: Routledge, 1933), p. 13.

31. Jacob, *Fifteenth Century,* p. 355.

32. Exactly which members were in attendance is difficult to say, although the audience might well have included primarily the liveried, and hence most substantial, members of the corporation; see the discussion of the goldsmiths' feasts on St. Dunstan's day, the principal election feast, in Herbert, *History of the Twelve Great Livery Companies,* 2:234–39.

CHAPTER 13

POSTCOLONIAL CHAUCER AND THE VIRTUAL JEW

Sylvia Tomasch

> *Despite the Expulsion of 1290, the perpetuation of the "virtual Jew" remained essential to English religious devotion and national identity. Allosemitic constructions of the Jew, fostered by medieval English postcolonial conditions, were manifested in fourteenth-century literary and artistic productions, including the Holkham Bible Picture Book, the Luttrel Psalter, and the poetry of Geoffrey Chaucer.*

In the *Canterbury Tales,* Geoffrey Chaucer alludes to Jews more frequently and more explicitly than the almost exclusive critical attention paid to the *Prioress's Tale* would indicate.[1] Chaucer's allusions, ranging from the faintly positive to the explicitly negative, present Jews as proto-Christian prophets, wandering exiles, blasphemers and torturers, and anti-Christian murderers—all familiar depictions in his time. Some medievalists have found Chaucer's reiteration of the sign "the Jew" puzzling, Jews having been expelled from England 100 years earlier. In fact, it is perfectly consonant with the late medieval circumstances that perpetuated the presence of the "virtual Jew" in the absence of actual Jews. Denise Despres puts the case for such simultaneous "absent presence"[2] most cogently when she writes: "Despite the fact that no practicing Jews were permitted to reside in fourteenth- and fifteenth-century England, late-medieval English devotional culture is rife with images of Jews, from the Old Testament patriarches [*sic*] in the Corpus Christi Plays to the blasphemous, terrifying host desecrators dramatized in the *Croxton Play of the Sacrament* and legitimized in Middle English sermons."[3] Although some scholars have tried to explain away "the paradoxical centrality of Jews to late-medieval English literature and art" by "asserting that Jews function in this literature to represent a generic 'Other,' or as a displacement for the Lollard sect," Despres concludes that, to the contrary, "Jews were not merely symbols of alterity in English culture, whether generic or specific, but rather . . . their presence was a necessary element in the devotional world of the later medieval English laity."[4]

Following Despres, and along with Colin Richmond and James Shapiro, I argue in this chapter that "the Jew" was central not only to medieval English Christian devotion but to the construction of Englishness itself.[5] As Shapiro writes, "The desire on the part of the English to define themselves as different from, indeed free of, that which was Jewish, operated not only on an individual level but on a national level as well: that is, between 1290 and 1656 the English came to see their country defined in part by the fact that Jews had been banished from it."[6] The centrality of Jews to English religious devotion and national identity certainly helps explain the persistence of "the Jew," both pre- and post-Expulsion. But in addition, we can understand this enduring sign as marking the persistence of colonialism in England from the thirteenth into the fourteenth century. For although the Expulsion signaled the exile of the Jews, it did not entail an utter break with England's colonial past. That is to say, the English colonialist program did not end in 1290, and its pernicious effects continued to be felt, postcolonially, by the colonizing subjects, the English themselves.[7]

Some scholars have insisted on using "colonial" and "postcolonial" only in reference to the modern period. And indeed, if we define these notions exclusively in terms of European imperialism or the rise of capitalism or the birth of nationalism,[8] then they will not serve to delineate conditions in the Middle Ages. But if we attend to Kathleen Biddick's assertion that "[t]he periodization of colonialism . . . begins to look very different if one includes Jews,"[9] then it is possible to employ these terms to explore certain very troubling aspects of late medieval culture. To that end, recent theorizations of the relationship between colonialism and postcolonialism provide a critical grammar for describing the mentality of Chaucer's England. In addition, recent theorizations of the idea of the virtual contribute to a more nuanced understanding of late medieval representations of "the Jew." Considering Chaucer's poetry through the double lens of the colonial and the virtual provides grounds for refuting those who would either save him from charges of anti-Semitism or damn him accordingly. Rather than try to do either, I intend here to explore the complexities of medieval representations of Jews so as to understand the ways in which post/colonial English conditions fostered the creation of virtuality and the paradox of Jewish absent presence.

The acme of English depiction of Jews occurred in the thirteenth century as prelude to and, no doubt, stimulus for the 1290 Expulsion.[10] In thirteenth-century England, Jews served all sorts of theological, political, social, and economic purposes, being alternately commended or condemned according to the interests of their observers. For example, Matthew Paris, in his *Chronica majora,* extended "his condemnation when the Jews advanced royal power and, conversely, his unconditional support whenever the Jews either obstructed the centralising aims of the king or became the victims of royal policy."[11] Similarly, other monastic chronicles, such as the *Annals of Burton,* distinguished between blameworthy contemporary English Jews (thought to be demonic descendants of Judas) and their praiseworthy ancestors.[12] Such inconsistent, even contradictory, attitudes are common, and, according to Jeremy Cohen, correlate with contemporary theological shifts in conceptions of the "hermeneutical Jew."[13] This shift followed from the "traumatic encounters" of Christian Europeans with Muslims, encounters that led to a new perception of Jews as allied to external adversaries such as Tartars, Saracens, and Turks. Perceiving Jews as aligned with many threatening Others helped justify violence against them on the "assumption," in Sophia Menache's words, "that they constituted an actual danger to the physical survival of Christendom."[14] This new perception of Jews was thus one crucial part of religio-political trends that led not only to the 1290 Expulsion from England and Aquitania but also to subsequent expulsions throughout Europe. This new perception also led to the paradox of English post/colonialism: For the sake of security, Jews had to be removed; for the sake of self-definition, "the Jew" had to remain. The English shift from colonialism to postcolonialism is thus marked both by the expulsion of the actual and by the persistence of the virtual.

It is not surprising, therefore, that artistic productions of the period depict Jews in a striking variety of roles. Thirteenth-century English apocalypse manuscripts, for example, portray Jews in a wide variety of guises, some positive, such as Old Testament prophets or the allegorical personification of the Old Testament itself, and some negative, such as beast worshippers, resistant listeners to Franciscan sermons, or captives of demons.[15] As Suzanne Lewis's magisterial study shows, these manuscripts also depict various others as Jews, including John the author of Revelations, the Four Horsemen of the Apocalypse, the sponge wielder at the crucifixion, and two figures from Canticles used to symbolize the nation of Israel—the Bridal Soul and the Shulamite. In these manuscripts a single visual panel often contains more than one Jewish representation or allusion. For example, in the illustration showing John consoled by the Elder (Lewis's figure 33), the Old Testament patriarchs are embodied three times, by the angel, the Elder, and John. The angel represents those who prophesied Christ as the redeemer, while the Elder and the weeping John symbolize those who, believing only literally, "held the Old Testament but did not see it."[16] Thus throughout the thirteenth century, "the Jew" appears in multiple, sometimes contradictory variations that are repeatedly reinscribed—even after the Expulsion.

The persistence of Jewish representation in fourteenth-century cultural productions is well illustrated, albeit often with a diminution in intensity. For example, according to Michael Camille, although the *Luttrell Psalter* still contains "distorted hook-nosed semitic stereotypes of Christ's torturers," such images are "notably less emphatic" than their counterparts in thirteenth-century psalters.[17] Similarly, as Martin Walsh shows, the *Holkham Bible Picture Book* only intermittently employs stereotypical Jewish characteristics; often it does so to emphasize basic theological distinctions. For example, one four-paneled illustration (folio 12) shows the course of Joseph's conversion from incredulous Jew to believing Christian by setting out a series of contrasting actions and attributes (figure 13.1). In the first panel, Joseph is fully denoted as a Jew, first by his placement among others of his kind and second by his hold on Old Adam's spade; however, in the second panel, as he lays his hand on Mary's womb, he is unmarked. In the third panel, during his encounter with Gabriel, Joseph wears the *pileus cornutus,* one of the sartorial signs of difference enjoined by the Fourth Lateran Council in 1215. But in the fourth panel, as he is reconciled with Christian truth, both "the Jewish hat and Adam's spade are now put behind him."[18] Lying as he does on the typological "fault line between the Old and New Testaments,"[19] Joseph thus attests not only to the multiple Jewish figurations available to Christian artists of the time but also to the continuing centrality of Jews to Christian self-definition. In these ways, both of these early fourteenth-century illustrated texts, the *Luttrell Psalter* and the *Holkham Bible Picture Book,* are typically post-Expulsion, for despite a diminishment in frequency and negative intensity, Jews remain what "they had already become in the thirteenth century: a ubiquitous presence in the English imagination established largely (and after 1290, entirely) through words, texts, and images."[20] Or as Camille says of Robert Mannyng's *Handlyng Synne,* its "minimal detraction of Jews . . . has been ascribed to the fact that there were no Jews [in England in the fourteenth century]. . . . But their non-presence in English society does not mean that they cannot still be attacked in the realm of the imaginary . . . as part of the very definition of a good society—that is, as excluded from it."[21] Turning to the words,

Figure 13.1: Four-panel image of Joseph. Used by permission of the British Library (ADD46780F12).

texts, and images of Geoffrey Chaucer, we can see the continuing post-colonial construction of the good society and of its negative exemplum, the virtual Jew.

In the *Canterbury Tales,* one crucial component of the fabrication of the good society is the construction of Englishness, both geographically and characterologically.[22] We see this construction in the tales of the Prioress and the Pardoner. In the *Prioress's Tale,* a polluted Asia—polluted through Jewish presence and actions—is implicitly contrasted with a purified England, whose sanitized state is founded on the displacement of the Jews.[23] The geographical removal of the Jews to Asia echoes their prior territorial Expulsion. On one hand, it *removes* the narrative from the context of English land, English people, English acts, and, especially, English Jews. On the other hand, it *requires* that forbidden identification and reasserts Englishness by including the coda recalling Hugh of Lincoln's martyrdom at the hands of the—now-expelled—Jews. This dislocation also enables an unremitting replay of perpetual Jewish crimes by containing Jews in an eternal, orientalized present. Because "translating Jews from time into space was a way in which medieval Christians could colonize—by imagining that they exercised dominion albeit in an [*sic*] phantasmatic space,"[24] the Prioress's "Asye" can be understood not only as the medieval orientalized East that replaces the familiar English homeground but also as the "phantasmatic space" that supplants in the English imaginary the actual, contested Asia of losing crusades. This is also an Asia, therefore, not only of subjugated Jews but of triumphant Christians; here actual victorious Saracens are displaced by virtual vanquished Jews.

If the Prioress's Asia substitutes for England as purified space, the Pardoner's Flanders stands for England as corrupted place. The *Pardoner's Tale* speaks to the vice-ridden conditions of English life that were blamed, at least in part, for the ravages of the plague. Representing the wicked English populace, the rioters are responsible for bringing Death upon themselves by seeking out its agent, the Old Man. In the tale, the Old Man emblematizes many of the most popular and pernicious anti-Judaic fantasies of the Middle Ages. Linked to the Wandering Jew,[25] the legendary figure punished for his mocking of Christ, the Old Man personifies not only Jews in general (nonbelieving exiles wandering through Christian time and space), but medieval European Jews in particular. Like them, he is intimately connected with gold—the unearned profits of avarice and usury—as well as with the massive population decimations of the mid-fourteenth century within which the Pardoner sets his tale. The evil nature that caused New Testament Jews to revile Christ and induced their Norwich and Asian coreligionists to kill innocent Christian boys also was believed to lead contemporary Jews to poison wells and spread the Black Death.[26] Precisely because he is undenoted as a Jew, the Old Man performs a perfect displacement of them.

A corollary component of the fashioning of the good society is the construction of Christianness, particularly as manifested in the material bodies of believers.[27] We see this dynamic in the tales of the Parson and the Monk. In order to dissociate good Christians from evil Jews, the *Parson's Tale* (like the chronicle of Burton) must first dissociate Jews from their own religion. Through traditional typological strategies, laudatory Old Testament Hebrew prophets are distinguished from blameworthy New Testament or contemporary Jews. Solomon, Moses, David, and others are cited with approbation, while post - Old Testament Jews appear in the context of deicide. The tale makes clear that medieval Jews are abominations to the sacred, embodied community their ancestors are used to authenticate. By linking words and bodies, the Parson specifically admonishes Christians not to swear and thereby emulate Jews: "For certes, it semeth that ye thynke that the cursede Jewes ne dismembred nat ynough the preciouse persone of Crist, but ye dismembre hym moore" (X[I].591). Such a focus on bodily dismemberment recalls not just the blood crimes of which contemporary Jews were accused (as in the *Prioress's Tale*) but also hints at their perverse physicality, voluntarily enacted in the continued self-dismemberment accomplished through the superseded ritual of circumcision.

As the *Parson's Tale* dissociates Jews from their own religion, the *Monk's Tale* dissociates them from their own bodies. The Prioress's murderous dismemberment of the Christian boy is countered in this tale by the salvific self-destruction of Samson. The Monk presents Samson, simultaneously the christianized proto-martyr and the judaized self-mutilator, in a number of ways, all of which dissociate Jews from their own bodies as well as from their own religion. First, the fact that he is an exemplary Israelite judge—or, as the tale puts it, "fully twenty wynter . . . / He hadde of Israel the governaunce" (VII.2059–60)—is almost completely elided. His generalized loss of power is specifically carnalized in his physical blindness, a blindness (like that of the allegorical figure of Synagoga) that symbolizes Jewish spiritual lack. Moreover, when Delilah cuts Samson's hair, the action makes visible—by metaphorical displacement—the self-castrating (i.e., the circumcising) impotence of Jews. What is particularly interesting, however, is that at the same time that the Monk presents Samson as a thoroughly impotent Jew, he also dejudaizes him. The very first lines of the episode—"Loo Sampsoun, which that was annunciat / By th'angel longe er his nativitee, / And was to God Almyghty consecrat" (VII.2015–17)—serve to reposition Samson within a famously Christian context.

In these tales, drawing on well-established representational conventions, Chaucer continues the post-Expulsion English practice of reiterating the sign "the Jew." As is typical in medieval postcolonial cultural productions, he assumes the factuality of blood guilt and bodily difference, without, however, ever matching pre-Expulsion artists and writers in their relish for portraying Jewish perfidy and perversity. As we have seen in other post/colonial texts, in the *Canterbury Tales* "the Jew" is never entirely or solely negative; in certain instances the sign can be understood, at least superficially, as philo-Semitic. The Man of Law, for example, speaks merely descriptively when he cites the "peple Ebrayk" (II [B].489), and the Pardoner himself mentions "hooly" Jews (VI [C].364). (In similar fashion, Bromyard praises Jews for their piety; Langland for their kindness; and Brunton, for their compassion for their poor.[28]) However, it should be obvious, especially when we remember patriarchy's complementary valorization of Mary and denigration of Eve, that all stereotypical assertions, both positive and negative, are merely isotopic variants. Like phonemes, they have no base term. The two sides—Jews as wicked murderers / Jews as generous alms-givers—are not merely conjoined, but, as with Mary and Eve, they are the same. By the later Middle Ages, every Jew is both evil and good, murderous and charitable, for all Jews can be characterized as "the Jew." Following Zygmunt Bauman, therefore, a better term to describe such indivisible, isotopic variation is "allosemitism."[29] What is important for appraising a writer such as Chaucer, therefore, is not whether he is anti- or philo-Semitic—he was, I believe, inevitably both—but rather that, given his Englishness and his Christianness, Chaucer could not help but contribute to the ongoing allosemitic construction of the virtual Jew.

What does it mean for an entire people to be virtual? And how does that virtuality correlate with their actuality? We can begin to address these questions by contextualizing medieval Jewish virtuality within the shift in England from a condition of colonialism to one of postcolonialism. Anne McClintock's definitions of "colonization" and "internal colonization" are helpful here:

> Colonization involves direct territorial appropriation of another geo-political entity, combined with forthright exploitation of its resources and labor, and systematic interference in the capacity of the appropriated culture (itself not necessarily a homogeneous entity) to organize its dispensations of power. Internal colonization occurs where the dominant part of a country treats a group as it might a foreign colony.[30]

The case for understanding pre-Expulsion medieval English Jews as an "internally colonized" people is a complex one.[31] On one hand, although Jews were not, strictly speaking, a separate "geo-political entity" within England, they were a distinct religious entity, with separate political and social responsibilities, privileges, and liabilities.[32] There is no question that their Christian overlords "systematic[ally] interfer[ed] in [the Jews'] capacity . . . to organize [their own] dispensations of power." Neither is there any question that in their use and abuse of Jews, the English did their best to "forthright[ly] exploit . . . [Jewish] resources and labor"—until, that is, such exploitation no longer suited their needs. Finally, "direct territorial appropriation" occurred, most vividly although not uniquely, at the Expulsion itself. Thus, while this case is not one McClintock considers, the situation of thirteenth-century English Jews fits her definition of internal colonization all too well.

On the other hand, the internal colonization of medieval English Jews was not territorial in any simple fashion. Three paradoxical aspects are important for understanding not only the decolonization of the Jews but also postcolonialism itself. First, however long Jews had been in residence in England (and most scholars agree that it closely followed within 100 years of the Conquest of 1066), they were by no means the indigenous inhabitants. The nonnative nature of their English habitation was important to monastic chroniclers of the Expulsion. Whereas some accounts (i.e., the *Annals of Waverley*) stressed the continuity of Jewish residence, others (i.e., the *Annals of Dunstable*) stressed the justness of such punishment because of their sins (especially that of blasphemy). One consequence of their second-order status, therefore, was that during the troubles of the thirteenth century, Jewish resources could more easily be appropriated by the very same Christians who expressed pity for their plight. The post-Expulsion image of the Jews is thus the familiar double one: ancient inhabitants, whose exile after their long sojourn is to be pitied (according to the Cistercians of Waverley) versus threatening interlopers, enemies of Christ whose exile is deserved (according to the *Annals of Osney*).[33] Creatures of such unresolvable duality are obvious dangers to and therefore must be rent from the body of Christian society.

This state of inassimilable difference leads to the second paradox: At the very same time that Jews were understood as secondary in terms of territorial occupation, in more important ways—important, that is, in terms of Christian supersessionist theology—they also were perceived as necessarily prior.[34] While domination in the medieval English case involved the exploitation of land, resources, and labor, even more fundamentally, it involved the appropriation of religious truth and the true religion. For the ultimate territory at stake in medieval English post/colonialism was theological. Although the Expulsion was unarguably a consequence of a multitude of economic, political, and social factors, underlying all was the fact that the Jews were reviled, massacred, and expelled because they were not Christians, because they were not (truly) English, and because Christians/English were not (could not be, must not be) Jews. Although Judaism provided the foundations for Christianity, Jews threatened the definitions of Christian society. Jews were expelled not merely because they first possessed (English) lands and goods from which they needed to be displaced, but because they first possessed the (Christian) book—from which they needed to be displaced. In their priority lay the rationale for their alterity, the justification for their abuse, and the roots of their destruction. The Christian dilemma set the stage for English action: the "dreadful secondariness" (to use Edward Said's phrase[35]) of medieval Jews was thus a consequence of their intolerable primariness.

Third, and contrary to the usual modern postcolonial scenario, in medieval England it was the dominant group (the Christian English) that expelled the subordinate group (the English Jews), and not the other way around. It was the dominant group that then suffered from inevitably disappointed utopian fantasies of a purified and liberated state. It was the dominant group that exhibited the "pathology" resulting from "persisting colonial hierarchies of knowledge and value."[36] In a word, it was the Christian English, not the English Jews, who suffered from the postcolonial condition. When Leela Gandhi asserts that "[t]he postcolonial dream of discontinuity is ultimately vulnerable to the infectious residue of its own unconsidered and unresolved past,"[37] she is referring to the condition of the formerly colonized. In the case of medieval England, however, the "postcolonial dream of discontinuity" was that of the colonizers, the English. As ever, that dream failed. In their attempts to liberate themselves from intrusive foreign elements, thereby purging their country of religious difference, the English expelled the Jews. Yet, as our examination of the *Canterbury Tales* and other texts has shown, while the English may have eliminated the Jews, they never eradicated "the Jew."[38]

Terms proliferate to describe this reiterated sign: "hermeneutical," "theological," and "notional Jew" have all been proffered.[39] Yet none of these speaks directly to the postcolonial condition; for that purpose, I am proposing the term "virtual Jew." Although I derive "virtual" from cyberspace studies, "virtual Jew" is meant to foreground the condition of historically specific oppression as well as the concomitant illusion of liberation from history that is postcolonialism as its most pernicious. "Virtual Jew" stresses the integral connections between imaginary constructions and actual people, even when they exist only in a fabricated past or a phantasmatic future. In cyberspace studies, "virtual" is used most often to modify "worlds" or "narratives."[40] Marie-Laure Ryan explains the usual "two senses of the term":

> One is the philosophical meaning, which invokes the idea of potentiality. The virtual is the field of unrealized possibilities that surround the realm of the actual in a system of reality. . . . [Within a narrative universe] the potential type of virtuality is represented in two ways: in the as-yet unrealized representations formed by the [text's] characters, such as wishes, goals and plans,

and in the horizon of possible events surrounding the textual actual world. . . . The other sense of "virtual" describes an optical phenomenon. According to Webster's dictionary, a virtual image is one formed of virtual foci; that is, of points "from which divergent rays of light seem to emanate but do not actually do so." This meaning can be metaphorically transferred to a type of narrative discourse that evokes states and events indirectly as they are captured in a reflecting device that exists as a material object in the textual actual world. This reflecting device could be a mirror, text, photograph, movie, or television show.[41]

Building on Ryan's definitions, we see that the virtual does not actually refer to the actual, although this is what it claims to do. Rather, the virtual "surround[s] the realm of the actual in a system of reality," thereby creating a simulation that, by seeming to be more authentic than the actual, may be mistaken for it. When we examine the virtual Jew, for example, we see that it does not refer directly to any actual Jew, nor present an accurate depiction of one, nor even a faulty fiction of one; instead it "surrounds" Jews with a "reality" that displaces and supplants their actuality. In fact, following the trail of the virtual guarantees that one will never arrive at the actual, for the referent of any virtual is always irretrievable. Thus, rather than being surprised at or having to explain the continuation of English reference to Jews after the Expulsion, we might better acknowledge that Jewish absence is likely the best precondition for virtual presence. For wherever in Western culture actual Jews come to reside, they encounter the phantom that follows and precedes them. By virtue of its virtuality, therefore, "the Jew" maintains its frightful power.

To further understand the subtle workings of this medieval phantasm, it will help to situate the virtual Jew within Homi Bhabha's discussion of colonial truth production. In his well-known essay, "Signs Taken for Wonders," Bhabha writes that

> the field of the "true" emerges as a visible effect of knowledge/power only after the regulatory and displacing division of the true and the false. From this point of view, discursive "transparency" is best read in the photographic sense in which a transparency is also always a negative, processed into visibility through the technologies of reversal, enlargement, lighting, editing, projection, not a source but a re-source of light. Such a bringing to light is never a prevision; it is always a question of the provision of visibility as a capacity, a strategy, an agency.[42]

In Bhabha's terms, the virtual Jew is a "transparency," "processed into visibility through [various] technologies." More than simply a projection of the Christian gaze in the psychological sense, the sign is a projection in the optical sense: an image that is necessarily an illusion. The virtual Jew is not a source of emanations of the actual in itself but a "re-source," a reflection constructed by means of such processes as "reversal, enlargement, editing," and so on. "The Jew" reflects not any actual Jews but the "capacity, strategy, agency" of the observer. In this sense, we do not start with the actual existence of actual Jews, then consider how the depiction of Jews in various forms of discourse in the Christian Middle Ages matched or distorted the actuality. Rather, we understand from the start that the virtual Jew is an invented "reality" that does not depend on actual medieval Jews for its connotations, let alone its denotation. For even if we were to observe actual medieval Jews, we could only come to the conclusion that they do not, in themselves, possess the "true." The widespread medieval use of phrases such as "*verus Israel*" and "*Hebraica veritas*" confirms Bhabha's assertion that the determination of true and false has been made *prior to* the reading of the true, for having determined that Jews are not the "true Israel," Christians then could claim to be those who, truly, possess "Hebrew truth."[43] When Christians become the true Hebrews and Jews the false, the need for Jews as augustinian "bearers of the book" is superseded. And as we have seen, such dispossession of Jews is actualized in colonial displacement, particularly, in England, in the Expulsion of 1290.

Despite—or because of—its *a priori* determination of the real, the virtual contains almost unlimited potential for proliferation. Bhabha argues that such proliferation is an essential aspect of the stereotype, which functions in a "continual and repetitive chain . . . [so that] the *same old* stories of the Negro's animality, the Coolie's inscrutability or the stupidity of the Irish *must* be told (compulsively) again and afresh, and are differently gratifying and terrifying each time."[44] To these compulsive retellings we can add the multiple medieval reiterations of "the Jew" that recur in the *Canterbury Tales* as well as in apocalypse manuscripts, the *Luttrell Psalter,* and the *Holkham Bible Picture Book.* Reiterating the sign, "the Jew," is thus an act that releases possibilities of image—but also of event, with actual consequences for actual Jews. When Jews (whose basic religious tenets forbid blood contamination) are accused of blood crimes, or when Jews (who place little or no emphasis on proselytizing) are denounced for judaizing, the resulting persecutions are "effects of knowledge/power" of the virtual Jew upon actual Jews. The sign is thus the equivalent of an optical "reflecting device" ("not a source but a re-source of light"), by means of which the post/colonial "system of reality surrounding the actual" is constructed. According to this system, it is actual Jews who must suffer for the sins of the virtual Jew, and their punishments arise, in Louise Fradenburg's words, "from the very need to substantiate an irreality populated by hallucinations."[45]

However irreal, however phantasmatic, the power of the virtual is with us still. In thirteenth- and fourteenth-century England, social, political, and religious conditions ensured that artists, writers, and theologians participated in the paradox of continually ridding England of Jews while continually repatriating them. But as we have seen, the ongoing colonial construction of the virtual Jew did not end with the Expulsion of 1290; rather, it began to gather steam so that by the sixteenth century, "[m]ost European kingdoms had expelled their Jews . . . [as the] idea of a Europe *Judenrein* began to take its place in the mentality of Western Christendom."[46] When Despres notes that "[l]ike the Canterbury pilgrims, Chaucer's audience lived in a post-expulsion world,"[47] she is alluding to the aftereffects of colonialism on Chaucer and his English contemporaries. But modern medievalists also live in a post-Expulsion world, and the England we construct for Chaucer is most often as *judenrein* as the England of the *Canterbury Tales*. In light of the history that followed the Expulsion— the history of European Jews as well as the history of Western imperialism—it therefore becomes imperative to consider the Middle Ages from the perspective of postcolonial studies as well as to consider postcolonialism from the perspective of medieval studies.

When Ella Shohat famously asks, "When exactly, does the 'post-colonial' begin?" nowhere in her answer does she indicate that a reconfigured, nonhegemonic "notion of the past" might include the European Middle Ages.[48] I am not suggesting here that the Middle Ages is that origin; medievalists such as Allan Frantzen already have pointed out the dangers inherent in such a position.[49] Rather, I am suggesting that we need to recognize the many connections between medieval English Christians and Jews that constituted a colonial, then postcolonial, relation: The English acted as colonizers, using their power to exploit and deterritorialize; the Jews were an internally colonized people, achieving release from English colonialism only at the cost of exile; the English/Christians constructed "the Jew" as part of their fabrication of national/religious identity; and English artists and writers, such as Geoffrey Chaucer, participated in the ongoing, postcolonial, allosemitic production of the virtual Jew. When we consider all of these connections, then we also must recognize that the 1290 Expulsion, while marking a turning point in English Christian and Jewish relations, constitutes but one episode within a postcolonial continuum whose tragic effects persist to the present day.

Notes

1. Surveys of the critical literature on Chaucer and the Jews are included in Florence Ridley, *The Prioress and the Critics,* University of California Pub-

lications, English Studies 30 (Berkeley: University of California Press, 1965); and Louise O. Fradenburg, "Criticism, Anti-Semitism, and the Prioress's Tale," *Exemplaria* 1 (1989): 69–115. Most notable among the articles written on the subject in the 1990s is Denise L. Despres, "Cultic Anti-Judaism and Chaucer's Litel Clergeon," *Modern Philology* 91 (1994): 413–27. All references to and citations from the *Canterbury Tales* are from Geoffrey Chaucer, *The Riverside Chaucer*, 3rd ed., gen. ed. Larry D. Benson (Boston: Houghton Mifflin, 1987).

2. On Jewish absent presence in the *Divine Comedy*, see Sylvia Tomasch, "Judecca, Dante's Satan, and the *Dis*-placed Jew," in *Text and Territory: Geographical Imagination in the European Middle Ages*, ed. Sylvia Tomasch and Sealy Gilles (Philadelphia: University of Pennsylvania Press, 1998), pp. 247–67. For the case in medieval England, see Michael Camille, *The Luttrell Psalter and the Making of Medieval England* (Chicago: University of Chicago Press, 1998), p. 284; Christine Chism, "The *Siege of Jerusalem*: Liquidating Assets," *Journal of Medieval and Early Modern Studies* 28 (1998): 319; Despres, "Cultic Anti-Judaism," 414; and Colin Richmond, "Englishness and Medieval Anglo-Jewry," in *The Jewish Heritage in British History: Englishness and Jewishness*, ed. Tony Kushner (London: Frank Cass, 1996), p. 56. For the case in early modern England, see James Shapiro, *Shakespeare and the Jews* (New York: Columbia University Press, 1996). For a modern instance that reverses the usual sequence of absence following presence, see Leo Spitzer, *Hotel Bolivia: The Culture of Memory in a Refuge from Nazism* (New York: Hill and Wang, 1998), p. 166.

3. Denise L. Despres, "Immaculate Flesh and the Social Body: Mary and the Jews," *Jewish History* 12 (1998): 47. See also her "Cultic Anti-Judaism"; and "Mary of the Eucharist: Cultic Anti-Judaism in Some Fourteenth-Century English Devotional Manuscripts," in *From Witness to Witchcraft: Jews and Judaism in Medieval Christian Thought*, ed. Jeremy Cohen (Wiesbaden: Harrassowitz Verlag, 1997), pp. 375–401.

4. Despres, "Cultic Anti-Judaism," 427. See also Thomas Bestul, *Texts of the Passion: Latin Devotional Literature and Medieval Society* (Philadelphia: University of Pennsylvania Press, 1996), esp. chap. 3.

5. Richmond, "Englishness"; and Shapiro, *Shakespeare*.

6. Shapiro, *Shakespeare*, p. 42.

7. Postcolonial theorists agree that since the effects of colonialism are ongoing, the "post-" cannot be taken to mean a simple "after"; as Ania Loomba, *Colonialism/Postcolonialism* (London: Routledge, 1998), writes, "a country may be both postcolonial (in the sense of being formally independent) and neo-colonial (in the sense of remaining economically and/or culturally dependent) at the same time" (p. 7). But since England was not colonized from without, was colonizing the Jews within, and was therefore not neocolonial in the ways Loomba indicates, I use "postcolonial" here to link both the shift in chronology and the continuation of colonial culture that inhered in

England during Chaucer's lifetime. On occasion, I use "post/colonial" as shorthand for "colonial and postcolonial."

8. On these widely held positions, see Loomba, *Colonialism/Postcolonialism,* chap. 1.

9. Kathleen Biddick, "The ABC of Ptolemy: Mapping the World with the Alphabet," in *Text and Territory,* ed. Sylvia Tomasch and Sealy Gilles, p. 291 n 2.

10. On causes of the Expulsion, see Shapiro, *Shakespeare,* pp. 46–55.

11. Sophia Menache, "Matthew Paris's Attitudes Toward Anglo-Jewry," *Journal of Medieval History* 23 (1997): 158; on Henry's policy, see pp. 160–61. Kenneth L. Stow, "The Avignonese Papacy or, After the Expulsion," in *From Witness to Witchcraft,* ed. Jeremy Cohen, cites a parallel case of papal pragmatism (what Zygmunt Bauman calls allosemitism, see below) when he describes the "precarious situation" of Jews under the Avignonese papacy as resulting not from "the alternation of repression with toleration or kindness, but of an integral policy in which all principles operated simultaneously" (p. 277).

12. Sophia Menache, "Faith, Myth, and Politics—The Stereotype of the Jews and Their Expulsion from England and France," *Jewish Quarterly Review* 75 (1985): 360.

13. Jeremy Cohen, "The Muslim Connection or On the Changing Role of the Jew in High Medieval Theology," in *From Witness to Witchcraft,* ed. Cohen, p. 159. David Nirenberg, *Communities of Violence: Persecution of Minorities in the Middle Ages* (Princeton, NJ: Princeton University Press, 1996), has countered the emphasis of Cohen and other historians on the perceived shift from toleration to persecution.

14. Menache, "Matthew Paris's Attitudes," p. 144; see also Chism, "The *Siege of Jerusalem.*"

15. Suzanne Lewis, *Reading Images: Narrative Discourse and Reception in the Thirteenth-Century Illuminated Apocalypse* (Cambridge: Cambridge University Press, 1995); the illustrations cited in this paragraph are, in order, Lewis's figures 48, 83, 117, 177, 231, 9 (plus 17, 21, 33, etc.), 42 (plus 45, 48), 224, 233, 251, and 33.

16. Lewis, *Reading Images,* p. 72.

17. Camille, *Luttrell Psalter,* p. 282.

18. Martin W. Walsh, "Divine Cuckold/Holy Fool: The Comic Image of Joseph in the English 'Troubles' Play," in *England in the Fourteenth Century: Proceedings of the 1985 Harlaxton Symposium,* ed. W. M. Ormond (Woodbridge, Suffolk: Boydell Press, 1986), p. 284. We should note that Joseph also wears the *pileus cornutus* in subsequent scenes (e.g., the Nativity). Other figures (e.g., Pharisees, torturers) are presented as grotesque, sometimes wearing peaked caps suggestive of the Jewish hat, but none is as explicitly marked as "a Jew" as is Joseph. Four-panel image of Joseph used by permission of the British Library (ADD46780F12).

19. Ibid., p. 297.

20. Robert C. Stacey, "From Ritual Crucifixion to Host Desecration: Jews and the Body of Christ," *Jewish History* 12 (1998): 25.

21. Camille, *Luttrell Psalter,* p. 284.

22. On Englishness and Jewishness, see the essays in *The Jewish Heritage in British History: Englishness and Jewishness,* ed. Tony Kushner (London: Frank Cass, 1992); also Shapiro, *Shakespeare.*

23. On the locational politics of "Asye," see Fradenburg, "Criticism, Anti-Semitism," 98. Both Fradenburg and Despres, "Cultic Anti-Judaism," stress the importance in this tale of a purified England.

24. Biddick, "ABC," p. 270.

25. Nelson Sherwin Bushnell, "The Wandering Jew and *The Pardoner's Tale,*" *North Carolina Studies in Philology* 28 (1931): 450–60, argues that only since the seventeenth century is the wanderer understood as Jewish; but Despres, "Mary of the Eucharist," cites an example from the thirteenth-century de Brailes Hours (384).

26. On Jews and the plague, see Seraphiné Guerchberg, "The Controversy Over the Alleged Sowers of the Black Death in the Contemporary Treatises on Plague," in *Change in Medieval Society: Europe North of the Alps, 1050–1500,* ed. Sylvia Thrupp (New York: Appleton-Century-Crofts, 1984), pp. 208–24. Also see Anna Foa, *Ebrei in Europa: Dalla peste nera all'e-mancipazione* (Latera: Bari, 1992); and Nirenberg, *Communities of Violence,* esp. "Epilogue."

27. On Christian and Jewish bodies, see Steven Kruger, "The Bodies of Jews in the Late Middle Ages," in *The Idea of Medieval Literature: New Essays on Chaucer and Medieval Culture in Honor of Donald R. Howard,* ed. James M. Dean and Christian Zacher (Newark: University of Delaware Press, 1992), pp. 301–23. See also the articles in Sarah Kay and Miri Rubin, eds., *Framing Medieval Bodies* (Manchester: Manchester University Press, 1994).

28. Philo-Semitic examples are cited by Stephen Spector, "Empathy and Enmity in the *Prioress's Tale,*" in *The Olde Daunce: Love, Friendship, Sex, and Marriage in the Medieval World,* Robert R. Edwards and Stephen Spector (Albany: SUNY Press, 1991), pp. 211–28. On Brunton, also see Sister Mary Aquinas Devlin, "Bishop Thomas Brunton and His Sermons," *Speculum* 14 (1939): 324–44. For another view of Langland's citation of Jews, see Elisa Narin van Court, "The Hermeneutics of Supersession: The Revision of the Jews from the B to the C Text of *Piers Plowman,*" *The Yearbook of Langland Studies* 10 (1996): 43–87.

29. Zygmunt Bauman, "Allosemitism: Premodern, Modern, Postmodern," in *Modernity, Culture, and 'the Jew',* ed. Bryan Cheyette and Laura Marcus (Stanford, CA: Stanford University Press, 1998), pp. 143–56. See also Bryan Cheyette, "Introduction: Unanswered Questions," in *Between "Race" and Culture: Representations of "the Jew" in English and American Literature,* ed. Bryan Cheyette (Stanford, CA: Stanford University Press, 1996), pp. 1–15. Although, strictly speaking, "allosemitism" is anachronistic in reference to the Middle Ages, I believe it is useful for encompassing the contradictions

inherent in medieval Christian European attitudes toward and representations of Jews.

30. Anne McClintock, "The Angels of Progress: Pitfalls of the Term 'Post-Colonialism,'" *Social Text* 31/32 (1992): 88 (her emphases).

31. For another discussion of premodern Jews as internally colonized, see Jonathan Boyarin, "The Other Within and the Other Without," *Storm from Paradise: The Politics of Jewish Memory* (Minneapolis: University of Minnesota Press, 1992), pp. 77–98.

32. On thirteenth-century English anti-Jewish measures, see: Jonathan A. Bush, "'You're Gonna Miss Me When I'm Gone': Early Modern Common Law Discourse and the Case of the Jews," *Wisconsin Law Review* 5 (1993): 1264, on the statutes of 1233, 1253, 1271, and 1275; Lewis, *Reading Images,* p. 216, mentions the synods of Oxford (1222), Worcester (1240), Chichester (1246), Salisbury (1256), Merton (1258), and Lambeth (1261). On medieval Anglo-Jewry see: Menache, "Faith, Myth, and Politics" and "Matthew Paris's Attitudes"; Richmond, "Englishness"; Shapiro, *Shakespeare,* pp. 43–55; Robert C. Stacey, "The Conversion of Jews to Christianity in Thirteenth-Century England," *Speculum* 67 (1992): 263–83; and "Recent Work in Medieval English Jewish History," *Jewish History* 2 (1987): 61–72. On Jewish-Christian relations in medieval Europe, see Anna Sapir Abulafia, "From Northern Europe to Southern Europe and From the General to the Particular: Recent Research on Jewish-Christian Coexistence in Medieval Europe," *Journal of Medieval History* 23 (1997): 179–90.

33. Throughout this paragraph, I rely on the discussion of monastic accounts in Menache, "Faith, Myth, and Politics."

34. On Christian supersessionism, see Daniel Boyarin, "The Subversion of the Jews: Moses's Veil and the Hermeneutics of Supersession," *Diacritics* 23 (1993): 16–35; also Narin van Court, "Hermeneutics of Supersession."

35. Edward Said, "Representing the Colonized: Anthropology's Interlocutors," *Critical Inquiry* 15 (1989): 207; quoted by Leela Gandhi, *Postcolonial Theory: A Critical Introduction* (New York: Columbia University Press), p. 7.

36. Gandhi, *Postcolonial Theory,* p. 7.

37. Ibid., p. 7.

38. See Richmond, "Englishness," p. 56.

39. "Hermeneutical Jew": Jeremy Cohen, "Introduction" in *From Witness to Witchcraft,* ed. Cohen, p. 9; "theological Jew": Gilbert Dahan, *Les intellectuels chretiens et les Juifs au Moyen Age* (Paris: Cerf, 1990), p. 586; "notional Jew": Bush, "'You're Gonna Miss Me When I'm Gone.'"

40. I know of only one other linking of medieval and cyberspace studies: Jeffrey Fisher, "The Postmodern Paradiso: Dante, Cyberpunk, and the Technology of Cyberspace," in *Internet Culture,* ed. David Porter (New York: Routledge, 1997), pp. 111–28, who speaks of a body-transcending "will to virtuality" shared by medieval and cyberspatial texts.

41. Marie-Laure Ryan, "Allegories of Immersion: Virtual Narration in Postmodern Fiction," *Style* 29 (1995): 262–64.

42. Homi K. Bhabha, "Signs Taken for Wonders," in *The Post-Colonial Studies Reader,* ed. Bill Ashcroft, Gareth Griffiths, and Helen Tiffin (London: Routledge, 1995), p. 32.

43. On *verus Israel,* see Friedrich Lotter, "The Position of the Jews in Early Cistercian Exegesis and Preaching," in *From Witness to Witchcraft,* ed. Cohen, pp. 163–85; also Marcel Simon, *Verus Israel: A Study of the Relations Between the Christians and Jews in the Roman Empire (135–425)* (1948; 1964; reprinted Oxford University Press, 1986).

44. Homi K. Bhabha, "The Other Question," in *Contemporary Postcolonial Theory: A Reader,* ed. Padmini Mongia (London: Arnold, 1996), p. 47 (his emphases). I distinguish "virtual" from "stereotype" in that although "virtual" also has a psychological component, it is not tied narrowly to the construction of the individual colonial subject; see also Robert Chazan, *Medieval Stereotypes and Modern Antisemitism* (Berkeley: University of California Press, 1997). I also distinguish "virtual" from "simulacrum," for although they share a technological component, "virtual" does not depend on the globalization of capital nor is it tied directly to the posttextual, commodified postmodern; see Jean Baudrillard, *Simulacra and Simulation,* trans. Sheila Faria Glaser (Ann Arbor: University of Michigan Press, 1994). Most important perhaps, I use "virtual Jew" in contradistinction to Jean-Francois Lyotard's undifferentiated, universalized, lower-case "jew" as standing for the ultimate postmodern intellectual predicament— what Max Silverman, "Re-Figuring 'the Jew' in France," in *Modernity, Culture, and "the Jew,"* ed. Cheyette and Marcus, calls "the judaizing of alterity in postmodern theory" (p. 199); see Lyotard, *Heidegger and "the jews,"* trans. Andreas Michel and Mark S. Roberts (Minneapolis: University of Minnesota Press, 1990).

45. Fradenburg, "Criticism, Anti-Semitism," p. 83.

46. Jeremy Cohen, "Traditional Prejudice and Religious Reform: The Theological and Historical Foundation of Luther's Anti-Judaism," in *Anti-Semitism in Times of Crisis,* ed. Sander L. Gilman and Steven T. Katz (New York: New York University Press, 1991), p. 97.

47. Despres, "Cultic Anti-Judaism," p. 427.

48. Ella Shohat, "Notes on the 'Post-Colonial,'" in *Contemporary Postcolonial Theory,* ed. Mongia, pp. 325, 330. Shohat shares an assumption of the necessarily post-Columbian origins of colonialism with other postcolonial theorists; see, for example, Ashcroft, Griffiths, and Tiffin, eds., *Post-Colonial Studies Reader,* p. 2.

49. Allan J. Frantzen, *Desire for Origins: New Language, Old English, and Teaching the Tradition* (New Brunswick, NJ: Rutgers University Press, 1990).

CHAPTER 14

IMPERIAL FETISHISM:
PRESTER JOHN AMONG THE NATIVES

Michael Uebel

> *This chapter discusses the colonialist utopia of Prester John in terms of the
> revolutionary potency of fetishism.*

Taking as its focus stories of India's legendary ruler, Prester John, this
chapter suggests something of the social and psychic relays between
the utopic imaginary of twelfth-century colonialism in India and the
geopolitical crisis of twentieth-century imperialism in Africa. Condensed
in the twelfth-century version of the legend of Prester John, and some of
its important late medieval and early modern incarnations, is a narrative
of Western European political failure that gets displaced, or redeployed,
across the material body of the fetish. And, I suggest, condensed in John
Buchan's *Prester John,* his 1910 colonialist story for boys, is the failure of
turn-of-the-century liberal humanism, a failure that gets played out
through a process of reduction, where the aggressivities of imperialism
become partially neutralized in the material fetish. In both cases, Prester
John stages the pathologization of power relations, indeed, in such an urgent way that, "magically," fetishism helps evacuate violence and inequality from the social scene. Yet while fetishism works dialectically to control
violence, by formally recoding it, at the same time it perpetuates the violent project of imperialism. In the case of both medieval and modern
colonial narratives around Prester John, I am interested in linking perverse
strategies to survival in the face of the breakdown of culturally sanctioned

identities (political and personal) as well as attending to the ways in which fetishism immerses the subject in the political field.

Prester John's Gift: The Ecstasy of the Imperial Fetish

The fetish is situated in the space of cultural revolution.

—*William Pietz, "The Problem of the Fetish, I"*

This section considers how symbolic exchange haunts medieval imperial formations, calling into question the seemingly unrelated mechanisms of social valuation employed in both political and epistemological economies. In a late medieval version of the story, Prester John's gift of precious gems to a Western ruler who fails to discover their esoteric powers poses a sharp challenge to European epistemology, ways of knowing and perceiving that ground the formation of social utopia. What Prester John offers can, however, never be reciprocated, for his gift radically alters the terms of political economy itself by operating outside a principle of reversibility, or the countergift, thereby putting an end to accumulation and diminishing the power of the fetish. This section suggests why this annulment of accumulation, this effacement of the fetish, was crucial as Western medieval economies prepared for further war with the East.

After the failure of the second crusade in 1148, a mysterious letter begins to circulate throughout Europe. Addressed to Western emperors such as Frederick Barbarossa and Emmanuel Comnenus, the *Letter of Prester John* holds out many promises, including aid in liberating the Holy Land, gifts of vast material wealth, and a utopic future modeled on the peaceful coexistence of church and state. Structurally, the *Letter* amounts to a vast list, a superabundance of things available for the asking: "Because of the usual munificence of our liberality," the *Letter* promises, "if there is anything you should desire for your pleasure, make it known to us through our delegate through a small note of your esteem, and you shall have it" (§ 5).[1]

The *Letter's* list of inalienable gifts plays a crucial role in the production of imaginary relations into which the document's Western readers are interpellated. By offering the illusion of reality in a state of absolute plenitude, the *Letter* works both to compensate for what is lost, namely, the Holy Land and its treasures, and to safeguard what is already possessed. The classical and medieval encyclopedia, genres to which we might compare the *Letter* in terms of ideological utility, compile *facta* as a response to the urgency of cultural disruptions.[2] In the process of preserving culture, medieval encyclopedic narratives, like the *Letter,* taxonomize the world, provisionally sheltering it against ever-present threats of disorder and oblivion.

The absorption of the list form by that of the letter renders the *Letter of Prester John* a rather special document, one that spatializes its *facta* into a containing coherence and temporalizes them as part of a dynamic process wherein devolution to disorder is inescapable—and, as I argue, potentially transformative. Or to put it otherwise, in terms of its generic form, the *Letter* guarantees its own longevity and integrity through a kind of chaos management while inexorably moving toward novelty and disorder. The *Letter* functions as both *thesauros* (treasury, treasure trove), conserving a rich knowledge about the East, and *montage,* consistently attracted to the paratactic, the fragmentary, the unfinished.

In the Middle Ages as now, collections and inventories fashion a consumer fascinated by his relation to and identification with alterity. In his famous essay "Towards a New Middle Ages," Umberto Eco identifies in the conception of art as *bricolage* one of the most salient points of contact between medieval culture and our own: "the mad taste for collecting, listing, assembling and amassing different things . . . due to the need to take to pieces and reconsider what is left of a previous, perhaps harmonious, but now absolute world."[3] The kind of indiscriminate collections possessed by rulers such as Charles IV of Bohemia or the Duc de Berry have as their discursive analog documents that amass, in a nonsystematic manner, information about things, events, and places so remote in space or time that, if never assembled, either would remain unknown or else would be forgotten.[4] However, in the *Letter,* the impulse to collect is not wholly reducible to the need to bring into temporary alignment two different realities—say, the marvelous and the mundane—but rather signals a more profound need to designate the seam itself between realities as the site for grasping cultural difference.

Assessing the significance of the space between cultures opened up by the differentness of objects collected and cataloged is a powerful form of cultural (self-)analysis. "By its very nature," Patti White observes, "the list provides a cultural perspective that is at once grand and microscopic, since it implies everything while mentioning only selected items. . . . essentially, the list exhibits the cultural episteme writ small."[5] Such a dialogic perspective thus possesses "a peculiar intensity," what Gaston Bachelard has called "intimate immensity."[6] Indeed, grasping the *relatio* of one culture to another is possible only under conditions that foster the production, in the imaginary, of a gestalt constituted by smaller relational intensities. These conditions include above all the rapid-fire additive style of the *Letter,* the movement of one list image quickly followed by another such that a disjunctive shock is produced that impels further movement. Despite the chaotic potential of the list formation, despite its violence to the notion of how things may be coordinated and subordinated, a sense

of the way things of varying intensity fit together within a phenomeno-
logical field does emerge.

A fine example of this occurs in the *Letter*'s obsessive accumulation of
imagery concerning precious gemstones. Enumerated are gemstones possessing magical powers (§§29–30; 66; E 8–20); precious stones gathered
from flowing rivers (§§22; 32–33; 39–40); gems used in the construction
of palaces or other monuments, such as the magical mirror tower or marvelous mill house (§§68; B 87–93; D w-y; E 29); gems used for architec-
tural purposes but primarily ornamental (§§47; 57–60; 62–63); and gems
whose value is particularly high because of the difficulty of their attainment (§38). The *Letter*'s multiple interpolations suggest that such a catalog
of fantastic riches can be extended ad infinitum, such that the following
claim in the earliest version seems fully credible [7]: "Of all the riches that
are in the world, our magnificence exceeds in abundance and surpasses"
(§50). The pile-up of gemstones of varying utility and intrinsic value draws
attention to the desire for or fantasy of accumulation itself as the real subject of the images. Here precious stones do not represent the otherness of
vast wealth or marvelous virtue associated throughout the Middle Ages
with India so much as the force of fantasy itself that creates the possibility
for a meeting of self and other across the space opened up by their putative differences.[8]

One form that the fantasy takes, one field in which it might be con-
textualized, involves the contrasting of Eastern with Western ways of assessing an object's true value. Because precious stones, given their relative
rarity and manifest aesthetic properties, have immediately recognizable and
exoteric value, their absolute or hidden worth may never be known. Two
documents from the later Middle Ages, a fourteenth-century Icelandic tale
of India and a fifteenth-century Italian Prester John *nouvelle*, center on a
gift of three precious gems from Prester John to a Western potentate who
fails to discover their esoteric powers.[9]

In the Icelandic version, the king of Denmark is given three stones by
one of his own subjects, a man who has just returned from India, where
he himself was given the stones by a local ruler. Although the Danish king
admits he knows nothing at all of the stones' value, he keeps them in case
the giver should ask one day for reciprocation. As it turns out, a messenger from India does arrive at the king's court with a request for something
in return, to which the king replies: "I don't know how they merit any rec-
ompense, for I do not see what can be done with them."[10] The Indian then
demonstrates their virtues: One multiplies gold, the second protects against
wounds in battle, and the third transports the user to India—whereupon
the Indian vanishes. In the Italian story, the plot trajectory is similar: An
emissary from Prester John arrives at the court of a Western potentate to

explain the significance of precious stones already possessed, only to vanish with the stones after elucidating their virtues. But the Italian story is from its outset a moral tale: "the form and intent of the mission was double: a desire to put to the test whether the emperor was learned in speech and in deeds." Having received the three stones, the emperor is supposed to indicate "what is the best thing in the world." The emperor, however, fails to inquire about the stones' virtues, choosing to praise their beauty instead. The emperor concludes, somewhat ironically given the great opulence of his own court, that the best thing in the world is *misura* (moderation; the golden mean). After hearing report of the emperor's words, Presto Giovanni judges the emperor "very wise in word, but not in deed, in as much as he had not asked about the virtue of such precious stones." Prester John then dispatches his jeweler (*lapidaro*) to retrieve the stones. Once the jeweler holds all the stones, he becomes invisible, returns to India, and presents the stones to Prester John "con grande allegrezza" [with great happiness].[11]

Both tales clearly illustrate the failure to understand an object's intrinsic significance, a failure that has ultimately less to do with the mysterious nature of the objects themselves than with the social field in which they were exchanged.[12] In the Maussian view of gift exchange, the gemstones are transacted as part of cultural relations, but the crucial thing to underscore is the extent to which they are, as Marcel Mauss puts it, "parts of persons." In contrast to commodities produced by labor, these gemstones bear a substantial relation to their giver. It is their status as inalienable that binds giver and receiver together, such that the gift is to be properly experienced as a kind of test regarding how it will eventually be consumed. Prester John issues this challenge to his Western counterparts: whether in accepting the gifts they will also accept the alternative, magical world of which the gems are symbolic.[13] By failing to discover or even investigate the stones' esoteric powers, the Western rulers display their fascination with the outward signs of material wealth and with the sheer act of accumulation itself. As aesthetic objects, material things whose value is rooted in the present, the stones become substitutes for a lost faith in the mysteries mediating between this world and another possible one. We might even say that the stones, as the West experiences them, are nothing other than symptoms of a kind of "petrification of the faith," the deadening of popular mythology that, according to Frederick Turner, characterizes cultures no longer animated by their interaction with "an infinitely larger and more beautiful design."[14] Thus the gems provide an example of utopia as self-critique, but of a special kind of critique, wherein Prester John's gifts do not provide an education in what this world is or should be like but instead gesture toward the possibility of what *another* world might be like. Placing a burden upon their receiver, the gifts structure new imaginary relations with what is other.

Prester John's gemstones are less objects to be admired, or marveled at, than identifications, bridges to another "reality." The *Letter* has the peculiar function of presenting its reader with an unorganized perceptual wealth, wherein the immediate reality of *things* is eclipsed by the active *relations* into which a reader is placed. If things, as they are given meaning in language, imprison subjects through their circumscription of cultural space, they also may serve as the very vehicles for transforming or transcending one's own delimited social reality. Wilhelm von Humboldt was one of the first to suggest how things furnish a sense of bounded reality: "Man lives with his objects chiefly—in fact, since his feeling and acting depend upon his perceptions, one may say exclusively—as language presents them to him. By the same process whereby he spins language out of his own being, he ensnares himself in it; and each language draws a magic circle round the people to which it belongs, a circle from which there is no escape *save by stepping out of it into another.*"[15] It is the fetishization, in language, of objects like gemstones that transforms them into "magical" things, more *real,* we might say, than reality itself. That is, objects condition a way of looking at and living in reality that finally has little to do with their specific materiality or utility. Not merely the inert "stuff" of reality, things bear directly on, and thus can come to dominate, as if by magic, the perceptions and realities of life. The fetishistic value of objects resides, then, in the magical potencies they harbor.[16]

If things do possess the magical power to take over the space of their production and consumption, then they also possess the power to circumscribe entirely new fantasmic spaces into which subjects might step—or, I suggest, leap. This leap into a new identificatory relation is, as I hinted earlier, encouraged by none other than the *Letter's* own artificial list structure, a formal arrangement that, because of rather than in spite of its artificiality, provides the truest index of the real, the surest, and most assuring shape of reality, especially reality to come.[17] Neither in its elements nor as a totality does the utopic text come to rest in the form of a "'realized' vision of this or that ideal society or social ideal"; rather it moves continuously forward by means of "logically unmotivated associative transition[s] from one theme to another."[18] In its cognitively abrupt transitions, the text's fully "ideological aspect" is fully revealed. I propose here, apropos of the theories of Russian filmmaker Sergei Eisenstein, that the *discursive* relations found in the *Letter's* list structure cannot be construed independently of the *existential* relations such a generic structure urges.

The force of cinema's intervention into reality depends, for Eisenstein, not on the fetishization of reality, of real things, that the montage seems to promote but on its mode of "cutting the spectator into and beyond the film in a (multi-) position of reading" and living.[19] Montage film is a manifestly material-based and, as Eisenstein would have it, "agitational" or "aggressive" medium—aimed at "moulding the audience in a desired direction"—and in this it has structural, if not political, affinities with literature that emphasizes linguistic effect over plot motivation.[20] In order to concentrate one's emotion in a desired direction, montage art creates cognitive dissonances in the *subject* (in both senses of the term), shocks or collisions between two or more disparate units of meaning that, despite obvious incongruity, constitute a whole, an impression in the mind. This impression is the seed of a transformation, the conflict inherent in the art having been transferred to the onlooker. "Agit cinema" compels a special kind of fictive collaboration, one centered on "an effective construction . . . according to which it is not the facts being demonstrated that are important but the combinations of the emotional reactions of the audience."[21] The figurative tendencies of the "agitational spectacle" ("What does it mean?") are secondary to its productive qualities, that is, to its ideological effects on a subject who has internalized a series of dynamic relations, what Eisenstein refers to as the "shocks" between spectacles. The dialectical instabilities of montage guarantee its provocativeness, its constant, often overwhelming, challenge to seek out and inhabit another—perhaps better—state of existence.

This distillation of Eisensteinian film theory should provide a backdrop for investigating the utopic dimensions of the medieval montage mechanism. With respect to the utopic impulse, montage does double duty: It conserves a past, by indulging cultural nostalgia for lost unity with the others it portrays, and it maps out possible futures for subjects in whom it installs the desire for alternative worlds. In the *Letter of Prester John* this tension of nostalgic desire and its sublimation assumes the shape of a dynamic, often rhythmical oscillation between the poles of conservation and loss, enjoyment and interdiction. Pleasures and desires fulfilled are perpetually lived *through* rather than arrived at. Never entirely achieved or lost, the pleasures of Prester John's utopia constitute less a final *bonheur terrestre* than a passageway to composing, and confronting, the problem of their own enjoyment. The utopian is never wholly within or without (both outside of and lacking) a kind of earthly happiness and satisfaction:

38. Near the desert between the uninhabited mountains a certain rivulet flows beneath the earth, the entrance to which is not accessible except by chance. Indeed, sometimes the ground opens up, and if someone at that moment crosses over from there, he is able to enter; but he must quickly get out, if by any chance the ground may close up. And whatever he snatches

up from the sand is precious stones and gems, for the sand and gravel are nothing but precious stones and gems.

The enjoyment of utopia is risky and fleeting: Quickly snatching up jewels, one faces entombment in the utopic space (within a utopic space) one has entered. Access to and attainment of utopic pleasure are not givens but are determined by chance and even by the extent of one's greed and the ability to curb it. This liminal space tests the limits of the utopian's desire, measuring how much he is willing to risk for a taste of utopia proffered now and again.

Such moments as these are much more than seductive signs of wealth and abundance; they are the key or guide to a process of radical self-estrangement that originates in idealization.[22] Clearly Prester John's catalog encourages, indeed dramatizes, the capacity of its Western European reader to confer on his Eastern "better half" the things and attributes he does not or cannot possess at home. Thus the *Letter*'s montagelike structure works to accumulate—or, better, pile up—images of the marvelous and extravagant, upon which are instantly conferred an ideality. In this manner, the montage structure functions as a way of making sense beyond its status as a collection of images, each moving abruptly, as in a filmic "cut," from one to the next.

Montage, in order to have any social effect, must be a meaningful, that is, meaning producing, operation. Individual images, whose relation to one another the montage manages, should "add up" to a greater organic and expressive whole. However, in the *Letter,* the montage arrangement of individual images works slightly differently. The symbolic whole, to which all the parts supposedly add up, is nothing other than a surplus, whose excessive meaning exceeds the total of its combined parts. In other words, the anatomizing of Prester John's kingdom into parts, into a catalog of gifts, is an operation that cannot be undone, or reversed, by reassembling the parts into the whole. New sets of relations—among parts and between reader and text—intervene, ones that produce irreparable changes in the whole. Innocent reflection on the utopic text/event is never (again) possible.[23]

Such new relations, although in a sense supplemental, are not, however, the by-products of some useless expenditure;[24] instead, they are meant to be recycled as stimuli for the abandonment of one's familiar social relations. Within the network of montage relations, abandoning the familiar necessarily entails discovering the alien. The medieval utopic text points to what readers would immediately recognize as strange, a social state where there is no poverty, no crime, no vice, no dissension. Such an ideal social condition, having been broken down into its constitutive elements and conveyed as a list of local attributes, functions dialectically as prescription and description. While each element signifies something desirable in and of itself, each element, as Fredric Jameson puts it, "is also *at one and the same time* taken as the *figure* for Utopia in general, and for the systemic revolutionary transformation of society as a whole."[25]

The *Letter's* list structure places the reader right in the midst of a relay of displacements, tensions, and contradictions, a circuit that provides the dialectical energy for redirecting identificatory relations. In utopic lists like this, the logic of the selfsame has little transformative force. The fetishistic insistence that the other is only some ideal version of the same collapses the space of difference, whereas immersion in the utopic process makes sure that there is always something "ungraspable" out ahead of the place where one has momentarily settled. Prester John presents us, in what I have been calling a montage mode, with things that are just alien or ideal enough to limit severely the self-reflexivity and immobility inherent in the idealizing impulse.

Eisenstein, as I have suggested, was acutely attentive to the formal possibilities of social transformation. His montage compositional method aimed above all at effecting an ecstatic relation to otherness, what he called a "maximum 'departure from oneself.'" In his essay "The Structure of the Film" (1939), Eisenstein notes two crucial facts about montage: It is "*an arrangement of phenomena, which themselves flow ecstatically*"; it is "the representation of phenomena as distributed in such a way *among themselves, that each of them in relation to each other seems a transition from one intensity to another.*"[26] The moving image is designed to provoke or "shock" the subject into moving "from quality to quality" on the way to "a new condition" of social existence. This is the "fundamental ecstatic formula" of the utopic impulse:

the leap "out of oneself" invariably becomes a leap into a new quality. . . .
Here is another organic secret: a leaping imagist movement from quality to quality is *not a mere formula of growth,* but is more, *a formula of development . . .* [that] makes us, instead, *a collective and social unit, consciously participating in its development.* For we know that this very leap, in the interpretation of social phenomena, is present in those revolutions to which social development and the movement of society are directed.[27]

The "organic secret" of the *Letter* is the way that it carries "the montage principle over into history" by discovering "the crystal of the total event in the analysis of the small, individual moment."[28] The inherent instability of the paratactic gift list, its frequent violation of logical order and diegetic expectation, even its internal ambiguities, spark an abandonment of singular and familiar selfsameness in search of ecstasy, collectivity, utopia.[29] The analogy between montage and the list structure is, I think, most useful *as* an analogy—one that allows us to formulate the revolutionary nature of identification as an ecstatic transition to something else.[30]

Prester John's Empire: India to the Indies to Africa

In 1530, a year or two before Bartolomé de las Casas would begin to edit and transcribe Columbus's *Journal of the First Voyage,* an imperial coronation was being celebrated in Bologna. Its climactic event, the crowning of Roman German Emperor and Spanish King Charles V by Pope Clement VII, was interrupted by a most fantastic event, an intervention of myth into history. The moment was captured by Charles's biographer, Ludovico Dolce: "At that time, to Clement and to the Emperor were delivered the letters of Prester John the greatest and most powerful king of Asia, who informed them how he had been baptized and how he had embraced the Christian faith; and he declared to the Emperor that he would be his lawful vassal, and to the Pope his obedient son."[31] The dream of a Christian East, the fantasy animating the crusades, is here, over 400 years later, fulfilled in the name of political propaganda. Emperor Charles claimed what many religious and secular leaders since the mid-twelfth century had: knowledge of and communication with the legendary Christian ruler of the East. However, what distinguishes Charles from some of his predecessors is his absolute confidence in declaring rulership over a universally Christian world, one encompassing its religious others. This is nothing other than a dream of Christianity without boundaries, an Eastern fantasy of unselfconscious coherence and homogeneity, a fantasy whose content Gilles Deleuze and Félix Guattari aptly describe: "the Orient . . . only exists in the construction of a smooth space."[32]

The Prester John legend in the fifteenth and sixteenth centuries, and beyond, is mobilized to foster the goals of secular and religious harmony within Christian empire. Indeed, the perfection of Prester John's earthly paradise in the East offers the tantalizing possibility of triumph over an imperfect or impure cosmos. But, as I suggest, such a triumph must be renewed constantly due to the fetishistic strategies upon which imperialism obsessively relies. In what follows, I will place in a genealogy two different conceptions of Prester John's utopia—in Asia and Africa—in an effort to bring us closer to an understanding of the imaginary contours of what it means to discover, describe, and claim to possess a genuinely new or alien world. Toward this goal, I borrow from psychoanalysis a general notion of (perverse) fantasy and fetishism as those activities by which representations of, and solutions to, personal enigmas and social contradictions are gener-

ated. Fantasy, especially in its so-called perverse forms, is vital to both individuals and collectivities as the process by which identity is consolidated,
protected against loss and the threat of dissolution. However, such a process
should not be viewed strictly in terms of its defensive or reactive operation; rather, its function is active and generative. Fantasy, and the perverse
activities it supports, represents ways of reconstituting the world in order
to generate a new, utopic one. Perverse fantasies thus should be viewed, according to Janine Chasseguet-Smirgel, within the larger frame of historical man's attempt "to go beyond the narrow limits of his condition."[33]
Fantasy, it is not going too far to say, is the true generator of ideology.[34] At
the very site of fantasy and its objects (its fetishes), boundaries, which enforce the line between self and other, are spectacularly contested. What results, says Chasseguet-Smirgel, are "historical ruptures which give an
inkling of the advent of a new world."[35] I now examine briefly the ways
the legend of Prester John as ideology, as fantasy, is appropriated by
Columbus in the record of his exploration and colonization of what he
called the *otro mundo* (other world) and then by the fictional figure Reverend John Laputa in John Buchan's colonialist novel of revolutionary
South Africa, *Prester John*.

What I would call the colonial fantasy of Prester John functioned, in no
small way, as the stimulus for Columbus's voyage to the *otro mundo*. A won-
derful condensation of all that was current in discourses concerning the
"marvels of the East," the *Letter of Prester John* served as an important stimulus for Asian exploration. Messengers carrying letters to the Priest-King
were dispatched and missions were sent to his court, as Europeans expected
to find an ally in their losing crusades against the Saracens. Even after the
crusading impulse had withered, the search for Prester John thrived. Some
dates around the time of Columbus's voyages to the Orient: 1487, Pedro de
Covilham is sent by the king of Portugal to look for Prester John; 1492,
Martin Behaim of Nuremburg places Prester John in Cathay, or China, on
his famous map inspired by Marco Polo's travel account; 1497–1499, Vasco
de Gama, on his first journey to India, carries with him a letter of introduction from King Manuel to Prester John; and the Borgia map of the second half of the fifteenth century locates "Prespiter Johannes" in India next
to the marker for paradise, "locus deliciarum" (place of pleasures).

But, increasingly in the fourteenth and fifteenth centuries, the fantasy
locating Prester John in India runs parallel to an alternative history of the
legendary Priest-King, one placing him in Africa, as the Christian king of
Ethiopia. This is the same history that, twisted and extended, lends authority to the Great Kaffir Rising charted in Buchan's *Prester John*. The
quest for Prester John in Africa recurs constantly in the history of European exploration. After Dominicans are sent to Abyssinia in 1316 by Pope

John XXII, stories return from that region about Prester John and his magnificent empire. A story of the king is told in 1391 to King John I of Aragon by a priest who had spent several years at his court. In 1427 two ambassadors from Prester John, one a Christian and the other an infidel, arrive at the court of Alphonso V of Aragon. In 1441 Prince Henry the Navigator, responding to Antão Gonçalves's proposal that any African of rank captured on the west coast of Africa should be returned and ransomed in the hope of learning about the interior, asks for information about the Indies and Prester John. While Friar Jordanus, in the fourteenth century, places Prester John in Africa, Fra Mauro, in the middle of the fifteenth, identifies him on his map with the king of Abyssinia. After the Pedro de Covilham mission to India, the Portuguese send out another; this one, under (Dom Rodrigo) da Lima, reaches Abyssinia in 1520 and confirms the existence of the Ethiopian potentate.

Coinciding with the structure of imperial fantasy and fetishistic pleasure itself, Prester John functioned as the fetish par excellence of medieval and early modern European imperialism.[36] He became the symbolic ground upon which problems of cultural exchange could be negotiated. In her reading of the ideological value of the imperialistic fetish, Anne McClintock observes that the fetish serves as the preeminent site for the simultaneous embodiment of contesting systems of value. The fetish is "an impassioned object" of irresolution, a concentrated object whose social and psychological value, always more complex than its surface suggests, never merely replays, recodifies, or reaffirms the structures of the dominant ideology.[37] In order to localize the multiple ideological positions Columbus assumed relative to his historical experience of Prester John, we turn now to the prologue of Columbus's logbook of the first journey.

Columbus, addressing his imperial benefactors, begins at an end: "This present year of 1492, . . . Your Highnesses had brought to an end the war with the Moors who ruled in Europe and had concluded the war in the very great city of Granada."[38] He continues with a recollection of January 2, the day he witnessed the royal standards secured on the towers of the Alhambra and the Moorish King Boabdil formally surrender, kissing the hands of Ferdinand and Isabella. Columbus is acutely aware that he has witnessed the end of the Reconquista, a Spanish Christian enterprise begun nearly 800 years earlier. But, for Columbus, the impulse animating the Reconquest, the wish for an orthodox and universal Christianity, remained incomplete, unfulfilled. And so, he writes:

> because of the report I had given to Your Highnesses about the lands of India and about a prince who is called "grand Khan," which means in our Spanish language "King of Kings"; how, many times, he . . . had sent to

Rome to ask for men learned in our Holy Faith in order that they might
instruct him in it . . . ; and Your Highnesses, as Catholic Christians . . . lovers
and promoters of the Holy Christian Faith, and enemies of the false doctrine of Mahomet and of all idolatries and heresies, you thought of sending
me . . . to the said regions of India to see the said princes and the peoples
and the lands . . . to see how their conversion to our Holy Faith might be
undertaken.

Situating himself at the historical juncture of the successful Reconquest
and the potential conquest of a new world, Columbus sees himself as the
agent who will effect the transition from crusade to colonization, from
consolidation to expansion.

The reference to the Grand Khan who sends for instruction in the
Christian faith continues to puzzle historians and critics. Stephen Greenblatt recently declared that "it is not entirely clear whom the Spanish imagined the Grand Khan to be or how they conceived of his rule," and he let
it rest at that.[39] There is, however, some agreement that the title probably
refers to Kublai Khan, the grandson of Genghis Khan and first Mongol
emperor of China (1215–1294).Columbus, we know, owned a Latin
Marco Polo, which he copiously annotated, and probably learned about
the Grand Khan there.[40] Columbus also owned the *Travels* of that
renowned liar Sir John Mandeville. In the Englishman's writings he found
not only descriptions of a Great Khan, who, as in Marco's account, is explicitly placed in China, but also an account of another khan, Prester John
the Emperor of India. I wish to entertain the possibility that, for Columbus, behind the historical identity of the Great Khan lies Prester John.[41]

According to legend, Prester John, enemy of Islam, ruler of the Indias,
had asked for instruction in orthodox Christianity, for he was always considered in the West to be a proto-Christian, a Nestorian, an ally against
Islam, "even if," says Mandeville, "[he] doesn't have all the articles of the
faith as clearly as we do."[42] Missions to China bringing the articles of faith
to the Orient were celebrated and established accomplishments since the
mid-thirteenth century. Therefore, Columbus's assertion that the Grand
Khan, if indeed he is the Chinese emperor, needed instruction seems, at
the least, unusual. Furthermore, it seems unlikely that, given Columbus's
Franciscan religiosity, he was ignorant of the successes of his own order,
renowned for its missionaries—from those first sent by Pope Nicholas IV
in the thirteenth century to Odoric of Pordenone in the fourteenth.

However, the point I want to make is more ideological than historical:
Prester John symbolizes for Columbus the tantalizing possibility of catholic
universal empire, a paradise of resolution and fulfillment, richness measured
spiritually and materially. When Columbus, anchored off Cuba, writes for

November 27, "I say that the whole of Christendom will do business in these lands," he means business in both a commercial and sacred sense, a conflation of mercantile and crusading impulses.[43] The obsessive search for ever-elusive gold and spices—traditional resources of abundance in the Orient, in Prester John's kingdom—must persist, Columbus says repeatedly, in the name of funding another crusade to Jerusalem in order to free the Holy Sepulcher from Muslim possession. Columbus writes on the day after Christmas, 1492, weighing anchor in Christmas Harbor, having left behind the first beachhead—thirty eight Christians in a fort made of the timbers of the fabled *Santa Maria*—that he hopes, on his return from Castile, to

> find a barrel of gold that those who were left would have acquired by ex-
> change; and that they would have found the gold mine and the spicery, and
> those things in such quantities that the sovereigns, before three years are
> over, will undertake and prepare to go conquer the Holy Sepulcher; for thus
> I urged Your Highnesses to spend all the profits of this my enterprise on the
> conquest of Jerusalem, and your Highnesses laughed and said that it would
> please them and that even without this profit they had that desire.[44]

Read against the grave logic of exchange value motivating colonial practice, the ambiguity of the imperial laughter, expressing at once assuring approval and disbelief, surprise and discomfort, may be linked to the
uneasiness or instability of the utopic fantasy itself. If the dream of recon-
quering the Holy Lands was anachronistic, the colonial project whose
profits would fuel such a campaign was not. The success of the sacred enterprise of colonizing the East—and, in Buchan's novel, South Africa—
rests on the efficiency of the exchange mechanism.

In light of recent postcolonial criticism, there may be another way to
read this imperial laughter. If I am right in identifying an ambiguity here,
then it is an ambiguity that can be related to the complexities and instabilities of the colonialist text itself. I have in mind the textual typologies
offered by Abdul JanMohamed, namely his classification of the colonial
text (and attitude) into "the imaginary" and "the symbolic."[45] Imaginary
texts are structured by a strong fetishistic drive that fixes the opposition between self and other, while symbolic texts are more open to dialectical
play, even to the point where the barriers of racial difference begin to
crumble. Of course, the two categories are not mutually exclusive; indeed,
colonialist writing predominantly exhibits the economy of a "Manichean
allegory," an ideology that bolsters European authority at the same time it
obsessively and fetishistically puts on display the native's inferiority.
Columbus's logbook takes advantage of the Manichean allegory that is

constantly generating the stereotypes fixing the other in place and, through its fetishizing strategy, tends to affirm moral and civilizational differences. The consequence of this strategy is, as JanMohamed points out, a denial or blockage of the movement of history. Colonialism, in tending to refuse any cultural syncretism, fastens itself to the status quo, thereby foreclosing any sense of utopic becoming.

Prester John inscribes not only a "imaginary" ideal of religious unity and conquest but, in the context of developing colonialism, a "symbolic" ideal of resistance to that very same project of imperialism. To see how Prester John, as a figure for sacred empire, gets ideologically reinscribed, we will glance at Buchan's adventure book, *Prester John*. The novel describes the adventures of David Crawfurd, a Scot sent to a remote part of South Africa, "where white men are at a premium," as an assistant storekeeper for a large trading and shipping company. Crawfurd is sent into the veld with the sole purpose of returning to Scotland a rich man. Upon departure his uncle gives him twenty sovereigns: "'you'll not be your mother's son, Davie,' were [the uncle's] last words, 'if you don't come home with it multiplied by a thousand.'" The surest way to multiply his gold is to open new trade with the natives, an exploitative project, as the schoolteacher Mr. Wardlaw, the other figure of imperialism in the hinterland, summarizes it: "You'll exploit the pockets of the black men and I'll see what I can do with their minds."[46]

When Crawfurd arrives at the place where he is to set up shop, Blaauwildebeestefontein, or Spring of the Blue Wildebeeste, he is struck by its similarity to a *locus amoenus* in *Pilgrim's Progress,* the Delectable Mountains. He concludes that "whatever serpent may lurk in it, it was a veritable Eden I had come to." But Crawfurd's fantasy of an edenic arena for the projection of his commercial desires quickly crumbles. The place of colonial fantasy resists, rather than invites as Columbus saw it, capitalistic representation. This resistance begins to terrify Crawfurd and his companion Mr. Wardlaw, who feel greatly outnumbered, as a white minority, in the hinterland. Wardlaw admits that he is "black afraid," terrified the Kaffirs might "organize a crusade against the whiteman." Crawfurd shares his fear: "I felt I was being hemmed in by barbarism, and cut off in a ghoulish land from the succour of my own kind."[47] Whiteness itself fails to provide any real security. The unity and power of colonialist utopia, as the site upon which are projected both the comfortable positioning of the other and the borders distinguishing civilization from barbarism, are threatened. For Crawfurd and Wardlaw, the boundaries and hierarchies by which they are able to reinforce their own culture are disrupted, blurred by the historical order of another, alien conception of utopia.

The utopic place of Crawfurd's imperial fantasy is challenged by one symbolically tied to the legendary empire of Prester John and the African empires successive to it. Crawfurd's sleuthing uncovers the beginnings of a united tribal revolution, the center of which is the image of Prester John, a conqueror who extends his lineage, through southward tribal movements, from the fifteenth-century Abyssinian king to the nineteenth-century Chaka Zulu. The African story of Prester John is here transmitted as a religious cult, Christian and pagan at once, built around the notion that Prester John's spirit, as father of the tribe, will be reincarnated with the possession of a fetish object known as the Snake. The serpent that spoils Eden, Crawfurd's scene of fantasy, is literalized in the novel as the ruby necklace that confers the strength of empire. Possessing the talisman, the magisterial Reverend John Laputa masquerades as the incarnated spirit of Prester John, successfully uniting the tribes in revolution against their white oppressors.

Laputa, an anticolonial reincarnation of Prester John, preaches the concept of historical renewal, the idea that if the natives had a glorious empire in the past, they would have an even better one in the future. Laputa thus "spoke of the great days of Prester John . . . he pictured the heroic age of his nation, when every man was a warrior and hunter, and rich kraals stood in the spots now desecrated by the white man, and cattle wandered on a thousand hills . . . he concluded . . . with a picture of the overthrow of the alien, and the golden age which would dawn for the oppressed." Laputa's reclamation of ancestral land rights and his reassertion of native values and power in a postrevolution golden age recalling the glorious kingdom of Prester John constitutes, for Crawfurd, "the secret of Africa." Like all secrets, however, once disclosed, it loses its power. The novel closes with Crawfurd witnessing the suicide of Prester John's avatar and recalling Laputa's last words: "My race is doomed." The secret of Africa, the ideological reincoding of the medieval Prester John legend, is at once exposed and reconcealed when Crawfurd snatches the necklace and declares "I had in my pocket the fetish of the whole black world." Without its sacred leader and the dream of unity he represented as concentrated in the fetish, the native revolutionaries are easily contained and silenced. His fear arrested, Crawfurd can be assured of his own vision of history: "All of a sudden I realized that at last I had come out of savagery. . . . Behind me was the black night, and the horrid secrets of darkness."[48]

But the fantasied world of Prester John strangely recurs in Buchan's "history of the Great Rising." Its last page describes the new prosperity of the native population, its access to and enthusiasm for education, and its increasing similarity to the colonizer's world—in short, a landscape of perfect colonial domestication. However, it would be hasty to conclude from this that Laputa/Prester John's revolution turns out to serve a purely colonialist dream. The figure of Prester John actually interrupts imperial space: "There are playing fields and baths and reading-rooms and libraries just as in a school at home. In front of the great hall of the college a statue stands, the figure of a black man shading his eyes with his hands and looking far over the plains . . . on the pedestal it is lettered 'Prester John,' but the face is the face of Laputa. So the last of the kings of Africa does not lack his monument."[49] This intense gaze, ranging far over the plains of South Africa, recovers a crucial element of resistance lost in the failed uprising, namely, the communifying (and fetishistic) power of Prester John.

For Columbus, the fetish of Prester John marks a vision of absolute possession, the inscription of everything within one boundary. To recognize Prester John is to disavow difference, to find, at the site of his fantasy, only oneself. By contrast, the anticolonialist Prester John brings into play another possible relation, one of ecstasy rather than possession. Buchan's fiction portrays the oppositional value of Prester John, the recognition, rather than the disavowal, of difference that effectuates any dialectical or revolutionary leap into a new collectivity or identity.[50] Alhough it surrenders to the imperial view of history that suppresses otherness, the modern novel imagines utopia, the nonplace of projected fantasy, in dialectical relation to the specular structure of fetishistic identification. I suggest that the fetish, by embodying the boundaries delimiting and separating self and other, can only generate an ambiguous situation, one analogous to the situation of colonial history itself. In the fetish resides a deep rapprochement of self and other, an annihilation of differences that opens up historical becoming. The imperial fetish forever oscillates between its temporary effacement and its permanent memorialization.[51] That Prester John narratives, from the twelfth to the twentieth century, crucially hinge on the fetish object that often serves as a test or model for identity reveals something of the dynamic, revolutionary nature of the fetish itself.

Notes

1. All references to the Latin *Letter of Prester John* are in "Der Priester Johannes," ed. Friedrich Zarncke, *Abhandlungen der philologisch-historischen Classe der königlich sächsischen Gesellschaft der Wissenschaften* 7 (1879): 909–24; translations mine. References are indicated by section number (with letters for interpolations).
2. See Nicholas Howe, *The Old English Catalogue Poems* (Copenhagen: Rosenkilde and Bagger, 1985), pp. 30–32; Fritz Saxl, "Illustrated Medieval Encyclopedias," in his *Lectures* (London: Warburg Institute, 1957) 1: 228–54; and Simone Viarre, "Le commentaire ordonné du monde dans

quelques sommes scientifiques des XIIe et XIIIe siècles," in *Classical Influences on European Culture, A. D. 500–1500,* ed. R. R. Bolgar (Cambridge: Cambridge University Press, 1971), pp. 203–15.

3. Umberto Eco, "The New Middle Ages," in *On Signs,* ed. Marshall Blonsky (Baltimore: Johns Hopkins University Press, 1985), p. 502.

4. For a list of the objects from the treasure of Charles IV of Bohemia and from that of the Duc de Berry, see ibid., n.

5. Patti White, *Gatsby's Party: The System and the List in Contemporary Narrative* (West Lafayette, IN: Purdue University Press, 1992), pp. 108–9.

6. Ibid., p. 165 n. 20; Gaston Bachelard, *The Poetics of Space,* trans. Maria Jolas (Boston: Beacon Press, 1969), p. 193.

7. Here I account for only the interpolations in the Latin text. Interpolations to the vernacular MSS, especially the late ones, are extensive. Common to these later interpolations is the kind of information found in lapidaries. See, for example, the interpolation in BM Egerton 1781 (152r), an Irish text of the fifteenth century, which introduces a list of gems and their properties. For the Irish text, see David Greene, "The Irish Versions of the Letter of Prester John," *Celtica* 2 (1952): 125.

8. The twelfth-century MS Berlin 956 (fols. 24–25), a lapidary ascribed to St Jerome, opens with the description of a journey to India, the land of the carbuncle, emerald, and other gemstones, a place so remote that navigating the Red Sea alone takes six months, while crossing the ocean to India requires another year. For William of Auvergne and Albertus Magnus, India was the proper site of the fantastic precisely because gems of marvelous virtue were easily found there. See Lynn Thorndike, *A History of Magic and Experimental Science* (New York: Columbia University Press, 1923), 2: 236–37.

9. A transcription of the fourteenth-century MS appears in *Fire og fyrretyve for en stor Deel forhen utrykte Prœver af oldnordisk Sprog og Literatur,* ed. Konrad Gislason (Copenhagen, 1860), pp. 416–18; the Italian tale appears in an edition of Carlo Gualteruzzi, *Il Novellino. Le ciento Novelle antike* (Bologna, 1525). A French translation of the Icelandic text, along with the Italian version, appears in Reinhold Koehler, "La nouvelle italienne du Pretre Jean et de l'Empereur Frédéric et un récit islandais," *Romania* 5 (1879): 76–79.

10. Koehler, "La nouvelle italienne," p. 77; translation mine.

11. Ibid., pp. 76–78; translations mine (with the assistance of Professor M. Roy Harris).

12. The ideological significance of gift exchange is most famously discussed by Marcel Mauss, *The Gift: The Form and Reason for Exchange in Archaic Societies,* trans. W. D. Halls (New York: Norton, 1990). See also Jacques Derrida's recent reading of Mauss and the problem of exchange in *Given Time: I. Counterfeit Money,* trans. Peggy Kamuf (Chicago: University of Chicago Press, 1992), pp. 34–70.

13. An alternative view of Prester John's gift-giving, which centers on the ideal of largesse, is given by Katharina M. Wilson, "Social Behavior as Iden-

tity Formation: Prester John and his Largesse," *USF Language Quarterly* 24 (Fall–Winter 1985): 39–42, 48.

14. Frederick Turner, *Beyond Geography: The Western Spirit against the Wilderness* (New Brunswick, NJ: Rutgers University Press, 1983), p. 89. In his polemical book, Turner suggests that attitudes toward gems and metals mark important differences between cultures. The crusaders, Marco Polo, and Columbus were united, he suggests, in their quest for things: "gold, silver, and stones, [which] like technology, are pathetic substitutes for a lost world, a lost spirit life" (p. 90).

15. Wilhelm von Humboldt, "Uber die Verschiedenheit des menschlichen Sprachbaues und ihren Einfluss auf die geistige Entwicklung des Menschengeschlects (1830–1835)," in *Einleitung zum Kawiwerk,* vol. 7 of *Wilhem von Humboldts Werke,* ed. Albert Leitzmann (Berlin: B. Behr, 1907), p. 60; my emphasis.

16. For a splendid reading of historical discourses on the fetish, framed within a discussion of mercantile imperialism, from the late medieval Portuguese *feitiço* to Enlightenment social theory, see the series of articles by William Pietz, "The Problem of the Fetish, I," *Res* 9 (Spring 1985): 5–17; "The Problem of the Fetish, II," *Res* 13 (Spring 1987): 23–45; "The Problem of the Fetish, IIIa," *Res* 16 (Autumn 1988): 105–23. See also chapter 10 in this volume.

17. For an alternative reading of the utopic effects of the *Letter*'s list structure, see Martin Gosman, "Le royaume du Prêtre Jean: l'interpretation d'un bonheur," in *L'idée de bonheur au moyen âge: actes du Colloque d'Amiens de mars 1984* (Göppingen: Kümmerle, 1990), pp. 213–23.

18. Fredric Jameson, "Of Islands and Trenches: Neutralization and the Production of Utopian Discourse," in *Syntax of History, The Ideologies of Theory: Essays 1971–1986* (Minneapolis: University of Minnesota Press, 1988)2: 80–81. Sergei M. Eisenstein, "Literature and Cinema: Reply to a Questionnaire" (1928), in *Selected Works, Writings, 1922–34,* ed. and trans. Richard Taylor (Bloomington: Indiana University Press, 1988) 1:96.

19. Stephen Heath, "Lessons from Brecht," *Screen* 15 (1974): 112.

20. Eisenstein, "The Montage of Attractions" (1923), in *Writings, 1922–34,* 1:34, 40; and see Eisenstein, "Literature and Cinema: Reply to a Questionnaire," in *Writings, 1922–34,* 1:95–99.

21. Eisenstein, "The Montage of Film Attractions," 1:49.

22. An excellent example from the *Letter,* too long to quote here, is §§42–50.

23. I am reminded here of Berthold Brecht's treatment of Chinese painting, a fragment of which Stephen Heath quotes and discusses: "Chinese painting leaves room, the eye can wander, dispersed: 'the things represented play the role of elements which could exist separately and independently, yet they form a whole through the relations they sustain among themselves on the paper without, however, this whole being indivisible.' Not an organic unity— *a* meaning—but a series of meanings and remeanings . . . a multi-perspective without the fixity of depth. Instead of representations, displacements—of eye,

of subject (in both senses of the term) [—] a materiality of texture which baf-
fles the 'innocence' of reflection": Heath, "Lessons from Brecht," p. 105.

24. In Georges Bataille's notion of *dépense* (unproductive expenditure), his theory of the need for absolute loss, is implicitly a critique of any materialist
enterprise (such as montage) that seeks some order of reality beyond the
phenomenal. I would emphasize precisely what Bataille leaves out of his
account: the harnessing, to human and social ends, of the agitational energy of ideality. See Bataille, "The Notion of Expenditure," in *Visions of Excess: Selected Writings, 1927–1939,* ed. and trans. Allan Stoekl (Minneapolis:
University of Minnesota Press, 1985), pp. 116–29.

25. Fredric Jameson, "Pleasure: A Political Issue," in *The Ideologies of Theory*
2: 73.

26. Sergei Eisenstein, "The Structure of the Film," in *Film Form: Essays in Film
Theory,* ed. and trans. Jay Leyda (New York: Harvest, 1949), pp. 150–78,
quotation at p. 170.

27. Ibid., pp. 173, 167, 172.

28. Walter Benjamin, "N (Re: the Theory of Knowledge, Theory of Progress),"
trans. Leigh Hafrey and Richard Sieburth, in *Benjamin: Philosophy, Aesthet-
ics, History,* ed. Gary Smith (Chicago: University of Chicago Press, 1989),
p. 48.

29. Considering the ambiguity and instability here in psychoanalytic terms, I
would suggest that they correspond to the latent ambiguity of objects that
are, in Klein's sense, not yet fully mastered. In other words, facing a world
of good objects and bad objects means that, as Michel Foucault puts it,
"ambivalence is established as a natural dimension of affectivity": *Mental
Illness and Psychology,* trans. Alan Sheridan (Berkeley: University of California Press, 1987), p. 20. The potential here for anxiety is great; loss of an object (the Holy Land) necessitates the search for a substitute (Prester John's
kingdom); the successful search is ecstatic: "In considering the dynamics of
the process, the concept of anxiety is clearly needed. Melanie Klein has laid
great stress on the fact that it is dread of the original object itself, as well
as the loss of it, that leads to the search for a substitute. But there is also a
word needed for the emotional experience of finding the substitute, and it
is here that the word *ecstasy* may be useful": Marion Milner, "The Role of
Illusion in Symbol Formation," in *Transitional Objects and Potential Spaces:
Literary Uses of D. W. Winnicott,* ed. Peter L. Rudnytsky (New York: Columbia University Press, 1993), p. 17.

30. Kaja Silverman's deconstruction of the dominant psychoanalytic paradigm
of cinematic identification (the experience of the film as introjective, ideo-
pathic) is the impetus for my reading of the ecstatic dynamics of the montage list and its centrality to the utopic project. Silverman was the first to
connect Eisenstein to the production of what she calls "political ecstasy"
(see *The Threshold of the Visible World* [New York: Routledge, 1996], pp.
83–121), an extension of her earlier work on heteropathic identification in

the dynamic of sympathy: *Male Subjectivity at the Margins* (New York: Routledge, 1992), pp. 205–7, 264–70.

31. The 1561 edition of *Vita dell'invitiss e gloriosiss Imperador Carlo Quinto;* trans. Alexander Vasiliev, *Prester John: Legend and History,* unpublished MS, Dumbarton Oaks Collection and Library, ca. 1950, p. 206.

32. Gilles Deleuze and Félix Guattari, *A Thousand Plateaus: Capitalism and Schizophrenia,* trans. Brian Massumi (Minneapolis: University of Minnesota Press, 1987), p. 379.

33. Janine Chasseguet-Smirgel, "Perversion and the Universal Law," *International Review of Psycho-Analysis* 10 (1985): 293.

34. In the colonialist context this is elaborated by Alain Grosrichard, *The Sultan's Court: European Fantasies of the East,* trans. Liz Heron (New York: Verso, 1998); see esp. Mladen Dolar's introduction, "The Subject Supposed to Enjoy," pp. ix–xxvii.

35. Chasseguet-Smirgel, "Perversion," 293.

36. See Vasiliev, *Prester John,* p. ii; also, Ernst Bloch's judgment: Prester John's "priestly kingdom in the East does not cease to be a focus of almost all medical, social and technological utopias in the Middle Ages . . . because in it the geographical wishful image of all wishful images played on the hopes of medieval people and . . . shone before them in a superstitiously moving, hopefully overhopeful way: the earthly paradise": *The Principle of Hope,* trans. Neville Plaice, Stephen Plaice, and Paul Knight (Oxford: Basil Blackwell, 1986) 2: 769.

37. Anne McClintock, *Imperial Leather: Race, Gender and Sexuality in the Colonial* Contest (New York: Routledge, 1995). p. 184; see also pp. 181–203.

38. All quotes from the logbook are from *The Diario of Christopher Columbus's First Voyage to America, 1492–1493,* ed. and trans. Oliver Dunn and James E. Kelley, Jr. (Norman: University of Oklahoma Press, 1989), p. 17.

39. Stephen Greenblatt, *Marvelous Possessions: The Wonder of the New World* (Chicago: University of Chicago Press, 1991), p. 171 n. 39.

40. Columbus's jottings include two references to Prester John. See Cesare de Lollis, *Scritti di Cristoforo Columbo,* 2 vols. (Rome: Ministero della Pubblica Istruzione, 1892, 1894) 2: 452, 454.

41. It has been suggested that *John* is a corruption of the title *Khan* or its Ethiopian equivalent *Zan;* for the first theory, see Gustav Oppert, *Der Presbyter Johannes in Sage und Geschichte* (Berlin, 1870), for the second, see Charles E. Nowell, "The Historical Prester John," *Speculum* 28 (July 1953): 435–45; for an alternative theory, see Vsevolod Slessarev, *Prester John: The Letter and the Legend* (Minneapolis: University of Minnesota Press, 1959), pp. 80–92. I will also mention here the medieval geographical confusion about the Indias. (There were, by most accounts, three, and they were notoriously fluid demarcations, often including China and Ethiopia.) The confusion dates from Isidore of Seville and persists well into the fifteenth century. For the impact of this confusion on the search for Prester John,

see C. F. Beckingham, "The Quest for Prester John," *Bulletin of the John Rylands University Library* 62 (1980): 291–310.

42. John Mandeville, *Mandeville's Travels,* ed. Paul Hamelius (London: EETS, 1919) 1: 181.

43. *Diario of Christopher Columbus,* p. 185.

44. Ibid., p. 291.

45. See Abdul R. JanMohamed, "The Economy of Manichean Allegory: The Function of Racial Difference in Colonialist Literature," *Critical Inquiry* 12 (1985): 59–87.

46. Quotations from John Buchan, *Prester John,* ed. David Daniell (New York: Oxford University Press, 1994), pp. 19, 20, 21.

47. Ibid., pp. 31, 54, 56.

48. Ibid., pp. 105, 103, 180, 124, 189–90.

49. Ibid., pp. 191, 202.

50. Daniell's critical introduction to Prester John goes some way toward underlining the difficulty contemporary readers must face interpreting Buchan's imperialist attitudes as they square with his particular colonial politics and his sense of history and morality. See ibid., esp. pp. xviii–xxvi.

51. It is the undecidability and oscillation of the fetish that produce its power to alter the terms of its own interpretation as well as that of the world that it figures forth. See Jacques Lacan and Wladimir Granoff, "Fetishism: The Symbolic, the Imaginary and the Real," in *Perversions: Psychodynamics and Therapy,* ed. Sandor Lorand and Michael Balint (London: Ortolan, 1965), pp. 265–76; and Leo Bersani and Ulysse Dutoit, "Fetishisms and Story-telling," in *The Forms of Violence: Narrative in Assyrian Art and Modern Culture* (New York: Schocken, 1985), pp. 66–72.

CONTRIBUTORS

SUZANNE CONKLIN AKBARI teaches at the University of Toronto. Her book *Seeing Through the Veil: Theories of Vision and the Development of Late Medieval Allegory* is forthcoming.

KATHLEEN BIDDICK is Professor of History and a Fellow of the Medieval Institute at the University of Notre Dame. She recently published *The Shock of Medievalism* and is finishing a book entitled *The Cut of Ethnography*

JOHN M. BOWERS is Professor and Chair of the English Department at the University of Nevada, Las Vegas. His numerous articles cover authors from St. Augustine to Shakespeare, and he has published *The Crisis of Will in "Piers Plowman" and "The Canterbury Tales": Fifteenth-Century Continuations and Additions.* He is currently completing a book entitled *The Politics of "Pearl": Court Poetry in the Age of Richard II.*

GLENN BURGER is Associate Professor of English at the University of Alberta and Codirector of its Medieval and Early Modern Institute. He is the editor of *A Lytell Cronycle, Richard Pynson's translation of Hetoum's* La Fleur des histoires de la terre d'Orient, and author of a number of articles on Chaucer and queer theory. With Steven Kruger he has coedited a collection of essays titled *Queering the Middle Ages/Historicizing Postmodernity.* He is currently at work on a book about sexuality and nation in the Canterbury Tales, titled *Chaucer's Queer Nation.*

JEFFREY JEROME COHEN is Associate Professor of English and Human Sciences at George Washington University. He is the editor of *Monster Theory: Reading Culture* and (with Bonnie Wheeler) *Becoming Male in the Middle Ages,* as well as the author of *Of Giants: Sex, Monsters, and the Middle Ages.*

KATHLEEN DAVIS is Assistant Professor of English at Bucknell University. She has published articles on medieval national identities, postcolonial theory, and translation and is currently working on a book entitled *Unbirthing the Nation.*

JOHN M. GANIM is Professor of English and Chair of the Department of English at the University of California, Riverside. He is the author of *Chaucerian Theatricality* and *Style and Consciousness in Middle English Narrative.*

GERALDINE HENG is Assistant Professor of English at the University of Texas, Austin, and is working on a book entitled *Empire of Magic: Medieval Romance and the Politics of Cultural Fantasy.*

PATRICIA CLARE INGHAM is Assistant Professor of English at Lehigh University. Her forthcoming book, *Sovereign Fantasies: Arthurian Romance and the Making of Britain,* analyzes the linkages between Middle English Arthurian romance and contestations over political and cultural identities in late medieval Britain. She has published articles on representations of chivalric masculinity in Arthurian tales and in Chaucer and has a forthcoming article examining the colonialist exoticism in the poem *Sir Gawain and the Green Knight.*

STEVEN F. KRUGER is author of *Dreaming in the Middle Ages* and *AIDS Narratives: Gender and Sexuality, Fiction and Science.* He has coeditied, with Deborah R. Geis, *Approaching the Millennium: Essays on Angels in America,* and, with Glenn Burger, *Queering the Middle Ages / Historicizing Postmodernity.* Professor of English at the University of Alberta, he is currently at work on a book about Jewish/Christian relations in the Middle Ages.

KELLIE ROBERTSON received her Ph.D. from Yale and is currently Assistant Professor of English at the University of Pittsburgh. She has published articles on Geoffrey of Monmouth and Milton and is at work on a book exploring the intersection of labor theory and literary production in late medieval Britain.

CLAIRE SPONSLER is Associate Professor of English at the University of Iowa. She is the author of *Drama and Resistance: Bodies, Goods, and Theatricality in Late Medieval England* and the coeditor of *East of West: Crosscultural Performance and the Staging of Difference.* She is currently writing a book entitled *Ritual Imports: Medieval Drama in America.*

SYLVIA TOMASCH is Associate Professor of English at Hunter College of the City University of New York. She is the editor (with Seally Gilles) of *Text and Territory: Geographical Imagination in the European Middle Ages.*

MICHAEL UEBEL is Assistant Professor of English at the University of Kentucky. His book on the inception of utopia in the early Middle Ages is in progress.

INDEX